INTERIOR DESIGN
RESEARCH
METHODS

INTERIOR DESIGN RESEARCH METHODS

Lily B. Robinson

FAIRCHILD BOOKS

NEW YORK · LONDON · OXFORD · NEW DELHI · SYDNEY

FAIRCHILD BOOKS
Bloomsbury Publishing Inc
1385 Broadway, New York, NY 10018, USA
50 Bedford Square, London, WC1B 3DP, UK
29 Earlsfort Terrace, Dublin 2, Ireland

BLOOMSBURY, FAIRCHILD BOOKS and the Fairchild Books logo are trademarks
of Bloomsbury Publishing Plc

Cover design: Louise Dugdale
Cover image: olaser / Getty Images

A catalog record for this book is available from the Library of Congress.

ISBN: 978-1-5013-2778-0

Typeset by Integra Software Services Pvt. Ltd.
Printed and bound in the United States of America

To find out more about our authors and books visit www.fairchildbooks.com
and sign up for our newsletter.

This book is dedicated to my father, Sherman Robinson,
who spent his life helping others and served as my mentor in all things.

contents

extended table of contents

preface

On the Intricacies of Creating
by Mae Villena Case
Some may call me a "creative" type
But aren't we all, in some way,
Afforded that kind of magic
In one form or another?
All that is tangible sprouts
From the what-ifs and the maybes
That lie in the intangible
Connections of our thoughts.
The concrete beneath your feet
As you weave through the bustle of
Your city
Moves you around the world so easily
That you don't even think about
The sorcery of how it came to be.
The secret is that we all play
A role in constructing all that surrounds us.
I am not more responsible for it
Because of these words that bring you that
truth.
I've just come to embrace it.
I've just come to embrace it.

A research textbook for creative people! How do you evaluate the success of a design solution for the built environment? What do you consider before beginning the design process, throughout the phases of a typical design project, and then after the solution is implemented and used? This textbook assists undergraduate and graduate students to confidently align themselves with time-tested, evidence-based design practices to defend their projects using valid arguments rather than conjecture, engage in dialogue with critics to produce innovative, inquiry-based design solutions, and ways to measure or assess the levels of success attained by the implementation of the design into everyday life. This book enables interior design students to have the terminology to communicate across a variety of disciplines and to the public. Building on the foundation established in *Research-Based Programming for Interior Design*, *Interior Design Research Methods (IDRM)* continues that educational pursuit and exploratory journey from the perspective that anyone with a mind for curiosity, creativity, and diligence can do research, given a strong philosophical background along with appropriate theoretical and practical tools. The text, tables, figures, and activities encourage students to brainstorm, compose, and implement their own research instruments to conduct qualitative, quantitative, and mixed method studies. *IDRM* supports both undergraduate and graduate-level, research-informed design curricula seeking to engage students familiar with the interior design process (which includes understanding and employing the five phases of design: programming, schematics, design development, contract documents, and contract administration) and expand their areas of expertise to include the research process, approaching research as a creative endeavor seamlessly integrated into the design process. This text will enable students of interior design to critically approach the research process, strengthen their research skills, and build on the creative process in which interior design practitioners wisely and appropriately apply quality information to solve human-centered problems.

COVERAGE AND ORGANIZATION

Chapter 1 links what designers do to what researchers do to prepare interior design students to become *design-informed researchers*. The skills and passion students have for design can easily be transferred to research. Designers are inherently curious which is the first step to becoming a researcher. Designers question the norms, seek to solve problems, tend to be intuitively connected and sensitive to the environment, and have an ardent attention for detail. Acknowledging and building on these skills allows students to become excellent observers, who can also compose sound research questions, interviews, surveys, and experiential activities to collect and analyze information.

Chapter 2 covers basic research terminology and concepts surrounding the scientific method, introduces systematic data collection practices, and building logical arguments which use *evidence* to support *claims*. Chapter 3 explores the philosophical underpinnings of different forms of research approaches and helps students clarify and reflect on their cultural, personal, social, and professional capital; what they bring to the table, so to speak. We hope to motivate students to do what they might have previously considered boring. Therefore, in Chapter 3 we also introduce how theory can be used as a lens to frame their study, view their data, or interpret their findings. Just as a design concept helps designers frame or guide design decisions, theory can help define observational categories and provide frameworks for categorizing, *coding*, or *reducing* data. Similar to concept imagery which provides visual metaphors for the aesthetics or function of a space, knowledge visualization is explored to help researchers express underlying relationships or patterns which emerge in the data.

Chapter 4 "Research Design for Design Research" explores types of studies, study components, and writing styles, and how to situate their study by using previously published sources commonly known as a *literature review* and *precedent*, or *case*, *studies*. Chapter 5 prepares students to design a study to gather their own data by providing a broad overview of methods, ethical considerations, and management tools which align with students' own value systems, appropriate to their type of inquiry and which support their question or topic.

Chapter 6, 7, and 8 expand and deepen understanding of the rich data-gathering techniques of interviews, surveys, and observation, offering students a range of possibilities in question wording, questionnaire design, distribution methods, how to conduct semi-experimental or experiential studies, and various documentation methods which yield raw data. In Chapter 9, "Data Analysis and Representation" delves into ways in which raw data can be reduced, analyzed, and represented to uncover qualitative findings or quantitative results, which can then be interpreted and discussed.

Chapter 10 offers insights into the multiple ways designers can conclude a design-related study. The chapter begins with traditional ways such as outlining a thesis paper and writing an abstract or research summary. It then explores the many ways study data can inform the practice of interior design, and how to share this information with a wider audience. It discusses communicating implications to possible end-users, potential clients, and the general public, as well as how to inspire future researchers in interior design.

APPROACH AND FEATURES

In this text, the author envisions interior design research as a crossroads to utilize both physical science as well as social science approaches, to propose a transformative, transcendent, or creative paradigm for design-related inquiries. The book does not promote a one-strategy-fits-all solution, but rather calls for innovation in research commensurate with the activity being studied.

> In a talk entitled *The New Frontiers of Design*, Paola Antonelli (2017), called for a process-oriented curriculum which emphasizes perspective, theory, implicit and explicit values, and expression of process [rather than focusing only on the product or design outcome]. Research-informed design curricula should underscore how systematically collected data, whether expressed quantitatively or qualitatively, can be viewed through a theory or theories, analyzed for patterns, trends or relationships with applications to practice and implications [for] further inquiry. Theory provides fields of awareness to help students make sense of data, making the research process more accessible and I believe this focus will help create a valuable connection between data and design.
>
> (Robinson, 2020, p. 18)

Interior Design Research Methods (IDRM) encourages students to explore ideas for studies related to interior design and promotes innovative data collection techniques. *IDRM* attempts to improve production of data, understand the various forms data can take, and how to analyze results to inform design. Data can be spatial, formal, relational, and communicated to form a narrative with data storytelling. Some qualitative data can be anecdotal, or subjective, and integrated with quantitative data gathered through experimentation. This text attempts to help students frame, interpret, represent, analyze, and translate findings to inform design solutions, and creatively apply information to the studio component of their thesis project.

IDRM offers two ways to approach the problem of integrating research into the design process in the education of an interior designer: (1) curriculum content and emphasis, and (2) emphasizing the role of theory. *IDRM* encourages student designers to conduct original research studies within the context of design curriculum to build familiarity with terminology, awareness of the variety of perspectives, and the research process in general. To make research attractive to interior designers, this textbook seeks to make information-gathering tasks rigorous yet creative. Students explore what constitutes evidence from beyond a dichotomy between physical (or "hard") science and social science perspective to a creative paradigm, which seeks to include, or transcend, both.

To this end, all chapters include two running boxed-text features: "Activities" and "Research in Action." Activities include a clear purpose along with step-by-step instructions to be used as homework, in-class, or both, opportunities to practice, contribute, and share knowledge. "Research in Action" features include examples, side-stories, and vignettes to facilitate understanding and as a source of inspiration. At the end of each chapter, students and instructors will find "Discussion Questions" to help promote seminar-style dialogue and reflection of the main points raised in the text. A list of references appears at the end of each chapter as well. It is hoped that students will revisit the resources which have informed the writing of this book for further inquiry and deeper understanding.

INSTRUCTOR RESOURCES

- The Instructor's Guide provides suggestions for planning the course and using the text in the classroom, including sample syllabi, in-class activities, and teaching ideas.
- PowerPoint® presentations include images from the book and provide a framework for lecture and discussion

Instructor resources may be accessed through www.FairchildBooks.com.

acknowledgments

My heartfelt gratitude extends to all who helped to realize this textbook. First, I acknowledge my graduate and undergraduate students who provided the inspiration and motivation to create this book particularly Meli Apone, Pierce Bryce, Emily Corless, Amanda Dowell, Nemo Kheem, Mary Kristovich, and Jesse Mitchell, who contributed many of the *Research in Action* examples. Second, I offer profound gratitude to my colleagues at ANFA (Academy of Neuroscience for Architecture), ACE (ANFA Center for Education), Salk Institute of Biological Studies, University of California, San Diego, Parsons School of Design, Cornell University, New School of Architecture and Design, Design Institute of San Diego, and San Diego Mesa College who have made essential contributions and have helped shape my thinking about research for the built environment, particularly Tatiana Berger, Dr. Maria da Piedade Ferreira, Crandon Gustafson, Dr. Chris Halter, Dr. Paula Levin, and Dr. David McGrevy.

I thank my family Chris Iandolo, Sandra Robinson, Binnie Robinson, William and Dawn Robinson (and Max, Sam, and Charlie), and friends Casey Green, Ellen Zimmerman, Alexandra Parman Pitts, Rise Walter, Sandra Pesante and Lidia Giaquinto, V. Williams, Dr. Alison Black, Dr. Amie Wong, Carlo Giurdanella, Deborah Wiley, Frederick Jackson, Frank Chindamo and Tashia Hinchliffe, Michaelle Goodman, Isabelle Odjaghian, Brandon Hilley and Tanya Snyder, Bradley Brown and Natasha Shapiro, Jack Beduhn, Dawn Borger, Gina Pollara, and countless others who have lovingly supported my endeavors. And, lastly but not least, the support of the editors and staff at Bloomsbury/Fairchild Books who patiently helped me navigate the writing process and fine tune this book, so that it can serve as a valuable resource for research-informed designers and design-informed researchers.

The Publisher wishes to gratefully acknowledge and thank the editorial team involved in the publication of this book:

Senior Acquisitions Editor: Emily Samulski
Senior Development Editor: Corey Kahn
Assistant Editor: Jenna Lefkowitz
Art Development Editor: Edie Weinberg
In-House Designer: Louise Dugdale
Production Manager: Ken Bruce
Project Manager: Joanne Rippin

Why Research?

LEARNING OBJECTIVES

After you complete this chapter, you will be able to:

- Contextualize the research process within the Information Age and beyond.

- Transfer design skills such as creativity, decision-making, and problem-solving to those needed for research.

- Envision research for interior design as a creative endeavor that begins with defining a problem to solve in the built environment.

- Generate ideas for research topics using brainstorming techniques.

- Compose focused and compelling research questions to answer throughout your research journey.

The Information Age has given us access to overwhelming amounts of data. What do we do with all of it? If social media has taught us anything, it would be that access to greater quantities of information does not necessarily mean that we are better informed. We need to evaluate the source, the perspective, the context, and integrate our own experience or prior knowledge in order to make sense of it.

(ROBINSON, 2020, P. 17)

BEYOND THE INFORMATION AGE

London Business School professor Julian Birkinshaw (2014) speculated that the Information Age, which emerged from the digital revolution in the mid-twentieth century, may quickly be replaced by a global society with too much information. He warns against four pitfalls: (1) paralysis through analysis, a state in which no one feels as if they have enough information to make an educated decision, (2) intellectual laziness in which we rely on "big data" or artificial intelligence to make decisions for us, (3) impulsiveness and lack of focus as we juggle multiple means of communication and sharing of information, and (4) shallow understanding of complex issues due to inability to perceive quality information from speculation in which experts have rightful authority. For example, he cites misuse of the Internet for patients who incorrectly self-diagnose their illness, rather than seeking a doctor. We can see also the plethora of strong opinions held by people with little or no understanding of certain kinds of facts. As society becomes more transparent, that is, as information becomes more readily available or more easily accessed by people, the ability to discern truth from falsehood becomes more difficult. Overall, in the post-information age he sees a need for a return to deep understanding, which balances individual experience with critical thinking, and a greater commitment to make quality decisions, an act which combines intuition with rational judgment.

> So what are the consequences of a business world with "too much information"? At an individual level, we face two contrasting risks. One is that we become obsessed with getting to the bottom of a problem, and we keep on digging, desperate to find the truth but taking forever to do so. The other risk is that we become overwhelmed with the amount of information out there and we give up: we realise we cannot actually master the issue at hand, and we end up falling back on a pre-existing belief.
>
> (Birkinshaw, 2014)

How can we empower ourselves to focus our attention, question our assumptions, and foster an understanding of the complexity of issues surrounding a problem without falling back into old patterns or relying on outdated solutions? The first way is to situate ourselves into the cultural and technological assumptions of the present era, to reflect on how it came to be as well as where it might be headed; that is, getting the overall big picture of human history and how we fit in to it. For the ease of identifying and differentiating overarching patterns within human history, social scientists identified classifications of human technological evolutions: beginning with the Stone Age, Bronze Age, and Iron Age; ages based around progressive use of materials to perform assistive functions in daily life.

As shown in Figure 1.1 the Information Age, as well as our current, ever-evolving built environment, has been influenced by the technological ages of the past such as the Renaissance for its emphasis on humanism, the idea of man as inventor, a proliferation of literature that fostered secular ideas, forever changing our understanding of what it means to be human. This influence has resulted in the emergence of the importance of human-centered design. The Industrial Revolution brought about the factory system of fabrication, new

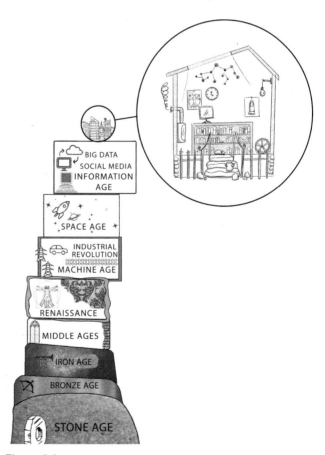

Figure 1.1
What is the influence of the past technological ages on your current surroundings? What era could be next?

methods of fossil-fuel-based transportation and electric manufacturing machinery, and an emphasis on people as consumers which has had a profound effect on economic, social, and cultural conditions around the world. The Space Age introduced the idea that we could transcend the earth to interact and influence environments beyond the planet and limitlessly into the universe.

When it comes to the field of *interior design* or any design of the built environment, we must ask ourselves more basic questions. What is interior design and how can we add to knowledge in the field of interior design? **Interior design** is a distinct profession with specialized knowledge applied to the planning and design of interior environments that promote health, safety, and welfare while supporting and enhancing the human experience. Founded upon design and human behavior theories and research, interior designers apply evidence-based methodologies to identify, analyze, and synthesize information in generating holistic, technical, creative, and contextually appropriate, design solutions (NCIDQ, 2019). The practice of interior design follows a cross-disciplinary process (shared with architecture, landscape architecture, and allied engineering disciplines) which typically encompasses **five phases of design:** (1) Pre-Design/Programming, (2) Schematics, (3) Design Development, (4) Contract Documents, and (5) Contract Administration which can also be seen as the industry standard of five billable stages of a design project for the built environment. For a comprehensive look at the first few phases of this process in interior design education, please refer to the publication which is complementary to this textbook, *Research-Based Programming for Interior Design* (2020).

Researchers interested in design for the built environment position themselves at the forefront of what is next. The Information Age initiated a global network through computerization, to the point where social media and aggregated data promote unprecedented entrepreneurship, the concept of "global citizenship," and a recognition of interconnectedness of life on the planet and its fragile ecosystems. Design researcher Stephen R. Kellert termed this phenomenon **social ecology**, the speculation that people may be able to solve these global environmental issues by working together. Many designers, such as architect Michael Murphy of MASS Design Group, use the power of design not only to address environmental issues, but

as a transformative force for positive social change. Some emerging terms such as *Social Age* and *Big Data* indicate that we are already transitioning to another technological era. Perhaps expansion of **augmented reality** (the use of virtual effects such as filters and digital overlays to enhance real world experience) and **virtual reality** (interaction in 3-dimensional digital spaces) in the "metaverse," by Facebook founder, Mark Zuckerberg acts as a key transition point (*https://about.facebook.com/meta/*).

As researchers in the field of design, we must become aware of what has led us to this moment. As practitioners of design, we must discern what will be the next big thing. We must anticipate change and help society through our dedication to the craft of design and to our research efforts. Just as Tim Berners-Lee (credited with inventing the World Wide Web), Steve Jobs who revolutionized computers with the *Apple 1*, and Bill Gates who developed the software which runs the world, we need to be innovators and active participants in the evolution of the built environment as we head into the next era.

WHAT IS RESEARCH-INFORMED DESIGN?

In an Association of Collegiate Schools of Architecture (ACSA) lecture titled "Positive Psychology as a New Lens for Architecture," architect and design educator, Philip Mead (2020) offers insight into a new focus in design education: to measure and value the effect of buildings on human well-being. His interest comes from a psychological perspective, which lies between the social and biological sciences, particularly **positive psychology**, the scientific study of how an environment supports the emotional well-being of the occupant, promotes confidence, empowers, or encourages an uplifting emotional state. He suggested that how a proposed design solution supports the "five pillars of well-being: positive emotions, engagement/flow (creativity), relationships, meaning/purpose, and achievement" (originally identified by Martin Seligman) may form the basis for a new direction in the way we evaluate the built environment. As quoted by Ruff (2018), architect Chuck First, author of *A Place to Be Happy* envisioned the workplace as an appropriate testing ground, with a particular focus on elevating the lives of people who work there. Interior design research in the workplace would emphasize the experience over time, rather than initial visual impact. "People who work in offices can be there for years." First stated, "So it's more of a life experience rather than a wow experience that is needed."

Recent breakthroughs in neuroscience have led to a theory of **neuroplasticity**, an understanding that the brain and nervous system are not fixed, but continually change throughout an individual's lifetime. Change occurs in the number of cells (neurons), the health of the cells, and their ability to make new connections or pathways. With billions of neurons stretching from our brain, down the spinal cord, throughout our body, continually transforming its own networks, researchers now view our brains through the theory of **embodied cognition** (Goldhagen, 2017; Mallgrave, 2010) which no longer categorizes our brain as a passive recipient of sensory information but as a mutable organ responding to its surrounding. Designers now have a renewed responsibility to create ideal surroundings for our nervous system; ones which support healthy brain function, cognitive development or learning, creativity, and emotional wellness. As both designers and design researchers, we can continually seek out, identify, implement, test, and propose built environments that are optimal for the function of our brain and nervous system. Research in interior design must respond to the challenge of basing our design decisions on credible evidence, provided by physical, or natural science, from diverse fields such as biology and neuroscience, as well as behavioral, anthropological, or sociological scientific ways of knowing.

Research-Informed Design (RID) is the most recent iteration of **Evidence-Based Design (EBD)**. It is an approach to design for the built environment that bases design decisions and decision-making processes (such as space planning, material selection, lighting, and so forth) on the results of scientific inquiry. Historically, EBD gained wide notoriety following the publishing of an article in *Healthcare Design* magazine by design-researcher D. Kirk Hamilton which categorized four levels of practice for those who use research studies in the design process (Hamilton, 2003). At that time, the areas of concern were primarily in safety (preventing accidents and injury), stress-reduction, and reduced time of stay for patients in healthcare environments. Championed by interior designers such as Jain

Malkin, EBD expanded to include even more kinds of studies, including psychological, cognitive, biological, and neuroscience for outcomes related to healing environments, including visitors and healthcare workers as important end-users.

According to Malkin (2008) "The Center for Health Design (CHD) defines EBD as 'the deliberate attempt to base building decisions on the best available research evidence with the goal of improving outcomes and of continuing to monitor the success or failure for subsequent decision-making.' An evidence-based model can be used for all design decisions" (p. 3). EBD tends to emphasize results from experiments with measurable outcomes, appealing to the empirical, generalizable evidence produced from the scientific method as espoused by most of the physical or "hard" sciences. There is also statistical evidence garnered from social sciences as well. Currently, in research-informed design practice other studies are included in the areas of art, humanities, education, philosophy, sociology, and the mind. Research-informed design now leads as the preferred practice in professional trade organizations as well. In 2021, **American Society of Interior Designers (ASID)** virtual conference introduced the Outcomes of Design (OOD) initiative which encouraged interior design professionals to participate in building a body of knowledge based on collecting empirical data of their own projects to show positive outcomes of good design.

Research-informed design is an approach which recognizes that the study of the built environment falls into both the physical world and the realm of imagination and, therefore, there may be a discrepancy between how architects, designers, and planners produce, adopt, use, and understand what constitutes evidence (results or findings from research studies), and the research process (the act of researching itself), particularly when it comes to exploring space and design of the built environment from a human-centered design perspective.

As you will see in Chapter 2 multiple perspectives in research exist, from the more objective, post-positivist to phenomenological to interpretivist, and beyond. This has led to a seemingly disparate chasm between multiple modes of operation in the sciences, which has led to confusion or disagreement between branches of science. Chapter 2 will help elucidate the differences and the overlaps for clarity and help promote dialogue.

The field of interior design bridges the worldviews of objective and subjective realities, from physical or hard science and soft or social sciences and delving into humanities, communication, and education, into art and movement studies. All these arenas can inform design, but we must be vigilant and help them to create logical arguments which connect appropriate evidence to support claims or design decisions. An extension of this view is to see all "creative" design decisions as arising or originating from information including a research-informed design concept, in addition to the typical research-based programmatic requirements.

Research-informed design emphasizes how information enhances the creative process and fosters innovative information-gathering techniques involving images, drawings, movement, and cross-disciplinary interactions. Systematically collected data, whether expressed quantitatively or qualitatively, through a theory or theories, can be analyzed for patterns, trends, or relationships (not necessarily a causal relationship) with applications to practice and implications for further inquiry. Research-informed design students use information to expand:

- Programmatic requirements and problem statements,
- Concept development,
- Site-specific data,
- Potential design solutions, to overcome assumptions about what the design should be to what it could be.

Aspects of design research provide fields of awareness, making a valuable connection between the research process and the design process. When we consciously choose where we find our area of interest (along the continuum) we can then match the research design to align with that paradigm. Our study can be a combination of efforts used to triangulate data, approaching research as one would approach design. As interior design educator Ellen Fisher so aptly summarizes research-informed design:

> Interior design education covers a multitude of knowledge areas: design, art, history, philosophy, technology, and science. It is the research and original thinking in each of these areas that generates new knowledge that has the potential

to improve the lives of people, the wellbeing of communities, and the health of our planet.

> (Fisher, 2020, p. 5)

This textbook is designed to help interior designers become *design-informed researchers* as they navigate and make sense of research. It engages the designer as an active participant in gathering their own evidence, practice designing their own study, using terminology associated with scientific method, and systematic inquiry in general. The goal, of course, is to seamlessly integrate research into the design profession, so we can cultivate *research-informed designers*. However, the search for advancement in research-informed design does not lie solely in producing more data, but to make compelling arguments that connect claims (design decisions) with credible evidence to support those claims.

Design as Creative Problem-Solving

> The natural response to a problem seems to be to try to get rid of it by finding an answer—often taking the first answer that occurs and pursuing it because of one's reluctance to spend the time and mental effort needed to conjure up a richer storehouse of alternatives from which to choose.

> (Adams, 2001)

Design Is a Decision-Making Process

We have, most likely, read many definitions of design, but the one we think gets to its essence is a simple one, **design** is a creative process that emphasizes making decisions. Optimizing an interior requires deliberate choices, selecting one thing over another, or deciding to encourage one set of values over other competing demands, be they visual, spatial, or conceptual. When our design solution needs to meet so many needs—physical, emotional, psychological, ergonomic, spiritual—we find ourselves organizing, prioritizing, and arranging elements to meet as many needs as possible in a holistic solution that also adheres to principles we value of harmony, balance, and proportion. Lest you think this confines us to an overtly rational, empirical, and transparent process, we remind you that the seeds of design decisions are explored in many ways: sketching, modeling, and simply daydreaming not least among them. The origins of intuitive decisions may not always be visible to us, but they have agency *as* decisions, nonetheless.

Design Is a Creative Process

We believe design-as-a-decision-making process activates another meaning of design: it is a *creative* process. Rattner (2019) defines **creativity** as the act of developing novel and useful ideas for products, services, and systems. A novel combination of ideas, a connection between two known parts previously unknown to each other, and the unexpected joy in a new interpretation of the familiars of our world is not accidental, but rather is founded on our *agency*, our capacity to act independently and to make choices. Being creative in this sense may be deliberate *or* intuitive. It does not have to be a mysterious "black box" but is subject to our understanding. Which brings us to the good part: the act of being creative is a skill that can be learned. To discover new patterns and put into form new combinations, we can access the myriad "building blocks" of a designed interior setting.

In 1977 architect and builder, Christopher Alexander led a team of researchers at U.C. Berkeley to produce an inspiring new way of looking at design of the built environment. The team published a series of books including *The Timeless Way of Building* and *A Pattern Language* which, when used together, offered a ground-breaking strategy for designers of the built environment. Using observation, the team identified essential atmospheric or practical qualities of built environments at three scales: towns and neighborhoods, buildings and gardens, and interior rooms and features. The researchers generated what they considered generic or neutral descriptions of these qualities, independent of style or culture, hoping to capture a universal language that would operate across time and location. Much like the discussion of technological ages earlier in the chapter to categorize human evolution, these qualities called "patterns" were described and numbered, systematized so that they could be referred to and used in practice by designers. In all, they identified 253 patterns, each with a succinct poetic description and accompanying sketch or diagram to help a designer concretize abstract concepts. Once understood individually, these patterns can be assembled by a designer to be experienced sequentially, simultaneously, or overlapping in an actual space.

For an example, in the introduction to *A Pattern Language*, Alexander asked us to consider several patterns for the design of an entry sequence into a home: "Private Terrace on the Street" (#140), "Sunny Place" (#161), "Outdoor Room" (#163), "Six-foot Balcony" (#167), "Ceiling Height Variety" (#190), "Front Door Bench" (#242), "Raised Flowers" (#245), and "Different Chairs" (#251). The ability to see each pattern as a distinct entity that could be interpreted and organized in infinite ways gave designers a new way to describe a building to a potential client, understand why a certain environment produced a pleasing human experience, or articulate why another environment was unpleasant and offer ideas on how it could be fixed. Overall, this project visualized the component pieces of everyday environments as elements that were available to us to use in combination, just as the elements of spoken or written language can be formulated in countless ways to yield a poem, an aria, a recipe, directions to the coffee shop, or *Hamlet* (Alexander, Ishikawa, & Silverstein, 1977).

Understanding and control of the creative process, along with the agency to intervene in settings and manipulate their component parts, brings us to the application of research in the interior design process. The "building blocks" of an interior consist not only of their physical and spatial properties; the behavior of the occupants with their surroundings and with each other are also building blocks interior designers will seek to understand and organize to achieve the spatial outcomes that people desire and need. This kind of building block is also subject to the designer's decision-making. And to drill down just a little deeper, this decision-making begins to play a role phenomenally *early* in the process: before we apply behavioral data to design, we are making decisions about how to gather that data and what it means. These early decisions will affect the use of research in design, and therefore we see an understanding of interior design research methods as an essential contributor to the creative process.

In the creative process, research is often seen in a supporting role, providing real-world evidence for sound design decision-making. We intend to expand its role in this chapter. Our aim is to promote research to the status of marquee player, so we will explore the role of research itself as a creative endeavor. While it does indeed serve creative ends in a practical role, the research activity at its best is driven by creative motivation just as other phases of the design process are. The pursuit of evidence can spark those mood-elevating centers in our brains that tell us we are enjoying the kind of pleasure we get from a brilliant concept diagram or a rendering that captures the play of light on a surface that doesn't yet exist. You know the feeling, as does the poet, composer, choreographer, and painter. Who else knows that feeling, and what does it tell us?

What Is Creativity?

Most designers count creativity as a primary motivator for choice of profession. It is right up there with the desire to create something beautiful and useful, and serving others by supporting their needs with appropriate and functional environments. The promise of doing something creative is the juice that keeps us going, through countless obstacles, frustrations, and all-nighters, to enjoy the reward of having brought into the world something new.

Some would say creativity is like comedy: if it must be explained, it's no longer funny. We do not believe that, nor do Henri Bergson or Jerry Seinfeld (about comedy). In the arts, the social and "hard" sciences, and the study of organization management (yes, that can be creative, too!), we see creativity being defined in new ways. This dynamism is useful to us, because it gives us formulations that not only explain the work of a Leonardo da Vinci, but that of DiCaprio; it reveals tools that we can use and apply to our activities today.

Design and other professions in the arts share the valorization of creativity with another group: the sciences. Consider the stories of discovery, whether they feature the sudden insight, as in Isaac Newton's manipulations of a simple glass prism delivering the theory of color; the slow-moving hunch begun in Darwin's journal on the *HMS Beagle*; or the dream-inspired revelation of the structure of the DNA molecule achieved by Watson and Crick. Creativity delivers not only the sounds, shapes, and movements that give us aesthetic pleasure, it gives us the tools to understand the way our universe works. Some would say that, too, is an aesthetic fulfillment.

In recent years we have seen multiple disciplines converge on a definition of creativity that is not only (1) novel, in the sense of bringing something new into the world, but (2) useful, in contributing to a domain of knowledge within or at the edge of its boundaries, and (3) collaborative or collective, drawing for its essence on a group, or emerging from an immersive and supportive environment (Amabile & Pillemer, 2012; Hautala & Ibert, 2018). This definition is gaining international consensus across cultures (Farmer, Tierney, & Kung-McIntyre, 2003) and can be accepted in its time ("crowd-pleasing") or, sometimes, not (Sternberg, 1999).

In the 1970s this definition was augmented by the characterization of creativity by a growing number of theorists as "a process through time, rather than a static trait of individuals or of certain creative products"—one that relies on the combination of parts and pieces (Sawyer, 2003). Phrased thus as the first tenet of the "emergent" theory of creativity, this conception of a process could apply to our traditional view of da Vinci (the notebooks!), and equally well to the collaboration of an ensemble where creativity is of necessity a product of multiple players, roles, the limitations of a given medium, and the passage of time within a matrix of space (DiCaprio). For us, the good news is that the walls of exclusivity are broken down. We no longer must "be" creative in the sense of the solitary genius, we can now access a process, the rules of which are discoverable and shareable.

Examining Habits

According to Duhigg (2012) **habits** are formed with a psychological pattern of environmental cue, behavior, and reward. When performed over and over these routine behaviors form strong neural pathways which allow the behaviors to become more automatic. Habits are traced to the parts of the brain associated with emotion, memory, and pattern recognition, which are different from the parts of the brain associated with decision-making. The habits that human beings form, our acquired modes or patterns of behavior, allow us to solve the infinite list of intellectual problems that come our way, through rapid and efficient methods. Habits have been essential to our survival as a species because we would never get anything accomplished if we had to formally process all of the stimuli that come into our perception. Habits of thought and behavior ensure our survival by allowing us to focus our attention on only what is needed to accomplish the task or goal of the moment (Adams, 2001).

This tendency toward habit is the functional reason why we adopt the assumptions mentioned previously—which can include stereotypes, labels, categories, and associations—as well as adopting systems of organization and operation. Habit is like an automatic filing system (Adams, 2001). From a professional standpoint, this forming of habit can result in a designer always drawing upon an existing list of "solutions" that come from preconceived notions, assumptions, and categorizations of what a design solution *should* be, rather than contemplating and exploring the infinite possibilities for what a design solution *could* be. There is value in building an interior design project and design solutions based on improving upon what you already have. But do not overlook the potential for imagining a new definition of what it could be (Adams, 2001, p. 61).

For Twyla Tharp, habit is a good thing. An unexpected approach to creativity can be found in her emphasis on the importance of rituals, of daily habits that both trigger and support creative activity. "A lot of habitually creative people," she writes, "have preparation rituals linked to the setting in which they choose to start their day." She describes her own prosaic routines involving getting up, stretching, dressing, grabbing the paper, and cabbing it to the studio. This may sound boring, but each one of these serves as a micro-preparatory act leading up to her achieving the mental state of being "ready" to create. The newspaper, really? Yes, one of the steps. Compare this to the cliché of stormy, angst-driven struggle we sometimes associate with the creative process. If angst is your thing, make it a habit so you know when the creative juices can be expected to flow, but if not, think about those daily steps, whether it is cleaning the bathroom or laying out your favorite gel markers that settles you in and sends your brain the right signals.

A dancer or an athlete's stretching routine deliberately touches those muscles that don't get used in the standard activities of daily life. Designers have imaginative muscles that need "limbering up" too—including the ones that make connections between the things we think about all the time, like space or form or color, and the things we may not think of as frequently: the user's experience of a space, or form, or color, and how we can make hypotheses about these things, and test them. How often do you use that muscle?

Getting in the Flow

We hear about dancers and athletes achieving a "flow" state, one of focused concentration in which they lose themselves in performing the activity at hand. In flow, challenges stretch but do not overmatch skills, time slows down, and extraordinary levels of creation seem natural. The basketball player "catches fire" and any shot from anywhere on the court is going to fall. Chess players and rock climbers describe having these experiences, and yes, designers, too. Dr. Pfeiffer's "neural pathways" are wide open, external objectives fade in importance, and we become absorbed in the activity purely for its own sake.

If our goal is to bring creative flow to our work, can we understand and apply its mechanisms to a design *charrette* (an intense, time-limited collaborative session focused on solving a problem) or the formation of a research paradigm? Behavioral psychologists Jeanne Nakamura and Mihalyi Csikszentmihalyi have investigated the "flow" experiences of diverse subjects and add to what we know about this admittedly subjective condition. Intrinsic motivation, they found, is much more important than extrinsic motivations. In a state of flow, what happens in any moment is responsive to what happened immediately before. Sports and games, they note, have goals and feedback structures that make flow more likely (Nakamura & Csikszentmihalyi, 2001).

Some people achieve "flow" ironing shirts. They find the "feedback structure" that makes a well-ironed shirt a source of pleasure. Can we as designers strive for an elegantly phrased research proposition for its own sake? Can we build feedback structures into our *charrettes* and research activities, or discover beneath their surface the places they already exist? We are more likely to achieve a state of flow when we are intrinsically motivated; if we are doing the work out of an inner motivation, we are more likely to be able to exercise our creative faculties.

Creativity asks you to go beyond what is considered the norm or the accepted "right" answer. While habits are safe, creativity is daring. Sometimes it is our habits of thinking and doing that make up the filter of judgment that blocks young ideas that could have been great. Uninhibited free-thinking and writing techniques are essential parts of the creative process. They provide a safe environment in which you can practice breaking your habits, allowing you to conjure creative options in response to any question or problem (Adams, 2001).

RESEARCH IN ACTION 1.1
Designing a Space to Enhance Creativity

By Amanda Dowell

Take a look around your home. Do you feel inspired? Do you feel creative? Or do you feel guilty about the pile of dirty socks in the corner? As an interior designer I am fascinated by the way our surroundings affect how we feel and how we act. I moved into a little condo last year and one of the first things I noticed were the high ceilings and picture windows. Painted canvases adorn my walls, sketchbooks stacked knee high, and mason jars filled with paint brushes. I wondered if my space is making me more creative which led me to look into the science connecting environment and creativity.

If you do have high ceilings like me, you are in for a treat. Researchers discovered that people in a room with ten-foot ceilings scored higher on creativity assessment tests than those who took the same test under eight-foot ceilings (Rattner, 2019). It seems that if our space is open, our minds are open. This also applies to lateral directions, in front and behind us, or side to side, and to the space above us.

Another study using fMRI brain scans showed that a part of the brain that deals with exploration activated when looking at a picture of high ceilings. When the subjects looked at pictures of low ceilings this activation was not found. The experiment showed that our brain activity changes depending on the apparent height of the ceiling. High ceilings open our minds to new and innovative ideas (**divergent thinking**). On the flipside, lower ceilings foster detail-oriented and more focused thinking (**convergent thinking**). William Lidwell refers to this relationship between ceiling height and cognition as **cathedral effect** (Lidwell, Holden, & Butler, 2010).

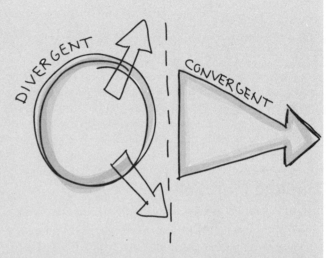

Concept of Divergent–Convergent Thinking. During divergent thinking our minds are opened to new ideas, whereas during convergent thinking we are more detail-oriented and focused.

In our design office we have large windows and I believe it makes me more creative and productive. According to Rattner (2019), "windowed environments can facilitate creative task performance by restoring cognitive capacity, reducing stress, mental fatigue, and perceived risk, and promoting a sense of freedom and openness" (p. 47). A study conducted in 2014 showed that people who worked in a room without windows suffered a lack in sleep quality than those with windows. A theory by Jay Appleton, known as **prospect–refuge theory**, proposes that due to our biological need for survival, people relax when they can clearly view what is available to them (*prospect*), while feeling protected from unseen danger (*refuge*).

The theory stems from the way our ancestors lived, as this type of setting was vital to their survival (Appleton, 1975). Although, we don't need to worry about being eaten by wild animals in our urban settings, this preference of *prospect–refuge* is still with us today. Brain scans show that people would rather sit with their backs to the wall in public spaces

with an expansive view of a space. Gazing out a window with the door closed makes us feel relaxed and safe, which allows our brains to switch from a more logical, planning and risk-aversion mode of thinking, to a creative and expansive state of mind (Rattner, 2019).

Prospect–Refuge Theory. People need a safe but inspiring place, balancing the ability to view what is in the distance with the possibility to retreat, as shown in this sectional diagram.

The Aha Moment

Insight, a sudden comprehension, or an **Aha Moment** is an important aspect of human thinking. If you have ever had a sudden moment of clarity, think back to the situation you were in. Many times, our environment has an impact on our frame of mind, our thoughts, and emotions, and therefore the connections that we make in our mind that leads to a realization or solution to a nagging problem. We may not be aware that our brain has been working on the problem. Although the experience of insight is sudden and can seem disconnected from the immediately preceding thought, according to Kounios and Beeman (2009), studies using the tools of cognitive neuroscience (measuring brain activity through EEG and fMRI), show that insight may happen as a result of brain processes over time. This means your brain is working in the background, and that you can facilitate or expedite the process of insight by preparing your brain through feeding your brain positive imagery, laughing at a joke, or periodic resting.

According to Vincent Ryan Ruggiero (2008) *The Art of Thinking: A Guide to Critical and Creative Thought*, the human mind has two phases: the production of ideas and the judgment of ideas (p. 97). The way humans go back and forth between these two conditions can be enhanced by cultivating playfulness, forging courage, seeking out input from others, being independently resourceful and just plain hard work (including industriousness and refusing to give in to frustration or disappointment). These are what Ruggiero refers to as the "characteristics of creative people" (p. 100). When

we apply our cultivated personal habits of the mind to a particular problem or issue, we activate *motivation* which is an essential ingredient to the creative process. Ruggiero gives us a few avenues by which we can come up with a good problem to exercise our creative muscle. We can take a novel approach to an old problem (such as homelessness or unemployment), modify an existing process or system (such as cooking or serving food), invent a new type of space or institution (such as a recreation center for preventative medicine), or we can find a new use for outdated items (i.e. convert an old library to a school). Overall, we can be on the lookout to improve something in terms of its usefulness or helpfulness for people in their daily lives.

Bryce (2014) suggests a kind of brain calisthenics, or step-by-step practice to exercise your brain's ability to be innovative. First, explore multiple ideas, then focus, allow a particular idea to incubate, and then wait for an insight. "Flashes of insight are markers of the creative process and may help elucidate what happens in the brain during creative problem solving" (p. 40). Simply put, if we feed our brain with quality information, and immerse ourselves in situations that balance this wealth of information with relaxed but focused attention on the problem, we may be able to facilitate, or create the ideal situation for, this sudden moment of insight or clarity. Have you ever heard the adage that people make their own luck? If we can foster flexibility of thinking we can more likely arrive at an appropriate, and novel, idea.

IDENTIFYING A PROBLEM TO SOLVE

In his book *Creativity* (2006), Robert Weisberg references a "Model of Creativity" developed by Teresa M. Amabile. The essential element in this model of creativity is the role of motivation. In her 1983 study, Amabile found that

> a person's attitude toward a task is critical in determining whether he or she will respond creatively to it. If the person finds the task intrinsically motivating—that is, if he or she is interested in the task for its own sake and not because of some extrinsic reward that might come about as a result of a successful performance—the chances of the person's producing an innovative response will be maximized. One hears individuals who work in creative fields—writers, artists, scientists—say again and again that they do what they do because they love it, and the fact that they make a living doing it is only a bonus.
>
> (Weisberg, 2006, p. 99)

In *Conceptual Blockbusting* Adams says, "Motivation is essential to creativity" (2001, p. 69). The reality is that no matter how talented you are, problem-solving and the design process involve tedium, frustration, and challenges. Adams goes on to say that "unless you truly want to solve a problem you will probably not do a very good job" (p. 69). That means that unless you are convinced that a change needs to happen in a certain area within the realm of interior design, you are not likely to question or hypothesize and propose a solution for how that change can and will happen (Adams, 2001).

If you do not carefully select a design problem that you are motivated to solve, your research project could be tedious and arduous. So, choose an area that will maintain your interest throughout the process. The greatest satisfaction comes when you are presenting your project to your jury of critics, and you see an audience of academic and professional peers who are there because the problem you have chosen to solve and the topics you have explored and incorporated in this process matter to people. You have embarked on a design journey that is meaningful not only to you but to others as well, and the conclusions you draw will be added to the body of knowledge that makes up the foundation of the interior design field (Adams, 2001).

Within every project type you encounter, whether in school or in the professional world, there are areas of focus and design issues you will be faced with and will be excited to learn more about. Some of the time, the area of focus or issue will be of great interest to you and you will enjoy learning about it and adding it to your list of skills. Other times, the topic will be less familiar to you.

These are times to remember the words of James Webb Young, who literally wrote the book on how to get ideas in advertising: "Every really good creative person in advertising whom I have ever known has always had two noticeable characteristics. First, there was no subject under the sun in which he could not easily get interested … Second, he was an extensive browser in all sorts of fields of information" (Young, 1940). Curiosity, he tells us, is the most important trait a creative person can have. Young's formula for creativity in advertising works for the design professions, too. In fact, his five-step creative process mirrors the one interior designers use today: (1) gather materials—this is where the curiosity and the browsing come in; (2) chew on it for a bit—look for connections and patterns; (3) incubation—allow time for your unconscious mind to work; (4) the Aha moment; and (5) submit your idea to the consideration of others—and watch it expand!

We talked about your motivation to solve a problem, beginning with your commitment to create positive change in the built environment. Don Koberg and Jim Bagnall, the authors of *The Universal Traveler*, remind us that most of the design problems we will address in our careers will have been brought to us by others. Whether that is the case, or there is simply an aspect of your self-chosen project that is less appealing to you, it is helpful to think of Koberg and Bagnall's phrase for that good feeling you get when you take on a problem and you're juiced to do something positive: they describe it as one of the "energy states" you will experience as you move through the design process, called Acceptance (Koberg & Bagnall, 1974). This is the point where you assume responsibility for the problem, and in so doing, re-order your own priorities to align with the problem's needs.

The energy state of Acceptance isn't required, but it makes a difference in how you feel about the project and, ultimately, how creative you will be in its solution. While some self-discipline is needed at many stages of design, we also recognize Acceptance cannot be artificially manufactured. Be attuned to your own feelings. If you are about to take on a problem, try confirming your commitment through reflective and interactive exercises. Koberg and Bagnall have fifteen of these exercises; we suggest trying at least one of the three that our students have found to be the most successful:

- Put yourself on the spot. Gather "witnesses" you respect and trust, tell them you are taking the problem on, and identify some measurable expectations and due dates.
- Imagine yourself as the end user whose life will be diminished if the problem is left unsolved. Keep a journal of your thoughts and feelings.
- Become the problem. Immerse yourself. Wear its clothes, talk its language, adopt its beliefs, until you are so like it that your friends remark on it.

These are ways of taking ownership. At the end of this chapter are activities designed to get you started. After completing them, you should know whether you want to own the problem.

The interior design topics and issues you investigate and address in your project work may well play an important role in your career direction and job search. They present you with a chance to set yourself apart from other applicants as being an expert in the design topic or issue you explored extensively in school. Whether or not a firm you are interested in is looking for a designer who has a particular specialization or study in your field of experience, the story you can tell about your research and design can support your unique qualifications, and mark you as a designer with the curiosity to look beneath the surface of a project brief.

Brainstorming

One way to use the freedom of the creative process is to expand our "adjacent possible"—to search the larger realm of ideas available to us by simply reaching for them outside our original pool. In *Where Good Ideas Come From*, Steven Johnson says nature in its proliferation of species does this (as found by our friend Darwin) through new combinations, and that we can do it, too, by accessing the fertile environments of cities, new communication media, and the evolving tools that enable us to connect what we know to what we don't know yet. Begin, Johnson says, in a metaphorical house, in a room with four doors, "each leading to a new room that you haven't visited yet. Those four rooms are the adjacent possible. But once you open one of those doors and stroll into that room, three new doors appear, each leading to a brand-new room that you couldn't have reached from your original starting point" (Johnson, 2010).

Among the many methods of tapping into the adjacent possible, one of the most fertile may be **brainstorming**, popularized by A. F. Osborn in his book *Applied Imagination* (1953). As a method of problem-solving that leveraged the resources of a group, brainstorming sessions were conceived as occurring under a set of rules that facilitated members of the group contributing to a conversation that explored a problem in a freewheeling, non-judgmental way. W. J. J. Gordon promoted the efficacy of the technique as being superior to the ability of individuals to creatively solve problems working on their own and described case studies in group brainstorming in *Synectics* (1961). While later studies found a lack of evidence of the superiority of group brainstorming over individual efforts, it became a staple of group problem-solving across multiple fields.

Osborn and Gordon's process built on the simple observation that a stimulating conversation between two persons can result in the emergence of a thought structure that belongs to neither of them alone. Brainstorming succeeded when participants checked their critical analytical tendencies at the door. Key to the process was every group member's ability to add an idea without fear of it being criticized or dissected. In practice, this is quite hard to do.

In design, we have been educated within a teaching model of the design critique and its unique method of responding to creative ideas. The drama of standing up in front of peers and instructors alongside one's design has become a rite of passage, to good effect and bad. For brainstorming, the downside is that we tend to adopt the persona of the insightful critic that we've learned. It is quite easy to pick apart a new idea that attempts to solve a problem in a different way, and at the same time it is quite difficult to skip the opportunity to demonstrate our critical skills when we find ourselves in a group.

While brainstorming has become the default term for group ideation, it seldom creates the kind of safe space that allows participants to look forward to the event. To make ideas happen, we need to establish an environment of trust, in which we can rediscover the sense of unlimited possibilities latent whenever two or more of us are gathered. Where can we find such a place? We have to create it in our own daily practice.

As we have seen, creativity is free: a process for bringing forth new ideas, and pushing boundaries, with the support or in the company of others. What can we do with that freedom?

RESEARCH IN ACTION 1.2
The Improv Club—Where Something Is Made from Nothing, Nightly

Two people alone on a stage wearing their everyday clothes. One starts it off with a remark, or a random phrase offered by the audience. The other takes that remark and does something with it: builds on it or sends it in an entirely new direction. The actors don't look particularly imposing. There is no script and no advance preparation. Nothing stands between them and public failure. Yet, minutes later, the club is engulfed in laughter! Why does this work?

Leonard and Yorton (2015), a couple of *Second City* producers outline key points of improvisation: there's no starting over, no passing up a line to wait for a better one, no second-guessing, and no criticism. Leonard and Yorton (2015) distill the elements that open the creative gates, the first of which is "*Yes, And*"—the principle that every idea deserves its chance to be acted on (and acted out!). The second is the element of *Ensemble*—you don't have to be right; you don't have to be better, and you don't have to pretend you're in control when you're not. Third is *Dialogue*: it pushes the story to places monologue can't take it. Number four, being *Authentic* means you don't pretend that problems don't exist. Number five happens all the time: *Failure*—that moment onstage when a mistake happens—the whole audience knows it … But by acknowledging the mistake and incorporating it into the narrative, something new and unexpected happens that makes the audience go wild. The sixth element of *Follow* which allows any member of the group to take leadership when needed, then just as easily return to the ranks when it's better for someone else to take over. The seventh and final element is *Active Listening*. We've all made the mistake of mentally rehearsing our follow-up instead of listening to what the current speaker is saying. That doesn't work in Improv. We need to be in the moment.

As designers we often find ourselves in the position of creating something out of nothing. Yes, we might have a brief, and the constraints of an existing site, but the blank sheet of paper at the beginning is daunting. The same is true of a research *hypothesis* (defined in Chapter 2). The first statement of your inquiry is usually not the best and playing it out with a trusted ensemble will save time and get you to a place you hadn't foreseen when you first drafted the statement. Recruit your own Second City troupe and have a go. Every idea gets a chance. That's it—a simple model for collaborative creativity (and you're not required to be funny). In Improv, you know you've got back-up. You don't have to fear carrying the scene by yourself. As Leonard and Yorton (2015) quoted Dr. Mark Pfeiffer, "Every time you learn to be unafraid, your brain changes. [Improv is] the quickest way to get to the neural pathway change, because it puts [people] in a situation where they're facing their fears." While Dr. Pfeiffer suggests fear can be overcome through neural pathway change, how do we face fear if we're not Improv comedians? Designers often face fears of unoriginality—"someone has done it before." To be judged unoriginal is a fear shared by performers. The dancer and choreographer Twyla Tharp says this: "Someone has done it before? Honey, it's all been done before. Nothing's really original. Not Homer or Shakespeare and certainly not you. Get over yourself" (Tharp, 2009).

If you can master the idea of **conceptual block-busting** or breaking through the "mental walls that block the problem-solver from correctly perceiving a problem or conceiving its solution" (Adams, 2001, p. 13), then you have mastered the secret to innovation: breaking down your preconceived notions and letting your mind go beyond what it already knows and understands. The following are some of the fundamental elements of conceptual blockbusting:

- Avoiding analyzing or judging too early in the problem-solving process
- Avoiding taking only the first answer that occurs
- Using your brainstorming capacity to create as many alternative questions, answers, or solutions as possible
- Developing confidence in your work and ideas

In his book *New Think*, Edward De Bono speaks of the difference between **vertical thinking** and **lateral thinking**.

Vertical thinkers take the most reasonable view of a situation and then proceed logically and carefully to work it out. Lateral thinkers tend to explore all the different ways of looking at something, rather than accepting the most promising and proceeding from that. The great thing about vertical and lateral thinking is that you don't have to accept one over the other; you can use them both to reach the best outcome. You can use lateral thinking to generate your ideas and use vertical thinking once you are focused and ready to develop one of those ideas.

(1968, p. 23)

Once you have these two concepts in your mind, consider this further observation from De Bono:

It is possible to deal with a subject by carefully proceeding from one point to another. It is possible to describe a building by studying the architect's plans, starting first with one elevation and then going on to another, working one's way methodically over the details. But there is another way of getting to know a building, and that is to walk around it, looking at it from all sorts of different angles. Some of the views will overlap, but in the end a good general view of the building is obtained, and it may turn out to be more real than that obtained by a detailed study of the plans.

(De Bono, as quoted in Adams, 2001, p. 34)

In the quote just above, the first approach—carefully reviewing all the details—is an example of vertical thinking, while the second approach—looking on from many angles—is considered lateral thinking. This combination of approaches could be applied to our previous discussion about how, by nature, design is a circular process rather than a linear one. Some steps might overlap or even be revisited, but in the end the overall approach is more complete, thoughtful, and responsive to the evolving needs of the project. The value of taking an exploratory approach to a creative problem, rather than following a systematic predetermined path, becomes clear.

Activity 1.1
Writing a Catastrophic Expectations Report (CER)

Purpose: To build confidence in your work and to sell your ideas to an instructor, a critic, or a potential client.

The next time you are having difficulty deciding whether to push an idea, ask yourself the following questions and write a short Catastrophic Expectations Report (CER) inspired by *Conceptual Blockbusting* (Adams, 2001, p. 46):

1. First, looking at your idea, write down EVERYTHING you could be criticized for or judged on with regard to it. Be specific as you get into the minds of your critics.

2. Now look at the same idea and precisely detail exactly what would happen to you if EVERYTHING went wrong with the idea. What is the worst-case scenario?

3. Now that you have dumped your fears onto a piece of paper outside of yourself, look at what you have written and make some evaluations of the situation. Can you separate the subjective judgments from the objective issues that can and should be addressed now to make your idea stronger?

Use the CER process as an opportunity to make your idea even stronger. By putting yourself in the mind-set of the critics, you give yourself an opportunity to find the answers to their questions. You will be confidently prepared to answer those questions, realizing that the worst-case scenario to your idea proposal probably is not something you can't handle if you are just willing to step out on a limb. Ask this question: What is the worst that can happen? And as Cameron (1992) advised in *The Artist's Way*, "Leap and the net will appear" (p. 2).

Activity 1.2
Creating a Concept Map

Purpose: This activity is intended to facilitate brainstorming and innovative connections to help you come up with a research topic.

Concept mapping supports brainstorming in that the process allows you to explore many ideas, without getting lost, judgmental, or overwhelmed in the process. Concept mapping also helps you retrace your way back through earlier ideas, often finding exciting new paths as you navigate from one idea to the next. The goal of the **concept map** is to brainstorm ideas and then mark the meaningful relationships among them. It can look very similar to the relationship diagrams you might draw up in the schematic stages of a design project, but it has the potential to become much larger, as it branches out in different directions.

Concept mapping translates easily from academics to the interior design profession. It would be used in much the same way at work as it would in your academic process. It can help you sort out challenging and complex concepts and ideas. For now, use it to help you find connections between ideas that might eventually lead to your asking questions that could become the foundation for your research or thesis project.

1. Place a word or phrase (your initial idea) at the center. Begin to add related words or ideas around it. Use color, graphic annotations, and symbols to create connection and meanings among related ideas, as illustrated below.

2. Now take a highlighter and trace a path from the center out along a branch that you find MOST interesting or compelling. Continue until you have made a clear connection that results in a project direction.

3. When you are ready share your concept map with others for their insight and opinions.

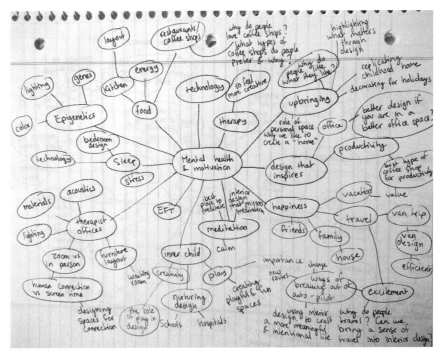

Some initial, broad terms such as "Mental Health" and "Motivation" as drawn in the center connected with other words that come up during a concept mapping session may lead you in many exciting and innovative directions.

Activity 1.3
Focusing and Narrowing Your Research Topic

Purpose: This fill-in-the-blank sentence prompt can be used to help focus and narrow your research project ideas.

Using some of the words and ideas generated in the previous activity, complete the following sentence:

My interest lies in helping _____ (end-user type) with/overcome/enhance (circle one) _____ (issue) in a _____ (project type) setting or situation.

Consider the following examples:

1. My interest lies in helping <u>students and instructors</u> enhance <u>social interaction</u> in a <u>virtual classroom</u>.

2. My interest lies in helping <u>servers</u> with <u>efficiency as well as safety</u> in a <u>restaurant (or hospitality environment)</u>.

3. My interest lies in helping <u>aging adults</u> with <u>finding their way</u> in an <u>assisted living environment</u>.

Keep in mind that your end-user can be defined through their age, gender, culture/heritage, socioeconomic status, occupation, abilities/disabilities or other physiological or demographic characteristics. The "issue" you choose to address can be drawn from design-related areas of expertise that you specialize in or have an affinity towards (such as aesthetics, functionality, sustainability, efficiency …), more humanistic concerns (such as cognition/learning, motivation, accessibility, privacy, safety …) or socially oriented issues (such as equality/justice, ceremonial/religious, entertainment, or recreation, to name just a few). The project type you select can be from a broad category such as residential, commercial, hospitality, or institutional, or can be more specific such as a restaurant or research laboratory, or it can be a newly invented kind of built space. Please use this activity to further your brainstorming skills. You may have more than one answer at this point, which is understandable!

Activity 1.4
Developing a Research Question

Purpose: To develop a compelling and focused research question.

Sometimes a research study is built around a statement, but it is often more powerful if we can turn it into a question. A research question should be carefully crafted, considering each word choice. For example, asking *if* something is valid or *should* exist ends up eliciting a *yes* or *no* answer, whereas asking *why* seeks a causal relationship between two things, and asking *how* leaves the possible answers open to perceived relationships or patterns that may not be causal in nature.

It may help to ask *what* the relationship is between two phenomena, and to continually ask it throughout the research process so that the answer could become more and more clear. Followed by asking *who* is potentially in a position of power to address it? And then, asking *what* can be done to solve the problem? In addition, we can restrict or focus our question to target a certain subcategory or instance and then narrow it to a certain geographic location, time period, or project type. Consider the following iterations or variations on a question about a problem:

1. Can homelessness be solved? (Yes or no question)

2. Why do we have homelessness in our society? (Seeking a causal relationship)

3. What is the relationship between mental health and homelessness? (Recognizing that the relationship may exist but not be causal one)

4. How can homelessness be addressed in our community? (Open-ended)

5. How can we address the issue of single-parent families in this community and reduce the risk of them becoming homeless again? (Focused and narrowed)

Reflect on the examples in Tables 1.1, 1.2, and 1.3. And then write your responses in the blank boxes provided. Share your questions with your instructor, colleagues, or peers to see if it makes sense to them.

This activity will help you develop a compelling research question or thesis statement. A research question is often open-ended (not a yes/no question) and can logically emerge as you restrict and narrow your broad topic.

Table 1.1 Focusing a Broad Topic into a Specific Research Question

Broad Topic	Transportation	Affordable Housing	Universal Design	Fitness	Hospitality
Restricted Topic—chooses a direction	Airline travel	Efficient use of space	Wheelchairs / Mobility tools	Specialty gyms	Integrating green design into hotels
Narrowed Topic	Traveler experiences in airports including check-in, security, and boarding	Flexibility and adaptability in multi-family residences	Resistance to aesthetics of federal accessibility regulations	Children as "users" of a gym	Promoting and designing for "green behavior" among hotel guests
Research Question	How can airports adapt to the changing needs of passengers while reducing stress?	How can the principles of flexibility and adaptability help us to create smaller footprint for homes without losing comfort and usability?	How can Universal Design also be aesthetically pleasing?	What is an effective way to promote health and fitness for children?	How do we design a hotel to promote and facilitate sustainability and promote "green" behaviors in guests and hotel staff?

Table 1.2 A Simple Topic Leads to Multiple Research Questions

Broad Topic	Coffee	Coffee	Coffee
Restricted Topic	Coffee houses and social gatherings	Coffee scent	Coffee house innovations
Narrowed Topic	Appropriate scale and proportion for intimate social interaction in U.S. culture	Coffee as used on airplanes and other forms of transportation	Innovations in travel and coffee service/coffee on the go in Western Europe
Research Question	Could the size and scale of recycled shipping containers be an innovative solution to coffee house design?	How can scent of coffee be used in interiors to reduce stress and offer comfort?	Can the coffee house come to the customer rather than the customer having to go to the coffee house?
Proposed Answer			

Table 1.3 Composing Your Research Question

Broad Topic	(Example) Dining Practices	(Example) Marriage	Your Broad Topic Here:
Restricted Topic	Dining Practices in Japan	Non-Traditional Wedding Ceremonies	**Your Restricted Topic Here:**
Narrowed Topic	Japanese Tea Ceremony and Tea Houses	Churches/Sacred Spaces	**Your Narrowed Topic Here:**
Research Question	Has the traditional Japanese tea house changed over time to reflect modern culture?	Is the traditional church an appropriate setting for today's non-traditional wedding ceremonies? What type of space would best suit this activity?	**Your Research Question Here:**

A RESEARCH-INFORMED INTERIOR DESIGN SOLUTION

A research endeavor can lead to many different forms. Research can be communicated via a project, such as a large-, medium-, or small-scale proposed interior design solution, innovative custom furniture or product design. Findings from a study can also be turned into a conference presentation, a poster, a published article or book, a workshop, a business model, or some other product or artifact. We conclude this chapter with a look at an example of a research-informed, interior design project proposed by a student of interior design.

RESEARCH IN ACTION 1.3
Euphadose: A Safe Injection Facility

By Mary Kristofich

According to the CDC, from 1999 to 2018 more than 115,000 Americans died from overdoses related to using heroin. Addiction to intravenous drugs results in outcomes that affect other avenues in our society as well. Sharing syringes increases the chance of spreading diseases, such as HIV and Hepatitis, while used syringes contaminate our water sources and contribute to environmental pollution. It has been estimated that the average heroin user in the U.S. costs taxpayers $50,000, while incarcerated heroin users cost taxpayers $74,000 (NCBI, "Societal Cost of Heroin Use Disorder in US"). Along with the cost, heroin user's risky behavior can contribute to public harm due to DUIs (Driving Under the Influence) and other criminal offenses such as burglary and robbery.

Taking on this subject matter as part of my thesis project, I proposed an interesting solution: What if addicts had a safe place to use drugs? I found that in Canada, and various countries in Europe, safe injection facilities combat problems such as overdose and spread of disease. These facilities also empower addicts to help end their usage of heroin through positive interaction and access to counselling. *InSite*, a safe injection facility located in Vancouver, have had 3.6 million clients in total since 2003, and have successfully intervened all overdoses. Providing a snack and a counselor to talk to, *InSite*'s clients report feeling accepted and human. In 2018, 443 of *InSite*'s clients accessed their detox facility. A similar facility in Copenhagen called *H17*, used color coding to help distinguish different sections of the facility and color theory to influence their well-being. Upon entering, the patient experiences an immersive blue palette. As the patient continues to walk through the facility, the colors gradually become warmer. This transition from cool to warm is intended to subconsciously awaken the patient to help them re-enter society.

Although some cities in the United States have needle exchange programs, they do not yet provide the necessary facility to handle the country's addiction crisis. The interior design solution I have proposed (see images at end of boxed text.) provides a human-focused approach using a variety of evidence-based design solutions. *Euphadose*'s safe injection facility anticipates approximately 800 visits per day, with users spending 30 minutes in the facility. With such a high turnover rate, the materials in the facility must withstand the durability and maintenance. All fabrics are antimicrobial and able to be cleaned with bleach. Seamless fiberglass benches were implemented in waiting rooms to make it easier to wipe down and sanitize. LVT flooring used throughout with carpet tile in the acoustically quiet areas, making it easier to replace. From an image-based survey I conducted on *Reddit*, 64% of users were drawn to an image of forest and ocean which led me to create a color palette of greens and blues. In fact, the most popular image from the survey adorns the privacy partitions in each booth.

Curves in architecture have been shown to reduce anxiety and promote calmness, rather than sharp or straight edges. Curves and organic patterns have been integrated into the flooring, built-in cabinetry, and in the walls. A clear curving path allows for easy wayfinding throughout the building, while creating a sense of flow. The curves also create areas of prospect and refuge, such as in the waiting room.

Similar to the variation of color in *H17*, I created a progression of natural light. Upon entering *Euphadose*, there are clerestory windows to allow diffuse light from above which maintains privacy. As one exits the Injection Room, floor-to-ceiling windows help them awaken through a greater exposure to daylight and views of greenery.

▶

In case of an overdose emergency, a nurse needs to be able to tip a patient chair backwards and administer an overdose reversal such as *Narcan*. The injection room has been planned with this procedure in mind with more than 25% additional circulation space and a radial floor plan which helps the nurses on staff keep an eye on their patients.

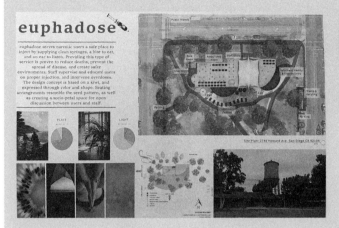

Euphadose Concept board and site plan

Euphadose Entry perspective, reception desk elevations and finish materials.

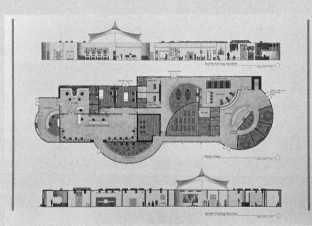

Euphadose Furniture plan and building sections

Euphadose Interior elevations and furnishings.

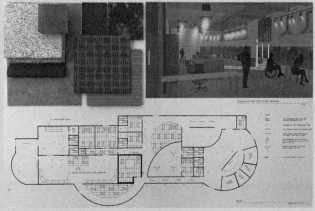

Euphadose Perspective rendering and lighting plan.

CONCLUSION

While the research process may seem daunting at first there are many commonalities between design and research. First, students of interior design research should understand how scientific studies reflect both the ideological and technological age in which they are conducted, and how trends in research methods depend on the tools and techniques available to conduct them. Students should take the time to explore the various research techniques using their penchant for design, including curiosity, creativity, and problem-solving, and previously developed design skills such as interviewing, observation, problem identification, conceptualization, ideation, diagramming, and other visual presentation skills. Designing a study takes a commitment to rigor, while also examining our unspoken assumptions, being flexible in our lateral and vertical thinking, and deliberate risk-taking associated with creative endeavors.

Broad research topics, narrowed to highly specialized questions, generated from activities in this chapter should be written down and kept close on hand as they are the springboard for the remainder of the research journey. It is normal for these questions to change over time or be modified through preliminary testing, sharing them with colleagues, and incorporating feedback. Maintaining awareness of your interests, your research goals, and continually checking in with your underlying motivation will also serve to guide you, especially when the tasks seem particularly difficult to do. The questions you have generated will remain the driving force behind each of the subsequent decisions you make in the process: in how you frame the problem, design the study, collect your data, and formulate usable findings. They may also influence how you present yourself in the academic arena, share your results with others, or implement your results into future design projects.

Key Terms

"Aha" moment	Creativity	Interior design
American Society of Interior Designers (ASID)	Design	Lateral thinking
	Design-informed researchers	Neuroplasticity
Augmented reality	Divergent thinking	Positive psychology
Brainstorming	Embodied cognition	Prospect-refuge theory
Cathedral effect	Evidence-Based Design (EBD)	Research-informed design
Concept map	Five phases of design	Social ecology
Conceptual blockbusting	Habits	Vertical thinking
Convergent thinking	Information Age	Virtual reality

Discussion Questions

1. What are the technological ages of human history? How would you describe research in the current age?

2. What is the relationship or connection between creativity and research? Can you give an explanation through an example of your own experience?

3. Do you think that research *limits* or *expands* your potential to be creative? In other words, does the act of doing research, collecting information, or using data, increase or decrease innovation in the design process? Give several examples to support your answer.

4. Identify and discuss one resource mentioned in this chapter that you would like to explore further. What is interesting about this source?

5. What direction do you see your research taking? At this current point in time what would you consider to be your broad topic? What question(s) would you pose? Or what statement comes to mind?

6. Overall, how would you like to see interior design contributing to the field of research, or research contributing to the field of interior design? What are some practical applications and/or approaches you can take?

References

Adams, J. L. (2001). *Conceptual blockbusting: A guide to better ideas*. Cambridge, MA: Basic Books.

Alexander, C., Ishikawa, S., & Silverstein, M. (1977). *A pattern language: Towns, buildings, construction*. New York: Oxford University Press.

Amabile, T. & Pillemer, J. (2012). Perspective on the social psychology of creativity. *The Journal of Creative Behavior, 46*. 10.1002/jocb.001.

Appleton, J. (1975). *The experience of landscape*. New York: Wiley.

Birkinshaw, J. (2014). Beyond the information age. *Wired insights*. Conde Nast. Retrieved February February 24, 2020 from https://www.wired.com/insights/2014/06/beyond-information-age/

Bryce, N. V. (2014, July/August). The AHA! moment: A step-by-step guide to your next creative breakthrough. *Scientific American Mind*. Retrieved from https://www.nessabryce.com/_files/ugd/09e18a_94e74c787504431c86c1a94472927252.pdf

Cameron, J. (1992). *The artist's way: A spiritual path to higher creativity*. New York: Tarcher/Putnam.

De Bono, E. (1968). *New think*. New York: Basic Books.

Duhigg, C. (2012). *The power of habit: Why we do what we do in life and business*. New York: Random House.

Farmer, S. M., Tierney, P., & Kung-Mcintyre, K. (2003). Employee creativity in Taiwan: An application of role identity theory. *Academy of Management Journal, 46*(5), 618–630.

Fisher, E. (2020). Who put the evidence in evidence based design? *IDEC Exchange: A Forum for Interior Design Education*, Issue 1, Spring 2020, 5. Retrieved from https://idec.org/wp-content/uploads/2021/04/IDEC_Exchange_2020_FNL.pdf

Goldhagen, S. W. (2017). *Welcome to your world: how the built environment shapes our lives*. New York: Harper.

Gordon, W.J.J. (1961). *Synectics: The development of creative capacity*. NY: Harper & Brothers.

Hamilton, D. K. (2003). The four levels of evidence-based design practice. *Healthcare Design, 3*(9), 18–26.

Hautala, J., & Ibert, O. (2018). Creativity in arts and sciences: Collective processes from a spatial perspective. *Environment and Planning A: Economy and Space, 50*(8), 1688–1696.

Johnson, S. (2010). *Where good ideas come from: The natural history of innovation*. London: Penguin Publishing Group.

Koberg, D., & Bagnall, J. (1974). *The universal traveler: A soft-systems guide to creativity, problem-solving, and the process of reaching goals*. Burlington, MA: W. Kaufmann.

Kounios, J., & Beeman, M. (2009). The Aha! moment: The cognitive neuroscience of insight. *Journal of the Association for Psychological Science, 18*(4), 210–216.

Leonard, K. & Yorton, T. (2015). *Yes, and: How improvisation reverses 'no, but' thinking and improves creativity and collaboration—lessons from The Second City*. New York: Harper Business.

Lidwell, W., Holden, K., & Butler, J. (2010). *Universal principles of design, revised and updated: 125 ways to enhance usability, influence perception, increase appeal, make better design decisions, and teach through design*. Beverly, MA: Rockport Publishers.

Malkin, J. (2008). *A visual reference for evidence-based design*. Concord, CA: Center for Health Design.

Mallgrave, H. F. (2010). *The architect's brain: Neuroscience, creativity, and architecture*. Chichester, West Sussex, U.K: Wiley-Blackwell.

Mead, P. (2020). Positive psychology as a new lens for architecture. *Conference Proceedings for 108th Annual Meeting of ACSA (Association of Collegiate Schools of Architecture)*. San Diego, CA: March 12–14, 2020. https://www.acsa-arch.org/conference/acsa108-virtual-conference/108th-annual-meeting/full-schedule-saturday/

Nakamura, J., & Csikszentmihalyi, M. (2001). Catalytic creativity. The case of Linus Pauling. *The American Psychologist, 56*: 337–341. DOI: 10.1037/0003-066X.56.4.337

NCIDQ (2019). Retrieved from https://www.cidq.org/_files/ugd/0784c1_16c47b1a47de44f7b8f-3f87367e483ac.pdf

Osborn, A. F. (1953). In *Applied imagination: Principles and procedures of creative thinking*. New York: Scribner.

Rattner, D. M. (2019). *My creative space: How to design your home to stimulate ideas and spark innovation*. New York: Skyhorse Publishing.

Robinson, L. (2020). The role of theory in research-informed design. *IDEC Exchange:*

A Forum for Interior Design Education, Issue 1, Spring 2020, 17–18. https://www.idec.org/files/IDECExchange_2020_FNL.pdf

Ruff, M. (2018, May 29). Elevating workplace architecture and design with Positive Psychology. NAIOP/Commercial Real Estate Development Association. Retrieved May 5, 2021 from https://blog.naiop.org/2018/05/elevating-workplace-architecture-and-design-with-positive-psychology/

Ruggiero, V. R. (2008). *The art of thinking: A guide to critical and creative thought*. 9th ed. New York: Pearson Longman Publishing.

Sawyer, R. K. (2003). *Improvised dialogues: Emergence and creativity in conversation*. Westport, CT: Greenwood Publishing Group.

Sternberg, R. J. (1999). A propulsion model of types of creative contributions. *Review of General Psychology, 2*, 83–100.

Tharp, T. (2009). *The creative habit: Learn it and use it for life*. New York: Simon & Schuster.

Weisberg, R. (2006). *Creativity: Understanding innovation in problem-solving, science, invention and the arts*. New York: John Wiley.

Young, J. W. (1940). *A technique for producing ideas*. Detroit. MI: Crain Communications.

Systems of Inquiry and Evaluation

CHAPTER 2

LEARNING OBJECTIVES

After you complete this chapter, you will be able to:

- Use terminology associated with research and scientific inquiry.

- Explain the scientific method.

- Distinguish between *qualitative* and *quantitative* data and discover the value of each in interior design research.

- Explore methods associated with physical (natural) and social sciences.

- Differentiate *systems of inquiry* (data-gathering methods) from *systems of evaluation* used to analyze data.

THE RESEARCH PROCESS AND SCIENTIFIC METHOD

Like design, *research* has meaning as both a noun and a verb. As a *noun*, **research** means reliable information retrieved or discovered through systematic inquiry. **Basic research** serves to inform general understanding about a subject matter while **applied research** seeks to solve a particular problem. Application of knowledge to the design process may not be direct; it asks us to first understand the discovered results within a systematic pursuit of knowledge. Research as a *verb* has connotations and an understanding by both scientists (generators of research) and the general public (consumers of research) as a rigorous, systematic approach and process.

The word *research* can also be used as an adjective! *Research methods* and *research methodology* are two phrases that are often misunderstood. **Research methods** refers to tools and techniques for gathering and processing data, while **research methodology** is the framework used to justify the methods. In other words, research methods describe *what* the researcher did, while research methodology shows *why* they did what they did, *how* they were able to reach a conclusion or result, and the overall meaning, purpose, or contribution of the study. Research methodologies, philosophies, and underlying worldviews will be discussed in more detail in Chapter 3. Chapters 4 and 5 will focus on how to align your research methodology with your **research question**, and help you decide when methods apply. An in-depth look at individual methods for gathering your data (interviews, surveys, and observation) will be addressed in Chapters 6, 7, and 8, respectively.

Developed over millennia (since the time of Greek and Persian philosophers) the **scientific method** is a standardized method of procedure that has characterized natural science since the seventeenth century, consisting of systematic observation, measurement, experiment, and the formulation, testing, and modification of *hypotheses*. According to Barnet, Bedau, and O'Hara (2020), "**experiments** are deliberately contrived situations … designed to yield particular observations … often in controlled situations and with the help of laboratory instruments" (p. 108). Figure 2.1 shows that published **results**, *findings*, or conclusions of a study, can serve as fodder for new studies which

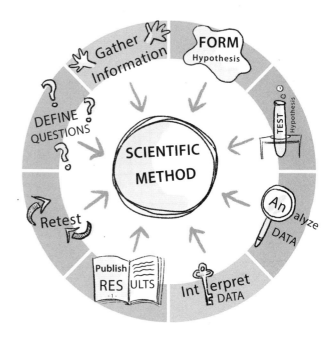

Figure 2.1
Illustration depicting the circular nature of the research process using the scientific method.

seek to confirm, refute, or build on previous findings in an unlimited circular or cyclical process.

Through the scientific method, researchers first recognize and formulate a broad question. Then they carefully design a study to collect data, typically through observation and experiment. Overall, the commonly accepted steps are as follows:

1. Make an observation.
2. Ask a question.
3. Form a **hypothesis**, or testable explanation.
4. Make a prediction based on the hypothesis.
5. Test the prediction.
6. Iterate: use the results to make new hypotheses or predictions.

According to Blakstad (2008) "steps of the scientific method are shaped like an hourglass—starting from general questions, narrowing down to focus on one specific aspect, and designing research where we can observe and analyze this aspect. At last, we conclude and generalize to the real world" (see Figure 2.2).

Additionally, the six steps (five main steps plus one feedback step) of the scientific method try to ensure that the resulting data be reproducible, given the same circumstances, and as **objective** as humanly possible, which means free from bias,

Figure 2.2
The steps of the research process can resemble an hourglass.

At the heart of the scientific method is a need to maintain control over the process to try to maintain objectivity. For example, if a neuroscientist were conducting a controlled experiment to study aspects of *way-finding* in architecture and interior design, she might focus on how the human brain processes visual cues in the environment being navigated, such as color or images. This would be a useful study for hospitals, where visitors are likely to be under physical and emotional stress and need to find their way to a patient's room easily and quickly, especially in the case of an emergency. The neuroscientist must maintain control over the experimental process so that the results gathered from many different subjects can be measured and analyzed to produce accurate and reliable conclusions to the medical, interior design, and architecture fields.

So, you might ask, what does this have to do with my designs? You've just read about the connection between the scientific method and the interior design process, but you might still be asking, "Isn't interior design an artistic field, and by nature isn't artistic expression **subjective**?" That is, ideas arising from the mind, based on, or influenced by, personal feelings, tastes, or opinions. Weisberg (2006) agreed: "Artistic creativity is an inherently subjective process since the artist brings objects into existence as he or she carries out the artistic process, while scientific discovery is an objective process that deals with objects that exist 'out there' independent of the scientist" (p. 54). So, yes, interior design tends toward artistic creativity, and artistic creativity seems to be an inherently subjective process. However, interior design is not purely art—nor should it be—for design is problem-solving, while art is usually an expression or communication of meaning.

If creativity is considered *subjective*, scientific discovery, in contrast, could be seen as *objective*. Objects, events, and facts available to all of us are what scientists "discover" (Weisberg, 2006, p. 6). For example, if there had been no James Watson and Francis Crick, the two men credited with discovering the double helical shape of DNA, the DNA would still have been there, waiting for its nature to eventually be uncovered. Watson and Crick had the foundation of knowledge and comprehension that put them on a path to uncovering the truth. As scientists, they did not create or invent the DNA molecule; rather, they discovered and uncovered its true shape and composition (Weisberg, 2006).

chance, individual human perception, and error. There is an underlying notion that a systemization of research, or a very regimented and procedural approach, where the process and results can be easily reproduced, reveals a "right" answer (Groat & Wang, 2002). The scientific method in its purest form strives to be objective and, if used properly, should provide accurate results.

If our goal is to apply information toward the solution of interior design problems, we can start by searching for existing knowledge and listening to the expertise or experience of others. We can continue by observing behavior and drawing on opinions and beliefs formed in the mind based on experience, *a priori* beliefs (those arising from the mind, not based on direct experience but deduced, or requiring no evidence), kinesthetic awareness, and more. This step-by-step methodology separates research from informal conjecture. As you will see in the next chapter, there is a place in research for hunches, speculation, personal experience, and anecdotal evidence. But the fundamental definition of research involves the formalized nature of inquiry.

Interior Design Research: Physical Sciences Versus Social Sciences

In 1984, E. O. Wilson sought **consilience**, a convergence of knowledge from the diverse fields of science. More recently, **Academy of Neuroscience for Architecture (ANFA)** sought a similar confluence to advance design in the built environment. They fostered collaborative research efforts which paired architects with scientists only to discover that each profession speaks different academic "languages." The designers often misunderstood what constituted *evidence* to support a *claim* to a scientist, usually stemming from divergent views of the nature of reality. Neuroscientist Sergei Gepshtein (2019) offered a path for how to bridge the gap between the professions. As illustrated in Figure 2.3, he described the differences as belonging to a continuum or spectrum.

On one end of the spectrum, scientific research seeks to determine *causal* relationships while on the other it aims to recognize patterns and describe that which cannot be quantified or analyzed statistically. Each end of the spectrum represents very different assumptions about the world and the nature of science in that world causing conflict or confusion. Does science seek an underlying cause for an effect, or should science seek to describe patterns? Both are valuable to the research-informed designer. For example, the physical properties of a surface material help us determine whether it will meet the functional requirements for a kitchen countertop. On the other side of the research spectrum, an in-depth look at how a family prepares dinner within a cultural setting will also help us choose the materiality (color and texture) of the countertop. While a unified vision or consilience has an allure, a plurality of perspectives towards research may be necessary in the application of research to design of the built environment. Unfortunately, misunderstandings about what constitutes research, miscommunication between researchers, and confusion will continue until this realization occurs. Perhaps designers becoming adept in research procedures, familiar with terminology, and more practice conducting their own research will help bridge the gap.

Referring again to Figure 2.3, Gepshtein suggested designers and neuroscientists meet in the middle. He advocated for research for the built environment to be conducted in the *phenomenal* realm that concentrates on the study of consciousness and the objects of direct experience. As you will see explored more in the next chapter, there are multiple philosophies, perspectives, and points of view from which to view science. Interior design researchers can choose from this variety of perspectives based on their personal values (explored in Chapter 3) and the focus of their study. In other words, identification of differences may not move us closer to a *consilience* but rather to a *transcendence of boundaries*. With awareness of this spectrum, a designer may engage at the level to which they believe their project's

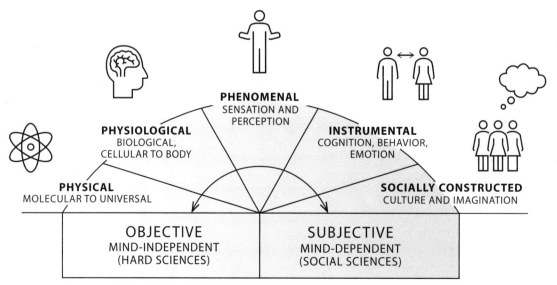

Figure 2.3
Scientific spectrum along which design research is conducted (Adapted from Gepshtein, 2019).

issues lie and can cross boundaries, mixing traditional information-gathering techniques with more artistic ones while still producing clear, reliable evidence which supports their subsequent design decisions.

The goal of this textbook is to seamlessly integrate research into the interior design process, so we can cultivate design-informed research in the field of interior design. As generators of original research, interior designers can become comfortable with, and fluent in, the terminology associated with a wide variety of study types, from controlled experiments to quasi-experimental activities using *mock-ups* to *participant observation* and *ethnographic* studies in naturalistic environments. Creative research assignments found throughout the rest of the textbook allow you to design and conduct studies until you feel as comfortable and excited with the process of research as you do with the design process.

RESEARCH TERMINOLOGY OVERVIEW

As you embark on your research journey, it is important to speak the language of your fellow researchers to build confidence and credibility, and to avoid miscommunication with others in the field. This next section helps build your vocabulary by establishing definitions for a formalized inquiry. To test out your prior knowledge of research terms, read the following statement about beginning your research made by Martyn Shuttleworth (2008) and see if you understand the highlighted words (italicized here to stand out):

> Defining a research problem is the fuel that drives the scientific process and is the foundation of any research method and experimental design, from true *experiment* to *case study*. It is one of the first statements made in any research paper and, as well as defining the research area, should include a quick synopsis of how the hypothesis was arrived at. *Operationalization* is then used to give some indication of the exact definitions of the *variables*, and the type of scientific measurements used. This will lead to the proposal of a viable *hypothesis*. As an aside, when scientists are putting forward proposals for research funds, the quality of their research problem often makes the difference between success and failure.

Linking Claims to Evidence in a Logical Argument

According to Barnet, Bedau, and O'Hara (2020), "every argument has a purpose, goal, or aim—namely to establish a claim (conclusion or thesis)" (p. 338). An **argument** is a term used in **logic** which refers to an attempt to persuade someone to adopt our point of view, with a distinctive purpose: "one that elevates the cognitive or intellectual capacity for reason" (Barnet, et al., p. 85). We can view our thesis project, or any outcome of our research endeavor, as a logical argument in which we make *claims*. A **claim** is an assertion or statement that you would hope others will agree with and endorse. Of course, if your claim is something that is already agreed upon or accepted as fact, then there is little reason to undertake the research. We encourage you to take a stand and risk being challenged. It will make the research process uncomfortable but well worth it in the end.

Shuttleworth (2008) reminds us, "Look at any scientific paper, and you will see the research problem, written almost like a statement of intent." The intent is typically to persuade the reader to look at something in a new way and add to the body of knowledge on a certain subject matter. In the field of interior design, a claim can be a proposal for a new facility. It can also be a design decision such as a furniture layout, signage system, or material selection.

The *Toulmin Method* of argument in law, in Figure 2.4a and 2.4b, shows that a claim needs to be supported with *grounds*, *warrants*, and *backing*, as well as *qualifiers* (language that establishes character and scope of the argument) and *rebuttals* (anticipated counterarguments). In interior design, a counterargument could be critique from a seasoned professional serving as a guest critic or member of your thesis committee. In the professional world, anticipated counterarguments for your design decisions are likely to come from clients. Whatever the situation, to support your claim (or design decision) you will need to provide **evidence** (reasons, premises, or grounds).

So, what constitutes evidence? Evidence may come in many forms. In a court of law, evidence is very specific and subject to rules of jurisprudence. In scientific research, evidence can be the result of experimentation in controlled situations and measured with specialized laboratory instruments. In some social

Figure 2.4a
A successful claim is linked to credible evidence using a warrant. A successful researcher prepares to defend their claims against anticipated critique.

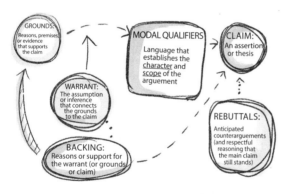

DEFENDING A RESEARCH STUDY

Figure 2.4b
Linking claims to evidence in a logical argument. From Barnet, Bedau & O'Hara (2020, p. 338) based on Stephen Toulmin, Richard Rieke and Allan Janik's *An Introduction to Reasoning* (1979; second edition 1984).

sciences, humanities, as well as in daily life, evidence can also be clearly articulated examples of experiences, cultures, events, and previously built or proposed designs solutions. An interview with a client, for example, can give extremely helpful evidence of one (very important!) person's perspective. As in law, quoting an

expert's opinion, can function as **testimony** to further give reasons why a claim or choice has been made. The **peer-review** process in which authored research is reviewed by other experts before it gets published helps to ensure that information appearing in those sources can be cited as reliable evidence.

Understanding Theory, Constructs, and Propositions

In general, a **theory** is a currently accepted conclusion about a topic. More specifically, a theory is "a set of interrelated ideas or a set of relationships, and it provides a system or a filter for planning and conducting research and then for making sense of its findings" (Guerin & Dohr, 2007, Research 101 Part II, p. 1). Theory offers an explanation and is usually associated with the theorist or person responsible for first recognizing a relationship or inventing a term or phrase to describe what they have observed through philosophical discourse or experimentation. Some theories are widely accepted as truth, due to the fact they have not been proven to be otherwise. Theories can be described as our "latest version of what we call truth" (Glesne, 2011, p. 37), a currently accepted conclusion which has arisen after being modified or challenged by philosophy and experimentation. Further inquiry or testing can support and uphold the theory as true, or it can prove the theory wrong, in which case the theory is discarded, a new theory takes its place, and the process continues.

Theory can be very general about design as a practice, or very specific, applying design principles, such as balance, symmetry, hierarchy, and unity, to design elements, such as color, texture, and shape (Guerin & Dohr, 2007). Multiple theories can be layered and incorporated both into the research methodologies and ensuing design solution, as you will see later in the textbook. As theory applies to your design research, keep in mind that

when researchers are about to begin working on a research problem, they look for a theory to guide their work. It is important, however, to make a distinction in the difference between research methods and theories in the study of interior design. On the one hand, with research methods, we have the information or data that you will collect and the method or technique you use to collect that data, and on the other hand we have the theoretical interpretation that you apply to that data.

(Weisberg, 2006)

Theory helps address difficult concepts, such as "the public." What is "the public"? You reframe it with a theoretical discussion in the studio before you even design a public space (R. Vaccarino, quoted in Hodge & Pollak, 1996, p. 46).

Design researchers use these components of theory to guide their system of inquiry, and designers can use them to guide their design decisions (Guerin & Dohr, 2007). In their article "Research 101" (2007), Guerin and Dohr dissect the example of color theory

to illustrate the components of the theory: **constructs**, **propositions**, and **assumptions**. Table 2.1 defines, explains, and provides examples for each of these components as it relates to color theory.

As you conduct research for your interior design project, you will determine if your research findings agree or conflict with the **propositions** (rules) put forth by the theory that is guiding your research. This is how you then add to current theory, propose revisions to a theory, or develop a new theory. It is also one of the ways you are contributing to the body of knowledge in interior design and providing other researchers with more information about how people may behave in a built environment (Guerin & Dohr, 2007).

Table 2.1 Basic Components of Theory

Components of Theory	Definition/Explanation	Example: Color Theory
Constructs	The components, concepts, or parts that comprise a theory.	Color theory constructs include "hue," "value," and "chroma."
Propositions	The rules within the theory which establish relationships among the constructs or concepts.	"Dark, bright, and saturated colors advance and cool, light, and muted colors retreat." "Warm colors such as red and orange make us hungry or stimulate our metabolism, while cool colors such as blues make us feel calmer." (These propositions have been established through research.)
Assumptions	Positions that cannot be proved or disproved but are assumed and must be agreed upon for the designer to explore and use the theory.	One color theory assumption, posited by Newton in his theory of optics that has stood the test of time, is that colors we perceive are portions of the visible light spectrum. "White light" is a mixture of the full spectrum of colors.

RESEARCH IN ACTION 2.1
The Earth Has "Furniture"

While touring the North Pacific Beach cliffside revegetation project, interior designer Pierce Bryce, found himself looking at the environment through the lens of a theory. He had just read James J. Gibson's (1986[2015]) book *The Ecological Approach to Visual Perception* and learned a new term: *affordance*. The term **affordance** refers to the opportunities for interaction provided by a particular object or environment. Gibson (1986[2015]) argued that when we encounter something in the environment, we perceive what actions it allows us to take. He further clarifies affordances:

I have described the environment as the surfaces that separate substances from the medium in which the animals live. But I have also described what the environment affords the animals ... the terrain, shelters, water, fire, objects, tools ... affordances of the environment are what it offers the animal, what it provides or furnishes, either for good or ill. The verb afford is found in the dictionary, but the noun affordance is not. I have made it up ... It implies the complementarity of the animal and the environment. (p.119)

Pierce observed that despite posted signs that read "dangerous unstable cliffs—stay back," people

►

were using what the crumbling coastline afforded them. People, he mused, must love the unobstructed ocean view and all the beauty the cliff has to offer, whether it is checking the surf, walking their dog, taking selfies, or basking in the warm sun. The cliff, about 70 feet above the waterline, has slowly eroded to the point that there could be a possible landslide at any moment. Why then are people still hanging out on the cliff edge? As shown below, he noticed a woman using the top of a retaining wall as a headrest. Further to the right, he saw another woman also using the gentle incline of the cliff's mesa as a natural lounge chair. And finally, he noticed the dog using the curb as its own raised sidewalk, the affordance of being elevated alongside its owner!

Gibson's theory of affordances offered a radical approach (or hypothesis) to viewing the environment—he implied that the values or meanings of your surroundings are directly related to what the features in the environment offer you. What do they allow you to do on a physical, emotional, and psychological level? Gibson wrote, "a horizontal, flat, extended, rigid, surface affords support … The flat earth lies beneath the attached and detached objects on it. The earth has 'furniture'" (p.123). The cliff is falling, slanting, sliding, and unstable—it is no longer suitable for support. That is apparently clear. But the slanting and man-made efforts to stabilize it may offer something else to the potential user. Pierce now understood that the combination of perceived affordance of the cliffs by the beach-goers proved irresistible despite the advertised quality of being potentially dangerous!

Interior designer, Pierce Bryce, looked at the North Pacific Beach cliffside restoration revegetation project through the lens of Gibson's theory of affordances.

What Is a Testable Hypothesis?

In research, a **hypothesis** is a suggested explanation of a phenomenon (Blakstad, 2008). A *testable hypothesis* is a statement or an "educated guess" that suggests a specific relationship(s) among a theory's constructs or components. Researchers test hypotheses to form new knowledge about an existing theory (Guerin & Dohr, 2007, Research 101, Part II, p. 3). Based on whether the hypothesis is found to be correct or incorrect, "it serves as a starting point for further research and investigation" (Zeisel & Eberhard, 2006, p. 80). Referring back to the color theory example in Table 2.1, a testable hypothesis related to color theory explains a specific relationship among the constructs of hue, value, and chroma. For example, you could form the hypothesis that colors applied to create a high level of contrast (a relationship between hue and value) between horizontal and vertical surfaces in an assisted-living facility will result in a reduction of accidents and injuries among elderly residents. You could test this hypothesis by recording the current rate of injuries in an existing assisted-living facility, applying the suggested change to the space, and making a record of subsequent injuries. You would compare the two sets of data and determine if your hypothesis is correct or incorrect.

The Null Hypothesis (Ho) and Alternative Hypothesis (Ha)

According to Blakstad (2008) "a *null hypothesis* is a hypothesis which a researcher tries to disprove. Normally, the null hypothesis represents the current view/explanation of an aspect of the world that the researcher wants to challenge." The researcher tests the hypothesis to disprove the null hypothesis, because it would mean coming closer to finding an answer to a specific problem. The research hypothesis is often based on observations that evoke suspicion that the null hypothesis is not always correct. Research methodology also involves the researcher devising an alternate way to explain the phenomenon, called an *alternate hypothesis.*

This brings us to two kinds of logical reasoning. **Deductive reasoning** formulates a hypothesis using a predetermined theory to be predictive, otherwise known as a series of "if–then" logical statements. **Inductive reasoning** begins with gathering data to identify patterns, pose a theory, or make a generalization, in a bottom-up approach. As you can see in Figure 2.5 both types of reasoning can be used in the generation and testing of hypotheses. However, as you will see in the next two chapters, deductive reasoning is typically associated with physical sciences and laboratory experiments, while inductive reasoning is associated with social sciences studying cultural, anthropological, and sociological issues in naturalistic settings.

Defining Variables

A **variable** is an object, event, idea, feeling, time period, or any other type of category you are trying to measure. There are two types of variables: *independent* and *dependent*. An **independent variable** is one that stands alone and is not changed by the other variables you are trying to measure. For example, a person's age may be an independent variable. Other factors, such as his favorite food, the school he attends, or his grade point average, are not going to change the person's age. Age is a constant. In fact, when you are looking for a relationship between variables, you are looking to see if the independent variable causes, or is linked in some way, to a change in some other variable that you have deemed associated with the first one. A **dependent variable** is something that changes and relies on other factors for that change. For example,

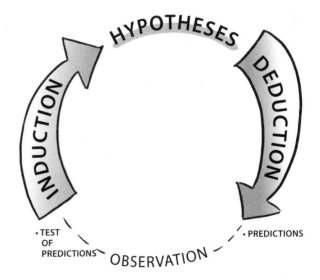

Figure 2.5
Inductive and deductive reasoning in scientific inquiry occur in a cyclical fashion.

a test score could be a dependent variable because it could change depending, for example, how much you studied, how much sleep you got the night before you took the test, or the noise level in the room where you took the test. Usually, when you are looking for a relationship between two things, you are trying to figure out what makes the dependent variable change the way it does.

Many people have trouble remembering which variable is the independent variable and which is the dependent variable. An easy way to remember this is to insert the names of the two variables you are using in the following sentence:

(Independent variable) causes a change in (Dependent variable), and it is not possible that (Dependent variable) could cause a change in (Independent variable).

For example:

(Time spent studying) causes a change in (Test score), and it isn't possible that (Test score) could cause a change in (Time spent studying).

We see that time spent studying must be the independent variable and the test score must be the dependent variable, because the sentence wouldn't make sense the other way around.

Operationalizing a Concept

Have you ever had a good idea about what to do at your place of work or in your community that turned out very difficult to implement in practice? Perhaps you would like to see more people recycle in your homeowners' association. Or you wanted to figure out a way to track down the owner of lost pets. Or a new way to celebrate your colleagues' birthdays at work. At first you have a vague idea of how to improve a situation, but as you try to go about getting the idea adopted, institutionalized, and enacted by others, the task becomes more complicated, difficult, or even impossible? This is the idea behind the research term **operationalize**. How does one take a fuzzy concept, construct, or variable and try to measure it by specific observations? For example, how would you *operationalize* "happiness" in a study to determine whether a space promoted positive feelings in the occupants? You can measure happiness by asking people to rate their feelings on a scale. What are some other ways to operationalize the same concept? The broad idea

of operationalization, and how it may be applied to many stages of the research process is illustrated in Figure 2.6.

After operationalizing what is to be measured, a researcher develops **instruments** such as questionnaires or checklists for gathering data. **Triangulation** is a strategy for increasing the level of validity by employing several different kinds of instruments to collect complementary data. (Harkiolakis, 2018). These concepts will be explored further in Chapters 4 and 5 when we attempt to design our own study.

Examples of Hypotheses and Variables in a Study

A hypothesis tests a theory by defining and operationalizing the constructs in a particular study or experiment. The variables in an experiment are the properties or characteristics in the research question

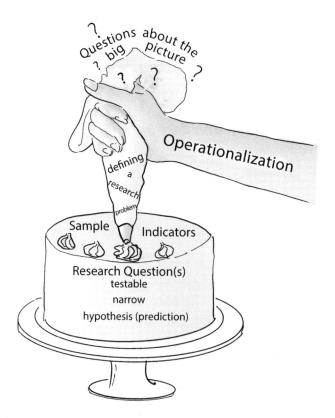

Figure 2.6
Operationalization helps researchers narrow and measure vague or broad concepts shown here as using icing to decorate a cake. It is the process by which you define your sample, decide how to measure indicators, and choose a specific set of circumstances for your study.

that can take on different values. The property that is changed or manipulated is the independent variable and the expected outcome is the dependent variable. In an assisted-living facility, for example, an independent variable could be the application of high-contrast treatments to the edge of horizontal surfaces such as stair treads and countertops and the dependent variable would be rate of injury among residents (Guerin & Dohr, 2007, part II, p. 4). Or we could design a study to determine the effect of class size on student learning in schools. The study could be conducted with a class size of twenty and compared to a class size of 100 to determine if class size (independent variable) affects student learning (dependent variable) (Guerin & Dohr, 2007, part II, p. 4). In both examples, one variable must remain constant to determine its relationship with the other variable(s). Examples might be maintaining the same age range among residents in the assisted-living facility or having the same teacher and/or assignments for both class sizes (Guerin & Dohr, 2007, part II, p. 4). Outside of the independent and dependent variables, all other variables should be constant to eliminate their having an impact on the results.

To paraphrase and simplify this process, forming a testable hypothesis is like saying, "If I do this, this will happen." It is your best "guess" about the outcome of research based on existing literature, research, or theory about the topic. It can be said that every design solution is a hypothesis or a prediction by the designer that the design solution will work. The more "guessing" you can take out of the hypothesis, by applying research to the problem being solved, the more likely it is that the design solution will be functional, meaningful, long-lasting, and aesthetically pleasing.

Another hypothesis applied directly to interior design could involve an executive who believes that reducing the sound transmission of office walls will result in higher productivity and boost morale among employees. She and her interior designer persuade the board of directors to install soundproofing in three employee offices. The executive's hypothesis is that the effect of acoustical privacy (inability to hear adjacent coworkers) will be higher output, on average, than for employees in offices that are not acoustically separated (Fraenkel, Wallen, & Sawin, 1999). In this case, the independent variable is *soundproofing* while the dependent variables would be *employee productivity*

and *morale*. If the executive's hypothesis is correct, the experiment will reveal (1) that acoustics influence the productivity and morale of her employees and (2) that investing the money to install sound transmission barriers in office walls will pay off in the long run. Having this research to back up her proposal will make it easier for the executive to sell her idea to the board of directors.

Populations and Samples

A **population** is comprised of all the members of a group that you are attempting to study. This could be all the elementary school-age children in the world, in the country, or in a particular school. The **sample** is a small portion of that group who participates in your study which serves to represent the entire population. Typically, a researcher tries to get an objective representation, which is not biased by who he or she knows, so the members of the sample are often randomly selected. See Figures 2.7 and 2.8 for different types of *random* sampling: *convenience*, *purposive*, and *stratified*.

If you are trying to generalize your findings to all members of the population, the sample size may be an issue to examine. As you will see, a small sample size can be used in some kinds of research, but the larger the sample size, the greater chance your findings will be respected by fellow researchers and consumers of research, and a greater chance you will be able to generalize your findings to the entire population.

Figure 2.7
Random samples of a population of all children in a playground. If children are selected as participants because they are closest to you, we may call it a *convenience* sample. If you selected children because you knew they had attributes of interest to your study, we could call it a *purposive* sample.

POPULATION: FIFTY STUDENTS: (60% GIRLS, 40% BOYS)

SIX GIRLS

FOUR BOYS

STRATIFIED RANDOM SAMPLE: TEN STUDENTS (20%) WITH PERCENTAGES REFLECTING
THE PERCENTAGES OF THE POPULATION VARIABLE

Figure 2.8
Stratified random samples mean that the percentages of
the sample reflect the percentages found in the population.
In this example, we see the sample stratified to match the
variable of two genders.

Activity 2.1
Terminology Check-in

Purpose: This brief activity summarizes the concepts
explored in the first part of the chapter and tests
how well you have internalized the terms related to
research.

Objective: To create a paragraph of text that flows
accurately, reflecting your understanding of terms
introduced in this chapter.

Requirements: Fill in the blanks with the
appropriate key terms listed at the end of the
chapter.

If we want to study the effect of lighting on buying
behavior in a retail store, _____ would be
the independent variable and _____ is the
dependent variable.

When two research variables move consistently
in relation to each other, we can say there is a
correlation between them, but we <u>cannot</u> necessarily
conclude _____, in which the value of one of
the variables is determined by the movement of the
other variable.

When we see data that demonstrates relationships
between variables greater than that which would
occur randomly or by chance, we can say it
demonstrates _____ significance.

A single data point is generally not useful, because
_____.

If you begin with a concept that is so broad that
you are unable to begin gathering useful data, you
should first _____ it to narrow
your focus and measure things that provide greater
understanding.

TYPES OF DATA

There are many ways to categorize **data**, facts, and statistics collected for the purpose of reference, comparison, or analysis. Data (which is plural) can be *continuous* or *discrete*. **Continuous data** can be expressed as a "rational number," for example, test scores or a person's height. **Categorical** data is **discrete**, or "not connected." It could be *nominal* (name) or *ordinal* (ranking) which are defined and explored in more detail in Chapter 7. See how data can be categorized in Figure 2.9.

You can have an individual data point (or datum) such as a single reading of temperature or one player's score in a game. Data only becomes meaningful when there is an accumulation that can be measured or compared. Data also comes in many forms. Data can be in numbers and sizes, but it can also be individual words, verbal or text description, and archived documents. Visual data can be in photos, models, and drawings such as an aerial view, three-dimensional globe, or map showing a route or expedition.

The field of **statistics** is made up of a set of techniques for obtaining knowledge from incomplete data, by managing data throughout collection, organization, analysis, presentation, and interpretation, in a variety of numeric forms. *Social statistics* deal with the study of human behavior and interaction in a social environment. Such phenomena include activities of groups of people like households, societies, and nations and their impacts on culture, education, and other areas of social life (C. Halter, personal communication, November 10, 2020).

There are two forms of statistics: *descriptive* and *inferential*. **Descriptive statistics** focus on representative amounts commonly displayed in visual charts and graphs. They also refer to the three **measures of central tendency** commonly known as **mean**, **median**, and **mode** (see Figure 2.10) as well as **standard deviation**, a measure of deviation from the average (see Figure 2.11).

Inferential statistics focus on relationships and associations which express differences within the data. They are used to test hypotheses about differences in populations based on measurements made on samples of subjects. For some research results to be accepted, statistical significance will need to be established. **Statistical significance** is the claim that a result from data generated by testing or experimentation is not likely to occur randomly or by chance. This significance can be mathematically established using a **P-Value** which is a measure of the probability that an observed difference could have occurred just by random chance (0.05, 0.01, 0.001). The lower the p-value, the greater

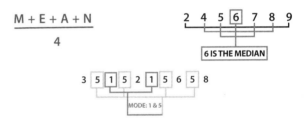

Figure 2.10
Graphic depictions of three ways to calculate central tendency (or average) of data: mean, median and mode (Halter, 2020).

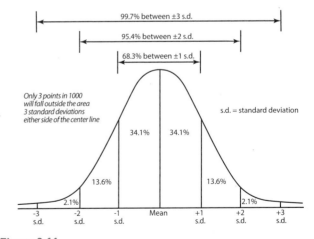

Figure 2.11
Graph illustrating *standard deviation* to show how much of the data falls outside the average (Halter, 2020).

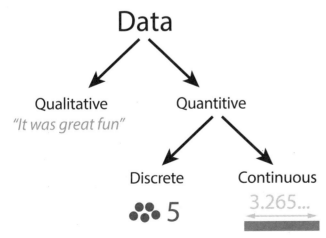

Figure 2.9
Visual display of two broad categories of data: qualitative and quantitative. Quantitative data can be discrete (individual points or numbers) or continuous (Halter, 2020).

the statistical significance of the observed difference being outside of a chance occurrence. In social science research, we often select the 95% significance level which gives us the critical p-value of 0.05.

We use inferential statistics to see how groups of data relate to each other which can be:

- **Correlation**: measures the degree to which two variables move in relation to each other. See Figure 2.12 for how scatter plots illustrate various degrees of correlation.
- **Causation**: measure that shows how one action causes, or leads to, an outcome.

Although two variables may show a high degree of positive correlation, it is important to recognize that may not indicate that one variable *causes* another. For example, if you ask a bunch of your friends whether they like chocolate, and most of them do, you could say that there is a high positive correlation between people being your friend and the fact that they love chocolate. But you could not jump to the conclusion that their love for chocolate *caused* them to be your friend, or that being your friend *caused* them to love chocolate.

Once we understand the types of questions asked in a typical study and the types of data that may be collected and analyzed, we can begin to form relationships between the two. Figure 2.13 shows the possible interrelationship of types of research questions with types of data to be collected.

Quantitative and Qualitative

According to Groat and Wang (2002) in their book *Architectural Research Methods*, "At its most basic level, quantitative research depends on the manipulation of phenomena that can be measured by numbers, whereas qualitative research depends on non-numerical

evidence, whether verbal (oral or written), experiential (film or notes about people in action), or artifactual (objects, buildings, or urban areas)" (p. 25).

An easy way to distinguish between the two is to identify the word *quantity* within the word *quantitative*. *Quantity* is often used to refer to a measurement of something—or "How much?"—**quantitative** information connects a phenomenon to a measurable and often numerical result. Similarly, you can derive the word *quality* from *qualitative*, from which you might ask, "What kind?" **Qualitative** information discusses the character or attributes of a situation, a place, or an experience. Often associated with a subjective experience or opinion, qualitative information might include a personal report of feeling inspired by a worshipper viewing natural light emanating from above in a sacred space, or the emotional or psychological effect of a dynamic range of sounds (from a whisper to a cymbal crash) heard by a listener in a concert theater.

Although *quantity* and *quality* are clearly delineated separately in the explanations above, research in interior design often uses a combination of both types. For example, you could calculate light levels to *quantitatively* describe the amount of light within a kitchen, or you could note the effectiveness of the light to highlight decorative features which alters the aesthetic appearance to *qualitatively* describe the effect of light within the same space.

At times, it may be challenging to differentiate between *quality* and *quantity*, because the distinction is not only influenced by your selected research method but also how you collect, record, organize, or prepare your data for analysis. In fact, sometimes qualitative data can become quantitative and vice versa, further blurring the lines between them. But the difference

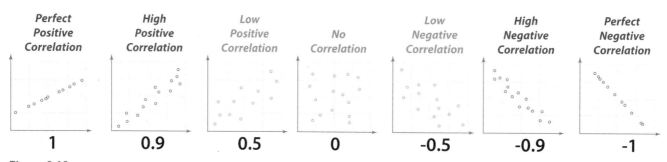

Figure 2.12
Data points on a scatter plot can show degrees of correlation from positive to negative.

Good research is a partnership of *questions* and *data*	What types of data are collected?	
	"Categorical" Data	"Continuous" Data
What kinds of question can be asked of those data? — "Descriptive" Questions	• *How many members of the class are women?* • *What proportion of the class is fulltime?* • *... ?*	• *How tall are class members, on average?* • *How many hours a week do class members report that they study?* • *... ?*
"Relational" Questions	• *Are men more likely to study part-time?* • *Are women more likely to focus on high school education?* • *... ?*	• *Do people who say they study for more hours think they'll finish their doctorate earlier?* • *Are computer literates less anxious about statistics?* • *... ?*

Figure 2.13
This matrix shows an interrelationship of types of questions asked by a researcher and types of data that can be collected (Halter, 2020).

is important. A quantity constitutes something that can be measured while a quality is anything that can be described. Quantitative data will help support a concept due to statistics, and qualitative data will assist in documenting a cultural, behavioral, or environmental phenomenon which relies on its ability to be understood through detailed and relatable description.

Let us consider the following research scenario: A high-end boutique hotel has hired you to redesign their lobby because guests at the hotel seem to make little use of it. In fact, guests have often complained that the hotel lobby and reception space seem cold and uninviting, a qualitative description.

You begin your information-gathering with a site visit to view the existing conditions. You might bring a clipboard with a notepad, a printed floor plan, or camera/audio recorder with you to make written or narrated notes on as you perform an informal observation in the lobby, watching guests walk through, check in, use amenities, all while noting their behavior within

the space. If you describe what you are seeing by writing field notes, taking photos, using colored pens to outline paths of travel, or a combination of video/audio recording which show/describe how people use the space, these would usually be considered qualitative data-gathering methods. Data gathered from what you see, hear, touch, taste, and smell typically fall into the qualitative data category. You might also sketch what you are observing as shown in Figure 2.14, which depicts important aspects of what the researcher observed. The original notes, photos, drawings, and audio/visual recordings would be considered raw qualitative data.

Next, you may begin to ask questions. You may have put together a list of questions, or you may spontaneously decide to ask guests (based on your curiosity), about their seating choice, why they remained standing, or what they would like to see added to the lobby to make them more comfortable. If you collect quotes or record interviews, that may also be considered

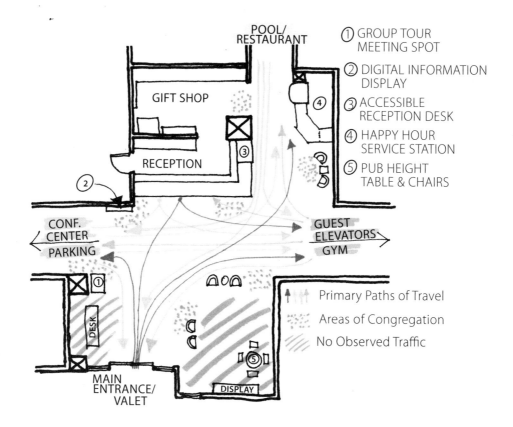

Figure 2.14
Field notes on a sketched floor plan generated by researcher to represent her observation of traffic patterns in a hotel lobby serves as qualitative raw data.

qualitative data, since it still consists of descriptions of qualities.

After this initial observation and based on your analysis of the plan, you may begin to see patterns of behavior emerge. You *hypothesize* that the layout of the lobby in relation to the main entrance, hotel access, parking garage, and restaurant functions more as a main circulation route rather than a gathering space, and therefore the guests report that it feels hurried and impersonal. You might also conclude that the linear, side-by-side, fixed seating, as one might find in an airport terminal, do not foster conversation. Rather, the inflexible seating arrangement causes guests to wait there briefly and to seek other locations when they want to interact.

To support or refute your initial conclusion, you could perform another research method—this time quantitative. You might return to the hotel lobby to count the number of people who occupy the space at various times during the day (see Table 2.2). If your initial educated prediction is true, chances are that your chart will show an increase in usage during the typical lunchtime and dinnertime hours, as guests are using the lobby to access the bar and restaurant. You could use a chart such as the one below to quantitatively record your observations.

When completed, your chart indicates an increased usage of some lobby areas during the typical lunchtime and dinnertime hours. Perhaps there was also an increase in usage around 3 p.m., which corresponds to the hotel's guest check-in time. These results support your hypothesis that the lobby is a circulation route used primarily to access the restaurant and bar. Notice that on both visits to the hotel, your research method was an observation. However, the conclusions from the initial qualitative note-taking and sketching were further supported by your quantitative method of data collection and charting. This broad and thorough understanding of the current use of the lobby will help you redesign it to fit the hotel management's goals to create an inviting atmosphere for hotel guests to linger and socialize.

Table 2.2 Quantitative Data Collection Chart for Hotel Lobby Observation

Instructions: Record number of people in each area at each time slot.

Date of Observation: _____

Day of Week (circle one): M T W Th F S Su Holiday or Special Event: _____?

Time of Day	Valet Entrance	Street Entrance	Reception	South Seating	West Seating	Central Waiting
7:00 A.M.						
8:00 A.M.						
9:00 A.M.						
10:00 A.M.						
11:00 A.M.						
12:00 P.M.						
1:00 P.M.						
2:00 P.M.						
3:00 P.M.						
4:00 P.M.						
5:00 P.M.						
6:00 P.M.						
7:00 P.M.						
8:00 P.M.						
9:00 P.M.						

RESEARCH IN ACTION 2.2
Corporeal Architecture: The Body as Learning Medium

Architect and interior designer, Dr. Maria da Piedade Ferreira's on-going research integrates performance art and neuroscience into the architecture and interior design curriculum. Her innovative methods develop students' *corporeal* (related to one's body) awareness, as well as to heighten sensitivity to social and ecological issues and embed those firmly in design education. Interest in this research began in response to Maria's experience in architecture school and design practice where she found herself enduring prolonged hours sitting passively in front of a computer screen. Maria began to critique the current paradigm in which she found herself producing seductive, yet disembodied architectural images designed to persuade clients. She found this endeavor an alienating experience. Current design practice did not engage the designer's body but rather, she felt, it disconnected the designer from the environment. To her dismay, this disconnection seemed to be accepted as normal by most of her fellow colleagues and triggered her desire to create an alternative mode of thinking and working in design.

Dr. Maria da Piedade Ferreira's research revolved around the central question, "How can architecture influence emotions?" More specifically, she asked, "What is happening in the body while it is engaged in the built environment?" A first step towards this long-term goal was to pursue a doctoral degree, grounding her efforts in theory and scientific rigor. Maria's dissertation study explored the neglect of the body in architecture theory and practice. Inspired by pre-historic cultures, Ancient Egyptian, Greek, and Roman thought and practice, she found a basis for design which connected humans to landscape as well as to the cosmos, created meaning through ritual, and viewed architecture as a place for purposeful action. Her research spanned millennia from Vitruvius, who stated that the origins of architecture most likely related to the instinctive human gestures protecting the body, to Le Corbusier who attempted to express the need for a scientific aesthetic in modern architecture. Her historical inquiry also included

Oskar Schlemmer's "stereometry of space," Joseph Beuys, and extended into the work of twentieth-century performance artists such as Rebecca Horn and Matthew Barney. Through this literature review and focused investigation, she discovered that advances in neurosciences gave new insights into the brain and nervous system. This connection with contemporary science helped her to bridge the traditional split between body and mind. Tools which informed science could also be utilized to inform the study and practice of architecture and interior design. The common element or thread is seeing the body as experimental medium for receiving and responding to stimuli within a continuous multisensory experience.

As exemplified by the famous drawings by Schlemmer shown at right, space is created by our movements. Space is not static but dynamic; not a finished product but viewed as a complementary extension of our bodies which simultaneously affords and restricts motion and behavior. The built environment can be a source of pleasure, allow us to reach our highest potential, or unfortunately serve to frustrate us by thwarting our needs. Biometric data, psychophysiology such as heartbeat, muscular tension, brainwaves, electrodermal activity, body temperature, and eye movement can act as important data reflecting aspects of the body engaged in activity. Data is also seen as a design material. And the built environment can be seen as manifestations of a mental world, allowing us to connect deeper or express who we are. The continued question, "what is happening to the body when we change design parameters?" allow us as design researchers to create situations and measure them and share our findings with others in a community of practice.

After more than ten years of a cycle of experimentation, conversations, and reflexive teaching, *Corporeal Architecture* brings the body back to architectural discourse, starting from the designer's body, and radiating out to the environment. Maria's creative research process integrates costume, temporary structures, and body-mediated explorations to inform art, architecture, interior design, and cross-disciplinary theories. Maria advocates a radically new approach to design education by using the body itself as a learning medium, through its potential for thought, creativity, and taking skillful action. In this way the body can be viewed

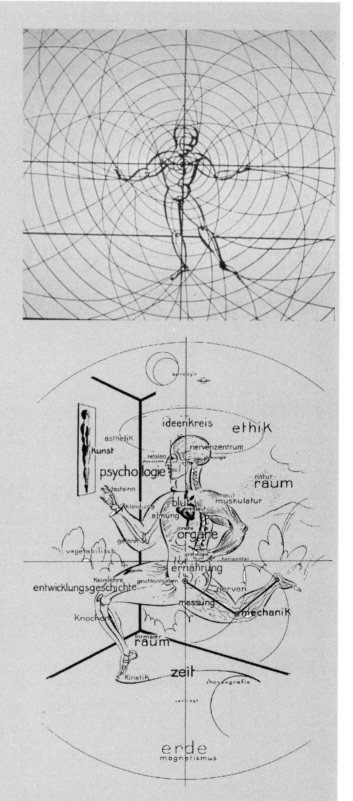

Oskar Schlemmer's (1921) drawing of man as dancer in space which illustrated his theory of "stereometry of space," that space is created by movements and can be felt or sensed by others. Schlemmer's (1928) drawing "Man in the Circle of Ideas."

as instrument for generating data, as well as for exploring its potential for action, through affordances and overcoming constraints which limit thought and action. Inspired by recent breakthroughs and discussion about the plasticity of the embodied brain as well as neurogenesis offers limitless potential for transformation—the idea that our bodies and brains can continuously change and evolve through time and exposure to new forms of thinking and acting or adaptation to changes in the environment.

Themes of body and space are addressed not only through the usual means of representation, such as drawing and model making, but also movement as a form of drawing and sculpting in space (as illustrated below left), as well as digital media which extend the possibilities of the body. The body as an agent in the environment is then investigated as a field for potential action, not only through its natural possibilities for movement but also in relation to the affordances acquired and developed through different technologies, at different scales. The Bauhaus motto "from the spoon to the city" is re-interpreted in today's context of digitalization and bringing awareness to the need to re-think social habits and patterns of action.

Each design task works within a particular conceptual framework which addresses a range of topics for reflection. Individually, the task is freely interpreted by each student who is encouraged to develop it through a mix of digital and material media, incorporating waste materials and repurposing them to create objects, settings, and installations, or adapting existing spaces to transform its character and create different atmospheres. The goal is to sensitize students to the creative possibilities present in existing objects and materials and to develop the capacity to shift one's previous bias and perception of materials initially viewed as objects to be discarded into objects that have value. Sustainability and life cycle are therefore recurrent concepts, important in the exploration of an *avant-garde* aesthetic which creatively incorporates waste material (as shown below right).

Ultimately, the goal of *Corporeal Architecture* (and the resulting projects), is a social transformation in design education, as well as incorporating the concept of neuroplasticity, that the environment has a direct impact on shaping the human brain. As an open-ended concept, *Corporeal Architecture* continues to take shape, organically and in many forms: as a teaching method, website, and a *YouTube* channel, where Maria archives lectures, conversations, and student work. *Corporeal Architecture* may well be seen as a virtual school of design, through an on-going cycle of conversations between architects, interior designers, design researchers, neuroscientists, and students of design.

Life Drawing Life (2020) performance art aimed to develop body and spatial awareness by using the entire body as a drawing agent. (Photo by Michael Hoschek for HFT Stuttgart.)

Wasteland (2019), a homage to Oskar Schlemmer's "Triadisches Ballett" to celebrate the 100 years of Bauhaus. The performance brought attention to the topics of waste, life cycle, and transformation. (Photo by Michael Hoschek for HFT Stuttgart.)

SYSTEMS OF INQUIRY

How you approach solving a design problem is referred to as your *system of inquiry*. Your system of inquiry will likely place interior design somewhere between art and science, combining innovative data gathering with more traditional methods. Among the many interior design programs in colleges and universities, some provide an art-based interior design education while others provide a science- or technology-based interior design education. What kind of degree does your school offer? Understanding your school's education philosophy will enable you to better understand the goals and expectations of your program. Your professors, advisors, and thesis committee members also have their own individual backgrounds in research, which may influence how they guide you toward or away from certain systems of inquiry.

In interior design, from the perspective of art-based design, we create something new with our minds where nothing existed before. Yet we are always building upon the work of the designers who came before us, and this process alone adds a level of objectivity (or science) to our creative process (Weisberg, 2006). Your information-gathering techniques may be more objective, such as collecting census data about the demographics of a community, or they may be more subjective, such as observing the people in a community and evaluating their behavior. If you are gathering information in a way that tends toward the subjective end of the spectrum, you need to be aware of and reflect on your personal background which may impact analysis and conclusion. This is covered in Chapter 3. For now, we will look at the information-gathering procedures that fall under the three main categories of quantitative, qualitative, and mixed methods.

Quantitative Research Methods

We use quantitative research methodologies to gather and analyze information that can be expressed in numbers. Many types of quantitative information are available to us. Numerical data can include, for example, calibrated measurements, such as the level of illumination falling on a working surface (measured in foot-candles), or the ventilation airflow in a space (measured in cubic feet per minute and/or air changes per hour).

Another broad area of quantitative measurement comes from naturalistic observation of occupants in an interior setting: we can measure spatial distancing in feet-and-inches, count the use of different seating arrangements, tally the number of occupants in selected locations, and clock the duration of people's stay in a space. We apply yet another kind of quantitative data gathering when we ask users to categorize their spoken or written perceptions about an environment, or to rank their preferences on a numerical scale. Thus, even though the content of our inquiry is qualitative in nature, such as feelings and opinions, we can gather and analyze that content using numbers that enable us to be systematic in our assessment of their meaning.

If you are engaged in a research project using quantitative data-gathering methods, your focus will be on distinguishing who will be studied, what key variables will be measured, how it will be measured, and how the data will be processed and communicated (see Figure 2.15). We will be exploring these big ideas in more detail in Chapters 4 and 5.

What we can do with the numbers, once we have collected them, is the key to their usefulness. Provided we design the data-gathering activity appropriately (see Chapter 4), this utility can go far beyond the obvious conclusions like "more students sit at the library tables with better lighting." We can find meaning embodied in the numerical data by performing various operations with the numbers. We will look at examples of these operations later in this chapter, *Data Analysis for Design Thinking*.

Qualitative Research Methods

In the section on Quantitative Research Methods, we examined methodologies of gathering and analyzing information that can be expressed in numbers. This is important; however, there are many ways to gain useful knowledge with which to solve a design problem that do not involve numbers. If we take research to mean *positivist* inquiry (explored in Chapter 3), that is, the asking of questions that can be answered through what can be observed; or, if we characterize research as an *empirical* activity, meaning "based on experiments or experiences rather than ideas," an interesting thing becomes clear: both words we have come to associate with the logic of mathematics do not have to be quantitative!

Qualitative Research is also empirical in method, but unlike its quantitative sibling it may ask questions

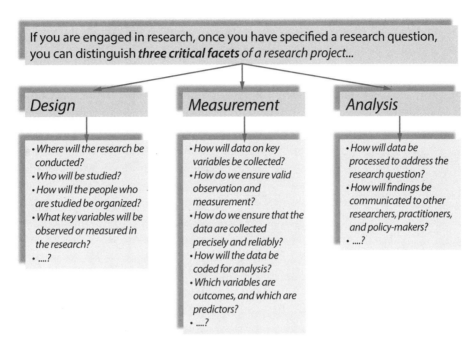

If you are engaged in research, once you have specified a research question, you can distinguish **three critical facets** of a research project...

Design
- Where will the research be conducted?
- Who will be studied?
- How will the people who are studied be organized?
- What key variables will be observed or measured in the research?
- ....?

Measurement
- How will data on key variables be collected?
- How do we ensure valid observation and measurement?
- How do we ensure that the data are collected precisely and reliably?
- How will the data be coded for analysis?
- Which variables are outcomes, and which are predictors?
- ....?

Analysis
- How will data be processed to address the research question?
- How will findings be communicated to other researchers, practitioners, and policy-makers?
- ....?

Figure 2.15
Answering questions with quantitative data involves designing the study to determine who will be studied, what will be measured, and how you will look at the data (Halter, 2020).

of the who, what, and why variety, not just how many, and employ words and images in both the gathering and reporting of information (Ormston, Spencer, Barnard, & Snape, 2013).

Some icons of anthropology come to mind: Margaret Mead reported "event analyses" of Samoan culture with the help of interviews, photographs, and personal testimony (Kincheloe, 1980); Jane Goodall brought only a notebook and a pair of binoculars to study the chimpanzees of Gombe Stream National Park. Qualitative researchers "study things in their natural settings, attempting to make sense of or interpret phenomena in terms of the meanings people bring to them" (Denzin, 2011, p. 3).

Examples of qualitative methodologies include:

- Fieldnotes, journals, and memos to self
- In-depth interviews and conversations
- Human–environment behavior in-the-field observation
- Photographs, video, and audio recordings
- Self-reports and journaling by participants
- Photo-manipulation, drawing, or sorting, encompassing a variety of non-verbal interview techniques
- Focus groups

Noting the diverse research methods gathered under the umbrella of "qualitative," Groat and Wang identify commonalities among these methods: their focus on naturalistic settings, interpretation and meaning, respondents making sense of their own circumstances, use of multiple research tactics, and application of inductive logic in interpretation of findings (Groat & Wang, 2013).

While quantitative research methods often require a narrow focus to collect numbers that can be reasonably compared using statistical methods, qualitative analysis may address its subject holistically, allowing the researcher to address complex phenomena in a behavioral setting. That is why the initial investigation of the hotel lobby setting in Figure 2.14 made sense as a qualitative study: it was too early in the analysis to start counting things or applying numeric value.

Interior settings and other designed environments and objects weave together a wide array of sensory inputs and social dynamics, making it a challenge to confidently analyze them based on dependent and independent variables. Was it the spacing of the chairs, or their color, or texture, or social status of the occupants that caused the observed behavior? Or perhaps the quality of light coming through the windows on an overcast day made the difference, or the time of day, or the state of the economy. Qualitative tools enable the researcher to capture and fully describe these phenomena in a scientific study. We will explore these methods in more detail in Chapter 5.

Design as a Research Method

Design itself can be a research method. In its processes of finding, producing, translating, and structuring, interior design questions how we use the environment and explores answers through drawing, modeling, and testing of hypotheses (Nijhuis & de Vries, 2019).

The outcome of design in the form of practical knowledge that informs our understanding of the built environment can be viewed in time spans: in the scale of decades, we learn from living in environments and adapting their solutions to new programs; in the scale of years, we may conduct *Post Occupancy Evaluations* of completed design projects, interviewing users, and examining trace evidence of use; in the scale of weeks and months we can prototype solutions at full-scale. Often a hotel room solution that will be replicated multiple times is mocked up with a complete outfitting of finishes, colors, furniture, and fixtures. The expense is well worth it, for the knowledge we gain from seeing the component parts assembled informs the designer's understanding of the occupant's experience as well as the construction team's efficiency in ensuring well-executed details. In the scale of minutes and hours we test solutions through manual and digital models and

fly-throughs, leveraging the learning that comes from an iterative process for improved solutions.

Research-Through-Design (RTD) was intuitively pursued by Antonio Gaudi. In the Sagrada Familia, in Barcelona, we find a model of Gaudi's upside-down force model of catenary arches, a design experiment to discover the most efficient curve of the arches by suspending weights in tension from cables, representing the gravity loads bearing in compression on the arches from above. In Figure 2.16a and 2.16b we can see the experiment done originally and a model which replicated the results in 2017.

Mixed Methods

According to Creswell and Creswell (2018), **mixed methods** involves the integration of both quantitative and qualitative data in a study. Mixed methods has garnered increasing popularity in recent years. There are three core research designs which combine both methods: (1) *convergent*, (2) *explanatory sequential*, and (3) *exploratory sequential*.

Figure 2.16a
Photo of Antonio Gaudi's Sagrada Familia concrete tower forms shown upside down.

Figure 2.16b
Re-creation of the original catenary model from a museum exhibit (2017).

In a *convergent* mixed methods approach, you would collect both quantitative and qualitative data using a single method such as a survey which has two main types of questions: closed-ended or multiple-choice that yield numerical data (statistics) and open-ended ones that yield description, photos, or drawings. You would then compare both kinds of data to see if they align with each other or not, and then interpret the results.

The other two kinds of mixed methods involve a sequence of typically two or more phases. An *explanatory* method "appeals to individuals with a strong quantitative background" (Creswell & Creswell, 2018, p. 221). Statistical results from a survey in the first phase would be analyzed. If the data turned out to be "confusing, contradictory, or unusual" you would then purposefully select some participants to be interviewed or otherwise provide qualitative data to explain or clarify (Creswell & Creswell, 2018, p. 222). On the other hand, *exploratory* sequential designs start with a qualitative data-gathering technique to help inform a subsequent experiment or survey. The idea is to use your experience observing or interviewing to get a sense of how to define variables or create an instrument for testing.

Activity 2.2
Proposing a Pilot Study

Purpose: A **pilot study** refers to a small-scale preliminary investigation which aims to test an instrument (such as a questionnaire), assemble a sample pool, try out a distribution method, or explore the feasibility of an approach. It is a preliminary test run which may yield important feedback on how to improve any of the content or implementation methods of the study components. The idea is to allow the pilot study to possibly fail so that we can learn from the mistakes or pitfalls of the practice run before we experience that challenge during the actual study.

Objective: To build on ideas generated in Chapter 1 regarding our research project. To discuss the design of a particular method to gather information for a research question generated in activities in Chapter 1.

Requirements: Reflecting on what you have learned so far, propose a simple pilot study that aims to test a research question you developed in Chapter 1 activities.

1. What is the research question?

2. What would be your population to study?

3. How many participants do you imagine you would need in your sample? How would you go about getting access to a sample of that size? How would you select your sample to maintain objectivity and minimize bias?

4. What kind of data-gathering method do you propose? Would it be qualitative, quantitative, or mixed methods?

5. Share your ideas with a colleague or partner.

6. Offer feedback on their ideas. Accept feedback on your ideas.

7. What questions do you still have about the research process?

SYSTEMS OF EVALUATION

While a *system of inquiry* is how you pose a question and the methods you use to answer this question, a *system of evaluation* is how you personally interpret the information gathered from your system of inquiry to draw new conclusions. In other words, a system of inquiry influences your method for gathering information, and a system of evaluation influences your interpretation and use of the information you gathered. Depending upon your role in the field, in addition to systems of inquiry, you will also employ one or more systems of evaluation, which will cause you to interpret information differently than other people working in the field. Systems of evaluation used by an interior design professional might include

- Functional or code compliance from an architectural or engineering perspective.
- Formal elements and principles in aesthetics, color, lighting, etc. as it relates to space and place.

- Environmental psychology—to interpret information as it holds meaning for the interactions between humans and their environment.
- Business model—to evaluate the viability of an operation, organization, or real estate proposal with respect to making money or creating value.
- Human-centered, end-user model—would involve active human participation, cognitive learning, or meaning within a culture or community.
- Health and well-being from a sociological, biological, or neuroscience perspective.

As you begin to examine your predilections and perspectives that have been shaped by your life experiences in the next chapter, strive to understand how your information informs and influences your project, as well as how it informs and influences the interior design field as a whole from many perspectives beyond your own. For example, you might propose a design solution, and immediately your engineer will be concerned with constructability, your client will be concerned with cost, your contractor will be concerned with available resources, neighbors might be concerned with the impact upon their ocean view, and so on. As a designer, you will want to look at problems and information from many viewpoints to see the big picture and find the answer that creates a balance for all parties involved.

Data Reduction Methods

When you start to collect data, you will see that sometimes it can be a very messy process. For example, you decide to observe children in a playground. As you stand outside surrounded by crowds of children running in multiple directions among the various pieces of play equipment, you may begin to get overwhelmed by the continuous, simultaneous, and multiple types of interactions taking place around you. You decide to come back with a video camera thinking that this will help alleviate some issues, only to find that video footage, while framed, focused, and recorded, giving you the ability to slow down, pause, and rewind still leaves you with an exhausting amount of information. Researchers in this situation have come up with tools that help focus their observation and reduce the confusion. Attempts to transform raw data to a more usable form by codifying or categorizing them are referred to as **data reduction** methods.

Sometimes color coding an interview transcript (as discussed in Chapter 6), helps to make isolated data points from a continuous stream of raw data. If we have established these categories *before* we start reading the transcript, listening to an audio recording, or watching video footage, we call these *a priori* codes. Grouping similar responses that we notice *after* we read the transcript, and naming them, is what we call identifying *emergent* codes. We can then look at the coded or reduced data to identify patterns and look for themes more easily. This method can transform qualitative data by counting the number of instances of a code, to yield quantitative data.

Data Analysis for Design Thinking

Statistical analysis of the quantitative data we have collected can yield insights about a design situation. Design researchers apply tools like analysis of variance and correlational analysis to inform their thinking about the relationships between people and their environments. In one example, researchers were curious about occupants' satisfaction with LEED-certified work environments. They used a questionnaire designed to obtain opinions from users of these spaces; they also asked respondents to self-assess their work performance in these environments (Lee & Guerin, 2010). This data became the researchers' dependent variables: the things they hypothesized would be affected by the work environment. The elements of the work environment itself—the illumination, partition heights, cubicles vs. private offices, and access to natural light—were catalogued and became the study's independent variables; the things that they hypothesized would account for variations in the workers' perceptions and performance. The study used analysis of variance as the tool to evaluate the questionnaire results and determine if their hypotheses were correct. We use **analysis of variance (ANOVA)** to analyze data when we want to determine whether an independent variable is related to variation in an outcome measure, the dependent variable. As we look at the numbers, we temporarily suspend judgment about whether the relationship we find between the independent and dependent variable is "causal," although our hypothesis may be that the physical environment could be the cause of satisfaction/dissatisfaction and/or work performance.

Innovative product design firm IDEO explains how they use data in their practice. "In addition to connecting with people and learning their stories, designers use quantitative data as a tool to gain empathy and inspiration. We learn from numbers the same way we learn from people, because we see numbers as a representation of people" (McClain, 2017).

Their "deep dive" approach involves immersion in information to help solve the problem at hand. Data helps designers explore the difference between what people say they do versus what they actually do. Quantitative as well as qualitative data help designers to create and test prototypes. According to Massa (2015) "Just as there are behaviors that can only be uncovered through human observation, there are behaviors that only data analysis can uncover."

Activity 2.3
Playing with Quantitative Data

Purpose: A highly scaffolded step-by-step guide to determine how data answers a research question about student satisfaction with the testing environment and the influence of the environment on quiz scores, this activity will help you to understand how quantitative data may be organized, aggregated, and prepared for analysis.

Objective: You want to know if there is a relationship between student satisfaction with classroom furniture (the independent variable) and learning levels (the dependent variable).

Requirements: Follow the application of analysis of variance and provide calculations where necessary.

In this activity we have similar groups of high school learners taking the same course, meeting in two different classrooms. Group A meets weekly in a room furnished with tablet-arm chairs, and Group B meets in a room with loose chairs at free-standing tables. The rooms are otherwise the same. There are 15 students in each group.

You have surveyed the students asking a simple question: "On a scale of 1 to 10, how satisfied are you with the seating in this classroom (with 1 being very dissatisfied and 10 being very satisfied)?" With the survey results, you have numbers for each student that represent their satisfaction with the furniture (on a scale of 1 to 10). We also have a measure of their performance: their scores on a recent quiz (worth 100 points). All of these are compiled in Table 2.3. Note that $n = 30$, meaning that there are a total of 30 participants in the study. The letter "n" stands for the number of individuals in the study, or your total sample size.

Table 2.3 With three data points for each student, we can compile our results in a table. $n = 30$

Room	Satisfaction	Quiz Score
A	6	65
A	4	82
A	3	73
A	2	48
A	7	74
A	9	81
A	5	70
A	3	75
A	5	63
A	6	83
A	2	63
A	8	89
A	5	82
A	4	67
A	3	59

B	9	98
B	8	96
B	6	88
B	7	69
B	6	87
B	9	79
B	5	68
B	3	52
B	7	88
B	8	78
B	9	87
B	7	90
B	10	96
B	9	95
B	8	94

Activity 2.3.a Calculate the average, or mean, quiz score for all 30 students. The formula is

$$\frac{sum\ of\ scores\ for\ students\ 1\ through\ 30}{n}\ \text{where } n = 30.$$

This is easy to do if you enter the data in a spreadsheet such as Microsoft Excel (if you use a spreadsheet now, it will make the next activity steps much easier). Round your result to the nearest whole number.

Activity 2.3.b Compare the average, or mean, score of the two groups of students, Room A vs. Room B. The formulae are:

$$\frac{sum\ of\ scores\ for\ students\ 1\ through\ 15}{n}\ \text{and}\ \frac{sum\ of\ scores\ for\ students\ 16\ through\ 30}{n}$$

where this time $n = 15$, because there happen to be 15 students in each group. Students 1–15 in Room A, it turns out, had a lower average quiz score than students 16–30 in Room B.

Activity 2.3.c Now, let's compare the level of *satisfaction* our two groups of students experienced with the furniture in their room. We will use similar formulae to find their *average* satisfaction on a scale of 1 to 10:

$$\frac{sum\ of\ satisfaction\ level\ for\ students\ 1\ through\ 15}{n}$$

and

$$\frac{sum\ of\ satisfaction\ level\ for\ students\ 16\ through\ 30}{n}$$

where again $n = 15$, because there are 15 students in each group. Students in Room A, it turns out, *also* had a lower level of satisfaction with their tablet-arm chairs than students in Room B had with their furniture.

In Activities 2.3.b–2.3.c you have used simple calculations of the mean (the average) to demonstrate a relationship: students in Room B liked their furniture more *and* performed better on the quiz. We don't know enough yet to say the furniture in Room A or even the unhappiness with it led to lower scores, but we've learned enough to tell the school facility manager to put a hold on the next order of tablet-arm chairs while we do further research!

Activity 2.3.d Visualize the relationship between low satisfaction and low quiz scores. In Excel, select/highlight two columns in your table: Satisfaction and Quiz Score. From the menu, select *Insert > Preferred Chart > Scatter*. The resulting graph will plot a point for each student with their quiz score on the y-axis and their satisfaction on the x-axis. Your graph should look something like the figure in this activity.

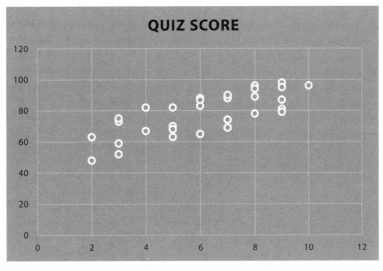

Scatter plot of quiz scores (y-axis) vs. satisfaction (x-axis).

Above, we have a picture of how the two variables (satisfaction and quiz score) relate for *each* student. Compare the pattern to the example scatter plots in Figure 2.12. Which one does it most resemble? There is a high positive correlation between the independent variable, furniture, and the dependent variable, quiz score.

CONCLUSION

In this chapter we discussed the scientific method, which includes variations involving the following steps (Cherry, 1999, p. 37), one of which is the formulation of a hypothesis:

1. Pose a question.
2. Collect pertinent evidence.
3. Form a hypothesis.
4. Deduce the implications of the hypothesis.
5. Test the implications.
6. Accept, reject, or modify the hypothesis.

In addition, we have become familiar with terminology used in research. As we start to read previously published studies and sources discussing the study results, it is important that you become a critical thinker, to be alert to the possible weaknesses in the methods, theories, and results.

Key Terms

A priori
Academy of Neuroscience for Architecture (ANFA)
Affordance
Analysis of variance (ANOVA)
Applied research
Argument
Assumption
Basic research
Categorical data
Causal/causation
Claim
Consilience
Constructs
Continuous data
Correlation
Data
Deductive reasoning
Dependent variable
Descriptive statistics

Discrete data
Evidence
Experiment
Hypothesis
Independent variable
Inductive reasoning
Inferential statistics
Instruments
Logic
Measures of central tendency (mean, median, mode)
Mixed methods
Objective
Operationalize
P-value
Peer-review
Pilot study
Population
Propositions
Qualitative

Quantitative
Research
Research method
Research methodology
Research question
Research-Through-Design (RTD)
Results
Sample
Scientific method
Standard deviation
Statistical significance
Statistics
Subjective
Testimony
Theory
Triangulation
Variable

Discussion Questions

1. What are the key components of the scientific method? How do they relate to the field of interior design?
2. What is the difference between quantitative and qualitative data? Give an example of each.
3. As interior designers and researchers, what should we be aware of before embarking on a research study? What are some of the issues that may be studied?
4. How does a system of inquiry differ from a data type? For example, how can a qualitative data-gathering method yield quantitative data? How can a quantitative data-gathering method result in qualitative data? How can qualitative data be transformed (or reduced) to quantitative data?
5. What are some ways we evaluate data?
6. Share some ideas about how the chapter influenced your ideas about your own research journey. What questions do you still have about the research process?

References

Barnet, S. Bedau, H., & O'Hara, J. (2020). *From critical thinking to argument: A portable guide* (6th ed.). New York: Bedford/St. Martin's.

Blakstad, O. (2008, March 10). *Research methodology*. Retrieved May 16, 2020 from Explorable.com: https://explorable.com/research-methodology

Cherry, E. (1999). *Programming for design*. New York: John Wiley.

Creswell, J. W., & Creswell, J. D. (2018). *Research design: Qualitative, quantitative, and mixed methods approaches* (5th ed.). Los Angeles, CA: Sage.

Denzin, N. (2011). The politics of evidence. In N. K. Denzin & Y. S. Lincoln (Eds.), *The Sage Handbook of Qualitative Research* (4th ed.). Thousand Oaks, 645–658. CA: Sage.

Explorable.com (2008, February 6). *Milgram experiment—obedience to authority*. Retrieved February 05, 2021 from Explorable.com: https://explorable.com/stanley-milgram-experiment https://www.khanacademy.org/science/high-school-biology/hs-biology-foundations/hs-biology-and-the-scientific-method/a/the-science-of-biology

Fraenkel, J., Wallen, N., & Sawin, E. I. (1999). *Visual statistics: A conceptual primer*. Needham Heights, MA: Allyn & Bacon.

Gepshtein, S. (2019). *Kinds of spaces*. Neuroscience for Architecture, Urbanism and Design Summer Intersession Program, August 15, 2019. New School of Architecture and Design, San Diego, CA.

Gibson J. J. (1986[2015]). The theory of affordances. In *The ecological approach to visual perception* (pp. 119–136). New York: Taylor & Francis.

Glesne, C. (2011). *Becoming qualitative researchers: An introduction* (4th ed.). Boston, MA: Pearson Education.

Groat, L., & Wang, D. (2002). *Architectural research methods*. New York: John Wiley.

Groat, L., & Wang, D. (2013). *Architectural research methods*. New York: John Wiley.

Guerin, D., & Dohr, J. (2007). *Research 101 tutorial*. InformeDesign, University of Minnesota. Retrieved December 25, 2007, from http://www.informedesign.umn.edu/

Halter, C. (2020). Quantitative analysis with JASP open-source software. Christopher Halter. Retrieved from https://www.christopherhalter.com/jasp

Harkiolakis, N. (2018). *Quantitative research methods: From theory to publication*. Middletown, DE: Nicholas Harkiolakis.

Hodge, B., & Pollak, L. (Eds.). (1996). *Studio works 4: Harvard University Graduate School of Design (No. 4)*. New York: Princeton Architectural Press.

Kincheloe, T.S. (Fall, 1980). Margaret Mead's early fieldwork: Methods and implications for education. *Journal of Thought*, *15*(3), 21–30.

Lee, Y., & Guerin, D. (2010). Indoor environmental quality differences between office types in LEED-certified buildings in the US. *Building and Environment*, *45*(5), 1104–1112.

Massa, J. (2015, October 9). *Medium design-x-data_ Your next hidden opportunity: finding the human angle in metadata*. Retrieved December 13, 2020, from https://medium.com/design-x-data/your-next-hidden-opportunity-7abc21e79efe

McClain, A. (2017, January 24). *IDEO design-x-data: How we use data to inspire design*. Retrieved December 13, 2020 from https://medium.com/design-x-data/how-we-use-data-to-inspire-design-ccc51327e904

Nijhuis, S. & de Vries, J. (January, 2019). Design as research in landscape architecture. *Landscape Journal*. *38*(1–2), 87–103.

Ormston, R., Spencer, L., Barnard, M., & Snape, D. (2013). The foundations of qualitative research. In J. Richie, J. Lewis, C. McNaughton Nicholls, & R. Ormston (Eds.), *Qualitative research practice: A guide for social science students and researchers* (2nd ed.), pp. 1–25. Los Angeles, CA: Sage.

Shuttleworth, M. (2008, October 2). *Defining a Research Problem*. Retrieved February 05, 2021 from Explorable.com: https://explorable.com/defining-a-research-problem

Weisberg, R. (2006). *Creativity: Understanding innovation in problem-solving, science, invention and the arts*. New York: John Wiley.

Zeisel, J., & Eberhard, J. (2006). *Inquiry by design: Environment/behavior/neuroscience in architecture, interiors, landscape, and planning*. New York: W.W. Norton.

CHAPTER 3

Philosophical Foundations and Meaningful Influences

LEARNING OBJECTIVES

After you complete this chapter, you will be able to:

- Explore your cultural and professional capital to see how these uniquely position you for design research.

- Explain the role of value systems in research and examine your own perspective.

- Become aware of underlying assumptions and bias and ways of overcoming them.

- Identify paradigms and worldviews and how they are subject to change or become obsolete.

- Understand how diverse philosophies and their use of reasoning and theory inform research methods.

- Consider a *Creative Paradigm* approach to research (using abductive reasoning) as you develop your own research and design philosophy.

"An unexamined life is not worth living."

SOCRATES

In Chapter 1 we discussed creative problem-solving as the heart of interior design. Have you ever considered the way you tend to solve problems? Inspired by Schön (1983) *The Reflective Practitioner: How Professionals Think in Action*, Gray and Malins (2016) call for design researchers to first be *reflective* practitioners. They advise designers to unite research and practice in a framework that encourages reflection-on-action, or "thinking about what we are doing and reshaping action while we are doing it" (p. 22). It is important, in both design and in research, to look at the way you do things.

As introduced in Chapter 2, your research methods, or tasks you plan to do, will be guided by your research methodology or overarching framework. If you wanted to know the temperature of a room, for example, you may use a thermometer. However, if you wanted to know if the occupants found the temperature of the room to be comfortable, you may conduct a survey. In this simple example you can see how what you are trying to learn greatly influences your choice of methods. How you solve a problem is guided by what you are looking for; what you aim to achieve influences the methods you use.

In addition to being aware of how you solve problems, would you also be able to explain that process to someone else? Not only should we be aware of our actions and the reasons behind them, but we should also cultivate the ability to make our process **explicit**, clearly communicating to others what we do and how they might duplicate the same procedure. This dynamic process of awareness and explanation, called **reflexivity**, is at the heart of human-centered, interior design research today.

BEGINNING YOUR RESEARCH JOURNEY

What you bring to any problem is unique—it is a combination of all your past experiences and what you have learned from them. Your method of problem-solving has been influenced by these past experiences including the culture you were born into, the languages you speak, the abilities you have, and the accumulation of sensations experienced by your physical body. Your perspective is a distinctive thing you bring to every problem you try to solve, one that no one else can. This chapter urges you to take some time to explore your unique perspective so that you understand how it influences how you view the world, what you deem important, and what you tend to focus on. In addition, awareness of these **implicit** or unspoken, underlying values and tendencies can help you reshape and refocus your research and design process. *Making the implicit explicit* is the first step in the research journey—it is the way one first becomes a researcher and not just someone interested in research. Just as this book shares information-gathering techniques for researching a design problem to find a successful solution, it also offers some techniques to help you clarify or gain some insights into yourself.

THE VALUE OF PERSONAL EXPERIENCE

Before you start problem-solving, this chapter guides you toward looking inward—to understand your unique perspective. Your *point of view* is a position or perspective from which you consider or evaluate experiences, ideas, or people or objects. It can also be referred to as your *perspective*. Everyone who experiences a certain person, place, or thing will come at it from a different point of view and will have a personal interpretation of the experience (Groat & Wang, 2002). Your point of view will also influence how you approach a problem.

Your point of view is invisible, but it is always present. As an example, think about a photograph. You cannot take a photograph without a point of view. And when you look at a photograph, the point of view is not in the photo but, rather, it is the combination of the camera lens, what you perceived as important, and where you were standing when you took the picture. When you look at a photograph taken by someone else, you are looking at something from their perspective, indirectly seeing their point of view about the subject in the image. Think how this could vary if a child and an adult each took a photograph of the same subject. Not only would the location of the lens be different due to height differences, but what the child perceived as important about the subject could be very different from what the adult perceived as important. Any experience is greatly influenced by the point of view or position from which that person approaches the subject. You have the greatest chance of seeing a thing, place, or experience clearly if you can gain an overall objective view of the situation. In any situation, there is always a bigger picture, a surrounding context, or a point of view to be considered.

The same principle applies to buildings, interiors, and the experiences that people have within these places. A great example is Seattle's Experience Music Project, designed by Frank Gehry. The exterior and interior of the building is a complex arrangement of geometries, colors, and materials, making each view of the exterior a unique one. Depending on where people are standing, each person might describe the experience of the building in a different way. From one vantage point the viewer might see the building as cold, gray, and metallic. From another vantage point the viewer might see the building as warm, red, and shiny, with undulating shapes and forms. The interior of the building is designed similarly, as each new space and point of view within the space provides the visitor with a new experience.

Add to this scenario the *subjective* opinion of the individual, often influenced by that person's previous exposure to architecture, interior design, art, and even music. In addition, we may have emotions tied to certain experiences. For example, what is "visually stimulating" to one person may be "chaotic" and "confusing" to another.

Building on Cultural and Professional Capital

In their book *Reproduction in Education, Society and Culture* (1990), Pierre Bourdieu and Jean-Claude Passeron use the term **cultural capital** to refer to the knowledge, experience, and connections that have enabled a person to succeed through the course of his or her life. *Cultural* could be summarized roughly as the customary beliefs, social norms, values, attitudes, language, symbols, and material traits characterizing experiences in a person's upbringing. *Capital* could be described as "something of great value," or as an adjective, "relating to or being assets that add to long-term net worth" (Merriam-Webster Online, 2012).

More recently, Hargreaves and Fullan (2012) propounded that one's own worth in any field, leveraged to accomplish desired goals, comprised one's professional capital. Building on the idea of business or financial capital, **professional capital** is "the product of *human capital*, *social capital*, and *decisional capital*" referring to an individual's talent, interconnection with others, and competence in making sound judgments or propensity for insight, respectively. "Making decisions in complex situations," they claim, "is what professionalism is all about … to have competence, judgment, insight, inspiration, and the capacity for improvisation." In addition, they state that professional capital also involves an "openness to feedback, and willing transparency … in a spirit of making greater individual and collective contributions" (Hargreaves & Fullan, 2012, p. 5). Applying that concept to your academic and professional experience, you could think of your value as resulting from all the life experiences that make you uniquely you. Such experiences shape and form your fundamental perspectives, the assumptions you make about the world, your opinions, your beliefs, and what you see as a good use of your time or a valuable contribution to society.

As we saw in Chapter 2, evidence for our claims comes in many forms. One form could be a compelling personal experience that serves to establish a need or give insight into a particular perspective that had not been given voice before. For example, many thesis presentations or dissertation defenses start out with the researcher giving a first-hand account of something that happened to them or a vivid description of something they had witnessed. This personal story, or **anecdotal evidence**, not only gets our attention and emotionally engages the listener, but it also provides **ethos** or helps to build the trust in and character of the speaker. It is an important part of being human as well as being a researcher.

Activity 3.1
Reflecting on Personal Capital for Anecdotal Evidence

Purpose: To reflect on your life experiences and the value they bring to decision-making.

Imagine you have been asked by someone you care about to help make an important decision.

Perhaps you have been asked to come along while they look at options for a new living place. It could be a grandparent evaluating independent living facilities, your favorite aunt moving to a new city, or your brother looking for his first apartment. You've toured some places together, evaluated cost, neighborhood safety, distance to the grocery store—researched all those things that can be answered with a number or a rating. Together you have researched all the options and listed the pros and cons of each, and this favorite person turns to you and says, "Now I want to know what *you* think."

Take twenty minutes to reflect: my friend or relative picked *me* to help make this decision. What are the unique personal resources I can draw on to support them? Visualize your "capital." Is it your knowledge of people that makes you feel comfortable sizing up each of the landlords? Is it your knack of listening to others that helps you to hear the underlying message in a casual conversation with one of the other tenants? Or your ability to see the signs of careful or careless use of the public areas of the buildings? Perhaps it is none of these but comes from somewhere else within you. Some sources might be your:

Experiences

- A place you have lived.
- A job or responsibility you have had.
- A life experience that changed the course of your life (for good or bad).
- A challenge you have faced (and overcome).
- A place you have been that you do not think anyone else has been.
- A memorable film you have seen, or a book you have read.

Aspirations

- Something you wish you could do.

- Something you find fun to do that you think no one else likes to do.
- A material possession you wish you owned.
- A wise person you would like to emulate.

Accomplishments

- A special talent or skill you have cultivated.
- All the languages you speak.

Likes

- A motto.
- A piece of artwork.
- A person or possession you treasure.

Motivations

- What makes you get out of bed in the morning?
- What scares you?

This is simply a starter list to get you thinking about your own personal capital. The categories might help you to think of things that aren't on the list, or you can make your own categories. If you think of each group as a "bucket" of personal capital, some buckets may be fuller than others. That is okay. That's you.

Share your answers in small groups or in class to see if you share common values or goals with anyone else. Where do your goals and passions differ, and where do they overlap? What does this information tell you about yourself?

OVERCOMING ASSUMPTIONS

Your point of view or perspective is based on your **value system** (a situation or condition you strive to maintain and will dedicate energy, time, and even money to maintaining). Your value system affects not only the decisions you make, but the sources you seek in informing your decisions (Cherry, 1999). If this concept is new to you, seek an understanding of your own value system simply by asking yourself, "What is important to me?" or "What will I exert energy on to gain or maintain?" In your journal or notebook, jot down your thoughts about these questions.

The challenge for each of us, as interior design researchers, is that our individual value systems have such a strong influence on the way we think that they can prevent us from seeking information or posing solutions that relate to a value system different from our own. This challenge becomes especially apparent in the information-gathering practices of interviewing or observation, as our value system determines the questions we ask and the questions we don't ask (Cherry, 1999), or the things we notice and those we don't, often referred to as "inattentional blindness" (Mack & Rock, 1998).

Your personal value system might have a far-reaching impact on your design process. Your value system influences the point of view from which you approach a design problem. Subsequently, your point of view influences the assumptions you make about the client, the user, the problem, the site, and so on. Often, we let our idea of what things *should be* influence how open we are to what things *could be* and how we could make conditions better than they currently are. Your assumptions influence the kinds of questions you will ask and the information you will seek. In the book *Programming for Design*, Edith Cherry uses a great example. A designer asks a corporate client, "How much growth do you want to plan for?" This question assumes that all firms want to grow, possibly based on a value system that believes company growth is good and all companies *should* want to grow. A better opening question might be "Do you want to plan for growth?"—thus taking a more neutral position and allowing the client to give more thoughtful and open answers (Cherry, 1999).

According to Barnet, Bedau, & O'Hara (2020), assumptions are "unexamined beliefs," taken for granted, which may be deeply embedded and hard to recognize (p. 104). Unstated or hidden assumptions can be very dangerous. They invite stereotyping, could waste time and money on unsound research in that they may obscure the real problem to solve. They can be false, implicit (unstated) or explicit (clearly identified). Assumptions are like small springboards along the path of information-gathering, where the goal is to find the truth or the right solution. Once you assume something about a situation, all other conclusions are built upon it. If the assumption is inaccurate or misguided, your subsequent conclusions will likely be wrong as well (Weisberg, 2006).

As seen in the previous example, if you ask your corporate client, "How much growth do you want to plan for?" you are assuming that all firms value growth as an asset. If you come to all your client meetings with that assumption in mind, you might misinterpret information the client shares with you. The client might say, "We would like you to help us find a new office space to better fit our needs." If you are assuming growth is inevitable, you might spend time seeking office spaces that in the end are completely unsuitable for the client's needs. You might seek a workspace in a high-rise office building with an open floor plan and plenty of open tenant space to grow, when what the client really needs is a smaller, more intimate-feeling space in a suburban office park.

Your interpretation of the information you gather will ultimately influence the design solutions you propose to the client. To maximize the potential solutions and outcomes for an interior design project, it is essential that you understand yourself and your own value system, that you are open to the value systems of others, and that you are able to maintain an open and neutral mind.

This discussion of value systems and assumptions applies to the interior design process at many levels (Groat & Wang, 2002). Just as your value system influences how you approach design, it also influences how you approach research, information-gathering, and programming. Believe it or not, it could influence other researchers and designers as well. If other researchers and designers apply your research-based conclusions to their own research process, you will indirectly influence their conclusions and solutions and even their design decisions (Groat & Wang, 2002).

The standards for evaluating the quality of the research and the accuracy of the findings depend substantially on the *system of inquiry* a researcher employs. A system of inquiry, as discussed in Chapter 2, is typically chosen when it aligns with the researcher's assumptions about the nature of the reality—and subsequently the methods by which the researcher seeks out answers to his or her questions (Groat & Wang, 2002). In a sense, the system of inquiry is the context in which the research is conducted. It is critical that the assumptions influencing your system of inquiry not be flawed in any way, or else your conclusions cannot be accepted.

You can tell a lot about your own value system by looking at the people you surround yourself with, the books you read, the activities you participate in, and the organizations you choose to join, just to name a few (Adams, 2001). Learn to recognize and identify the experiences that shape who you are and the point of view from which you approach the world, so that you are aware of the assumptions you carry and how they influence the decisions you make. Often your value system can be your greatest creative resource.

Creative design solutions could come from considering your value system from a new perspective or from adopting and extending the perspectives and value systems of others with whom you are in contact (Adams, 2001).

Acknowledging Bias

If you related Groat and Wang's statement about quantitative research back to the earlier definitions of *objectivity* and *subjectivity* in Chapter 2, you could make a correlation between quantitative research as objective and qualitative research as subjective. The most questioned aspect of your research approach is whether your system of inquiry is considered subjective or objective (Groat & Wang, 2002). According to Merriam-Webster Online, *objectivity* refers to research methods that express or deal with facts or conditions as perceived without any distortion caused by personal feelings or interpretations, while *subjectivity* refers to research that might be modified or affected by personal views, experience, or background.

Although this definition presents the distinction as cut-and-dried, the reality is more complex. There is a very common debate that there is no true objective reality—that, instead, there are many subjective realities based on the life experiences of the subject, creating the point of view from which the subject interprets the world. This is the impact of having a point of view that has unspoken, underlying assumptions about the nature of reality. Have you heard the expression "looking at the world through rose-colored glasses"? That expression refers to how that individual's life experiences influence their interpretation of the world around them, in this case reflecting an exceedingly optimistic view. We all look at a problem, question, and solution through "glasses" that reflect our life experiences—our lens of experience, so to speak. This lens affects what we see and how we see it. Unfortunately, this could mean that as we focus on one thing, we miss something else. In scientific research, where objectivity is valued as the key to finding truth, this influence could be considered unacceptable.

According to a phenomenon in the research world known as the *observer effect*, the observer always affects the observed, and may even contribute to the observed performance or inspired expectation; that is, you cannot separate yourself, the observer, from what is being observed. This is closely related to Heisenberg's Uncertainty Principle in quantum physics, where the observer, or measurer, disturbs that which is being measured, in the act of measuring it. For example, if we are trying to grasp or measure something submerged in water, the water surface is unavoidably disturbed, moving the object we are trying to grasp or measure and thus changing its true nature.

The **Hawthorne effect**, a term coined in 1958 by Henry A. Landsberger related to an experiment at a factory that failed to account for an *intervening* or **confounding variable**. The experiment tried to prove a causal effect of increase in light level on worker productivity. When researchers increased lighting levels, productivity also increased. But when the light level was reduced, productivity was still high. Researchers then knew that something else was attributing to the workers' productivity. Since workers knew they were being studied, they increased their productivity to meet the researcher's expectation. We could also call this the *placebo effect*. Performance or behavior by participants in a study may change due to the presence of the researcher or the knowledge that participants are being watched. If an interior designer is hired to observe employees in a corporate office there is a good chance that because an employee knows she is receiving increased attention, she might temporarily "be on her best behavior," thus influencing and possibly skewing the results of the study.

All these influences can impart a *bias* on whatever is being researched or studied. A **bias** is anything that produces a consistent error in the interpretation or presentation of data (Fraenkel, Wallen, & Sawin, 1999). Bias can affect both objective and subjective information-gathering. However, some information-gathering techniques are more subject to bias such as those dependent on the researcher's point of view. For example, in conducting a feasibility study to assist a client company in locating a new rental space, you might spend your lunch break driving around a prospective neighborhood to get a feeling for the area. You might conclude that the neighborhood is bustling with activity that seems safe and inviting. If you were to revisit the area around 6 p.m., however, you might find that there are significantly fewer pedestrians, less automobile traffic, and there is an unsafe or unwelcoming nature to the community, increasing the likelihood that security would be an issue for the client's business. In this example, your conclusions were *biased* by your lack of familiarity with the community, limited to midday hours.

Objective information-gathering is not immune to the influences of bias. For example, when evaluating rental space for the client company mentioned above to determine if a neighborhood is safe you might consult police reports to count the number of crimes reported by victims. While this data should be objective, it could be biased and inaccurate if victims in the area are reluctant to file a police report out of fear or negligence. You would want to consult multiple sources to verify the conclusions drawn from your information-gathering processes, whether subjective or objective.

Is there such a thing as truly objective research? There is, of course, the observable physical reality of the world and objects, which can be accurately defined and described through science (Groat & Wang, 2002). For example, look at a tree outside your window and describe the tree. Common responses about the tree's basic characteristics might be that it has a trunk, branches, and leaves and that the trunk and branches are covered in a material called bark. It will not be long, however, before what seem to be simple objective observations become influenced by your subjective experiences, assumptions, and perspective. You might refer to the leaves of the tree as green, while another individual might notice a sprinkling of brown and yellow. And still another individual, possibly color-blind, might say the leaves are gray. One person might say the tree is tall, but a person from northern California, who has grown up among the great redwoods, might scoff and say the tree is rather short or small.

All these distinctions exist because many of our methods of description are *relative* measurements, meaning that the characteristics of an object, a person, or an experience are measured or described through their relationship to something else. For example, we measure a sofa relative to the dimensions on a measuring tape. In the example above, the tree might be tall relative to a bush, but it would be short relative to a redwood tree. The same relative measurements influence the process of information-gathering and research; thus, you must understand the relativity of your conclusions as they relate to something else.

The world can also be measured not only in absolutes, but in degrees. So the tree discussed above could be described as kind of tall or very tall, depending on what it is being measured against. Or a person could kind of agree or strongly disagree, as might be the case when the person is filling out a survey. When you are conducting research, be aware not only of the information that provides an absolute measurement, but the degrees to which a measurement might fall upon a continuum of possibilities.

Barnet, Bedau, & O'Hara (2020) warn us that there are other obstacles to reason such as **rationalization** "a self-serving but dishonest form of reasoning which justifies our actions or confirms our beliefs" (p. 90). This **confirmation bias**, a cognitive tendency to seek out and employ information that aligns with our pre-existing beliefs, is very powerful and often difficult to overcome. Researchers Amos Tversky and Daniel Kahneman in 1972 introduced the idea of **cognitive bias** "a systematic error in thinking that occurs when people are processing and interpreting information … often as a result of your brain's attempt to simplify information processing" (Cherry, 2020, p. 1). Since then, many subsequent researchers have found that there are many kinds of cognitive biases, ranging from attention deficit and personality disorders (such as thinking you are smarter than everyone else) to being overly optimistic or lumping like things together which yields stereotyping or a "halo" effect. See Figure 3.1 which identifies many kinds of cognitive biases through illustrative quotes. Be aware if you find yourself saying (or thinking) any of these when you discuss your research, as they may indicate the presence of a nonconscious bias.

In summary, Cherry (2020) suggests that you train yourself to minimize your own cognitive biases by being aware that they may exist in your thinking process, considering the factors that influence your decisions, and then consciously challenging your biases by using critical thinking.

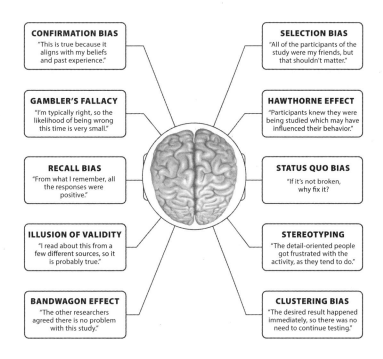

CONFIRMATION BIAS
"This is true because it aligns with my beliefs and past experience."

SELECTION BIAS
"All of the participants of the study were my friends, but that shouldn't matter."

GAMBLER'S FALLACY
"I'm typically right, so the likelihood of being wrong this time is very small."

HAWTHORNE EFFECT
"Participants knew they were being studied which may have influenced their behavior."

RECALL BIAS
"From what I remember, all the responses were positive."

STATUS QUO BIAS
"If it's not broken, why fix it?"

ILLUSION OF VALIDITY
"I read about this from a few different sources, so it is probably true."

STEREOTYPING
"The detail-oriented people got frustrated with the activity, as they tend to do."

BANDWAGON EFFECT
"The other researchers agreed there is no problem with this study."

CLUSTERING BIAS
"The desired result happened immediately, so there was no need to continue testing."

Figure 3.1
A chart listing a few types of cognitive bias identified by researchers, each through an illustrative quote.

Activity 3.2
Understanding Perspective/Points of View

Purpose: To gain an understanding of the differing nature of perspectives by individually observing an object or person, and then collectively determining the "truth" about that object or person.

1. As a group, select a complex yet common object, such as an upholstered chair, a sculpture, or a car. (This exercise could also work with an iconic, historical, or archetypal person, such as an image of a police officer, a medical doctor, or a political public figure.)

2. Each observer describes the object or person (using pen and paper) as each of you sees or experiences it, in as much rich detail as time will allow (~15 to 20 minutes).

3. Share your observations and descriptions with the group. Then consider the following questions:

   a. How did group members make their descriptions? Through words, images, shapes, feelings, adjectives?

   b. Which descriptive terms were most commonly used?

   c. Did individual descriptions vary slightly or extremely? When descriptions varied, what was the object being compared against? How might the description be relative to something else?

As you explore the object as a group, strive to put together a comprehensive understanding of what is true about the object, that is what would you consider is *objectively* true versus what was *subjectively* true? Is this easy or difficult to determine?

Activity 3.3
Identifying Underlying Assumptions

Purpose: To evaluate a series of statements to see whether you agree with each claim, and then identify the unspoken assumptions of each claim. The first step to overcoming assumptions is acknowledging that you have them!

Look at the statements listed below. You may agree with some of them, in which case they are part of your personal value system. You may disagree with others, and thus you would not consider them to be part of your value system.

Mark whether you agree with each statement. And then, using the diagram below as a guide, identify the underlying or unspoken assumptions of each statement.

- Responsible interior designers make environmentally friendly design decisions.
- Americans should take personal responsibility for their health and well-being.
- A strong military preserves a country's rights and personal freedoms.
- An interior designer's deep and meaningful understanding of the end-user allows the designer to design spaces that respond to the user's needs successfully.
- Children should be in environments that stimulate their intellectual, social, and emotional growth.
- Children have a right to play and schools should provide playtime during the school day.
- Family first.

- In medical spaces, it is the right of the patient to maintain a sense of peace, control, and dignity.
- Investing in our local communities preserves the hearts of our cities.
- Design helps people.
- You can never truly trust another human being.
- Employees must be closely supervised, or they will try to take advantage of the system.
- A strong hand makes an obedient child.
- Make peace, not war.
- If you don't vote, you don't have the right to complain.
- Without religion, people would behave unethically.

Did any of these statements ring true to you? Did any of them make you sad or angry? While value systems can be the result of lifelong experiences, often they are embedded in us from a very early age, perhaps by our parents or other authority figures. Or we may develop them later in life as a reaction to values that we first saw when we were children. Because of this, we tend to hold them tightly to us, and they can be hard to let go of or change.

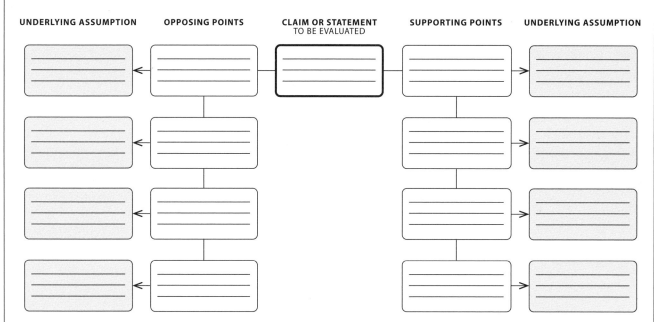

Put each statement in the bubble in the middle. List supporting points on the right and opposing points to the left. Then consider what may be an underlying assumption that causes a person to agree or disagree with that statement?

Figure 3.2 shows the first floor of a family home for a family of four that has recently moved from a country in North Africa to a small town on the east coast of the United States. As a simple informal activity, quickly sketch a design solution for the dining room area.

While the design solution shown in Figure 3.3 may work, it is laden with underlying assumptions, influenced by a designer's preconceived and customary notion of what a dining room in the United States commonly looks like, based on typical American values and experience. As you can imagine, the everyday living practices adopted by a family that has been living in North Africa might be very different from those of a designer from the east coast of the United States.

Figure 3.2
First floor plan of a family home of four who has recently moved to the United States. Quickly sketch a design solution for the dining room.

Figure 3.3
Did your sketch look something like this?

After reviewing your design, the client states,

We would like the dining room to be more of an entertaining space. We have also been known to have dancers and other entertainers join us, so to have an open space that could be used for this purpose and for mingling and cocktails when we host a party would be ideal. Sometimes, we have a couple of friends join us, but we might invite over twenty people or more, so flexibility is key.

The client continues,

All of the guests sit in a circle on the floor. Sometimes the meal consists of a whole lamb served on a large platter, along with another similarly sized platter of couscous and roasted vegetables. Both dishes are set out in the center of the circle of guests. However, if there is a 'guest of honor,' the lamb dish will be carefully positioned so that the lamb is facing this guest. We do not use silverware or individual plates, but instead dine directly from the main serving dishes and using our fingers and pieces of bread to serve ourselves.

Figure 3.4a and b show how this interview serves to help overcome our assumptions, to see that a traditional Western dining space was not the most appropriate solution. Instead, the answer was to create an entertaining space that combined the ritual of the client family's traditional dining practices within the context of a Western-style or American home.

The solution includes both a space for dining situated upon an elevated platform with banquet seating surrounding two small, round dining surfaces, as well as an open space for mingling and entertaining. In this alternative dining room, the concept of the experience is about flexibility and socializing around dining and entertainment, while in the previous floor plan the concept was more about formality and socializing around dining alone. Neither is right or wrong. Showing them both is meant to illustrate how your system of inquiry is influenced by your assumptions and how it shapes your interviewing questions and the eventual design solutions. It also illustrates the importance of following up an interview with participation

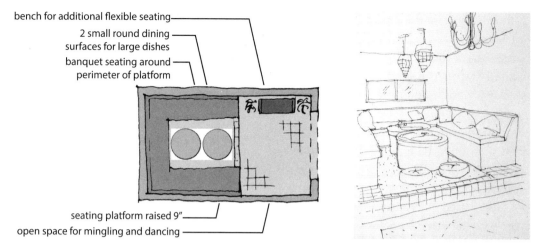

Figure 3.4a and b
Floor plan and perspective sketch of a design solution which reflects the culture and dining traditions of the client.

Labels on figure:
bench for additional flexible seating
2 small round dining surfaces for large dishes
banquet seating around perimeter of platform
seating platform raised 9"
open space for mingling and dancing

and observation to clarify the information you might gather during the interview.

Can you use this example to explore how value systems, assumptions, or expectations might shape your systems of inquiry and the context in which you gather information for your design process? What about how you evaluate or value the information you have gathered?

UNDERSTANDING PARADIGMS AND THE NATURE OF REALITY

To begin our discussion of paradigms, consider the following quote. As you read the quote, consciously replace the word *historian* with *designer* and *events* with *behavior*. According to Fischer (1970) "A *historian* is someone who asks an open-ended question about past *events* and answers it with selected facts which are arranged in the form of an explanatory paradigm." A *paradigm* may vary in form such as "a statistical generalization, or a narrative, or a causal model, or a motivational model, or a collectivized group-composition model, or maybe an analogy" (Fischer, 1970, p. xv).

Fundamentally, a **paradigm** sets an example, or model, for others to follow. Although this explanation sounds simple, the concept of paradigms can be difficult to grasp. Frequently, the word paradigm is used synonymously with the word *theory*, but although they are closely related, there is a distinct difference between paradigm and theory. Another way to define a paradigm is to explain that it is a means of communicating

ideas or theories among large groups of people which leads to a universal acceptance of how it is done. Once accepted and upheld, a paradigm then serves as a model or reference for how it *should* be done, and patterns of behavior then follow.

An interior design paradigm is an accepted and upheld example or prototype for how a theory *should* be expressed through its application to the built world. For example, one paradigm in the interior design field is that of the traditional single-family home in the United States, which includes a kitchen, a dining room, a formal living room, a family room or den, a master bedroom suite which includes a private bath, and several smaller bedrooms and baths in various configurations. That is the paradigmatic model for houses (that families look for when they go house hunting) and suburban land use (by developers and city planners). Recently the term "master bedroom" came under fire as it was identified as a reference to plantation homes and exposed an underlying hierarchy that existed in times of slavery. As you can see, paradigms change over time, influenced by historical theories about public spaces versus private spaces or by theories about cultural identity and an expression of prosperity.

What is exciting about paradigms is that simply through their existence they give us an opportunity to break free from them. Over time and as the world changes, we often outgrow paradigms; as we hold on to the idea of what "should be," the paradigm begins to hold us back. It is at this point that we use the development of new theories to guide us in how we can break out of an existing paradigm and begin a new one—this change is called a *paradigmatic shift*. According to a famous quote by Buckminster Fuller, "In order to change an existing paradigm you do not struggle to try and change the problematic model. You create a new model and make the old one obsolete."

A scientific revolution is marked by a radically new and more successful organization of the world. There is a paradigm shift and the old way of seeing things is replaced by a new vision. Thomas Kuhn's book *The Structure of Scientific Revolutions* (1970) expounds paradigms of scientific understanding, and the idea that people tend to stubbornly cling to old patterns of understanding for as long as possible before giving in to the weight of accumulating evidence demanding change. In Kuhn's narrative, it is only after the shift to a new paradigm has occurred, when the majority have gotten on board with it, that we perceive the outlines of the new model in the growing body of knowledge that had pushed the boundaries of the old paradigm. Kuhn (1970) noted that his book "portrays scientific development as a succession of tradition bound periods punctuated by non-cumulative breaks" (p. 208). Following a revolution, the old paradigm is displaced and there is a move back to normal science that works within the broad outlines provided by the new paradigm (Viney & King, 2003). For example, the paradigm of the traditional single-family dwelling is beginning to shift to a paradigm that dismisses rigid, compartmentalized rooms in exchange for spaces of flexibility and freedom that respond to the very diverse lifestyles of the new millennium. Some precedents of this paradigmatic shift came with the early-twentieth-century residences of Frank Lloyd Wright, breaking down traditional spatial compositions by creating open floor plans that escaped the boxed-in nature of traditional homes.

At the Salk Institute, Louis Kahn broke free of an existing paradigm for research laboratories by separating the functions of the traditional laboratory into spaces that would move knowledge forward. Kahn dismissed the standard laboratory scheme, a one-story box with a long corridor down the middle (Wiseman, 2007, p. 94). He envisioned the laboratory as a combination of three kinds of spaces: (1) space for experimentation, (2) space for private contemplation, and (3) the circulation space as connection between the lab and the study for social interaction. "The simple beginning requirement of the labs and their services expanded to cloistered gardens, studies over arcades and spaces for meeting and relaxation interwoven with unnamed spaces for the glory of the fuller environment" (Ronner & Jhaveri, 1987, p. 131).

Paradigms are essential to the development of your thesis, as they are the jumping-off point. You must understand current models before you can decide whether to support them with your design or to make a deliberate and meaningful break from them to construct a new model.

Multiple Modes of Knowledge/ Epistemic Frameworks

As one sets about framing a research proposal, become aware that the beliefs we hold will influence what questions we ask and the methods we use to answer them. Since our goal is to gain knowledge of a set of human–environment relationships, it might give us pause to think that another designer, starting from different beliefs than ours, might ask different questions about the same thing, and arrive at different answers. If that happens, which one of us has found the truth?

As discussed in Chapter 2 there is a continuum or spectrum of perspectives from which to view scientific inquiry. Neuroscientist Sergei Gepshtein (2019) identified two ways we can talk about the nature of reality: the physical world and the world of experience. Different views of the world are a direct result of what we believe. Do you subscribe more to the belief that there is an objective, mind-independent world outside of ourselves? Or do you believe there are multiple realities, depending on a subjective, inner world of experience? What is more real: the physical organs that make up your body or your thoughts and emotions? How you answer the question may indicate how you view the world. We can categorize *worldviews* based on how they frame or interpret the physical and non-physical aspects of the world. Some common *worldviews* are:

- Nativism
- Empiricism
- Positivism
- Post-positivism
- Constructivism
- Pluralism

- Pragmatism
- New pragmatism
- Transformative

The term **worldview** (used here in place of paradigm) refers to "a general philosophical orientation about the world and the nature of research that a researcher brings to a study" (Creswell & Creswell, 2018, p. 5). This section builds on the Creswells' concept of *worldview* and frames some common ways of thinking in a loose chronological narrative.

To find an example of a worldview in everyday life, we need look no further than our families to see how people can have fundamentally different orientations to the same situation. Our philosophy of life is different from our parents', because even though we are similar, they grew up under different economic circumstances, in a different political environment, access to different technologies, and with different expectations of how people behave. For example, they may recall a time before personal computers, whereas we have grown up with them. But we can recall a time before smartphones when we had to go to a library to check out a book if we needed to do research. They have their *worldview*, beliefs about the nature of reality and how the world operates, and we have ours. A philosopher would say our parents and ourselves also have different **epistemic frameworks**, which means we have different ways of knowing the world. In fact, this recognition, in and of itself, is a powerful **generational theory** (or *theory of generations*) developed by German sociologist Karl Mannheim. In 1928 he posited that people are significantly influenced by the socio-historical milieu they grow up in, creating a cohort called a "generation" which is defined by their shared experiences of technology and world occurrences. This contributes to a distinctive social consciousness experienced by each cohort which helps to explain this phenomenon of worldviews varying by generations and makes us aware of its implications.

Therefore, it is no surprise that differences in worldview often follow generational lines. The early twentieth century saw a dominant belief in *positivism*, a continuation of the idea that we should rely only on what can be verified through direct observation. You may have heard the term **empiricism** applied to this way of thinking (Samet & Zaitchik, 2017). Empiricists claim that all true knowledge is based on observed experience. Positivists tend to value quantitative reasoning over qualitative. As an alternative to unsubstantiated *nativist* or *a priori* beliefs, this objectivity makes sense and seems to be a generally more advanced worldview than earlier thinking. Nativism holds that our understanding of the world is fundamentally innate, or part of our initial condition. However, by the middle of the twentieth century leading thinkers increasingly noted the inevitability of *bias* influencing even the sincerest efforts at objectivity. Those who acknowledge this while agreeing generally with positivism may hold a **post-positivist** worldview, simply meaning after positivism. Post-positivist thinkers consider the pursuit of objectivity well-meaning but imperfect, and they often assert the value of qualitative as well as quantitative reasoning.

How does this apply to design research? As designers, we pursue knowledge of how people interact with their environments. We try to go beyond mere opinion and rules-of-thumb to find sound truths on which we can base our designs. If we think of this truth-finding as a journey, one of the first steps is seeing there is more than one way of knowing the truth. An *epistemic framework* is a way to think about these multiple ways systematically.

Post-positivism was not the only philosophical response to positivism. In fact, multiple ways of knowing gained interest in the mid-to-late twentieth century, including a revived *nativism* as suggested by research indicating innate characteristics of language; and a theory of **constructivism** advanced based on developmental cognition research. As the name implies, the constructivist worldview holds that humans actively construct their understanding of the world through a succession of learning experiences. In a case of societal development mirroring human development, researchers described their worldviews as *constructed*. Swiss psychologist Jean Piaget, who helped shape the Constructivist worldview, focused on children's growth and development, including the methods by which children come to understand and interact with their spatial and perceptual world. Designers may well ask if these self-constructed approaches to engaging with the built environment are the same for all, or if differences will require us to design for varying individual perceptions!

Is there a right or wrong epistemology (way of knowing about the world)? Is there one that is better than others? Fortunately, no. A black-and-white answer would mean we have come to the end of the line in advancing our ways of knowing. We are constantly growing our understanding in ways that can help our design research.

By the late twentieth century, scientists and philosophers were asking whether there was a sufficiently inclusive worldview that could take precedence, with many concluding that, at least for the scientific community, "no single disciplinary or interdisciplinary approach can provide a full account" (Kellert, Longino, & Waters, 2006, p. ix). *Pluralism* enables researchers to enact multiple approaches to learning about the world, and to gain insight from the diverse approaches of other researchers. Philosophers caution that pluralism itself is not a single, argument-ending approach.

A philosophy called *new pragmatism* (not to be confused with the earlier *Pragmatism* of Peirce, James and Dewey) "sets expectations for how inquirers conduct themselves" (Capps, 2019, p. sec. C) while allowing *pluralistic* approaches (Pedersen & Wright, 2018). It permits and accommodates disagreement between people who sincerely believe that they are solving problems and working toward true understanding. A *new pragmatic* approach expects researchers to take responsibility for the consequences of their actions and in doing so, it is like traditional *pragmatism* in addressing real-world problems.

To these ways of knowing, Creswell and Creswell add another late twentieth-century phenomenon, the *transformative* worldview, which includes a philosophical advocacy on behalf of marginalized peoples, thus changing "the lives of the participants, the institutions in which individuals work and live, and the researcher's life" (Creswell & Creswell, 2018, p. 9). We benefit, they continue, when we read others' research carefully to apprehend its underlying worldview. Likewise, we should strive to be self-aware and transparent about the worldview or views that shape our own research endeavors. All the worldviews discussed here have potential relevance and contribute to a critical understanding of research we will discover in literature reviews as we embark on the activities of Chapter 4.

To simplify this array of views, and according to Creswell and Creswell (2018), currently there are four common worldviews, beliefs about the world or the nature of reality:

- Post-positivism
- Constructivism (or Interpretivism)
- Transformative (Critical/Political)
- Pragmatism (Pluralistic/Practical)

Looking at Figure 3.5 we can see how each worldview forms a distinctly different logical background to research. It is our job as researchers to make our worldview explicit in a proposal for research in design. What do you believe is the true nature of reality? In reviewing the "four common worldviews" it is not quite as simple as it may seem. For example, post-positivist views should not be conflated with (or equal to) empiricism, as other views also use empirical methods.

Post-positivism	Constructivism
• Determination	• Understanding
• Reductionism	• Multiple participant meanings
• Empirical observation and measurement	• Social and historical construction
• Theory verification	• Theory generation
Transformative	**Pragmatism**
• Political	• Consequences of actions
• Power and justice oriented	• Problem-centered
• Collaborative	• Pluralistic
• Change-oriented	• Real-world practice oriented

Figure 3.5
Four current worldviews (from Creswell & Cresswell, 2018).

It is also key to understand that all, or portions of all, the worldviews can still be held by many people today and beyond. Understanding both the historical and overlapping nature of paradigms serves the interior design researcher—so long as you are aware that there are different epistemic frameworks, you can apply them from the standpoint of that awareness.

Derived from ancient Greek, **philosophy** means the love of wisdom. Often, philosophy is a tough concept to grasp because its abstract nature removes it from the concrete elements of the design field. Before explaining it, we would first like to show how it relates to the other terms discussed so far. As you move from paradigm, to philosophy, to theory, to a testable hypothesis, you move from the general to the specific. In other words, philosophy provides general overlying concepts that you can apply to direct your ideas into one or more theories. Theories, extracted from philosophies, summarize past experiences regarding beliefs, policies, or procedures and are proposed or followed as the basis of action. A hypothesis then tests a theory and either further supports it or potentially disproves it.

For example, you might adopt the philosophy that all interior design has the power to influence humans physiologically, emotionally, and even spiritually. From there, many theories emerge about the impact of interior design on human behavior and brain function. One of these theories, *biophilic design*, suggests that contact with nature has a positive healing effect on humans. To test this theory, you might develop a hypothesis that hospital patients in rooms with a view of nature will heal faster than hospital patients in rooms that have no visual connection to nature. This hypothesis could be tested through experimentation, through surveys, or observation.

In the early 1980s the *Planetree Model Hospital* project used *document analysis* of medical records which compared a group of patients in rooms with a view of a park with another group of patients in rooms with a view of a brick wall. Through the study, researchers found that patients recovering from surgery in rooms with views of nature took less pain medication and spent fewer days in the hospital than patients with no connection to nature. The results of this landmark study conducted by Roger Ulrich in 1984 (which we will dissect and discuss in Chapter 4) forever changed the status quo for the delivery of care in hospitals, and

it further supported the theory that a connection to nature has a positive healing effect on humans.

Another clear definition of philosophy is "the love, study or pursuit of wisdom in understanding the nature of the universe, man, ethics, art, love, purpose, etc." (Lister, 2008). In other words, *philosophy* is a methodical and systematic exploration of what we know, how we know it, and why it is important that we know it. The significant point is that philosophy is not a thing but a process. It directs us to develop theories—and in fact there can be competing philosophies about the same topic, with various theories within each one. Traditional categories of Western philosophic inquiry (*inquiry* being an action word) selected by Wheeler (2008) as important areas to consider in relation to interior design research are *logic, epistemology, ontology, empirical thought, aesthetics, ethical forensics*, and *metaphysics*. Table 3.1 provides an explanation and examples of each in relation to interior design.

The roles of logic and reasoning in each worldview are different. In Chapter 2 we defined inductive and deductive reasoning as associated with different research methods or data. Here we review the role of inductive and deductive reasoning, and introduce a third form, **abductive reasoning**, typically associated with pragmatism or a practical, real-world approach to solving problems. Barnet et al. (2020) define abductive as a "pragmatic approach to problem-solving, design, and artistic endeavors, making a probable or tentative conclusion from what you have experienced." This type of reasoning is the basis for what we call the *creative paradigm* for research in interior design, explored in the next section.

The Creative Paradigm

The word *paradigm* derives from Greek *paradeigma* which translates roughly as "an isolated example which illustrates a general rule." This is like a *parable*, a story with characters and events that can serve as an outstanding iconographic example, like the *Wizard of Oz*, where a girl travels far away only to discover "there's no place like home." We can use the story to explain the universal idea that although you may seek adventure you should never discount the importance of your roots. A design paradigm "exemplifies a distinct method of solving a problem which becomes a framework for explaining" (Wake, 2000, p. 2).

Table 3.1 Categories of Philosophical Inquiry

Area of Philosophical Inquiry	Explanation	Example of a Design Application within This Area of Philosophical Inquiry
Logic	The use of critical thinking—particularly binary Yes/No thinking and inductive/deductive reasoning—as a means of testing ideas and debate.	Active storage versus dead storage—placing frequently used items in easily accessed storage and infrequently used items in remote storage, such as in a kitchen or home office.
Epistemology	The study of how we know things with any certainty, and what limitations there may be to our ability to think, perceive, and understand.	What are "designerly ways of knowing"? How does a designer think and how does this influence his or her problem-solving? (Cross, 2007).
Ontology	The study of being, what constitutes objective and subjective existence, and what it means to exist.	Using phenomenological approach to studies to develop a deep understanding of how your end-users will experience a space.
Ethical Forensics	The study of what is right and wrong, why it is right or wrong, and whether a common basis for absolute morality can be found outside the individual mind in the laws of nature or the community.	The level of responsibility for interior designers to make environmentally conscientious design decisions.
Aesthetics	The study of what makes some things seem beautiful that have no practical benefit, and whether these things are necessary in some way.	The turn-of-the-century "Machine Aesthetic," exploring architecture and design as a reflection of the newly available technology of the era—for example, Le Corbusier's idea that houses should look and feel like "buildings as machines to live in."
Empirical Thought	The practice of controlling observable phenomena to test hypotheses with repeatable experiments (an idea that has become profoundly important for scientific proof, though it is not, as many people mistakenly argue, the only basis for scientific proof).	"View through a window may influence recovery from surgery" by Roger Ulrich (1984) contributing to evidence-based design (EBD) in healthcare.
Metaphysics	Speculative thought about matters outside the perceivable physical world.	What defines "sacred space"? Can meditation help reduce anxiety or increase creativity in a classroom setting?

The **creative paradigm** calls for the integration of research into problem clarification, based in user advocacy and human-centered design, and sees a multi-level transdisciplinary field of awareness as concentric circles. Weinthal (2011) organized and arranged her book, *Toward a New Interior: An Anthology of Interior Design Theory*, around the idea of expanding influence, from design for the human body (fashion) outward to design of society (cities). From molecules to emotion, this awareness of realms of inquiry extending both outward (and inward) is reminiscent of the classic video by Charles and Ray Eames. *Powers of Ten* (1977) took us on a journey that began with a couple having a picnic in a park setting. We start to view the scene at a distance which expands in concentric squares outward to the cosmos. The scale then decreases to journey inward to the level of cell, molecules, atomic and subatomic space, when the narrator claims that we've reached the limits of our current knowledge. This serves as an analogy for the breadth of research in human-centered design within the creative paradigm.

Designers embarking on research within the creative paradigm ask open-ended questions about the way people interact with spatial settings. They form explanatory, process-oriented, project-based theses that provide possible answers but often serve to prompt yet more questions. Much like the historian or scholar of social behavior, their "questions and answers are fitted to each other by a complex process of mutual adjustment" (Fischer, 1970, p. xv). The design researcher's *creative paradigm* may be seen as a dynamically evolving prototype, a model that simultaneously exhibits the quintessential nature of both problem and solution. The resultant explanatory paradigm may take many different forms: a statistical generalization, a narrative, a causal model, a motivational model or manifesto, a collectivized group-composition model, or an analogy or compelling metaphor. As expounded in Gray and Malins (2016), the assessment of the research lies in evaluating the design researcher's "specification of a research context for the questions … and what particular contribution this particular project will make to the advancement of creativity, insights, knowledge, and understanding in this area" (p. 3).

Seamlessly integrating original data collection and interpretation with synthesis in the design process, the creative paradigm seeks to flip the narrative from research-informed designer to design-informed researcher, particularly when it comes to developing or reinterpreting a written program, by abstracting, reframing, and then creatively resolving the problem—application of research with rigor, through the lens of a theory or theories. Design research within the creative paradigm is seen as an unlimited revision process. Design researchers continually tailor the design in response to incoming data while the form of data continually evolves from tools and technology. There is always research that can be done with a pen, paper, eyes, and some sort of measuring tool; always an opportunity for careful listening; always time to record a conversation that can later be deconstructed, analyzed, and the resulting ideas integrated into the design. Research, in this way, is ongoing and immersive, much like the design process.

THE ROLE OF THEORY IN DESIGN RESEARCH

As we discussed in Chapter 1, with so much information available to us, filtering and sorting becomes necessary to make meaning of it. The role of theory, as we saw in Chapter 2, takes a prominent position in the Information Age when we have collected piles of research data and want to know, "what does it mean?" In the field of interior design there exists

a clear parallel. The role of theory in research is comparable to the role of the design concept in the design process, as they both act as a filter to help sort, choose, and make decisions. As shown in Figure 3.6, in a typical interior design project, we run individual programmatic concepts through our overarching design concept to help us choose furnishings, finishes, and color. Similarly, we use theory to help us sort previously published data, define our variables, and choose data gathering methods. Additionally, we can use theory (the same one or a different one) to help us analyze the data and represent our findings. We can use different theories at different levels or tasks such as:

a. Frame or articulate the research question
b. Determine data collection methods
c. Analyze and represent data
d. Frame findings.

Theory helps give data meaning, describe patterns, recognize some sort of relationship. When a research

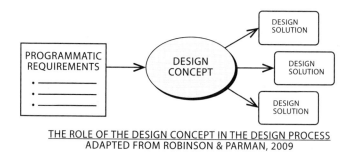

THE ROLE OF THE DESIGN CONCEPT IN THE DESIGN PROCESS
ADAPTED FROM ROBINSON & PARMAN, 2009

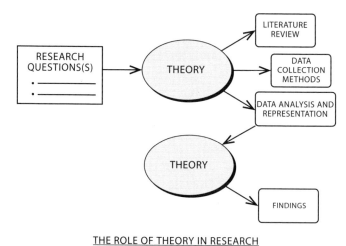

THE ROLE OF THEORY IN RESEARCH

Figure 3.6
The role of theory in research can be compared to the role of a design concept in an interior design project, as a lens to frame a research study, view data, or interpret findings.

study attempts to explain a causal relationship, the study must eliminate (or attempt to) extraneous variables. A theory can help us identify a variable. Theory is a filter through which we view information and determine applicability to a particular situation.

For example, when designing a kitchen, a design-researcher not only considers the physical properties of the materials and surfaces, but also the cultural customs of the people using the kitchen. How do the end-users store, prepare, and serve food? What can you learn from observing, or asking questions, about their use of utensils (artifacts), everyday habits, celebratory rituals, and symbolic meanings of color and form inherent in the end-users' customs. These underlying subconscious values, ideas, and learned beliefs, are often equal in importance to the conscious, physical, or functional design considerations, which bring to mind what cultural anthropologist Edward T. Hall called the "iceberg metaphor of culture" (Figure 3.7).

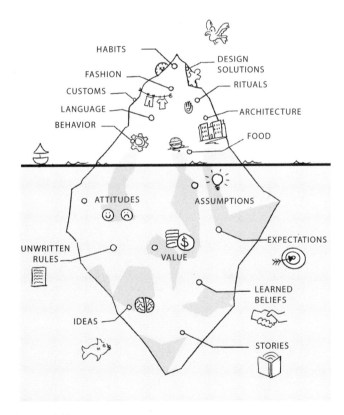

Figure 3.7
Edward T. Hall's "Iceberg Model of Culture" showing the manifest, outward appearance of culture above the water line, and the unseen, or subconscious aspects of culture below the water line.

Common theories in interior design address these hidden or unspoken psychological, sociological, cultural patterns, and forces, helping us to visualize what may be invisible to the untrained eye. Theories, like this one, help us make sense of observable phenomena. A few of these common theories are described in Table 3.2. You can see how each of these theories contains hypotheses and proposes a paradigm shift or new way of looking at the world.

For example, Universal Design theory functions as a lens through which we view design decisions for access and social inclusivity at all levels of the process and can also drive a research study about how to make a space usable by the greatest possible number of people. Biophilic Design plays an important role in articulating healthy aspects of an interior, as well as mental well-being, but can also help us identify what aspects of an interior to focus our attention on in our study. So too are cultural considerations.

The role of theory may be what separates social science from physical science, or, as you will see in Chapter 4, what differentiates quantitative approaches from qualitative, where theory is used in the research process deductively, rather than inductively.

Developing Your Personal Research/Design Philosophy

An understanding of philosophy is important for designers from two standpoints. First, for a design researcher "philosophy creates concepts that researchers can use to direct their testing of ideas. It helps to direct research from general concepts to very specific testable hypotheses" (M. A. Pitts, personal communication, December 2008). Second, the philosophies you buy into (similar to assumptions, discussed in Chapter 2) are often influenced by the value systems you have identified with, so your philosophy will also influence your system of inquiry and the direction of your research.

Frequently, the term *philosophy* is used somewhat nebulously. Speakers often mistakenly say, "My philosophy about X is … " when they really mean, "My opinion about X is … " or "My attitude toward X is … " (Wheeler, 2008). Your understanding and adoption of a design philosophy is a guide for your designs and how you make your mark on the design field. The next section of this chapter explores how you can use

Table 3.2 Common Design Theories Described and Applied

Theory	Description, Constructs, Hypothesis	Model/Paradigm, Examples in Practice
Affordances	*Description:* "animals, including human beings; secure the information from the world about them that is essential to their survival in it." (Gibson & Carmichael, 1966) *Construct:* An affordance is a term coined by Gibson as a property existing between the observer and an object related to cognition. *Hypothesis:* We observe, we act, and then we know. Aligning the visual qualities of an object with its intended function will help end-user.	*Model/Paradigm:* The environment offers places to work, play, hide, re-stand objects or furnishings shaped to easily engage a person ergonomically or perceptually demonstrates the characteristics of an affordance. *Examples in practice:* A baseball fits comfortably in the hand and its seams facilitate an easy grip for throwing; the lever handle on a door signals its use visually and accommodates the action of hand and wrist to open with a natural downward movement and minimal effort.
Biophilia, Biophilic Design	*Description:* Humans have an innate affinity for nature, and that there is a genetic basis for this tendency to positively value and seek out experiences that evoke natural settings (Wilson, 1984). *Hypothesis:* Implementing a combination of biophilic principles for biological, cognitive, and social well-being into interior spaces will improve lives of the occupants.	*Model/Paradigm:* The act of integrating nature into human-built habitations, evident throughout history, has a biological basis and should consciously and consistently be practiced by contemporary designers. *Examples in practice:* Egyptian stylized plant forms, the foliage-inspired Greek column capitals, the garden courtyards of the Alhambra in Spain, and Sullivan and Wright's use of "organic" forms in the architecture of the Prairie School. The use of plants in contemporary design with living green walls, healing gardens, views of nature, filtered sunlight, organic patterns in wallcovering, fabric, and furnishings.
Diffusion of Innovation	*Description:* The process by which new ideas are gradually communicated over time through a social system (Rogers, 1995). *Hypothesis:* Characteristics of end-users of technology can be determined and people can be categorized as "early" or "late" adopters of innovative tools.	*Model/Paradigm:* Acceptance of new technologies or ideas in design practice (CAD or sustainable design) can be facilitated by understanding individual tendencies and their position in influencing social organizations. *Examples in practice:* Clients could be identified who would accept innovative design solutions. Educational experiences can be developed to increase the use of the innovation and to educate those who are not comfortable with new technology.
Environmental Preference	*Description:* People process environmental information to increase their chances of "survival" and to improve their welfare. People need to make sense of, and acquire additional information about, their environment in order to better predict what might occur and to plan their actions accordingly (Kaplan & Kaplan, 1982). *Hypothesis:* Characteristics of end-users can be matched with environmental qualities that optimize performance and well-being.	*Model/Paradigm:* Certain interior design attributes add to people's preference for an environment. *Examples in practice:* certain amounts of complexity, mystery, coherence, or legibility are necessary for comfort, function, and stimulation. However, too much complexity can overstimulate and confuse people, causing decreased preference.

Theory	Description, Constructs, Hypothesis	Model/Paradigm, Examples in Practice
Human Ecosystem	*Description:* People interact with one another and with their environments, specifically the social, designed, and natural environments. People affect their environments, and environments influence how people behave (Guerin, 1992). *Hypothesis:* If a designer considers all aspects of an environment holistically, they can predict how spaces will be perceived and used.	*Model/Paradigm:* Useful in identifying all of the components that affect how a designed environment will be used. Can help determine how environments (social, designed, or natural) influence human behavior. *Examples in practice:* The success of school classrooms can be measured in observable behavior with the built environment, elements of nature, and levels of positive social interaction.
Maslow's Hierarchy of Human Needs	*Description:* Humans have a hierarchy of needs ranging from lower-level needs for survival and safety to higher-level needs for intellectual achievement and self-fulfillment. *Constructs:* Lower-level needs (survival, safety, belonging, and self-esteem) must be met before the higher-level needs (intellectual achievement, aesthetic appreciation, and self-actualization) can be addressed. *Hypothesis:* People's behavior at a particular moment is usually determined by their strongest need (Thompson, 2002; Woolfolk, 2004). If you design spaces to accommodate these needs, you can influence their behavior, and help them reach their highest potential (self-actualization).	*Model/Paradigm:* Prompts designers to look at the whole person and the interrelation of physical, emotional, and spiritual needs. *Examples in practice:* A child who is not fed before going to school may not respond as anticipated in a well-designed learning environment. If employees fear for their safety, they may be more concerned with their security and less with their productivity, no matter how supportive their work environment.
Narrative	*Description:* A process used in design to reveal and support meaning for people as it unfolds over time or through a sequence of spaces (Ganoe, 1999). *Hypothesis:* Personal meaning is expressed through unspoken or hidden narratives embedded in the environment. Explicitly writing or orchestrating a narrative helps determine the relationship between space and occupant.	*Model/Paradigm:* Demonstrates how people's experiences are connected to the interior environment. Development and use of design criteria are determined through a verbal or written narrative. Clients can relate their understanding and feeling about an interior space, which the designer can use to develop meaning for them through the design solution. Provides a way of identifying "meanings of places" for clients. *Examples in practice:* designing the entry sequence to areas in a hospital needs to respond to the variety of occupants. Visual cues for emergency room visitors should be designed differently than those for staff or other patients. Classroom design should accommodate students from a variety of abilities, socioeconomic, or cultural backgrounds and consider a variety of learning styles.

(continued)

Table 3.2 Common Design Theories Described and Applied (*Continued*)

Theory	Description, Constructs, Hypothesis	Model/Paradigm, Examples in Practice
Neurodiversity	*Description:* The idea that humans perceive information differently due to uniqueness and diverse abilities. Perry (2021) defined as the "individual differences in brain functioning regarded as normal variations within the human population." *Constructs:* Attention Deficit Hyperactivity Disorder (ADHD), Dyslexia, Autism Spectrum Disorder (ASD), Tourette syndrome, among others. *Hypothesis:* If designers consider neurodiversity, they will create products and environments that will be more widely appreciated and utilized.	*Model/Paradigm:* People from diverse backgrounds and abilities may experience the same space very differently. Overrides the idea of a "typical" end-user. *Examples in practice:* Utilize multiple modes of communication: visual, auditory, and tactile. Provide areas of low sensory stimulation (quiet, dark, etc.) for people who may experience stimulation overload and need a place to retreat.
Place Attachment	*Hypothesis:* Affective experiences, personal feelings, and emotions associated with a place are central to people's ability to attach meaning to environments and are based on subjective personal preference (Altman, 1992).	*Model/Paradigm:* A space becomes a place through attachment of personal feelings or subjective response to events. *Examples in practice:* Memorials for tragic or historical events can be designed keeping in mind the emotional attachment to objects, symbols, imagery, colors, and patterns such as national flags, city skylines, or architectural details.
Proxemics & Social Distancing	*Description:* Humans demonstrate a consistent way of managing distances between them that are dependent on the relationships among and between them (Hall, 1966). Distances kept between people interacting are culturally determined based on relationship and influence our vocal tone and gesture. *Constructs:* Personal Distances which can be measured: Intimate (up to 18 inches), Personal (18 inches to 4 feet), Social (4 feet to 12 feet), and Public (12 feet to 25 feet). *Hypothesis:* These measured distances, incorporated into spaces, support and encourage a variety of social interactions comfortably for members of the same culture.	*Model/Paradigm:* The model is the image of the four invisible space bubbles surrounding each individual which have a near and far phase. *Examples in practice:* Meeting tables or communal dining can be arranged to maintain sufficient social space distances, as seen throughout the pandemic to allow interaction without inadvertent sharing of biological or physical contact.
Human Habitat; Prospect and Refuge	*Description:* Humans are conditioned by their evolutionary roots to prefer settings which symbolically provide *refuge*, security, or a place to hide; and the *prospect* of opportunity or clear views of the surrounding terrain (Appleton, 1996). *Constructs:* *Refuge:* Actual or symbolic protection such as elevated sheltered or recessed in a hollow or void. *Prospect:* Opportunities to view surroundings from above, views or visual access to landscapes or public settings. *Hypothesis:* A person will naturally be attracted to places that provide prospect and refuge.	*Model/Paradigm:* Applied to settings which facilitate a view of the landscape from a protected area. *Examples in practice:* A house on a hilltop, a restaurant's terraced seating along a promenade, and a hotel room with views of the city simultaneously provide prospect (outward views) and refuge (feelings of protection).

Theory	Description, Constructs, Hypothesis	Model/Paradigm, Examples in Practice
Universal Design	*Description:* "The design of products and environments to be usable by all people, to the greatest extent possible, and without the need for adaptation or specialized design." The Center for Universal Design, NC State University. A term coined by Ron L. Mace, AIA in 1997 as retrieved at The Ronald L. Mace Universal Design Institute at Mace https://www.udinstitute.org/what-is-ud "A design process that enables and empowers a diverse population by improving human performance, health and wellness, and social participation." Inclusive Design and Environmental Access (IDeA) Center, University of Buffalo (2005) http://udeworld.com/goalsofud.html *Hypothesis:* Making the environment easier to use for people with disabilities will improve the lives of all people.	*Model/Paradigm:* Seven principles, which also may be viewed as constructs: *Equitable use:* The design is useful to people with diverse abilities. *Flexibility in use:* The design accommodates a wide range of individual preferences and abilities. *Flexibility + intuitive use:* Use of the design is easy to understand, regardless of the user's experience, knowledge, or language skills. *Perceptible information:* The design communicates necessary information effectively to the user, regardless of ambient condition or the user's sensory ability. *Tolerance for error:* The design minimizes hazards and the adverse consequences of accidental or unintended actions. *Low physical effort:* The design can be used efficiently and comfortably with minimum fatigue. *Size and space:* Appropriate size and space is provided for approach, reach, and use regardless of user's body size, posture, or mobility.
Wayfinding; Place Legibility	*Description:* People use spatial and environmental information to create "mental maps" which help them navigate to a destination (Lynch, 1960). *Constructs:* *Paths* are occupiable and may be directional such as a one-way street. *Edges* consist of non-occupiable barriers such as fences, walls, or boundaries *Districts* are perceived areas of similar characteristics such as public and private areas *Nodes* are strategic points from where you decide your next direction, and *Landmarks* refer to singular, outstanding, or unique reference points such as a sign, tower, or fountain. *Hypothesis:* Design that incorporates the five elements of wayfinding supports the way people naturally understand the environment. This will empower occupants, reduce confusion, and improve their quality of life.	*Model/Paradigm:* Five Elements of Wayfinding. *Examples in practice:* A red carpet clearly articulates an entry pathway and a sign with an arrow is a landmark at a decision-making point.

your understanding of existing architecture and design philosophy to develop your own personal design philosophy.

> Philosophy studies the *fundamental* nature of existence, of man, and of man's relationship to existence …. In the realm of cognition, the special sciences are the trees, but philosophy is the soil which makes the forest possible.
>
> (Rand, 1974)

A personal design philosophy is a critical element in guiding your approach to the design process. Design philosophy comprises the general concepts that form the foundation of interior design. Because your philosophy is reflected in what you do, the way you design will express your personal design philosophy. Just as any philosophy consists of many questions and concepts to be explored, there is not just one design philosophy but many, and you as a designer will benefit from knowing which design philosophy or philosophies you identify with or believe.

A way to identify your personal design philosophy is to spend time studying philosophies being discussed in the forums of other interior designers and philosophers. Your personal design philosophy does not have to be completely unique. As discussed previously, philosophies are general and broad, so it is common for a designer to adopt a philosophy that has been adopted by many others. Once you adopt a philosophy, you can focus on how that philosophy applies specifically to you.

For example, you might adopt the philosophy discussed previously: that all interior design influences humans physiologically and emotionally. You may further believe that interior design can affect us spiritually. From here, you could develop a new theory, perhaps related to the spiritual influence of space. Or you might adopt the theory that the use of contemporary architecture and design for sacred spaces is a denial of the transcendent and that contemporary architecture and design are too secular for a sacred space. On the other hand, you might adopt the theory that, through form, light, and color, using contemporary architecture and design for sacred spaces provides the freedom of expression required of a space dedicated to a spiritual pursuit. Either way, you are making a choice about what you believe in and you are designing according to that belief.

Your personal design philosophy can and should change over time. You will not be the same person in five years that you are today, so why should your philosophy not grow with you? Let the evolution of your philosophy reflect your evolution as a designer. The activities suggested here is a good place to start the process.

Activity 3.4
Exploring Your Personal Research and Design Philosophy

Purpose: To develop a philosophy by asking questions and contemplating the answers.

Note: This activity cannot be completed in a distracting atmosphere. Take yourself to an inspirational place, perhaps somewhere as simple as a park bench, a local coffee shop, or the beach. First jot down whatever thoughts come to mind in response to the questions in the following four parts. Later you can refine your words into a concise statement that extracts the essence of your thoughts.

PART 1: To What End? What are my objectives as a designer?
Start by describing where you want to end up. In other words, what are your objectives or goals as a designer? The rest of your philosophy statement should support these objectives or goals. (Note: These objectives or goals should be achievable and relevant to issues of design today, so avoid vague or overly grandiose statements. On the other hand, you will want to demonstrate that you strive for more than mediocrity or more than just nuts-and-bolts solutions to design problems.) What is your problem-solving strategy? What do you believe are your responsibilities as a designer: to the client, to the user, to society as a whole? Have you read philosophical discussions in journals, articles, or books that speak to you about the shortcomings or needs of the built world that you would like to address?

PART 2: By What Means? How do I accomplish these objectives?
When you have a clear idea about your objectives or goals as a designer, you can discuss the methods that you want to use to achieve those objectives.

Here is where you display your knowledge of design theory. You will want to explain specific strategies and techniques, tying them directly to your design objectives and explaining how each approach accomplishes that purpose. Discuss here how you make decisions about design principles such as form, balance, contrast, hierarchy, harmony, or unity. Furthermore, explore which principles of design are most important to you and your design objectives. Articulate your ideas by relating them to precedents and examples where you have found the same methods applied to architectural forms or interior spaces. You could even include images of other designers' work at this point, further supporting your ideas. Don't limit yourself to a local perspective but think nationally or even internationally as you search to identify how you will accomplish your design objectives.

PART 3: To What Degree? How do I measure my success?

Discuss how you intend to measure your success. If you have successfully applied the methods you outlined, how do you know when you have accomplished your design objectives? What is your scale of measurement? Is it the grade you get in class? Is it the opinion of others? Is it the response of the client or the end-users? Is it the aesthetic appeal to a certain group, such as your client, users, teachers, professional critics, or your peers? Who decides whether you have identified the correct design problem and solved the problem successfully? Exposing our designs to the subjective opinions of others can be a touchy subject, so it is important to establish your own criteria for success and achievement of objectives. What are your assessment methods?

PART 4: Why? Why do I do what I do?

Here is where you can be, if not grandiose, at least a bit grand. What, to you, are the great and wonderful rewards of interior design? Why is design important? How do you want to use design to make the world a better place? When you are overworked and feel undervalued, to what ideals do you return in order to rejuvenate and inspire yourself? How do you want your designs to make a difference in the lives of others?

From all your notes and writings from the activity, select ten (10) isolated phrases or sentences that you find to hold the most truth. Write these ten phrases or sentences on ten separate note cards. And then do the following:

1. Begin arranging and rearranging the note cards to create meaningful relationships. For example, some sentences might make similar points, or you might prioritize or rank the statements in some way, or perhaps you can create categories. As you categorize and organize, some of the statements will seem like tag-alongs that do not belong in the group. Discard those note cards.

2. From the remaining cards, see if you can extract a meaningful and concise message about design that you can relate to or that feels inspiring and truthful to you.

3. Practice simplifying your ideas into one or two statements that you can say out loud to yourself and then to a peer. When we hear ourselves say something out loud, we become very aware of the content of what we are saying and become better critics of our own ideas.

4. Finally, on another note card write your complete statement. This is your personal design philosophy. Post it where you can see it while you are working, so you can use it as a guide for instilling meaning and cohesiveness in your projects.

(This activity was inspired by Haugen, 1998.)

RESEARCH IN ACTION 3.1
The Best Posture is the Next Posture

In *The Chair: Rethinking Culture, Body, and Design* (1998), Dr. Galen Cranz documented the history of chair design from a sociological perspective making an argument that the form of a chair (and sitting, in general) has deep cultural and political bias, and does not align with our physiological needs. She proposed a new paradigm of chair design: the idea that the goal of the chair should be to support healthy, comfortable, and supportive body postures. According to Ames (2001) chair "designers have usually failed because they labored under the flawed assumption that comfort meant bodily stasis. The pivotal thesis in this book is that the human body, on the contrary, is actually a dynamic system" (p. 133). Through her understanding and practice of the *Alexander Technique*, a system of body–mind postural education, Cranz recognized that movement is a natural part of living, that the body "prefers being active to being still" (Ames, 2001, p. 133). When asked "what is the best posture" for sitting (by designers at a lecture), she stated, "the best posture is always the *next* posture" (Cranz, 2021). She was referring to a quote by designer Peter Opsvik, "the next posture is the best posture" (Cranz, 2019). Designers need to anticipate the dynamics of daily life and promote healthy movement in their designs.

Building on this manifesto and call for action, she helped found the International Association for Body Conscious Design and lectures on **Body-Conscious Design (BCD)**. According to Cranz, "the body and mind are related parts of a single system … body-consciousness means including ergonomic, psychological, and cultural perspectives all together" (Naranjo, 2019). In 2014, she collaborated on a study which tested the effect of body-awareness on designers using qualitative research methods. At right shows two drawings produced as data. From their study's abstract, Cranz and Chiesi (2014):

> We stimulated different levels of the brain–cortical and sub-cortical. "Experiential anatomy," "somatics," and neuroscience provide the theoretical framework. This quasi-experimental research compares and contrasts 136 sets of drawings of handles and lamps produced in 7 trials after stimulating the neo-cortex with those produced after stimulating sub-cortical parts of the brain. The two different cognitive states produced

What Cranz calls a "neo-cortical" drawing on the left and the subsequent "sub-cortical" drawing to the right. (Retrieved from https://ced.berkeley.edu/events-media/events/arch-exhibition-how-the-body-makes-marks).

> predicted design differences: straight, small, two-dimensional drawings morphed into curvilinear, large, and three-dimensional drawings of the same objects. Implications for design pedagogy and the history of "organic architecture" are discussed.
>
> (p. 26)

To summarize her use of theory in practice, Cranz described her ideal workplace as an aggregation of details of places she has admired. These elements included the sound of a Mozart violin concerto, the ability to walk barefoot on wood and wool carpet, surrounded by sunlight, natural ventilation, as well as the ability to choose from a variety of sitting and lying down options. Her advice to designers is to "honor your body, learn how to attend to it, and educate it to communicate with our culture. From this," she stated, "develop your own ideal environments … and become your own advocate for body-conscious design."

CONCLUSION

In this chapter we have developed an awareness that there is more than one method of gaining knowledge about the world for which we are designing. In fact, there are multiple approaches to knowledge acquisition, stemming from the diverse ways people comprehend their world. The philosophical tradition has given us names, categories, and structures for organizing these *epistemologies*, or ways of knowing.

This framework helps to read the work of scholars with critical understanding because we can place their work within the structure based on what we believe to be their *worldview*, or way of looking at the phenomena they are studying, and the lens through which they view it: their *paradigm* or model of reality.

Crucially, this awareness must extend to our understanding of ourselves as designers and researchers. We each bring a unique worldview to the work we do. We apply paradigms which seem right to us based on our experience and the role we play in the design and research process. This self-awareness becomes the platform upon which we can build appropriate ways of understanding environment–behavior settings. These methods can be multiple, reflecting a range of understandings of research, environments, end-users, and yes, ourselves.

As you move into the next chapter and begin searching the literature related to your topic and designing a research process to add to that body of knowledge, think of this chapter as a scaffold upon which you can start to organize the information you will be gathering, as well as a framework for your plan to act on that information. Return to the chapter whenever necessary to reinforce the ideas in your mind.

Key Terms

Abductive reasoning
Aesthetics
Anecdotal evidence
Bias
Biophilia/Biophilic Design
Body-Conscious Design (BCD)
Cognitive bias
Confirmation bias
Confounding variable
Constructivism/interpretivism
Creative paradigm
Cultural capital

Empiricism
Epistemic frameworks/
     epistemology
Ethos
Explicit
Generational theory
Hawthorne effect
Implicit
Logic
Narrative theory
Ontology

Paradigm
Philosophy
Positivism/Post-positivist
Professional capital
Proxemics
Rationalization
Reflexivity
Universal design
Value system
Wayfinding/Place legibility
Worldview

Discussion Questions

1. Which of the different "ways of knowing" comes closest to aligning with your own worldview?
2. What worldview or worldviews would be appropriate to consider as you undertake, for example, a low-income housing project? Why?
3. If you want to understand how people regard nature in interior settings, what theory or theories would form a potential starting point for your research?
4. How would these worldviews and theories guide your way of thinking about the problems of end-users? How would they affect the kinds of questions you would ask?
5. Describe an example of using a hypothesis to test a theory. How did your worldview affect the formation of the hypothesis?
6. Describe a personal bias that you became aware of through engaging with the examples of this chapter. How might you use this awareness in your research process?
7. Why is the exploration of the creative paradigm an unlimited, never-ending process?

References

Adams, J. L. (2001). *Conceptual blockbusting: A guide to better ideas.* Cambridge, MA: Basic Books.

Altman, I. (1992, July). *Place attachment and international relationships.* Paper presented at the International Association for People–Environment Studies, Marmaras, Greece.

Ames, K. L. (2001). Review of *The Chair: Rethinking Culture, Body, and Design,* by G. Cranz. *Studies in* the *Decorative Arts*, *8*(2), 133–136. Retrieved from http://www.jstor.org/stable/40662784

Appleton, J. (1996); (originally published 1975). *The experience of landscape*. Chichester: Wiley.

Barnet, S. Bedau, H., & O'Hara, J. (2020). *From critical thinking to argument: A portable guide* (6th ed.). New York: Bedford/St. Martin's.

Bourdieu, P., & Passeron, J. C. (1990). *Reproduction in education, society and culture* (2nd ed.). London: Sage.

Capps, J. (2019, March 21). The pragmatic theory of truth. Retrieved from *The Stanford Encyclopedia of Philosophy*, https://plato.stanford.edu/entries/truth-pragmatic/

Cherry, E. (1999). *Programming for design*. New York: John Wiley.

Cherry, K. (2020, July 19). What is cognitive bias? Retrieved February 21, 2020 from https://www.verywellmind.com/what-is-a-cognitive-bias-2794963

Cranz, G. (1998). *The chair: Rethinking culture, body, and design*. New York: Norton.

Cranz, G. (2019, November 4). The next posture is the best posture. *Galen Cranz Consulting*. Retrieved from https://galencranzconsulting.com/bcd-blog/the-next-posture-is-the-best-posture

Cranz, G. (2021, October 18). Conversation with Galen Cranz, *Corporeal Architecture*. Retrieved from https://www.youtube.com/watch?v=MIU9QhRjo68&list=PLL0bmMkpk_zB4UajHmi9nW55Sq_lQZV0E&index=17

Cranz, G., & Chiesi, L. (2014). Design and somatic experience: Preliminary findings regarding drawing through experiential anatomy. *Journal of Architectural and Planning Research*, *31*(4), 322–339. http://www.jstor.org/stable/44113090

Creswell, J., & Creswell, J. (2018). *Research design: Qualitative, quantitative and mixed methods*. London: Sage.

Cross, N. (2007). *Designerly ways of knowing*. Boston, MA: Birkhäuser Basel.

Fischer, D. H. (1970). *Historians' fallacies: Toward a logic of historical thought*. New York: Harper & Row.

Fraenkel, J., Wallen, N., & Sawin, E. I. (1999). *Visual statistics: A conceptual primer*. Needham Heights, MA: Allyn & Bacon.

Ganoe, C. (1999). Design as narrative: A theory of inhabiting interior space. *Journal of Interior Design Education and Research*, *25*(2), 1–15.

Gepshtein, S. (2019). *Kinds of spaces*. Neuroscience for Architecture, Urbanism and Design Summer Intersession Program, August 15, 2019, NewSchool of Architecture and Design, San Diego, CA.

Gibson, J. J., & Carmichael, L. (1966). *The senses considered as perceptual systems*. Boston, MA: Houghton Mifflin.

Gray, C., & Malins, J. (2016). *Visualizing research: A guide to the research process in art and design*. New York: Routledge.

Groat, L., & Wang, D. (2002). *Architectural research methods*. New York: John Wiley.

Guerin, D. (1992). Framework for interior design research: A human ecosystem model. *Home Economics Research Journal*, *20*(4), 254–63.

Hall, E. (1966). *The hidden dimension*. Garden City, KS: Doubleday.

Hargreaves, A., & Fullan, M. (2012) *Professional capital: Transforming teaching in every school*. New York: Teachers College Press.

Haugen, L. (1998). *Writing a teaching philosophy statement*. Center for Teaching Excellence, Iowa State University. Retrieved May 9, 2009, from http://www.celt.iastate.edu/teaching/ philosophy.html

Kaplan, S., & Kaplan, R. (1982). *Cognition and environment: Functioning in an uncertain world*. New York: Praeger.

Kellert, S. H., Longino, H. E., & Waters, C. K. (2006). *Scientific pluralism*. Minneapolis, MN: University of Minnesota Press.

Kuhn, T. (1970). *The structure of scientific revolutions* (2nd ed.). Chicago, IL: The University of Chicago Press.

Landsberger. H. A. (1958). *Hawthorne revisited*. Ithaca, NY: Cornell University Press.

Lister, E. M. (2008). *Glossary*. Miriam's Well. Retrieved June 18, 2008, from http://miriams-well.org/Glossary/

Lynch, K. (1960). *The image of the city*. Cambridge, MA: The MIT Press.

Mack, A., & Rock, I. (1998). *Inattentional blindness*. Cambridge, MA: MIT Press.

Merriam-Webster Online. (2012). Retrieved from http://www.merriam-webster.com/dictionary/

Naranjo, G. A. (2019, December 11). The body as a starting point. Retrieved from galos.blog/category/Body%20Conscious%20Design

Pedersen, N., & Wright, C. (2018, October 19). Pluralist theories of truth. Retrieved from *The*

Stanford Encyclopedia of Philosophy (Winter 2018 Edition): https://plato.stanford.edu/entries/truth-pluralist/

Perry, M. (2021, February 11). Addressing neurodiversity through universal design. Retrieved from https://www.progressiveae.com/addressing-neurodiversity-through-universal-design/

Rand, A. (1974, March 6). *Philosophy: Who needs it?* Address presented to the graduating class of the U.S. Military Academy, West Point, NY.

Robinson, L. B. & Parman, A. T. (2009). *Research-inspired design: A step-by-step guide for interior designers.* NY: Fairchild Books.

Rogers, E. (1995). *Diffusion of innovation* (4th ed.). New York: Free Press.

Ronner, H., & Jhaveri, S. (1987). *Louis I. Kahn: Complete work 1935–1974.* Boston, MA: Birkhäuser Basel.

Samet, J., & Zaitchik, D. (2017, September 13). Innateness and contemporary theories of cognition. Retrieved from *Stanford Encyclopedia of Philosophy* (2017 Edition): https://plato.stanford.edu/entries/innateness-cognition/

Schön, D. C. (1983). *The reflective practitioner: How professionals think in action.* New York: Basic Books.

Thompson, P. (2002). *The accidental theorist: The double helix of everyday life.* New York: Peter Lang.

Viney, W., & King, D. B. (2003). *A history of psychology, ideas and context.* Boston, MA: Allyn & Bacon.

Wake, W. (2000). *Design paradigms: A sourcebook for creative visualization.* New York: Wiley.

Weinthal, L. (2011). *Toward a new interior: An anthology of interior design theory.* Princeton, NJ: Princeton Architectual Press.

Weisberg, R. (2006). *Creativity: Understanding innovation in problem-solving, science, invention and the arts.* New York: John Wiley.

Wheeler, K. (2008). *Literary vocabulary.* Dr. Wheeler's Website. Retrieved May 9, 2009, from http://web.cn.edu/kwheeler/lit_terms.html

Wilson, E. (1984). *Biophilia.* Cambridge MA: Harvard University Press.

Wiseman, C. (2007). *Louis I. Kahn: Beyond time and style: A life in architecture.* New York: W.W. Norton.

Woolfolk, A. (2004). *Educational psychology* (9th ed.). Boston, MA: Pearson Education.

CHAPTER 4

Research Design for Design Research

LEARNING OBJECTIVES

After you complete this chapter, you will be able to:

- Match the appropriate methodology and methods to your research questions.

- Conduct a literature review using quality sources.

- Identify primary and secondary sources.

- Begin an annotated bibliography with domain areas related to your research topic.

- Be familiar with format and writing styles of a research paper, peer-reviewed article, and study.

- Acknowledge sources to avoid plagiarism.

- Document and analyze case studies in design for the built environment.

DESIGNING YOUR RESEARCH STUDY

To begin a discussion about designing a research study, we will turn to Umberto Eco for advice. In 1977, Eco wrote a short book entitled *How to Write a Thesis* (translated from the original Italian). It holds timeless and valuable advice to the novice researcher struggling to understand how they can contribute to the world of academics. Although Eco's target audience was graduate students in literature or the humanities, the advice applies to all students as they begin to embark on their own research journey. Eco (2015) defines a **thesis** as "a piece of original research in which one must not only know the work of other scholars but also 'discover' something that other scholars have not yet said" (p. 2). Before adding new knowledge, one must familiarize oneself with what has been done and said, the controversies involved in the topic area, and the varied opinions held by experts. Eco (2015) cautioned, "you must write a thesis that you are able to write" (p. 8). This means, your topic should align with or reflect your previous studies and life experience. You should have access to the resources necessary to do the study, and perhaps have some experience with the methodological framework that you will use.

After choosing something you can handle, you should clearly define your topic. In a section called "What Does It Mean to Be Scientific?" Eco advised that to be deemed *scientific* a work must

1. Identify and define all objects or concepts involved in the study.
2. Add to, or revise, previous work done in the subject area.
3. Be useful to others.
4. Provide the elements, principles, procedures, and instructions for future research, either by others to verify the results or to build on them.

Eco also described different kinds of theses derived from different types of studies. Your study can be focused on one example of a phenomenon which we consider a **monograph**, compare between two or more instances, a **comparative study**, or a comprehensive overview summarizing many cases which he called a **survey study**. If you are interested in the design of libraries, for example, you could examine one particularly innovative library design, you could contrast the design of two libraries, or you could discuss library designs in multiple locations, for different end-users, or repositories of different kinds of resources (not just books).

In addition, your study could look at the past, in a *historical* study, or a possible future event, as in a *theoretical* study. For example, you may look at the history of emergency housing in response to natural disasters (which have already occurred) or speculate about future possible events and propose innovative responses to that hypothetical disaster. Or you can conduct a study which involves looking at the past and proposing solutions for the future. Whatever you decide to study and however you decide to approach it, Eco (2015) reminds us, "the more narrow the field the better and more safely you will work" (p.13).

Matching the Study to the Research Question(s)

Hopefully by now you know what worldview you subscribe to, what your broad topic is, as well as some kind of research question you find compelling to address. This section will clarify what methods will help you design a study to answer that question.

In Chapter 2 we talked about research terms such as *quantitative* and *qualitative*, and corresponding reasoning or logic underlying each type of method, as *deductive* and *inductive*. In addition, we discussed options in combining these approaches using mixed methods such as *convergent*, *exploratory*, and *explanatory* (causal). In Chapter 3 we added the idea of *abductive* reasoning and the corresponding *creative paradigm* approach to interior design research. Earlier in this chapter we also identified different kinds of theses, the resulting paper that describes the research project, as focusing on one, two, or multiple instances of a phenomenon, and using an historical or theoretical approach.

In addition to these, a study can be **descriptive**, seeking to document and analyze existing relationships to gain a better understanding of a behavior, need, or condition. Or the study can be set up to be more of an *experiment* (as defined in Chapter 2) or **quasi-experimental** situation (where not all variables are accounted for) designed to test the relationship between variables to produce results which seek to determine a *causal* connection between manipulation of variables.

An experiment need not be done in a laboratory setting. It can be conducted, as we will see in

Chapter 8, using an application of a treatment, setting up a contrived experience in a naturalistic setting, and can be conducted either in person, or virtually using technology. The same research topic can be studied very differently by using unique combinations of these approaches and methods; you can design your study similarly as to how you would design an interior space. With use of a *theory* as a conceptual guide, an interior designer uses a design concept to frame the study and help define the variables or objects observed. Similarly, as a designer uses her understanding of elements and principles of design to arrange a room layout, the researcher employs appropriate information-gathering tools to conduct the study.

Now we can look at all these as interdependent choices you will make as you design the methods for your study. The first choice is research methodology. According to Barnet, Bedau, and O'Hara (2020), the *deductive* (derived from Greek "lead down from") reasoning starts with a generalization to a specific instance (see Figure 4.1), typically using **syllogisms**, a series of "if, then statements" designed to seek truth: "If_____is true, and _____ is true, then_____ is true." If the first statement, the *premise*, is true and the syllogism is *valid* or has **validity** (internal logic that cannot be proven false) then the reasoning is sound. An argument can be valid but not sound, or true but invalid, especially if there are missing or unstated premises (p. 91).

Alternatively, *inductive* reasoning involves the use of multiple observations to lead to a conclusion (see Figure 4.2). Arguments using this line of reasoning run the risk of being weak due to insufficient evidence (too small a sample) to support a claim.

Shown in Figure 4.3, an abductive or pragmatic approach to problem-solving, design, and artistic endeavors uses whatever evidence is available to make a probable or tentative conclusion. Typically, this line

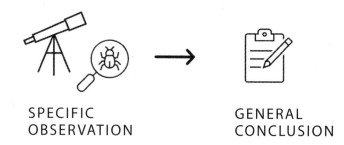

SPECIFIC OBSERVATION → **GENERAL CONCLUSION**

Figure 4.2
Diagram illustrating inductive reasoning.

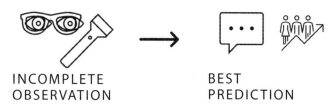

INCOMPLETE OBSERVATION → **BEST PREDICTION**

Figure 4.3
Diagram illustrating abductive reasoning.

of reasoning produces claims that can be argued in the following way, "from what I have experienced, I have found _____ to be true."

According to Barnet et al. (2020), persuasive appeals use ***logos***, Greek for logical appeal to persuade intellectually using the mind through evidence, ***pathos*** (Greek for appealing to the heart) evoking emotion to build empathy or convince you to believe something using passion, and *ethos* (previously defined in Chapter 3), inspiring trust, showing responsibility, and establishing credentials (p. 86). In research, establishing credibility with your audience is accomplished by offering your personal experience as anecdotal evidence, acknowledging your weaknesses or bias, considering other ways of looking at the problem, and, overall, being transparent, fully explaining your methods.

What are the criteria for selecting an approach or mix of approaches? Interior design is, by nature, interdisciplinary. That is, designers use several disciplinary perspectives when solving a design problem. Determine your perspective at the time you are setting up your research. Consider whether your topic falls in any of the varied disciplines of study such as anthropology, psychology, sociology, and many others listed in Table 4.1. Keep in mind, your topic may reside in more than one, or you can position your topic in the overlap of two or more disciplines.

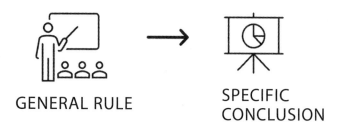

GENERAL RULE → **SPECIFIC CONCLUSION**

Figure 4.1
Diagram illustrating deductive reasoning.

Activity 4.1
Considering Multiple Perspectives to Frame Your Research

Purpose: to pose your research question and frame your research study using a variety of perspectives from diverse disciplines and consider both quantitative and qualitative approaches.

First look at Table 4.1 to see how the same research question, "How can we increase productivity in the workplace?" can be answered using four different disciplines: **anthropometrics** (the study of comparative sizes and ranges in human bodies) and **ergonomics** (the study of interaction of the human body with tools and furnishings while engaged in activity or work), business, biological/physiological, and psychological. Notice the difference between the examples of methods considering the quantitative and qualitative approach for each perspective—how the focus and methods change with each.

Then, fill in the blanks by framing the research question using an anthropological, sociological, and technological perspective. Discuss your answers with your colleagues. Did they have different research methods to answer the same question?

Now, consider your own research question that you composed in Chapter 1. Use Table 4.2 to reframe your research question and to consider each perspective. Would this lead you to a quantitative or qualitative approach, or could you see yourself using a mixed methods approach?

Did this activity help you see multiple ways of answering the question? Did you think of any disciplines or perspectives which were not listed here? Additionally, is your perspective practical or theoretical? Is it about market trends or historical precedence? Is it about trying to make sense of something that exists or proposing something new? Does your area of interest concern the experience of a single individual, interaction among two or more people, or more about the politics or social interaction of groups in a particular location? Are you trying to help a particular person, a type of person, or people in general? Answering these questions will help you get to the root of your research perspective, and help you make choices in your research design.

Table 4.1 Sample Research Approaches to Answer Research Question: How Can We Increase Productivity In the Workplace?

Discipline/Perspective	Quantitative Approach	Qualitative Approach
Anthropometrics/ Ergonomics	Measure productivity before and after implementation of new furnishings.	Provide new furnishings; seek feedback from end-users about satisfaction.
Business	Measure productivity using a standardized questionnaire distributed to all employees.	Observe employees and describe relationship between productivity and work environment.
Biological/Physiological	Compare temperature and air quality/flow in two different rooms and see if those measurements correlate with productivity.	Ask questions to employees about air quality and human comfort to see if there is a relationship between air quality and productivity.
Psychological	Create a controlled work environment with clearly a defined independent variable such as "visual interest" or "views of nature" and see if it corresponds with increased dependent variable "productivity."	Conduct interviews and surveys to see if current workers link productivity with work environment. See if patterns emerge in the responses.
Anthropological		
Sociological		
Technological		

Table 4.2 Disciplines of Study Related to Interior Design to Reframe your Research Question, Approach, and Design?

Discipline of Study	1. Write your reframed research question. 2. Propose one way you could answer your research question, considering this perspective. Note whether it is a quantitative or qualitative method (or mixed).
Anthropological/Cultural	1. _____ 2. _____
Anthropometrics/Ergonomics	1. _____ 2. _____
Architectural	1. _____ 2. _____
Biological/Physiological	1. _____ 2. _____
Business/Economics	1. _____ 2. _____
Educational/Cognitive	1. _____ 2. _____
Engineering: Structural, Mechanical, Electrical	1. _____ 2. _____
Art/Aesthetics	1. _____ 2. _____
Historical/Political	1. _____ 2. _____
Physical Science, Chemical, Material	1. _____ 2. _____
Psychological	1. _____ 2. _____
Philosophical/Theoretical	1. _____ 2. _____
Sociological/Political	1. _____ 2. _____
Technological	1. _____ 2. _____

According to Creswell and Creswell (2018), criteria for selecting an approach from among the three main approaches are:

- ❑ Quantitative approach is best when research problem and questions involve
  - Identifying factors that influence a particular outcome
  - Evaluating the utility of an intervention
  - Understanding best predictors of an outcome
- ❑ Qualitative approach is best when
  - The topic is new
  - The subject has not been addressed with a certain sample
  - Existing theories do not apply
- ❑ Mixed methods approach is best when:
  - Neither quantitative nor qualitative approaches alone are adequate to understand a research problem
  - The strength of each approach provides the best understanding, for example to use a quantitative approach to generalize findings and use qualitative to develop a detailed view.

As discussed in Chapter 2, your personal experiences and *professional capital* (what *you* bring to the research question or problem) should also be considered, such as your

- Training and past education
- Preferences/values
- Time available to devote to research
- Access to particular resources: experts, end-users, places where you could observe, etc.
- Stories about your experiences = *anecdotal evidence* which is a valuable starting point for research.

In summary, a research approach or methodology is a means by which a person gives order to answering questions and testing responses. Some researchers apply a very formal or systematic methodology that can be easily explained or replicated by another researcher, much like the scientific method. Using this approach, a researcher could design a system of investigation, similar to a controlled experiment, and then apply the same system in a step-by-step manner to research many different types of design problems (Guerin & Dohr, 2007). On the other hand, there is informal research methodology, in which a researcher does not have a rigid plan for conducting research (Guerin & Dohr, 2007). Instead, the researcher most likely follows a series of information paths or routes that develop and build upon one another, and the research process and the design project unfold in a flexible manner. In this informal methodology, the researcher's information-gathering responds to the research itself rather than following a prescribed system, and thus the researcher often has more freedom to follow unexpected twists and turns. The main drawback of informal research is that it may be difficult for another person to replicate. We will look at a variety of information-gathering strategies that fall under each of these approaches in Chapter 5.

The Role of Theory in Research Design

As we talked about in Chapter 1, the amount of information that is available to us all can be overwhelming; it can produce a sense of anxiety about researching a topic. A theory can help us differentiate and identify concepts which will help us sort through information more efficiently. Like a design concept in interior design which helps us choose colors, textures, or patterns, a theory can help us choose information sources, sort data, and ultimately, help us make sense of data. And as discussed in Chapter 3, theory can be used as a filter through which we view a research topic or question, and how we frame a study, using that theory's constructs, propositions, and underlying assumptions. The relationship of theory to research approaches varies in how and when theory is introduced into the study. A theory could be used to help design your research study by helping to identify constructs or concepts that you want to test. Or you may want to support or refute a particular theorist's proposition or hypothesis.

As illustrated in Figure 4.4, typically qualitative studies use theory as a frame through which to view a complex set of interrelated constructs occurring in a naturalistic setting, whereas quantitative studies use theory as a basis to predict or explain a hypothesis, using numerical data and statistical comparison.

In other words, a quantitative approach tests a theory. A new theory only emerges after researchers repeatedly test the hypothesis, getting a similar or same result, using the deductive approach as shown in Figure 4.5.

Qualitative

Quantitative

Figure 4.4
Using theory to frame your study.

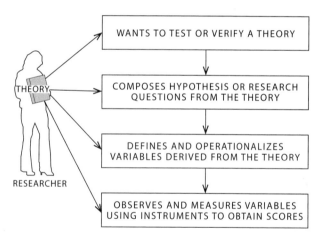

Figure 4.5
Deductive reasoning used in quantitative approach to test a theory (adapted from Creswell & Creswell, 2018, p. 58).

If the research is attempting to demonstrate causality, one would expect to see a relationship described, such as "variable X causes variable Y" for reasons stated in your study's narrative. True experiments test causal claims. The researcher would perform a correlation analysis (as discussed in Chapter 2) to see if there is a mathematical basis to claim a causal relationship. Recall our discussion from Chapter 2 about probability and

ruling out the idea that the cause happened by chance. *Predictor* variables may be used to predict outcomes of interest in survey-method studies. The *outcome* describes results or areas of interest in survey-method studies and often shares properties with dependent variables. **Control variables** are variables that are measured and statistically "controlled" to further show that the causal relationship did not happen by chance or accident.

True experiments are very difficult and time-consuming to design and implement because when we are looking at complex issues such as human behavior or response to the built environment there may be many variables we cannot control. *Confounding variables* (as discussed in Chapter 3) are third variables that may be the cause, like *intervening or mediating* variables, that stand between the independent and dependent variables and may transmit the effects that you attribute to the independent variable that you are trying to isolate. In setting up an experiment, one must consider what kind of theory they are testing; that is, on what level in terms of time, place, or number of people. According to Creswell and Creswell (2018), *micro-level theories* are limited to a small segment of time, place, or number of people. *Meso-level theories* link micro-level and macro-level theories. *Macro-level theories* attempt to explain phenomena at larger scales, for example "an entire society."

Theories in quantitative research may be stated in a set of hypotheses which are interconnected and demonstrate a process. A series of if–then statements (see syllogism earlier in the chapter) explain why one would expect an independent variable to influence or cause change in a dependent variable. **Visual models** like diagrams allow the reader to visualize the interconnections between the variables. Some attributes of quantitative theories:

- Placed towards the beginning of the study
- Used deductively
- Used as a framework for study
- Used as an organizing model for:
  - Research questions or hypotheses
  - Data collection procedure

In a qualitative approach, theory can be used in a variety of ways. Often a theory will provide a broad explanation used as a theoretical lens or perspective – for example, as an overall orienting lens for questions of gender, class, and race. When writing about a study, like the excerpt that appears in Figure 4.6, researchers

Murguia, Padilla, and Pavel (1991) studied the integration of 24 Hispanic and Native American students into the social system of a college campus. They were curious about how ethnicity influenced social integration, and they began by relating the participants' experiences to a theoretical model, the Tinto model of social integration. They felt that the model had been "incompletely conceptualized and, as a consequence, only imprecisely understood and measured" (p. 433).

Thus, the model was not being tested, as one would find in a quantitative project, but modified. At the end of the study, the authors refined Tinto's model and advanced their modification that described how ethnicity functions. In contrast to this approach, in qualitative studies with an end point of a theory (e.g., a grounded theory), a pattern, or a generalization, the theory emerges at the end of the study. This theory might be presented as a logic diagram, a visual representation of relationships among concepts.

Figure 4.6
Example of theory used to frame the study in a qualitative approach, which yielded a modified version of the theory (Creswell & Creswell, 2018, p. 65).

who use theory as a theoretical lens will generally place the description of the theory used upfront.

Theory is also typically the natural end point in an inductive approach as illustrated in Figure 4.7. While a qualitative research project may purport not to rely on any explicit theory, strive to identify underlying or unstated theoretical bases for your work. According to Creswell & Creswell (2018), "the case can be made that no qualitative study begins from pure observation" [because typically a] "prior conceptual structure composed of theory and method provides the starting point for all observations" (p. 64). In other words, there is no such thing as a study without a theory!

Ultimately, it falls upon the researcher (you) to make the underlying theory *explicit*, to bring attention to it,

including your own. Qualitative theoretical perspectives may also include those related to the human condition in a variety of ways such as a:

- Feminist perspective
- Racialized discourse
- Critical theory
- Queer theory
- Disability inquiry

Decide how you will use theory in your qualitative proposal and locate that theory early in your document to ensure the reader's understanding of your starting point. Studies with cultural themes or theoretical lens will typically state the operational theory in the opening passages. Studies with an *emerging* design of qualitative inquiry will also state the theory at the beginning, but seek to modify that theory at the end, in the conclusion. Studies based on **grounded theory** means that theory is planned to be derived inductively, therefore discussion of the theory is placed at the end, as it has emerged from interpreting the results of the study. See Figure 4.8 for an example of a study using grounded theory.

Mixed methods studies may include theory *deductively* (theory testing and validity) or *inductively* (an emerging theory or pattern). With a social science perspective, a mixed methods study uses a theory at the beginning as an *a priori* framework to guide composition of questions and hypotheses. Theory informs the explanation of the major variables in the study and can be used to diagram the causal links,

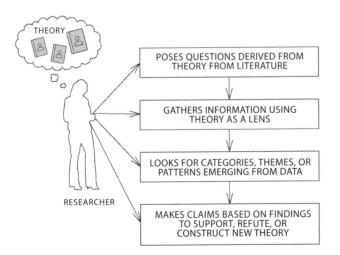

Figure 4.7
Inductive reasoning used in qualitative approach to generate a theory (Creswell & Creswell, 2018, p. 64).

Using a national database of 33 interviews with academic department chairpersons, we (Creswell & Brown, 1992) developed a grounded theory interrelating variables (or categories) of chair influence on scholarly performance of faculty. The theory section came into the article as the last section, where we presented a visual model of the theory developed inductively from categories of information supplied by interviewees.
In addition, we also advanced directional hypotheses that logically followed from the model. Moreover, in the section on the model and the hypotheses, we compared the results from participants with results from other studies and the theoretical speculations in the literature. For example, we stated the following:

> This proposition and its sub-propositions represent unusual, even contrary evidence, to our expectations. Contrary to proposition 2.1, we expected that the career stages would be similar not in type of issue but in the range of issues. Instead we found that the issues for post-tenure faculty covered almost all the possible problems on the list. Why were the tenured faculty's needs more extensive than non-tenured faculty? The research productivity literature suggests that one's research performance does not decline with the award of tenure (Holley 1977). Perhaps diffuse career goals of post-tenure faculty expand the possibilities for "types" of issues. In any case, this sub-proposition focuses attention on the understudied career group that Furniss (1981) reminds us of needs to be examined in more detail (p. 58).

Figure 4.8
Example of theory used at the end of a qualitative approach (Creswell & Creswell, 2018, p. 66).

guide the data collection process, and inform findings and results.

Overall, theory, in research, is used to provide an explanation or prediction about the relationship among variables in quantitative research, provide broad explanation, a theoretical lens, or as an endpoint in qualitative research, and inform the design, data collection, analysis, and interpretation in the mixed methods research. One of the ways we can find a theory or theories to guide our study is to look at what other researchers have used and developed. In the next section we will go about reading what others have written and become inspired by what we find. We will revisit the role of theory in Chapter 5 when we set out to design our data-gathering methods.

CONDUCTING A LITERATURE REVIEW

After developing a research question, we seek to start to answer the question by assembling and assessing previously published information from quality sources.

This process is referred to as a **literature review**, often shortened to "*lit review*." Eco (2015) explains,

> in a literature review the student simply demonstrates that he has critically read the majority of the existing "critical literature," or the published writings on a particular topic … the review can constitute an act of diligence on the part of the young scholar who, before beginning independent research, wants to clarify for himself a few ideas by gathering background information on the topic. (p. 3)

In this context, *literature* refers to "a body of information, existing in a wide variety of stored formats that has conceptual relevance for a particular topic of inquiry" (Groat & Wang, 2002, p. 46). In other words, it is a specially selected body of works and resources customized to fit the research question. A good starting point for a literature review could be linked to applying theory by identifying the theoretical influence on the studies, articles, or sources you find. The overarching purpose is to familiarize oneself with terminology, controversies, and breakthroughs and to get a sense of where you can grow your ideas from.

In some cases, a comprehensive review of projects, artwork, or artifacts can serve to inform and inspire. **Precedent research**, often associated with visual arts or other creative endeavors may be seen as an equivalent. Merriam Webster defines *precedent* as something done or said that may serve as an example or rule to authorize or justify a subsequent act of the same or an analogous kind. Precedent research categories related to architecture and interior design may include:

- Project type or building use
- Occupants, end-users
- Type of site, location, climate, culture
- Plan, layouts, configuration, circulation, size
- Construction methods, sustainable strategies
- Materiality
- Historic styles or "schools" of thought
- Use of technology
- Cross-disciplinary collaboration

This list is just a starting point. You could look at more esoteric or aesthetic categories such as the way landscaping integrates with built forms, how natural light enters the interior, how sound is enhanced or muted, or how colors, textures, or shapes reoccur over a comprehensive survey of past projects. Similar to Eco's *survey study*, a collection of cases can serve to establish context for your research project. This works well if you are interested in architects, artists, or designers who practice in a particular way or represent a way of doing something. Even an in-depth look at a particular case (recall Eco's monograph) from multiple points of view, or over time, can serve in place of a traditional literature review.

Design science refers to an area of research concerned with studying the design process itself, typically in the fields of engineering, human/computer interface, and social media/algorithms, but can also be applied to visual arts, music, education, or design. Towards this endeavor, Papalambros and Gero (n.d.), editors of the international open-source journal *Design Science*, publish articles concerned with "the creation of artifacts and systems, and their embedding in our physical, virtual, psychological, economic, and social environment" (https://www.cambridge.org/core/journals/design-science). In this arena, studying the way someone has produced a design is the focus of interest. It is therefore possible, as the focus of your study, to document the creative process of multiple people, look for patterns, and arrive at a theory about the process.

As part of conducting your precedent research or literature review, it is helpful to identify the "buzz words" of your realm of research to include as search topics. These buzz words are often descriptors of a reality that many people have accepted but few can fully define (Groat & Wang, 2002). An example of a buzz word in interior design is "sustainability." Recently, a student was interviewing a well-known architect to discuss her thesis about an environmentally responsible grocery store. She began the conversation by using the term "sustainability," at which point the architect asked if she knew what the word meant. The student gave her definition of the word, and the architect immediately corrected her, stating that the word is used far too much, used synonymously with green design and eco-friendly design, while few individuals truly understand the correct definition. For the student to continue her research, it is important that she define this word and understand its various applications and nuances, as the various associated disciplines might apply the term differently.

If your research topic uses specific terms or objects, first make sure you clearly define that term or object. According to Star and Griesemer (1989) "The creation of new scientific knowledge depends on communication as well as on creating new findings. But because these … objects and methods mean different things in different worlds … Scientists and other actors contributing to science translate, negotiate, debate, triangulate and simplify in order to work together" (pp. 388–389). Star and Griesemer defined a **boundary object** as "an analytic concept of those scientific objects which both inhabit several intersecting social worlds and satisfy the informational requirements of each of them" (p. 393). They take the position that people using the scientific method actually *create* knowledge. That, in and of itself, facts, concepts, and terms (scientific objects) used to describe them are *socially constructed*, and not inherently objective. As researchers, we need to understand that terms used in research, much like terms used in law or building codes, need to be defined as objects in order to be manipulated and studied.

The concept of the social construction of science was pioneered in French anthropologist Bruno Latour's controversial work *Laboratory Life: The Social Construction of Scientific Facts* in 1979. Along with his co-author Woolgar, Latour observed scientists conducting experiments at the Salk Institute for Biological Studies, as the scientists shared, and tried to make sense of, lab results. Latour and Woolgar's in-depth, qualitative study of the scientific method in action revealed that a large part of science involves making subjective decisions about what data to keep and what data to throw out. They showed that the study of physical science was not as objective as one would think. In summary, they presented scientific activity as operating within a system of beliefs and following prescribed culturally specific practices. Latour's thinking follows a Constructivist or Interpretivist worldview (discussed in Chapter 3).

To see how one researcher defined the concepts she studied let's look at a dissertation entitled *Museum Docents' Understanding of Interpretation* by Amanda Neill (2010). Before getting into the methodology of her study, Dr. Neill spends a considerable amount of time finding out what other people in the field of non-formal education have said about "museums," "docents," and the word "interpretation." In her dissertation's table of contents shown in Figure 4.9 we can see that, after writing about the conceptual frameworks (theories used to frame her study), she devoted sixty-five pages to explain definitions of these terms that she learned from her review of existing literature on the subject. Researchers **contextualize** their study, placing the study within the framework of past and current studies in similar research areas. From there, she attempts to show how the study contributes to the ongoing scientific conversation, or construction of knowledge, or how it helps fill a **gap in knowledge** discovered during the literature review. As you read the studies, articles, watch documentary videos, or sift through the visuals you collect, look critically at what is NOT there. Are you able to identify some of the areas or details that have been missed, overlooked, or ignored by previous researchers or practitioners? This missing piece of the puzzle might be the key to a new discovery and your project could fill that gap.

An important feature of a literature review would be a discussion of key concepts including clear definitions of the terms you will potentially use in the title. For example, if you were going to investigate the effects of lighting on viewers' perception of artwork in museums, you would first want to become proficient in terms associated with lighting, as well as those associated with fine art, exhibit

Figure 4.9
Partial table of contents from a dissertation showing the Review of Literature chapter and sublevels or domain areas within the broad topic (Neill, 2010, pp. v–vi).

design, and museums. There are professional associations and a perhaps commonly used **acronym**, a word formed from the initial letter or letters of each of the successive parts or major parts of a compound term, such as *IES (Illuminating Engineering Society)* and *LED (Light Emitting Diode)* you may have to define for your readers. Other examples include concepts specific to measuring light such as *wavelengths of electromagnetic radiation, color temperature* (typically measured in *Kelvin* scale), and *color rendering index* (CRI). You may also have to familiarize yourself with human biology and the neuroscience behind how the eye and brain produce vision. And you may also want to investigate common practices adopted by professionals to protect artwork from damage due to ultraviolet light, as well as other considerations such as safety (against theft or defacement) and energy efficiency (of the lamp and electrical systems).

We call these different aspects of one topic **domain areas**. It may be useful to identify these areas of domain, or subcategories within your broader topic. In the case of the example above those areas might be: Lighting Principles, Exhibit Design, and Protecting Artwork. You would start by making three folders to begin searching in a **database** (a large collection of data organized especially for rapid search and retrieval), and then download each article or resource into its appropriate folder.

As you work on getting quality sources, you may discover a new category that seems to pop up such as use of digital technology and immersive virtual environments to supplement traditional viewing to enhance understanding of the artwork by museum-goers. Or you may recognize an overarching theory common to, or emerging from, your various sources. You may then need to adjust your domain areas, and perhaps, your research methods to accommodate this new information. The beauty of research is that the process may lead you to surprising encounters and expand your awareness of the topic or it may alter your ideas altogether.

A first step, addressed in Activity 4.2, is to identify **keywords**, search terms used by librarians to link a document to an information retrieval system in digital databases, as well as search terms for search engines to identify content of the Web site. Your initial keywords may come from your concept map (developed in Chapter 1), or domain areas, to start. As you find more sources this list of keywords may grow—adding words you find that are associated with your topic. You will typically start with searching your keywords in a digital database at your school's library for recommended peer-reviewed journals and books. A library's online catalog will provide access to the collections of library materials owned by the library, and, unlike an online database, a **library catalog** usually includes a very diverse collection of options, such as books, journals, magazines, newspapers, video recordings, sound recordings, music scores, maps, and government documents. The Library of Congress—with the biggest library catalog in the world—can be accessed at http://www.loc.gov. Because this is a library catalog, the works themselves cannot be accessed through the site, but searches on this site enable many topical directions and connections to emerge (Groat & Wang, 2002).

General databases, available to you from your home computer, include *Google Scholar* (a highly recommended database), *Web of Science*, *EBSCO*, *ProQuest*, and *JSTOR* (for papers, dissertations, and theses of all disciplines). For specialized databases your school library may subscribe to *Avery Index to Architectural Periodicals*, *BuildingGreen.com*, *Corbis* (for stock photography), *Design and Applied Arts Index (DAAI)*, *ERIC* (for education), *Medline Plus* (for health and medical information), *Oxford's Grove Art Online* (for art, architecture, and design) and *PsycINFO* (for psychology and mental health). *Hoover's* database provides access to information about companies, people, and industries. See their Web site at http://www.hoovers.com.

Activity 4.2
Mining Databases in a Lit Review Treasure Hunt

Purpose: To explore vocabulary for your thesis title, that would be important to define early in your literature review. The following steps, inspired by Groat and Wang (2013) and Creswell and Creswell (2018), will help you to conduct a successful literature review:

1. What is the tentative title of your thesis? Take a moment to write down at least three possible titles for your study or the paper or project written about your study, which features results of your research.

(1)_____
_____
_____.
(2)_____
_____
_____.
(3)_____
_____
_____.

2. Are there terms that you are planning to use that may be new, unconventional, or potentially misinterpreted by your intended audience? List them here: _____

_____

_____

_____

_____

3. Select three of the terms that you listed above, do a keyword search in a database of your choice and locate at least one prominent author associated with each term. How do each of the authors define that term?

Keyword	Author (Date) Title of Publication	Definition of Term

4. Considering each of the terms above, how would you define your area of interest, or *domain areas*? Do there seem to be more than one? List your potential domain areas or subcategories into which your literature review may be divided:

Broad Area of Interest: _____

- Domain Area 1_____
- Domain Area 2_____
- Domain Area 3_____

5. Using several appropriate databases, locate at least 30 items (articles, books, etc.) for each domain area. You will need these for the annotated bibliography activity at the end of this section.

6. Employ a reliable and easy-to-use system for storing, sorting, labeling, organizing, retrieving, and citing individual sources. This system can consist of hand-written, color-coded note cards, a digital research tool specifically for **citation** (formal reference in an act of quoting) management such as *Zotero* or *EndNote* or develop a combination of complementary analog and digital elements you assemble for yourself such as a system of notebooks and array of desktop file folders for storage of digital documents, Web sites, books, articles, studies, videos, drawings, and photos. Develop a system to keep track of the difference between sources and label ones that seem to have the most promising information and ideas.

7. Skim each resource to determine its value, note whether it is a primary or secondary source and determine which sources to read more in depth later.

An optional, supplemental exercise might be to create a **literature map** (see below) or thesis outline, whichever is suggested by your instructor. Then, using information from the sources, as well as new ideas, begin to trace your path and fill in the blanks.

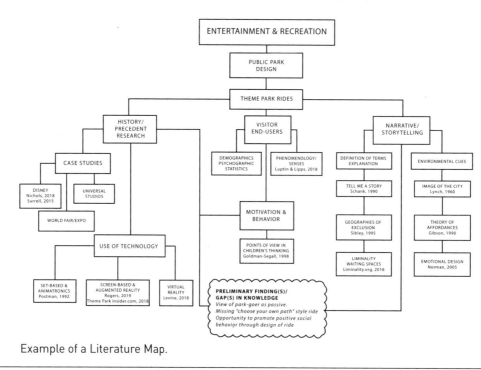

Example of a Literature Map.

Your literature review is not limited to the beginning of your research study (Groat & Wang, 2002, p. 57). As your ideas emerge, you can constantly trace the history of these ideas. Similar to your concept map, your literature review is the "Family Tree" of your literary research method, helping you to see the roots and branches of your design problem as you seek its solution. Creswell and Creswell (2018) call this a "literature map" (see example in Activity 4.2). Your literature review should identify sources as essential to framing the logic of your research study and how this information led to the formation of a new theory of your own (Groat & Wang, 2002, p. 63).

Think of your research project as a collection of ideas you will eventually defend in front of a jury of professional peers or in front of a client. To do this successfully, it is important that you continuously seek out valid and reliable sources that provide accurate information. Information based on erroneous sources will not allow you to draw valid conclusions, nor will it give you an accurate picture of the issues. Your project is only as solid as your information. A project built on faulty information is like a house built on a poor foundation. It will not hold up! So where can you find quality information?

Evaluating Sources

In academic and professional research, if you intend to use the Internet as a source you should view it critically. The Internet is a dumping ground for any and all information, with that information often placed on a Web site by unknown sources, each with their own agenda; thus, the accuracy of that information is always questionable. There is no system of checks and balances to establish the credibility of information, and many sites are operated by individuals with a particular bias (Ballast, 2006, p. 28). Online "blogging" is a perfect example.

When a professional submits a manuscript for publication as an article or a book, the manuscript is distributed to a variety of other professionals in the field for review. Through this *peer review* process (defined in Chapter 2), the accuracy of the information and its relevance to the field are verified. This helps to ensure that the published information is valid and accurate. Unfortunately, the Internet does not have the same system to verify the accuracy of information, so you must always be critical of information taken from the Web.

Despite this, the use of the Internet should not be discounted entirely. It can hold great value, especially in the preliminary stage of the research process, as a tool for planning your research. The Internet can also be used to find a source of information, and it can help you contact that source directly. For example, while "surfing the Net," you may find a blurb about a scientist who is studying the effects of lighting on retail environments. In this case, the Internet is the tool that informs you that the study exists and who performed it. Now you can track down the actual study to use as a source in your research, or you can contact the scientist to request an interview. The Internet is a great tool to help you brainstorm topics, track down sources or experts to talk to, explore online catalogs and databases, or research the background of a company or an individual. If you are seeking experts to interview for your project, the Internet can help you locate these experts, by providing professional background information as well as an e-mail address or other contact information.

There are various types of sites on the Internet, and each has its unique value to your research process:

- Local, state, and federal government agencies, with Web addresses ending in ".gov," such as the *Census Bureau* and *Americans with Disabilities* (Burkhardt et al., 2003, p. 72). These Web sites can provide authoritative information on building code requirements, laws, regulations, and permitting procedures (Ballast, 2006, p. 28).
- Educational institutions, with Web addresses ending in ".edu," such as universities, institutions, and museums like the *Smithsonian Institution*. These Web sites can often provide information on the latest trends in a field and how you might access more information about the topic.
- Nonprofit organizations and associations, with Web addresses ending in ".org," such as the *American Society of Interior Designers* and professional and trade associations like the *Architectural Woodwork Institute*.
- Commercial sites with Web addresses ending in ".com," the largest body of Web sites to be found on the Internet, which advertise a product or service (Burkhardt et al., 2003, p. 72). Recall the caution in the first paragraph of this section.

Although commercial sites usually are trying to promote a product that may make them inherently biased, they can also provide current and relevant data for a product, and they are valuable when they are specifying materials, furniture, lighting, and other architectural and interior design products. Manufacturers of furnishing systems such as Knoll, Herman Miller, Kimball (to name a few) have dedicated portions of their Web sites to publishing their in-house research, called **white papers**. Most manufacturers of interior finishes and building materials provide research summaries which may cite other sources which are useful for evidence-based design practitioners. For example, at the time this book was written, Sherwin-Williams offered free technical webinars entitled "How Do Cultures Influence Color?" and "Universal Design for Independent Living," as well as a seminar on the technical properties of paint and pigment. However, "if you need unbiased information to compare several manufacturers of the same product type, you should select another source" (Ballast, 2006, p. 28). Trade associations, such as the *Lighting Research Center*, are often a good source for this type of comparison information.

Just as a compass might help a hiker find his way in a complex forest, the Internet can help point you in the right direction. Once a direction has been found, it is your responsibility as a researcher to follow that path to appropriate and credible sources from which to make informed design decisions. When you are evaluating any source, your best approach is to do as Euripides advised: "Question everything." Do not automatically assume accuracy in any source of information. According to Adams (2001), incorrect information is like a runaway train and can carry you completely in the wrong direction. The following questions can help you ascertain the nature and value of material you are considering:

- How does the source know these details? Is the information coming from firsthand experience? (University Library, University of California, Santa Cruz, 2007)
- Where was this information obtained—from personal experience or from reports written by others? (University Library, University of California, Santa Cruz, 2007)
- Are the source's conclusions based on a single piece of evidence, or have many sources been considered? (University Library, University of California, Santa Cruz, 2007)
- What is the age or gender of the source?
- What is the political affiliation of the source, or what are the personal interests of the source?
- What is the background of the source? With what company, academic institution, or special interest group is this source affiliated?
- Under what conditions was the information gathered? Did the conditions provide for an honest and thorough collection of information?

Ultimately, source materials of any type must be assessed critically, and even the most scrupulous and thorough work is viewed through the eyes of the writer/interpreter. Anywhere there is room for interpretation or translation, there is the possibility of miscommunication, mistranslation, opinion, or bias. Take this into account when attempting to arrive at the "truth" of a piece or an event, as it can be concluded that no account is truly unbiased. Always maintain healthy skepticism about information sources. This will enhance your academic and professional credibility, whether you are defending your academic project or proposing a new and exciting design idea to a client.

In today's age of social media, it is easy to get distracted by interesting and enticing data that might sound exciting but is not likely to be useful for the focus of your specific research or thesis topic. The research process can be time-consuming, so you never want to waste time reading or pursuing a resource that is not relevant to your topic or project, regardless of its appeal. And, as mentioned earlier, you also do not want to waste time pursuing a resource that may not actually be accurate or valid.

While you want to remain focused and efficient, it is important to not limit yourself to only one perspective on your topic. For example, if two politicians write about the topic of affordable housing, one politician might conclude that it is the government's responsibility to provide affordable housing, while the other politician might conclude that the marketplace should control the cost of housing with incentives like low-interest loans that increase buyer purchasing power. In this instance, the topic of affordable housing is the same, but the ideas and solutions that the politicians have proposed are very different. Both perspectives are valuable for getting a more broad-based understanding of both the issues and the potential solutions. Acknowledging and including multiple viewpoints increases the chances of finding a successful solution to the design problem being investigated.

A thorough literature review can ensure that you can answer basic questions about the language used in this area, the scope of the issue, major players or experts in the field, and possible directions to situate your study within the field or to add to the body of knowledge on this topic. It will give you an overview of the latest information and lead you to the appropriate sources for gathering further information. Conduct your literature review with a critical eye to identify bias and other influences on the information presented and to be open to exploring varying points of view—as they will give you a more complete story.

Primary Sources

Primary sources include contemporary accounts of an event, written by someone who experienced or witnessed the event in question. These original documents can be diaries, letters, memoirs, journals, speeches, manuscripts, interviews, and other such unpublished works. They may also include published pieces such as newspaper or magazine articles (if they are written soon after the fact and not as historical accounts), photographs, audio or video recordings, research reports in the natural or social sciences, or original literary or theatrical works (University Library, University of California, Santa Cruz, 2007). Generally, primary sources are the "materials on a topic upon which subsequent interpretations or studies are based" (Hairston & Ruszkiewicz, 1996, p. 547). As we look more specifically into the fields of architecture, interior design, and other creative arts, there are many examples to draw from. These could be, but are not limited to, the following:

An Original Creative Piece as a Primary Source

- An original work of art, such as a painting or sculpture
- A building
- An historical site

- An interior space
- Construction documents
- A musical piece
- A novel
- A performance or event
- Data from a research study

Direct Documentation of the Original as a Primary Source

- Photographs of a building or interior space
- Personal interviews with architects, designers, or other creative professionals about their own work, or an audio or video of an interview with one of these professionals
- Audio or video about the construction of a project
- A professional peer-reviewed journal article explaining the results of a research study or the data from a research study
- A survey or questionnaire about the topic
- Personal observation about the place or topic
- Building measurements taken by a draftsperson for creating original floor plans
- Current satellite images
- Your direct observation of an environment or behavior

Statistics or Factual Information as a Primary Source

- Demographical statistics and census data
- Data from an academic or scientific study
- Building codes or regulations from a government Web site or codes book
- Specification information for a design or architectural product (for example, the Coefficient of Friction (COF) for a specified ceramic floor tile).

Secondary Sources

Secondary sources function to *interpret* primary sources, described as at least one step removed from the event or phenomenon under review. Secondary source material speculates, assigns values to, conjectures upon, and draws conclusions about the events or topics or things documented or observed in primary sources (University Library, University of California, Santa Cruz, 2007). Secondary sources are usually found in familiar places such as published books or magazine articles, but they can also be drawn from documentaries, TV specials, or simple observation of trace evidence left behind by humans interacting with an environment. Secondary sources can often yield contradictory information, as the "facts" are interpreted in different ways or are relayed in differing manners. Thus, in academic research, secondary sources are only as credible or as valuable as their circumstantial affiliations. Especially when drawing upon secondary sources, it is important for a researcher to include multiple points of view about the topic or issue to ensure that all perspectives are being explored and analyzed. In architecture, interior design, and other allied arts, examples of secondary sources could be, but are not limited to, the following:

- Reference material about the piece, such as a history book or a textbook
- A book about the piece or topic
- A discussion or debate on the topic
- A magazine or newspaper article on the piece or topic
- A TV special or documentary about the piece or topic
- Indirect observation of trace evidence associated with the environment or behavior.

If you were interested in studying a cutting-edge product and how it is being applied in interior design projects, you would have several choices: You could consult primary sources, such as research studies done on the product; or you could interview end-users of a space where the product is applied; or you could review secondary sources such as a magazine article about the product or project: "Primary sources are usually the topic that other sources comment upon" (Groat & Wang, 2002, p. 60). It is important to be able to distinguish between primary sources and secondary sources.

> Primary sources can be described as those sources that are closest to the origin of the information. They contain raw information and thus, must be interpreted by researchers. Secondary sources are closely related to primary sources and often interpret them. These sources are documents that relate to information that originated elsewhere. Secondary sources often use generalizations, analysis, interpretation, and synthesis of primary sources. Examples of secondary sources include textbooks, articles, and reference books.
>
> (libguides.furman.edu)

The fundamental difference between primary sources and secondary sources is in the "number of times the information has been reprocessed and resynthesized" (Burkhardt et al., 2003, p. 9). The closer you can get to the original source of the information, the study, or the work of art, the less biased your information will be. But primary and secondary also refer to how close the source aligns with your research question. For example, if you were doing research about the design philosophy of the architect Louis Kahn, original drawings, letters, or books that he wrote about his design philosophy, and a video recording of one of his lectures would all serve as primary resources. A documentary film by Nathaniel Kahn (his son) in which he takes us on a virtual tour of his father's built work and interviews people who worked with him would constitute a secondary source. Secondary sources would also include a book about Kahn's projects by an expert architectural historian or interviews with people who had been to his buildings. In contrast, if your topic addresses how Kahn's architecture is experienced and interpreted by the inhabitants, primary sources would be written or verbal responses of people who had been to his buildings and worked in them.

Consider this analogy as well: If you take an original photograph and make a copy on a copying machine, the reproduction will often vary in its exact representation of the original, based on the quality of the equipment and the operational accuracy. If you then make a copy of the copy, you again increase the chances that the integrity of the original document might be compromised and that some of the information from the original photograph might be lost or interpreted incorrectly. Someone viewing the second copy might mistake the identity of a person in the photograph or the identity of an object or a word. You can put the original photograph next to the copy of the copy and perceive an obvious difference between the two.

Eco (2015) warned students, "primary sources may not exist in an organized written form," especially about behavior of children in a playground, or occupants' opinions of their workplace (p. 45). "Instead," he stated, "you must gather and create your primary documents, including statistical data, interview transcription, and sometimes photographs or even audiovisual documents" (p. 45). This kind of data will be explored in future chapters (Chapters 5, 6, 7, and 8).

Activity 4.3
Categorizing Sources

(Inspired by and adapted from Burkhardt et al., 2003, p. 11)

Purpose: To develop your skill at discerning primary sources from secondary sources.

For this exercise:

1. Read the list of research sources below.

2. Look up any names or terms that are not familiar to you.

3. Identify each source as primary or secondary and as objective or subjective.

To help get you started, the following are examples of each category:

Table 4.3 Categorizing Types of Sources, Example

Types of Sources	Objective	Subjective
Primary	Medical records	Interview with a hospital patient
Secondary	Published research study done over time using medical records	Documentary film about patient's and family members' hospital experience

Let's say your topic is "Religious Practices in Garden Space" and your research question is "*How do religious practices held in outdoor, natural, or garden spaces differ from those held in indoor environments?*"

Place each of the following sources in the correct category in Table 4.4:

- You attend a guided tour of the meditation gardens at the *Self Realization Center* in Encinitas, CA.

- Notes and photos from your tour of the meditation gardens.

- Aerial photo of Tadao Ando's *Honpukuji Temple* (1991).

- Construction documents for church built around a courtyard that is open to the sky.

- A blog post about outdoor weddings in New York City.

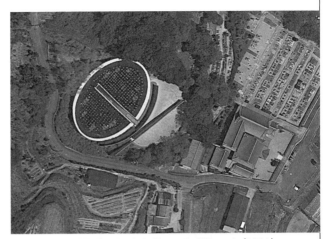

Aerial view of Tadao Ando's *Honpukuji Temple* (1991).

- Biometric data from a study about the effect of nature on a person's heart rate and blood pressure.

- Article from *Journal of Interior Design*, explaining the use of nature in the design of religious facilities.

- A textbook for your History of Interior Design class about use of gardens in historic religious facilities.

- A paper your classmate wrote about a religious retreat they attended over the summer that took place in a camp.

- An article from a local newspaper about a controversial sculpture of a religious cross in a public park.

- A site plan showing the cross sculpture in the park, with nearby parking and walking paths.

- An e-mail from an instructor approving your research plan.

- An interview with a rabbi answering your questions about the use of natural materials in the design of a *Sukkah* (an outdoor religious structure).

- An interview with a Buddhist monk about meditation practices.

- Documentary film *Journey to Mecca*.

- Excerpts from the *Qur'an*.

- Interview with a professional interior designer who specializes in religious facilities.

- A survey of all congregation members to generate ideas for the outdoor area adjacent to the church.

Table 4.4 Categorizing Types of Sources, Activity		
Types of Sources	**Objective**	**Subjective**
Primary		
Secondary		

Acknowledging Sources and Avoiding Plagiarism

Plagiarism is defined as the "unacknowledged use of another's words, ideas, or information" (Axelrod & Cooper, 2008, p. 748). Often it seems as though plagiarism does not apply to interior design, because interior designers are producing built environments and not necessarily papers or other written documents. But this is not true! The field of interior design involves written communication through proposals, project programs, and professional correspondence. It is also important to recognize that plagiarism is not just about written work. It can also apply to other works such as musical compositions, drawings, and even abstract ideas.

Plagiarism is not always about bad intentions. It can also result from irresponsible research methods. If you do not understand the appropriate conventions for acknowledging sources, you could plagiarize unintentionally—and suffer the same consequences as a student who simply does not want to do the work and hands in another student's assignment as his or her own. You should always familiarize yourself with the plagiarism policies at your own institution.

According to The Online Writing Lab (OWL) at Purdue University (2008), the way to avoid plagiarism is to "always give credit where credit is due." The following list from their Web site includes examples of when it is necessary to cite your work:

- Words or ideas presented in a magazine, book, newspaper, song, TV program, movie, Web page, computer program, letter, advertisement, or any other medium

- Information you gain through interviewing or conversing with another person, face-to-face, over the phone, or in writing
- When you copy the exact words or a unique phrase
- When you paraphrase another person's words or ideas
- When you reprint any diagrams, illustrations, charts, pictures, or other visual materials
- When you reuse or repost any electronically available media, including images, audio, video, or other media.

Resource Management Tools

The note card system referenced earlier is a tried-and-true method that will always be useful. Some evidence suggests that handwritten note-taking is associated with improved conceptual learning (Horbury & Edmonds, 2021). However, students and researchers are increasingly working on keyboards and screens without picking up a pen, often gathering resources while working on a tablet or smart phone. The process is becoming increasingly digital and mobile, and tools are evolving to make reference management more convenient and organized. You can begin your research in the library, continue it in a café, use the time on your bus ride home to pursue an avenue of interest, and continue from the comfort of your couch in the evening. The sources and notes you take can be accessible for use and modification any place you have a wireless connection.

The beginning of the second decade of the twenty-first century has seen the startup (and in some cases, discontinuation) of many software platforms for managing research resources. Before looking at these services, take a moment to understand the features of tools you are likely already using. Research is a very writing-intensive activity so word-processing software is likely to be integral to your work. That software has built-in reference management capability you are likely underutilizing. Familiarize yourself with the tools ribbon and try out some of the citation and reference tabs. Use the *Help* button for guidance and utilize a search engine to find video tutorials. Your word-processing document can function as a robust database capable of facilitating entry, management, and output of references. You can readily transfer your bibliography to a different citation style or another document.

The convenience of managing your sources within the word-processing software is that they are all in one file and update globally throughout the document. Multiple software platforms specifically devoted to the storage and use of resources have become available and are rapidly evolving. Most of these offer a cross-platform collection of tools that help you locate, access, organize, categorize, annotate, highlight, share, and properly cite research literature. Good quality programs have an easy-to-understand user-interface, a flexibility of multiple export formats, and additional digital options such as storing whole articles, tagging, excerpting, and marking up source documents using color-coded highlighting, notations, and even emojis! According to G2.com, a software rating service, the highest rated (along a satisfaction scale including ease of use and quality of support) were Mendeley, ReadCube, Zotero, EndNote, and EasyBib. As you investigate these to determine their value to your research effort, you will want to assess multiple parameters: cost (there are both free and paid options), integration with your word-processing software, operating system support, ease of importing and exporting, and supported citation styles are some of the features you will want to evaluate and compare.

Use your search engine to find independent, *current* comparisons of platforms. This information is constantly changing so do not rely on a comparison that was last published or updated more than a year ago. A search phrase like "independent comparison of reference management software" should get you some options. And before investing a lot of time in one of the platforms you will want to make sure it is something you will stay with for the long term. Take the software for a test-run. Use it for a week to be sure it fits your working style. A quick look at your phone may remind you that some apps have staying power and others do not. And a caution: many of these tools are often discontinued. It would be a shame to get your entire research bibliography and notes onto a platform, only to have to export it to another platform in the future.

Once you have settled on a resource management system, it is time to develop the habit of using it. Integrate it into your workflow. Many of the interfaces offer quick and easy saving and cataloging of sources as you go, so take advantage of this and err on the side of quantity. A large, well-maintained database will result in less search later in the process than having to go back and find that source you didn't bother to save in real-time. Some of the tools have add-ins that allow you to work with them directly in your word-processing document. Others can be kept open, running alongside your note-taking document. Some researchers work entirely within a platform for search, note-taking, and reference management. Whichever way you choose, you will appreciate the ability to publish a finished bibliography or reference list at the draft and end points of your research project, just by pushing a button!

Writing Styles and Citation Formats

It is important to consult with your instructor about the style of formatting that he or she prefers you to use for your project. While there is not one universally accepted system for acknowledging sources, a method commonly used by students for documenting bibliographical information is the **Modern Language Association (MLA)** format. However, based on your field of study, there are other options, such as **The Chicago Manual of Style (CMS)** and the **American Psychological Association (APA)**. APA style is more common to professional-level interior design research, while MLA style is more often used in schools. Have you noticed which format is used in this textbook?

- MLA style and format—Consult the *MLA Handbook for Writers of Research Papers* (6th edition), by Joseph Gibaldi, or the *MLA Style Manual and Guide to Scholarly Publishing* (2nd edition), also by Joseph Gibaldi.

- CMS style and format—Consult *The Chicago Manual of Style* (15th edition), by the staff of the University of Chicago Press, or subscribe to *The Chicago Manual of Style Online* at http://www.chicagomanualofstyle.org.
- APA style and format—Consult the *Publication Manual of the American Psychological Association* (5th edition), by the staff of the American Psychological Association. For more information about APA style, the Web site is http://www.apastyle.org.

There are two levels of citation you should be aware of:

1. Citing within the body of the text, *in-text citations*, occur at the end of a quoted sentence, paragraph of text longer than 40 words called a **block quote**, or with footnotes or endnotes, embedded so as not to be distracting to the reader, but to give credit for information taken from another source.

2. The bibliographic list of works cited, called **references** in APA format, is a summary of all sources drawn upon during the process of researching and designing your project.

In APA (American Psychological Association) style of writing and formatting, in-text citations appear throughout the document typically consisting of the author's name and publication date (to give credit for ideas that have influenced your work) and a page number when referring to an excerpt or quote from the original text. It is especially important to always give credit to anyone or anything that has offered an identifiable and significant contribution to the development of your research and design project, and this information must be represented within the bibliography of the project. A bibliography demonstrates your rigorous attitude toward the exploration of your project, as well as the breadth and depth of your research into finding both a real and relevant design problem and a successful solution (University of London, Postgraduate Online Research Training, 2008).

The only time you would not use an in-text citation for a source in your writing is when that written information is considered common knowledge or when you are including your own original ideas. Since the definition of *common knowledge* can be a bit hazy, it is advisable to cite everything in order to be as thorough as possible.

The basic formula for citing sources with the MLA format is to include—in parentheses at the end of a paragraph or after a direct quote or paraphrasing—the author's last name and the page number of the information being referenced. Other citing formats require that you include the author and copyright date of the published work being cited. Since each format varies slightly, it is important to carefully follow the rules of the format required by your instructor.

A *list of references* or *works cited* refers to a complete list of any and all sources used by a researcher—student or professional—in a research endeavor such as designing and conducting a study or producing a written artifact such as a paper, thesis, manuscript, or article for publication. Citations may even appear at the end of a *PowerPoint* presentation, a lecture prepared for a conference or class meeting, or at the bottom of a scientific poster. Sources includes any written works quoted or referenced, such as books, magazines, or newspapers, as well as all other materials drawn upon for information, such as interviews, audio or video recordings, statistical sources, maps and plans of existing buildings, and Web sites.

The Value of a Working Bibliography

A literature review can be both (1) a preparatory process and (2) a written document. As soon as you are able, begin a compilation of source summaries, organized chronologically, alphabetically by author's last name and/or grouped by domain area. This flexible, expanding, and ever-developing written document is called an **annotated bibliography**, and a shortened version simply, a *working bibliography*. At the end of this section, you will find an activity to help you get started on this useful document. An **annotation** is a summary and/or evaluation. Therefore, an annotated bibliography includes a summary and/or critical evaluation of each of the sources. The annotated bibliography looks like a list of references page but includes an annotation after each full citation. Annotated bibliographies can be part of a larger research project or can be a standalone document that serves to inform others of the valuable content you have found, and the authors who provided that content.

Activity 4.4
Beginning an Annotated Bibliography

Purpose: To compile a list of resources with notations about each source's usefulness to your research.

Start the document with an introductory statement of the general intent of the literature exploration. This includes suggestions for the ultimate direction of the proposed research to come. End your document with questions you still have, gaps in knowledge you may have noticed and other patterns or ideas that have arisen during your search.

Provide at least thirty entries/sources per domain area. If your research interests are an intersection of more than one domain or area of interest, please *organize the annotated bibliography first by topic*. Then, within each domain area, you can organize alphabetically by first author's last name, or if you are doing a historical survey, you can organize by date published. Each entry must include:

1. Summary
   ○ What topics are covered, or questions asked?
   ○ Who wrote the document? When and where was the document written?
   ○ What are the main arguments? What are the conclusions?

2. Assessment
   ○ Is it a primary or secondary source?
   ○ Is it peer-reviewed?
   ○ How does it compare with other sources in your bibliography?
   ○ Who may have funded or benefited from this study?
   ○ Has it been cited by others?

3. Reflection (what value does it add to your research?)
   ○ Is it useful?
   ○ How does it help shape your argument? How can you use this source in your research project?

Basic Writing and Format Tips:

1. Start with the same full citation format as a regular bibliography, list of references or works cited. Please choose (or seek advice from your instructor) one citation format to use for all the citations. Typically, you will choose from APA, CMS, or MLA.

2. After each citation, the annotation is indented two spaces from the left margin as a block.

3. Each annotation should be one paragraph, between three to six sentences long (about 150–200 words).

4. All lines should be double-spaced. Do not add an extra line between the citations.

5. Try to be objective and give explanations if you state any opinions.

6. Use the third person (e.g., he, she, the author) instead of the first person (e.g., I, my, me).

RESEARCH IN ACTION 4.1
Two Sample Annotations by Student

Ashbrook, R. (2018, June 07). *Screens: The future of theme parks*. WDWInfo. https://www.wdwinfo.com/walt-disney-world/animal-kingdom/screens-the-future-oftheme-parks/

This article focuses on screen-based rides lacking immersion. They do, however, mention the benefits of having screens as the main focus. Money is always a major factor. Original ride systems, like Star Tours, costs millions of dollars, but with release of the new films they have updated scenes in the attraction to feel new and fresh. The attractions also take up less space in the parks resulting in more space for other attractions, shops, and restaurants. She mainly gives examples of screen-based ride systems versus rides that are set-based and have animatronics. After reading the examples she provides, it is, in my opinion, superior to have set-based rides than screen-based. This article is not peer reviewed and strictly a fan's observation and opinion.

Clavé, A. S., & Clark, A. (2007). *The global theme park industry* (First ed.). CABI.

Salvador Anton Clavé is a professor at the Universitat Rovira i Virgili (URV) in Spain and his research concentrates on theme park design, urban and regional tourism planning, and the evolution of tourist destinations. This book is separated into three parts. The first focusing on the development of theme parks; the origin, globalization, operators. The second focuses on theme parks in the entertainment society. This section discusses commercial access to entertainment, the scope of spatial innovation, and the impact of theme parks. The final part explains the fundamentals of theme park development and management. This section dives deeper into the design and planning of a theme park. Section 11 dives deeper into the attractions. Understanding the flow and design of a theme park helps to understand what guests prefer the flow and experience of a ride.

READING A RESEARCH STUDY

According to Takooshian (Takooshian & Schiaffino, 2008), "the ability to share scientific discoveries is the basis of the accumulation and advancement of knowledge. A good scientific study builds on and furthers what is already known about a particular topic." In a video entitled "*How to Read and Understand a Research Study*," Takooshian goes on to say, "research papers are divided into seven sections, and include the abstract, introduction, methods, results, discussion, acknowledgments, and literature cited." In each section, we will discuss key terms used, and what you should look for to appropriately evaluate the quality of the information presented.

Abstract

The very first section of a paper is the **abstract**. It is a short summary, usually about 250 words, and is designed to summarize the research and get people interested in reading the paper. The abstract should include what is being studied and why, and in order to provide scientific justification, a brief description of the procedures used, and an equally brief explanation of the major results or findings. It may also include the significance of the results or implications for practice.

Introduction

The next section which provides background information on which the research is based is the *introduction*. It states the problem being tested as a question and a tentative hypothesis. It also situates the study in the body of literature that the researcher has reviewed. An essential goal here is that the researcher give some indication of why this research is important to the field, and if they are trying to solve a specific medical, social, behavioral, or functional problem or issue.

Methods

Typically, in the methods section, we will see how the original research was designed in terms of who participated in the study, how they were selected, and the sample size. It will address where the study was conducted, over what period of time, what instruments were used, and how the procedures were implemented, typically in a step by step narrative. How did the participants interact with the researcher? What was measured? How was it recorded? This information is extremely important especially if a future researcher would like to attempt the same experiment to see if they would get a similar result.

Results/Findings

In quantitative studies this section may be called *results*, while in qualitative studies they will typically be called *findings*. Sometimes a quantitative study will have a results section, which will contain all the numerical data, tables, charts, and calculations, followed by a findings section which will describe, expand on, or summarize the results. In either case, this section is typically where the reader will find a table, chart, or graph summarizing numeric data, or succinct text descriptions of emergent patterns found in the data.

Interpretation/Implications/ Discussion/Summary/Conclusion

Research papers differ in the way they conclude. Researchers differ in how they represent and interpret results or findings. Typically, the conclusion is carefully crafted to portray how these results impact the field, either for practitioners to use the data, or for future researchers. Researchers attempt to make a connection between the theory and the data, and to report whether the data supports the theory. In qualitative research this section usually provides an elaboration or modification to an existing theory or attempts to describe a new theory. The researcher might also attempt to influence future researchers calling on them to answer questions that were raised by their study.

Activity 4.5
Dissecting a Research Study

Purpose: To dissect and analyze a landmark study published in 1984 by Roger Ulrich, an urban geographer. This study has been cited countless times and serves to underscore the importance of views of nature in healthcare settings. Reviewing the following two-page article answer the following questions. You can share what you find in a small group or whole class discussion.

1. What was the sample size?

2. How long was the study conducted?

3. What data was gathered?

4. How was it analyzed?

5. What was the conclusion? What are the implications for the practice of interior design?

6. Is this a quantitative or qualitative approach? Or was it mixed methods?

7. If you were to design a study today to test these results how might you design one?

Page one of two of landmark study by Ulrich (1984).

Page two of two of landmark study by Ulrich (1984).

CASE STUDIES

This chapter concludes with a look at a comprehensive kind of investigation called a **case study**. The term *case study* is used in many fields. In the medical field, a case study would be a comprehensive look at a singular instance of a person who exhibited all the classic symptoms of a certain affliction. The story of the "elephant man" was a case study in which a man was afflicted with an extreme form of the disease called neurofibromatosis. Documentation of the way Joseph Merrick's body was deformed, the way he lived, and the way he died served to inform medical science. Even after his death, his remains, and the detailed story of his life, still serve to inform science.

Origins of the Case Study Approach

In academics, the method of learning about a phenomenon through a specific example, or examples, began with Harvard Law School dean Christopher Columbus Langdell's innovative introduction of the *Case Method* in the 1870s. Langdell was frustrated with the practice of teaching law through memorization, recitation, and drills, concluding that the actual learning of legal practice wasn't happening until after his students graduated and began working on legal cases in a firm. He drew on two principles discussed in Chapter 3, *inductive reasoning* and *empiricism*, proposing that lawyers needed to deepen their understanding of a small number of fundamental theories, and that reasoning from the application of these theories in practice developed one's ability to transfer understanding to new examples in different contexts (Garvin, 2003). Langdell's new approach called upon students to become deeply familiar with a few cases, and to submit to a Socratic series of questions-and-answers about them to interrogate their meaning within the framework of the law. The method demanded that students question the meaning of the examples (cases) and to make distinctions between cases—why was one decided one way, and another differently? A latter-day product of the *Case Method* of education, Senator Elizabeth Warren, says the mark of a good lawyer is "the ability to make fine discriminations, to think of two things that are closely interconnected but keep them separate from one another" (Garvin, 2003, p. 59).

This process of inductive reasoning from core theories, based on examples, was at first viewed as a radical approach, but by the end of the nineteenth century it became accepted at other elite U.S. law schools such as Columbia, Yale, and University of Chicago. The study of cases as a central learning process was adopted by Harvard Business School in the 1920s and rapidly became the model for other business schools; subsequently medicine and the social sciences adapted the approach, where it is practiced as an "in-depth, multi-faceted understanding of a complex issue in its real-life context" (Crowe, Cresswell, Robertson, et al., 2011).

Why is the method considered effective? One reason is it puts the student in the position of teacher: constructing and telling a story through examples helps one learn *how* to think, rather than *what* to think. The telling of the story, and the making of distinctions between cases, is a fundamental building block of persuasion. Most importantly, practice in the case study method gives students the tools to grapple with ambiguous situations. Educationally, writes William Ellet, the case represents "a monumental shift in the educational experience, from the comfort of authority and the officially sanctioned truth to the hard work of personal responsibility and the unease of ambiguity and multiple meanings" (Ellet, 2007). Ambiguity is one of the hallmarks of interior design, a profession where we seldom find right-or-wrong answers, one where the hierarchy of importance must be teased out of complex situations featuring an array of variables.

The effectiveness of the case study approach is potentially undermined when the term is used too loosely. Helen Simons warns it is often not clear what constitutes a "case"—since examples may be studies of a project, an organization or institution, or a person. Sometimes interviews are conducted and assembled into something called a "case study." The ground rules for applying lessons from case studies to broader problems, she warns, are not at all clear (Simons, 2009). Robert Yin bestows clarity on some of these issues with his recognition of a case study "foundational trilogy" consisting of:

- Case study research—the mode of inquiry
- Case studies—the method of inquiry, or research method
- Case(s)—the *unit of inquiry* or *unit of analysis* (Yin, 2017, p. xx)

A **unit of inquiry** or *analysis* is defined as the main entity you are going to compare. It may be an individual, a group, an institution, or an artifact. It can be one data point such as an exam score or an occurrence such as a classroom interaction. A case study can function as any of these. As you undertake case study research, it will be helpful to continually clarify your use of these terms, and to confirm that your instructors and peers are using them the same way. If there is some confusion, talk through the terminology to get consensus you can draw upon in discussions and presentations.

Case Study Characteristics

In addition to being a unit of inquiry, what is a *case*? The definition may vary across disciplines, but cases are generally characterized by boundedness. An analysis of the interior of the San Diego Central Public Library is a case because the topic of study has clearly delineated boundaries. "Public library reading rooms in Southern California 1996–2015" could also be considered a case, because the topic can be separated out and studied as an independent phenomenon. Each of these examples can be studied as a system with "a boundary and working parts" (Stake, 1995, p. 2). Under this definition, the topic "public library interiors" would not be considered a case. Only a particular example, or instance, of a public library project (either built or proposed) would be a case.

In *The Art of Case Study Research*, Robert Stake distinguishes between case study types. An *intrinsic case study*, he writes, is one we are given because we need to understand a specific situation, not because it sheds light on a broader problem. For example, complaints of insufficient lighting in the reading area of a junior high school library can be such a case study, as we would be interested in understanding the problem so we can fix it. Another type of case study is suggested by the occurrence of 5th graders fidgeting in classroom chairs where the insight gained from studying a specific group of elementary school students may yield valuable information on the need for furniture resiliency to be incorporated in the product development process. This would be an example of an *instrumental case study*—we are looking for findings that are applicable beyond a particular group of 5th graders. If we had the good (or bad) fortune to study all fidgeting 5th graders in public schools, we could call this a *collective case study*.

It is important to fully document, dissect, and examine each case study, to understand it on its own merits before applying the lessons you learn from it. Guard against the temptation to justify an *a priori* belief. This would be a form of confirmation bias, as described in Chapter 3. Next, remember that using case studies is a linear but iterative process. A feedback loop between steps of seeking out, documenting, analyzing on your own, and discussing them with others, informs the researcher of ways to sharpen the study while it is under way as shown in Figure 4.10.

Given the multiple strategies of research that are available, when is the case study the most appropriate? Yin (2017) reminds us that surveys, like case studies, are useful when the researcher is not in control of the events or variables under examination. Both are more focused on contemporary events than historical. Of the two, surveys are better suited to questions of *who*, *what*, *where*, and *how many*; case studies are often better for addressing questions of *how* and *why* (Yin, 2017).

Types of Interior Design Case Studies

In the field of interior design, the case study is an in-depth examination of a previously completed (or proposed) project that has conditions related to your own project, so that it can serve as an example to learn from. It can be either a successful or an unsuccessful design solution (so you can learn what has *not* worked in the past). There are different kinds of case studies to

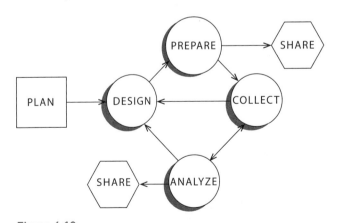

Figure 4.10
Diagram showing the iterative process of doing a case study (Adapted from Yin, 2017, p. 1).

explore. A **precedent study** usually refers to a project that exemplifies innovation in architecture or design, such as in its structural, technological, or formal (related to form) exploration.

The goal of precedent research in architecture is to understand what has come before and to use that knowledge to help define and develop your own design concepts. As we have seen in Chapter 1, as both a researcher and designer, your background is extremely important, as these experiences become influences you will bring to each design you produce. Precedent research is meant to expand and supplement these personal experiences. As you know more and understand what other designers have proposed, and why, you will be capable of producing a richer and more meaningful design solution.

Another type of case study is the *historic precedent*, as we often go back in time to the first project of its kind: an archetype, an architectural icon, or a pioneer study that led the way. Or we examine a project that exemplifies a certain historic style or time period.

We can also use recent or cutting-edge projects as examples to illustrate technological breakthroughs and possibilities or trends in philosophy and design theory. When many designers point to a project as an icon, it operates as a reference point and may function as a focus for the founding of schools of thought. Such a project is often referred to as a *paradigmatic case*. A good example is Le Corbusier's Villa Savoye (1929–1931). This building illustrated the five points of modern architecture as stipulated in Le Corbusier's manifesto, published in 1926. Its construction ushered in a whole new understanding of modern architecture. Thus, a case study can serve as a singular example that says, "Here I am. Learn from me."

Sometimes, the term *case study* refers specifically to an interior design project that solves a social problem or that benefits society, such as an innovative institutional program. The case study in this instance could also be used to document and explore how a project offered a unique solution to a problem faced by a certain user group or in a particular area—for example, a museum for the visually impaired or temporary housing in a disaster-stricken community.

The terms *document* and *explore* are key terms when learning from a case study. That is because the key to doing a case study is that you must gather a variety of aspects to get a multifaceted understanding of the project. Text descriptions are typically available when the project is featured in publications or can be gotten directly from the online portfolio of the design firm, archived documents such as floor plans, photographs, and maps (to be discussed in Chapter 5), interviews or documentaries interviewing people related to the project, and direct observation (if you are able to visit). A case study acknowledges the individuality and uniqueness of the participants and the setting (Guerin & Dohr, 2007) with a comparable project type, user group, or program and generalizes its applicability to the larger field of interior design.

An underlying assumption in science is that if you dissect something, you can find out the inner workings of an organism or discover how it functions in its environment. A fully documented case study is like a living organism. We can learn from its form, function, economy, and how it has stood the test of time. We can use case studies to compare the quality of designed environments, track current design trends, or to provide an historical framework for a proposal. Or we use them to explore the implementation of a brand-new material, innovative use of technology or construction method, or a fresh use of a design principle such as sustainable design.

To fully understand your project type, you may need to visit a few existing projects that are similar in scope, or that serve the same function or have the same user group or are in the neighborhood. When you find one that is innovative or has accomplished its goal successfully, you have found a subject for your case study. Next, you must document all the parameters of the project you found and dissect the project. What makes this project unique and a success? Or, on the flip side, what makes it a complete failure? We can also learn a great deal from another designer's mistakes, inappropriate use of color or materials, poor spatial configurations, or misguided assumptions about the way the users would use the space.

Activity 4.6
Learning From a Case Study

Purpose: To fully document and explore a previously built or proposed interior design project, that can serve as an example to learn from. Using one of the following case study collections, identify a project you would like to analyze.

Whole Building Design Guide (WBDG) at www.wbdg.org/additional-resources/case-studies

Academy of Architecture for Health (AAH) at network.aia.org/academyofarchitectureforhealth/viewdocument/case-study-library

Institute for Human Centered Design www.universaldesigncasestudies.org

Architectural Record www.architecturalrecord.com/topics/306-building-type-studies

AIA Committee on the Environment (COTE) at www.aiatopten.org/

Health Design at https://www.healthdesign.org/insights-solutions/open

Choose one project to document and explore ALL the following items:

1. **Project Basics:** location, year constructed, building type, size (SF), client, end-users, design team …

2. **Background and Context:** project goals, cost, neighborhood

3. **Function and Physical Appearance:** program, site plan, floor plans, diagrams, photos, key design details

4. **Implications for the Future:** Effectiveness? Impact on surroundings? Influence on other designers?

5. **Summary:** Applicability to your project. What did you learn?

As an optional or supplemental activity, prepare a list of questions that you still have about your case study. Are there any points you would like clarified or questions you would like to ask the designer, builder, owner, or staff member? In the next several chapters we will be talking about how to reach out via email or phone to contact the designer, owner, or staff member at your case study location which may provide additional information through interview, survey, or observation data gathering techniques.

RESEARCH IN ACTION 4.2
Case Study as Prototype: The Case Study Houses, 1945–1966

In 1945, *Art and Architecture* magazine sponsored a series of innovative new interpretations of the American single-family house. A set of relative newcomers, the architects and designers of these houses explored materials such as steel, glass, masonry, and concrete, which were theretofore uncommon in residential design. More importantly, they experimented with the boundary between inside and outside, designing the flow of space to continue seamlessly from interior living areas to exterior spaces. Images to the right show a proposed mid-century modern house that embraced and typified this radical notion of nested and layered spaces integrated with garden landscape.

According to Esther McCoy, more than a half-million people visited the first dozen case study houses. The houses were especially popular for the creative interior planning and furnishings they displayed. Lightweight "butterfly" chairs, sofas, and tables were smaller, more portable, and easier to rearrange than previous furniture for the home which was heavy and tended to stay in one place. The designers did not have manufactured pieces from which to choose, so they invented their own. Additionally, the program stimulated many small furniture manufacturing operations and enabled new designs for floor covering, textiles, lamps, tableware, and accessories (McCoy, 1977).

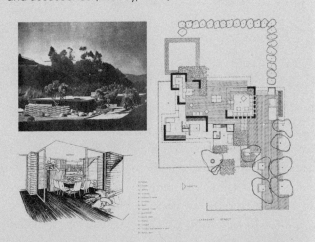

Designed, but never built, *The Loggia House* by Whitney R. Smith "creates a fluid living pattern particularly suited to Southern California."

CONCLUSION

In this chapter we examined a set of research tools that have become accepted and used widely within the academic community. These tools have become standards used across disciplines because they give us the ability to rely on the published work of other researchers. The methods covered in this chapter have applicability across many fields, including the natural and social sciences, and are fundamental to interior design research.

These tools form the basis for design of our research. They provide systematic ways of discovering, cataloging, and applying published work that allow us to be effective in the way we allocate our time to the research task. The research design methods presented in this chapter allow for appropriate use of theory as well as quantitative and qualitative approaches to discovering and augmenting existing knowledge. The activities of framing a research question, conducting a literature review or a comprehensive precedent investigation, discerning between primary and secondary sources occur both simultaneously and iteratively. We assess the information as we gather it to reflect on the work we've done so far, and to continually shape and reshape its direction.

Key Terms

Abstract
Acronym
American Psychological
   Association (APA)
Annotated bibliography
Anthropometrics
Block quote
Boundary object
Case study
Chicago Manual of Style (CMS)
Citation
Comparative study
Contextualize
Control variables
Database

Design science
Descriptive study
Domain areas
Ergonomics
Gap in knowledge
Grounded theory
Keyword
Library catalog
Literature map
Literature review
Logos (logic)
Methods
Modern Language Association
   (MLA)
Monograph

Pathos (empathy)
Plagiarism
Precedent research
Precedent study
Primary source
Quasi-experimental
Secondary source
Survey study
Syllogism
Thesis
Unit of inquiry/analysis
Validity
Visual models
White paper

Discussion Questions

1. Share your experience starting your literature review or precedent research. Are you concerned that you will miss something important in your search? What tips or advice can you give others in finding the relevant published work on their topic?

2. Give an example of a secondary source on your topic that referenced primary sources in their bibliographies or works cited. How can you determine if a cited source is primary?

3. On the topic of plagiarism, when does a source need to be cited? What do you see as the dangers of inadvertent plagiarism that may occur as an outcome of note-taking from digital source material? How might this happen, and what steps can you take to prevent it?

4. Describe your current method of keeping track of sources you gather during the research process. What are its advantages and disadvantages? Which new method do you plan to try, and why?

5. If you find a qualitative research article that does not explicitly identify a theoretical starting point, how can you reason from the information presented in the article to infer the author's operative theory?

6. Consider a topic that could shed light on your research question. How can the topic be structured as a case study? What are the boundaries that confine it to a small enough area that enable you to study it as a system?

References

Adams, J. L. (2001). *Conceptual blockbusting: A guide to better ideas*. Cambridge, MA: Basic Books.

Axelrod, R., & Cooper, C. (2008). *The St. Martin's guide to writing* (8th ed.). Boston, MA: Bedford/St. Martin's.

Ballast, D. K. (2006). *Interior design reference manual: A guide to the NCIDQ exam* (3rd ed.). Belmont, CA: Professional.

Barnet, S. Bedau, H., & O'Hara, J. (2020). *From critical thinking to argument: A portable guide* (6th ed.). New York: Bedford/St. Martin's.

Burkhardt, J. M., MacDonald, M. C., & Rathemacher, A. J. (2003). *Teaching information literacy*. Chicago, IL: American Library Association.

Creswell, J., & Creswell, J. (2018). *Research design: Qualitative, quantitative and mixed methods*. London: Sage.

Crowe, S., Cresswell, K., Robertson, A., et al. (2011). *The case study approach*. BMC Medical Research Methodology. doi:https://doi.org/10.1186/1471-2288-11-100

Eco, U. (2015). *How to write a thesis*. Translated from the original Italian *Come si fa una testi laurea: le materie umanistiche*. (1977/2012) Bompani/RCS Libri S.p.A. Cambridge, MA: MIT Press.

Ellet, W. (2007). *The case study handbook: How to read, discuss, and write persuasively about cases*. Boston, MA: Harvard Business School Press.

Garvin, D. (2003, September–October). Making the case. *Harvard Magazine*, pp. 56–65. Retrieved from https://harvardmagazine.com/2003/09/making-the-case-html

Groat, L., & Wang, D. (2002). *Architectural research methods*. New York: John Wiley.

Groat, L., & Wang, D. (2013). *Architectural research methods*, 2nd ed. New York: John Wiley.

Guerin, D., & Dohr, J. (2007). *Research 101 Tutorial*. InformeDesign, University of Minnesota. Retrieved December 25, 2007, from http://www.informedesign.umn.edu/

Hairston, M., & Ruszkiewicz, J. J. (1996). *The Scott Foresman handbook for writers* (4th ed.). New York: HarperCollins.

Horbury, S. R., & Edmonds, C. J. (2021). Taking class notes by hand compared to typing: Effects on children's recall and understanding. *Journal of Research in Childhood Education*, *35*(1), 55–67.

McCoy, E. (1977). *Case study houses: 1945–1962*. Los Angeles, CA: Hennessey & Ingalls.

Neill, A. C. (2010). Museum docents' understanding of interpretation. Doctoral dissertation. Pennsylvania State University.

Papalambros, P. Y., & Gero, J. S. (n.d.). Retrieved from https://www.cambridge.org/core/journals/design-science

ProQuest. (2008). CSA illumina. Retrieved February 5, 2009, from http://www.csa.com/

Simons, H. (2009). *Case study research in practice*. London: Sage.

Stake, R. (1995). *The art of case study research*. Thousand Oaks, CA: Sage.

Star, S. L., and Griesemer, J. R. (1989). Institutional ecology, "translations" and boundary objects: Amateurs and professionals in Berkeley's museum of vertebrate zoology, 1907–39. *Social Studies of Science*, *19*, 387–420.

Takooshian, H., & Schiaffino, K. (2008). *How to read and understand a research study*. Video. Sage. https://dx.doi.org/10.4135/9781483396750

The OWL at Purdue. (2008). Is it plagiarism yet? Retrieved January 11, 2008, from http://owl.english.purdue.edu/owl/resource/589/02/

Ulrich, R. (1984). View through a window may influence recovery from surgery. *Science*, *224*, 420–421. Retrieved November 8, 2017 from http://science.sciencemag.org/

University Library, University of California, Santa Cruz. (2007). How to distinguish between primary and secondary sources. Retrieved December 30, 2007, from http://library.ucsc.edu/ref/howto/primarysecondary.html

University of London, Postgraduate Online Research Training. (2008). Building up your bibliography. Retrieved January 25, 2008, from http://port.igrs.sas.ac.uk/bibliography.htm

Yin, R. (2017). *Case study research and applications: Design and method*. Los Angeles, CA: Sage.

CHAPTER 5

Gathering Original Data

LEARNING OBJECTIVES

After you complete this chapter, you will be able to:

- Plan a research strategy that seeks to fill the gap(s) in knowledge you have identified.

- Develop a proposal for conducting your own study.

- Analyze documents from project-related sources.

- Seek consent from participants of your study and approval from your Institutional Review Board (IRB).

- Gather, treat, and store data, ethically and responsibly.

- Integrate a variety of generalized, contextual, and site-specific data into programmatic requirements for a research-informed design project.

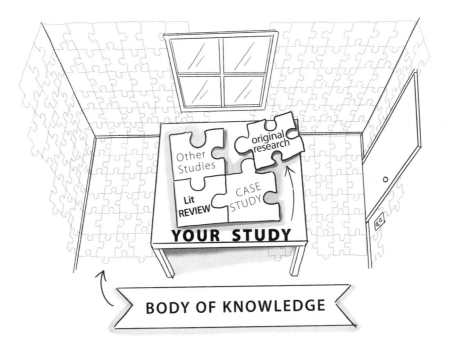

Figure 5.1
Visualize how your original research can fill a gap in knowledge (like a piece of the puzzle) and contribute to the body of knowledge of the interior design profession.

While most interior design projects require information-gathering to inform program requirements and project solutions, a proposal for original research that adds to the body of knowledge of the profession of interior design is unique to a master or doctorate level inquiry. Your review of literature explained previous research about your area of interest, helped you become familiar with terminology and concepts, and contextualized multiple points of view and other influences on the problem. In addition, the case studies you have documented and explored helped you to understand proposed solutions to the problem. Perhaps you have identified a clear gap in the research that only you can fill (Figure 5.1). Just like design concepts and imagery have inspired your clients, your proposed research methods to gather your own data should be communicated to your instructor in such a way that the endeavor seems both useful and doable.

SETTING UP A RESEARCH PLAN

At many schools, a **research proposal** or *research plan* to conduct original research consists of a written document as well as a verbal presentation and must be approved before the student can move forward. This proposal is the gateway to thesis design and the rest of the thesis process. Because of this, it is important to approach your thesis proposal with the same consideration you would give a position paper or persuasive speech. You should be clear, thorough, and, most of all, confident and enthusiastic about your ideas.

The thesis proposal must get the attention of the audience, which may consist of your thesis advisor and other members of a thesis or dissertation committee. It is up to you to establish your audience's interest in your project and get them to relate to at least some part of your project. Usually, the best way to do this is by sharing your inspiration, relationship, or familiarity with the subject matter, and a story from your personal experience. There is a good chance that the reasons you care will also be the reasons the audience will care. Your proposal must be very clear, communicating your ideas effectively. Plus, you must establish your academic and professional credibility with the breadth and thoroughness of your research and the thoughtfulness of your solutions.

Figure 5.2 provides a format to follow to ensure that the proposal covers all critical points. Manipulate the format here and there to tailor it to your unique project criteria. Remember, this is the core of your project intentions and ideas: Who, What, Where, and Why of your project! To relate the research proposal to an application in the professional world, a research proposal is often how you get the funding for your great ideas through grants, scholarships, and subsidies, and other monetary, commendations, or congratulatory awards. So, follow *Dr. Karen's Foolproof Grant Template* in Figure 5.2, and do not leave anything out. Do not assume that because your thesis advisor has been meeting with you throughout the quarter, thoroughness is not an issue. Write your proposal as though the reader knows *nothing* about your project. In some institutions, the professor or instructor is not the (only) person who approves the proposal, so if something is not in your document and presentation, your reviewers, critics, or jury might never see it.

Before you can gather information, you must know where to find the information and you must develop your *research strategy*. Your **research strategy** allows

you to decide, first, what information you need; second, where it might be found; and third, how you will get it. Consider the research approaches discussed in Chapter 4, and what methods are associated with each as illustrated in Figure 5.3. Quantitative approaches require developing methods and tools and refining those instruments and procedures before beginning your research study so that you can collect precise data for a statistical analysis. This often means designing a pre-test and a post-test, deciding what you are going to measure, how you will measure it, and attempt to control for the variables you identify. You will look for an increase in something positive (hopefully) such as better performance or higher satisfaction as a result of something you manipulate.

For example, a study can attempt to quantify *productivity* in terms of number of tasks accomplished before and after a change to the work environment. Here, you already have an assumption that the design of a room relates to productivity. You are attempting to prove or disprove a hypothesis that your design change will make tasks easier and lead to more tasks done in a set period of time. You would have to control for other variables that might interfere with the results, such as a person's familiarity with the task, or a change in behavior as a result of knowing that they are being studied (see discussion of the Hawthorne effect in Chapter 3).

In qualitative approaches, you can begin with asking open-ended questions, or observing a regularly occurring behavior, activity, or cultural event. Even though you will plan your study carefully, some elements such as your use of theory or your expectations will emerge rather than satisfy a predetermined hypothesis.

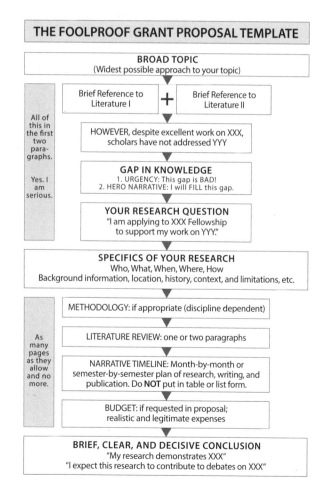

Figure 5.2
Dr. Karen's Foolproof Grant Template (Kelsky, 2015, p. 339).

Quantitative Methods	Mixed Methods	Qualitative Methods
Pre-determined	Both predetermined and emerging methods	Emerging methods
Instrument based questions	Both open- and closed-ended questions	Open-ended questions
Performance data, attitude data, observational data, and census data	Multiple forms of data drawing on all possibilities	Interview data, observation data, document data, and audiovisual data
Statistical analysis	Statistical and text analysis	Text and image analysis
Statistical interpretation	Across data bases interpretation	Themes, patterns, interpretation

Figure 5.3
Side-by-side comparison of methods (Cresswell & Cresswell, 2018, p. 16).

Perhaps you begin your study by watching workers in a fast-food restaurant assemble food for take-out and deliveries. Once again, you may encounter the Hawthorne effect, but you attempt to minimize it first, by keeping your study a secret from the workers (we will talk about *ethical* research methods at the end of this chapter) or by becoming a member of the staff (as a full participant). Or you attend regularly at a strategically placed table so that workers do not notice, or tend to disregard, your presence. You sketch a floor plan and draw color-coded lines to represent how you see different members of the assembly team move and interact. Over time you notice patterns of inefficiency where lines intersect too frequently, and you develop an idea to reorganize the storage shelves to locate more frequently used items at counter-height (more universally accessible) or grouped together so one worker can reach everything without crossing paths with another.

You may also decide to do a qualitative study activity first, followed by a quantitative one. Or a quantitative method followed by a qualitative one. These, of course, are *mixed method* studies. You could do a mixed method study administering the quantitative methods along with qualitative methods at the same time. And later you can turn the data gathered qualitatively into quantities to provide further quantitative evidence.

In addition, you also want to choose methods which align your personal research and design philosophy. In other words, look to match your approach with your underlying worldviews about the nature of reality as discussed in the previous chapter. Figure 5.4 compares the tendencies of the researcher and how they align or match with research methods. Study both tables carefully and make sure you understand the philosophical perspectives and how they compare to your worldview as we explored in the previous chapter.

Personal Reports and Observation Methods

Table 5.1 provides a general description of data-gathering methods an interior design researcher draws upon to create a research strategy organized into two broad categories: *Personal Reports* and *Observation Types*. It is important to point out that these categories are based on how the data is generated or collected rather than analyzed or interpreted. For example, a personal report is generated by a study participant, but when a researcher analyzes the document, the process is called *content analysis*. This difference will be discussed in Chapter 9. Table 5.1 also identifies the chapter that each data collection method is explored in more depth.

Tend to or Typically . . .	Qualitative Approaches	Quantitative Approaches	Mixed Methods Approaches
• Use these philosophical assumptions • Employ these strategies of inquiry	• Constructivist/transformative knowledge claims • Phenomenology, grounded theory, ethnography, case study, and narrative	• Postpositivist knowledge claims • Surveys and experiments	• Pragmatic knowledge claims • Sequential, convergent, and transformative
• Employ these methods	• Open-ended questions, emerging approaches, text or image data	• Closed-ended questions, predetermined approaches, numeric data (may include some open-ended questions)	• Both open- and closed-ended questions, both emerging and predetermined approaches, and both quantitative and qualitative data and analysis
• Use these practices of research as the researcher	• Positions him- or herself • Collects participant meanings • Focuses on a single concept or phenomenon • Brings personal values into the study • Studies the context or setting of participants • Validates the accuracy of findings • Makes interpretations of the data • Creates an agenda for change or reform • Collaborates with the participants • Employs text analysis procedures	• Tests or verifies theories or explanations • Identifies variables to study • Relates variables in questions of hypotheses • Uses standards of validity and reliability • Observes and measures information numerically • Uses unbiased approaches • Employs statistical procedures	• Collects both quantitative and qualitative data • Develops a rationale for mixing • Integrates the data at different stages of inquiry • Presents visual pictures of the procedures in the study • Employs the practices of both qualitative and quantitative research

Figure 5.4
Matching researcher with research approach (Creswell & Creswell, 2018, p. 18).

Broad Category	Method	Description	Chapter
Table 5.1 Methods for Creating a Research Strategy			
Personal Reports	**Self-Report/Diary**	Original source of text information elicited from experts or end-users to find out about their experiences, thoughts, memories, feelings, beliefs, motivations, or expectations. Reports of actions typically need another way of being verified.	6 and 7
	Photo Journaling	Original source of imagery or visual documentation from experts or end-users to find out about their experiences, values, thoughts about aesthetics, preferences, and encounters.	6 and 7
	Informal Interview	Very brief and often unplanned meeting or conversation to ask non-invasive questions. An informal interview may lead to a formal interview.	6
	Formal Interview	A predetermined list of questions given to an individual, ordinarily customized for the individual for the purpose of eliciting stories and quotes about experience, background, history, values, thoughts, beliefs, practices, and preferences. Can be for gathering factual or imaginative information to inform programmatic requirements, design concepts, or emerging themes and metaphors. Narrative or transcript can be reduced and quantified turning qualitative data into quantitative data for the purposes of comparison and evaluation.	6
	Focus Group	Purposefully assembling a group of people in which the primary goal is to generate a conversation that you can learn from. Can be used to help you identify your end-user, or current issues when this information is unknown.	6
	Survey	Using a standardized questionnaire—a predetermined list of questions given uniformly to a sample population	7
Observation	**Naturalistic/ Anthropological**	Observing behavior in an environment with an open-ended possibility for information-gathering. Usually this method adopts a "just looking" attitude; then, any information gathered can be used to establish a theory or conclusion about what was observed. Records data through video, photos, field notes, diagrams.	8
	Behavior Mapping	A technique for recording, encoding, tracking, and representing observed movement or interaction. Can document physical environment aspects as well.	8
	Environment Behavior (E-B)	Observing behavior in a space or an environment with specific goals in mind for information-gathering. Often, the designer uses this observation technique to enforce or dismiss a theory or conclusion already in place.	8
	Participant (Full)	Taking part in the activities or behaviors while simultaneously observing while being careful not to influence the outcomes. May be difficult to document. But you can record or talk about the experience afterward.	8
	Participant (Partial)	Engaging in the activity peripherally by asking questions or standing by.	8
	Identified outsider (most prone to elicit the Hawthorne effect)	Guided tours of a facility, attending a hosted meeting, observing an activity while being identified as an outsider, Shadowing is very common in interior design where the researcher follows someone on their daily activity to observe interactions and behaviors.	8
	Hidden (most prone to ethical considerations)	To gather the most natural behavior in a public or semipublic place. Researcher generates field notes and takes photos or supplements with sketches. Place-Centered Mapping and/or Person-Centered Mapping techniques can be used. Predetermined checklists may also be generated to facilitate focus when observing in the field.	8

Field Survey	Gather information about a site or a building in a comprehensive manner.	8
	Existing Conditions Report/As-Builts	
	Measure and record dimensions of existing building shell.	
	Inventory	
	List and photo-document client's existing equipment or furniture	
	Physical evidence	
	Observe objects left behind or removed after an interaction between people and a space.	
	Trace evidence	
	Accretion	
	Graffiti on a wall, a bicycle lying in a front yard, writing left on a chalkboard in a classroom	
	Erosion	
	A dirt pathway in the grass, a worn handrail, an empty trash can or dumpster	
Quasi Experimental/ Experiential	Usability studies, simulations, models, evaluating mock-up and testing prototypes could be systematic and/or cognitive.	8
Experimental	Conduct an observation in a controlled environment to test a theory or hypothesis. Typically seeking to establish a causal relationship involving variables which are controlled and/or manipulated.	8

Quantitative	Qualitative	Mixed Methods
• Experimental designs	• Narrative research	• Convergent
• Nonexperimental designs, such as surveys	• Phenomenology	• Explanatory sequential
	• Grounded theory	• Exploratory sequential
• Longitudinal designs	• Ethnographies	• Complex designs with embedded core designs
	• Case study	

Figure 5.5
Common study types for each approach (Creswell & Creswell, 2018, p. 12).

Figure 5.5 shows a more detailed list of common methods found within each approach. One way to look at this choice is to figure out whether your research questions seek to describe a phenomenon in as much detail as possible, such as "What is the patient experience in a typical emergency room visit?" or "How do concert-goers use wayfinding in outdoor music venues?" Or does your research question look for statistical or dimensional information to solve a clearly defined outcome such as, "How can we use interior design to reduce wait times in a typical emergency room visit?" or "How can use of lighting improve wayfinding in outdoor music

venue design?" In the first case, you may want to do a **descriptive** research study which seeks to describe the qualities of a situation in detail. In the second case, we may want to use surveys or a quasi-experimental situation which relates room design to wait time. And we may look for an independent variable such as light level to affect a dependent variable of wait time. This would be an example of a **causal** study, which hypothesizes that increasing light level would decrease wait time.

Another choice of methods would be how much time you have to conduct the study. A **longitudinal study** measures or describes change that occurs over time. If you would like to know how familiarity with attending outdoor music venues affects a person's ability to navigate one, you would have to have access to observing people attend multiple venues or shadow a particular person attending multiple venues (or the same venue multiple times). You might supplement this longitudinal study with a **cross-sectional study** in which you measure or observe multiple people at a music venue at the same time. Cross-sectional data allows you to make comparisons among participants at a single place and time, to look for patterns and differences in behaviors or preferences.

Looking again at Figure 5.5, we notice many new terms. Under the auspices of qualitative methods, *narrative research* is a study that leads to a description of the qualities of a situation, phenomenon, or event in terms of a story which unfolds over time and has a cast of characters—see Chapter 9 for an in-depth exploration. The researcher uses a combination of observation, interviews, and surveys to put together a cohesive, logical description of what they notice, supported by data. This type of study would answer the question, "How do concert-goers use wayfinding in outdoor music venues?" by allowing the researcher to reach conclusions about the importance of all elements in the venue (not just lighting) which emerge from the data that could serve to inform future designers and owners of music venues.

An innovative technique for both gathering information from end-users (or potential end-users) and interpreting it is to use an anthropological approach. **Ethnographies** are descriptive documentations of a culture, or a person as a representative of the culture. In other words, ethnography tells the story of a people. As interior designers, we can apply the same storytelling techniques as in the narrative study to understand and communicate information about our **end-users** or the people who are served by the interior design research project. An ethnography study can help you go beyond mere statistics to accomplish the following:

- Identify patterns in behavior.
- See "backstage."
- Capture emotional expression.
- Tell a story.

- Pay attention to detail.
- See from a new perspective.

Ethnography uses many of the same techniques we have already discussed, such as interviews and observation, but it can also employ creative documentation to extract the meaning of the information gathered. According to Hill and Knox (2021) these qualitative approaches have become accepted and embraced as empirical methods within the social sciences, with a recent evolution or branch called **autoethnography** which "involves a researcher writing about a topic of great personal relevance (e.g., family secrets), situating their experiences within the social context. Autoethnography thus requires deep reflection on both one's unique experiences and the universal within oneself" (p. 2). Refer to Chapter 8 for a more detailed and in-depth look at these types of studies and their associated methods.

Once you have written the research proposal and designed the research project, the breadth and thoroughness of your research and your subsequent conclusions should stand on their own, capable of being used by others, independently of you. Your conclusions will add to the body of interior design knowledge, and another researcher should be able to pick up where you left off and build upon your conclusions (Groat & Wang, 2002, p. 46). Be open-minded, think independently, and be prepared to potentially defy the crowd and advocate ideas that you believe in, but others may not agree with yet. Remember, a project that creates some controversy can be a good thing. It means your audience is engaged; it means they care (Weisberg, 2006, p. 100). When you prepare and present your research proposal you should be able to answer two questions:

1. Tell us why you care.
2. Tell us why we should care.

Your thesis project must pass the "So What?" test. You must teach your audience something new about something they care about, be it the topic, your users, your site or building, or some other aspect of your project. Your information must be current, relevant, and engaging and exciting to your audience. If you know the answer to the two questions above, then your project has likely passed the test.

OBTAINING SITE INFORMATION

As we have seen in the previous chapter, an interior design case study is an in-depth study of a particular example that we can learn from. Building on this idea, we can look at any interior design project as a case study, a unique combination of site, architecture, or building surrounding the interior space, which is owned and operated by a particular client, organization, or company, and seeks to serve a particular end-user or segment of the population. Many times, research for interior design revolves around a project, or coming up with a solution to a problem that exists within a specific context which needs to be included in the information-gathering.

As interior designers we are familiar with gathering information about the site, the client, and the end-users of a space, particularly when we are in the first phase of the design process known as **programming phase** or *pre-design*. We are aware of the difference between designing for a generic end-user or a specific client. This differentiation comes in to play, for example, when designing a multi-family housing complex in contrast to a custom home for a specific family. If we view a project as generic, we may be more apt to use *generalizable* results from a study rather than *context-specific* data. But both are very useful to interior design research. **Generalizable** data are those broadly or widely applicable to many different types of people or situations, contrasted with **context-specific** knowledge garnered from or identified as only occurring in a particular place, circumstance, or state. There may be a tendency to stereotype or group potential end-users using unspoken assumptions. Continuing the example of designing housing, you may be asked to design for people grouped by socioeconomic status, such as high-, middle-, or low-income, each with assumed values about preferences of size of unit, number of rooms, or type of finishes. Or maybe you have divided people into groups such as those affected by a natural disaster that need emergency housing, or people with a certain type of disability with a need for accessible housing. Whatever the issue, examine the underlying assumptions about your end-user group, and challenge those beliefs. Use both generalizable and context-specific data to solve the interior design problem.

Consider decisions regarding breakfast as an example of using generalizable versus context-specific data to solve a problem. There probably is an example of what is considered the ideal breakfast food for a human being based on nutritional content and environmental impact—perhaps a study done for nutritional science or culinary arts degree. If you are an interested consumer of research, you may seek out and use findings from this kind of study for criteria when considering what to eat for breakfast. But there will also be context-specific information to be considered in the selection of food as well, such as your metabolism, food allergies, or other medical considerations related to your diet. In addition, you also exist in a certain socio-cultural milieu in which some foods are readily available, and some are not. Thirdly, you also must take into consideration your personal preferences, your likes and dislikes for certain flavors or textures of food. Additionally, you may also look at cost, or ease of preparation, given your kitchen configuration, tools, and appliances.

This chapter continues with a look at how industry-related, context-specific data-gathering techniques supplement traditional research, and how this adds to the nature of interior design research methods. We will also explore the idea of documenting context-specific data so thoroughly that we can learn from it and seek to generalize, as in conducting an *ethnographic* study (defined previously in this chapter). As design-informed researchers we can build on our skills gathering context-specific information, not only as an expansion of the literature review (discussed in Chapter 4), but also to help introduce the research skill of *document analysis* (explored in Chapter 8) and as a bridge to interview, survey, and observation methods (discussed in Chapters 6, 7, and 8, respectively). As shown in Figure 5.6, a balanced research plan considers context-specific to generalizable data from a wide spectrum of information sources. We will refer to this figure throughout Chapter 5 as you assemble and refine data-gathering methods for your research project.

Considering Context

The site is the one unique thing to every project. There are two places inspiration comes from: the site and the client. And there's the unique combination of the two.

(Jennifer Luce, architect, personal communication, January 3, 2008)

Your **project type** defines the primary function of the space and is developed from your research and identification of the problem. Once you have identified your project type, you will need to familiarize yourself with the programming and design issues associated with the project type, such as sustainability, budgets, social responsibility, needs and requirements, terminology, controversy, and innovation. You should also understand the political, social, geographical, and historical context of the project type (Cherry, 1999). When designing a restaurant, for example, you might want to know about the dramatic origins of the restaurant in France after the French Revolution—as a place that served *essences*, broths made primarily from chicken and beef and served to restore strength to the sick. Knowing this historical reference might help to enrich your programming and design process and add meaning to your design decisions.

Familiarize yourself with issues common to your project type. In *Programming for Design*, Edith Cherry uses the example of a museum. Regardless of the uniqueness of a particular museum project, the museum project type always addresses issues of flow and how museum patrons will circulate through the building and the exhibits. Your project research should alert you to this issue, so that the issue can inform your thesis proposal and programming process (Cherry, 1999). Understand project-specific terminology and acronyms (as discussed in previous chapters). For example,

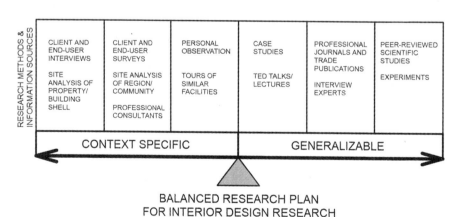

Figure 5.6
A balanced research plan considers context-specific to generalizable data from a wide spectrum of information sources.

in healthcare design, an M.A. refers to a "medical assistant." In commercial projects a T.I. project is a "tenant improvement" project. Knowledge of professional terms will increase your level of professional credibility with clients, end-users, and your research community.

Scale Versus Scope

The square foot area, or **scale**, the size of the project in relation to similar projects, is not as important as the depth of your investigation. In a thesis project, **scope**, or the depth, detail, and what is included, is most important. Designing a backpack would seem to be a small project in scale. However, an industrial designer could spend months integrating innovations such as a solar panel that collects energy to power a small reading light or adding waterproofing to allow the pack to be submerged in water (Smithsonian Institution, 2007). After the Columbine school shooting in April 1999, some backpacks were designed with Kevlar for bulletproofing in the case of another shooting, and after the attacks on the Twin Towers in New York City you could find an executive backpack that included a parachute! In light of more recent events and issues, what are other small-scale innovations related to interior design that could have a big impact?

The site investigation for a new project is a critical step because a building's interior is organically linked to its exterior surroundings. Buildings are like living creatures. They take in nutrients (deliveries, entrance of occupants, fresh air), they give off byproducts (trash removal, plumbing waste, off gassing), and change over time (deterioration, future growth, and alteration). Viewing the building as an organic entity will help you to envision the type of information you need to collect before starting the project. You must look outside the building at the outset to determine the constraints and possibilities of the site.

In the context of the interior design studio project, there are several different ways you may approach site selection:

- *Scenario 1(a)*—The instructor may have assigned you a site. There may be documentation of the site, such as a site plan, an existing conditions plan, a satellite view, a verbal description, and/or photographs. In this case, you are primarily responsible for interpreting the given evidence and responding to the site conditions with your design solution.
- *Scenario 1(b)*—Sometimes the instructor assigns a location, but obtaining the documentation is the responsibility of the student, which involves a site visit or field trip. In this case, the student is responsible for collecting data about the site and then analyzing the data.
- *Scenario 2*—In advanced studios, you may already have a user group (for example, autistic children) and/or a program (supervised play and treatment area for autistic children), but no assigned site or location. This would allow you to choose a building or space for your project. One possible assignment is *site selection*, which involves a combination of documentation and site data collection, as well as analysis to select the perfect site. An appropriate assignment in a Thesis Programming class might be for each student to document three possible sites for a project and present the sites in class. The site selection process is part of the work of the thesis.
- *Scenario 3*—In some instances, a site can be the inspiration or starting point for the whole project as illustrated in Figure B5.1.

RESEARCH IN ACTION 5.1
The Sage House: A Beautiful Starting Point

When I was in college, I was struck by the university's misuse of a beautiful, historic residence, *The Sage House*, as office space.

I documented the ill fit with photographs of file cabinets in the hallways, wires running across

a beautiful stained-glass window at the front of the house, and the like. It seemed to me that the house should be reverted to residential use, and I determined that due to its size and configuration, it would make an excellent bed and breakfast. I also determined, through analyzing the site as well as interviewing school authorities, that it would be an ideal housing facility for visiting faculty who traveled from various countries and who would stay varying lengths of time due to their teaching schedules—a

▶

few days if giving a lecture, or perhaps a few weeks, a few months, even an entire semester. From this example, you can see how the site was the catalyst for a new idea. Analysis of the site (The Sage House) led to an idea for a program (a bed and breakfast) and then to the user group (visiting faculty).

Exterior façade and interior views of the Sage House, an historic building on a university campus as the starting point for inquiry.

In professional practice it is often the client who determines the site because the client has already purchased or leased a property or wants to renovate a home that the family has lived in for years. But frequently, in both commercial and institutional design, a client will look to the designer to determine the best location for the project. The client may have a real estate agent assemble several choices for the designer's consideration. This kind of service is called a **feasibility study**. A designer not only determines whether the building is physically suitable to accommodate the needs of the program, but also may determine whether the local demographics (characteristics of the population living and working in the area) will support the new project, and whether the existing services or **infrastructure** (plumbing/sewerage/electrical) will support the new function, as when converting a warehouse into a restaurant.

Site Selection

In site selection, as in apartment hunting, you start with a set of parameters or criteria. For example, when you are looking for a place to live you may want to start with a list of the things that are most important: proximity to school, access to natural light, minimum square feet, number of rooms, cost or rent per month, pet accommodations, noise level. You could also include a "wish list" of amenities that you would love to have but that are not necessary, such as a view of the ocean, a fireplace, or a balcony. You may then further assign value by ranking the items. You can do the same exercise with your site selection process: set parameters. The parameters are going to be different for a commercial project than they would be for a residential project. You will want to determine, first, if the site's setting should be urban, suburban, or rural. Each of these types of areas has pros and cons. Urban environments are characterized by high density (number of people per square unit of measure), access to public transportation, and a variety of cultures, yet these positives may be offset by noise, pollution, and crowds. Suburban environments have less density and fewer people, but they may be farther from public transportation and not subject to a high volume of foot traffic. A rural environment is prized for its access to open spaces and the natural landscape, but it may be difficult for people to access. See Figure 5.7 for a comparison of the three settings in the context of density.

Site-Specific versus "Siteless"

Most projects are called "site-specific" because they are designed with a particular site in mind. But not all projects have a site. If you are designing a prototype or an interior space that can be applicable in more than one location, you may have a "siteless" project and would have to provide for general site conditions, but not for conditions that are specific to any particular area. For example, if you are designing emergency housing that can be shipped to a disaster area, your project would be independent of the site.

Figure 5.7
Relative population density of the built environment differentiates the building patterns in rural, suburban, and urban regions.

Surrounding Influences: Regional, Locale, Site, and Building

Research for interior design involves assembling and analyzing a series of complex relationships and connections. As referenced by Roberto Rengel (2007), the architect Cesar Pelli identifies at least eight:

1. Connections with the times
2. Construction techniques and practices
3. Place
4. Purpose
5. Culture
6. Design process
7. A project's constituents
8. Oneself.

In addition to these overall concepts, each individual location, building, or structure is rooted in a unique context—made up from the climatic conditions to the cultural settings. Each site is governed by an **Authority Having Jurisdiction (AHJ)**, the office, department, or person responsible for implementing and enforcing local codes. For your research interests about a particular project site, what do you think constitutes a thorough understanding of its environment and context? Imagine that the interior space is nestled within a series of concentric boundaries: within a structure (building shell); which is inside a property line (the building site); surrounded by a larger sphere of influence, such as a district or area (the locale); which is in a larger, politically demarcated, or economic sphere (the region). How far away from the building should you start gathering information? Figure 5.8 provides a

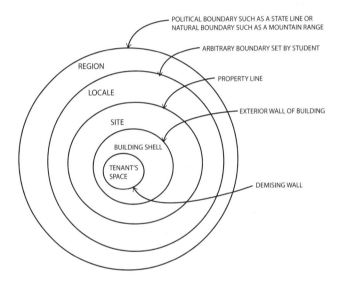

Figure 5.8
The project context as a series of concentric circles.

visual to help your visualize your site within a series of concentric circumstances. Table 5.2 serves as a menu of options from which to choose site information sources.

Get a sense of the **context** or the neighborhood. Who lives there? Anthropological information includes all aspects of human life: how people live, what they think, their customs and lifestyles. You may want to know about the culture (or cultures), local customs, lifestyle, and religious beliefs of people living in the region. Regional areas are often defined by boundaries, such as a city limit or state line—a formal legal border that would allow you to start your search for information by gathering political, social, and economic data. You can begin to collect statistical **demographic** information about the inhabitants of the region, such

Table 5.2 Site Information Sources

What	How	Where Do You Find It?
Regional	Maps Census Descriptive Text	Library Internet Travel Books History Books Articles
Locale	Satellite Images Direct Observation	Google Earth On location
The Building Site	Site Plan Direct Observation	Owner, Designer, Real Estate Agent, or local Building Department Records Office On location
Within Building Shell	As-Built Documents Field Measurements	Owner, Designer, Real Estate Agent, or local Building Department Records Office On location

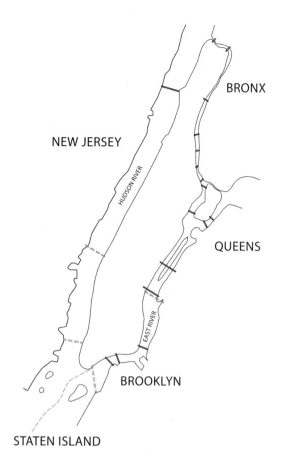

Figure 5.9
A regional view of the island of Manhattan reveals the natural edges or boundaries of the surrounding rivers and the man-made bridges and tunnels that provide access from the surrounding boroughs.

as their language, age, occupations, family structure, and income level.

Geographic information includes boundaries, the local climate, topography, and natural resources. The **topographic** features that determine the growth of the area include the shape of the visible landscape, including mountains, cliffs, valleys, forests, and bodies of water. Other physical regional information includes local industries, food sources, and man-made features such as transportation hubs like airports, ports, and train stations.

If a project is in Manhattan, you would look at maps of New York City. Manhattan is surrounded by the Hudson River to the west and the East River to the east. Noting these physical boundaries, you can start to understand the various ways that commuters travel into the city via bridges, tunnels, and ferry lines; this, in turn, can help you select a site based on ease of access. A regional view of the island of Manhattan reveals the natural edges or boundaries of the surrounding rivers and the man-made bridges and tunnels that provide access from the surrounding boroughs (see Figure 5.9).

A site in New York City relies heavily on public transportation and pedestrian (walking) traffic. Where is the nearest bus stop or subway station? In what direction does the traffic flow? What is the zoning (commercial, industrial, or residential)? This kind of information is essential to finding out whether your

project would even be allowed in the location you have selected. Regional information gives a broad understanding of an area socially, economically, and geographically.

The following is a list of items or issues you may want to look at within the boundaries of the region:

- *Natural resources/products of the region*
- *(Potential) Sources of pollution*—Industrial areas
- *Natural hazards*—*seismic* (earthquake zone) or flood plain
- *Cultural/historic implications*—Past inhabitants, former uses of the region, political struggles, cultural significance of region
- *Current regional ecosystem*—Economic influence of the region on surrounding regions
- *Demographics*—Languages, ethnicities, ages, income levels, education levels, values

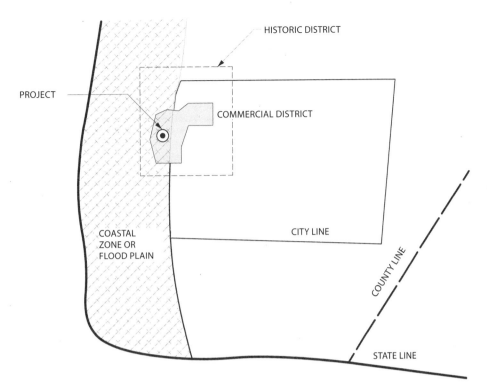

Figure 5.10
A project site may be embedded within a series of overlapping zones or districts related to natural and man-made boundaries.

- *Neighborhood/quality of life issues*—Local landmarks, sources of community pride or lack of pride, gangs, local community centers
- *Zoning*—Is the area zoned for commercial use, industrial use, or residential use? See Figure 5.10 for an example of a site in the midst of overlapping zones and other types of districts, boundaries, and areas.

When seeking information about a region, you will probably want to start with primary sources such as maps. There are several useful types of map, and each type presents different information. Most maps include a compass rose, which indicates the directions north, south, east, and west. Most maps also include a scale so you can estimate distances. Here's a look at some different types of maps:

- **Climate maps** give general information about the climate and precipitation (rain and snow) of a region. Cartographers, or mapmakers, use colors to show different climate or precipitation zones.
- **Economic or resource maps** feature the type of natural resources or economic activity that dominates an area. Symbols are used to indicate the kind of resource or product that is manufactured

there. For example, oranges on a map of Florida tell you that oranges are grown there. Business Improvement Districts (BIDs) use economic resource maps to impart a vision intended to improve business in the area.

- **Physical maps** illustrate the physical features of an area, such as its mountains, rivers, and lakes. The water is usually shown in blue. Colors are used to show *relief*, topography, mountains or land features, or differences in land elevations. Typically, shades of green are used to show lower elevations, and shades of orange or brown indicate higher elevations.
- **Road maps** show major—and some minor—highways as well as roads, airports, railroad tracks, cities, and other points of interest in an area. Interior designers would use this kind of map primarily to create the *vicinity map* for the cover sheet of the construction document set. Building officials use vicinity maps to determine zoning, and contractors use them for driving directions to find the project's location during the construction phase. It is important not to confuse a vicinity map with a site plan, which will be discussed later in this chapter.

- **Topographic maps** use contour lines to show the shape and elevation of an area. Lines that are close together indicate steep terrain, and lines that are far apart indicate flat terrain (Fact Monster, 2007).
- **Satellite Imagery** at the Google Earth Web site offers maps and satellite images for complex or pinpointed regional searches. The images allow you to see characteristics of the neighborhood that traditional maps cannot—such as shadows cast by adjacent buildings, the quality of open spaces, and possible views. The Web site's tools allow you to search for public amenities such as schools, parks, restaurants, hotels, and public transportation hubs.
- **Zoning and Land Use Maps** are an indispensable tool for urban planning. According to the New York City Department of City Planning Web site, "Zoning shapes the city" (NYC DCP, 2009). **Zoning** primarily determines two important things that can affect your project: (1) allowed **occupancies** or *uses* of buildings in a particular area (Residential, Commercial, Industrial, etc.) and (2) the **density** (number of people per square unit of land) or **bulk** (number of square feet allowed to be built on a particular lot). District regulations may also apply that control specific characteristics of a neighborhood, such as the materials that can be used on a building's façade, the number of parking spaces required, the amount of open space required, and the minimum distance required between buildings. Ordinarily, an architect would be responsible for obtaining this kind of information for a new building, but if the project is a tenant improvement or adaptive reuse project, an interior designer may be called upon to collect this kind of data.
- A **Sanborn Map** is a kind of historical map that was created for cities during the late 1800s and early 1900s. Scaled at 50 feet to 1 inch (1:600), these maps contain an enormous amount of information, including outlines of each building, building heights, property boundaries, street names, location of utilities such as sewers, and even the names of such public buildings as schools and churches. These maps are found primarily in archives and special collections in public and university libraries, but sometimes they are available in city offices as well (Sanborn Fire Insurance Maps, 2003).

Maps, of course, will not tell you everything you want to know about a region. For demographic information such as number of people, ages of people, and income levels, you will want to look at census data, which is available at www.census.gov. This Web site contains many powerful tools for collecting statistical data on your region, including population growth and other demographic trends, special maps, and articles related to demographics that highlight trends across the country. Which city is the fastest growing? Which city has the largest percentage of women with college degrees? Which city has the largest percentage of people living below the U.S. poverty level? Statistics are an important tool to use when determining the ideal region in which to set your project, or they can act as supplemental data to support the choice of site.

You can also find regional site information on some real estate Web sites such as *Zillow*, *Realtor.com*, and *Trulia*, which provide socioeconomic *vignettes*: holistic, multifaceted neighborhood profiles that provide a snapshot of the life of the area. Information includes cost of living, school statistics, crime rate, and local climate/weather. Demographic data include median age, marital status, unemployment rates, political affiliations, and education levels of inhabitants.

Psychographic variables are any attributes relating to personality, values, attitudes, interests, social class, or lifestyles. They are also called IAO variables (for "Interests, Attitudes, and Opinions"). They can be contrasted with demographic variables (such as age and gender) and behavioral variables (such as crime rate and education level). Psychographic profiles are used in marketing applications and advertising. This kind of information, along with other pertinent household information, allows you to formulate a qualitative, subjective description of the place.

Other secondary sources, such as *Scoutred.com* and *Property I.D.*, collect and organize a variety of information from a **municipality**, or local government agencies such as city-based archives, building department records, and property tax assessor documents. Occasionally, secondary sources will be more relevant or easier to digest than data from a more primary source such as a map or government census documents.

Once you have collected data on the region, focus on the more immediate area surrounding the project. The radius around the site varies from project to project. For a rural site along a river, for example, you may want to look at all adjacent properties for possible sources of view, noise, or pollution. This area could be a mile or so in diameter. For a suburban site, the area might be just the radius of one block in all directions for the sources of view, noise, or pollution. For the urban site, it may be more critical to study the height or use of the buildings directly adjacent to your site. The following is a list of items or issues you may want to look at within the boundaries of the locale:

- *Landscaping*—Hardscape (concrete, stone, brick, and paving that must pitch to a drain) versus landscape (grass lawns, soil, and vegetation that permits natural water permeation)
- *Water and wind*—proximity to bodies of water and prevailing winds
- *Adjacent uses*—Compatibility of uses of nearby properties
- *Adjacent structures*—Their height and configuration
- *Adjacent tenants*—Thoughts of people living or working nearby who may be affected by development of the site
- *Utilities infrastructure*—Water, sewer, electricity
- *Traffic types and patterns*—Pedestrian/car/public transportation.
- *(Potential) Sources of pollution*—Noise, odors, and other nonvisual qualities.

Since the site's locale involves a smaller area than the regional area, designers usually find this information by direct observation techniques, site-specific behavioral mapping (discussed in Chapter 8), and detailed photographic surveys. Also, since the population of a locale is more limited, you can distribute questionnaires to adjacent residents or business owners to gather demographic information or check out the public's opinion in the immediate vicinity. You can obtain sensory qualitative data such as views, odors, and noise by direct observation and descriptive journals. For this kind of qualitative data, you may want to wander through the neighborhood by car, bus, or bicycle or on foot, using unstructured or structured observation techniques and plenty of photographs, sketches, and textual descriptions. Figure 5.11 shows an interior design researcher's representation of a neighborhood after studying the locale.

Data collection within property boundaries includes documenting and exploring the existing conditions of the property to be developed, expanded (an addition), renovated (a tenant improvement), retrofitted

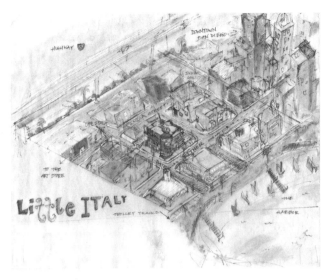

Figure 5.11
In this sketched view of "Little Italy" in San Diego, designer Leanna Wolff highlights a few elements which make up the locale, cultural character of a neighborhood.

for a new use (an adaptive reuse), or demolished. Construction documents can be obtained from a variety of sources depending on the building's type and age and the record-keeping habits of the previous owner. The following is a list of items or issues you may want to look at within the boundaries of the building site (see Figure 5.12 as an example):

- Existing structures within property lines—This includes buildings, outbuildings, storage sheds, garages, and other structures. This information would be found on a site plan, sometimes referred to as a *plot plan*.
- Existing natural and man-made site features—The locations of trees, rock formations, ponds, paths, and other such features should be documented.
- Existing access and entry points into the site—including curb cuts and driveways, fences, walls, and pedestrian walks.
- ADA/Universal Design—Accessibility to front entrance, height of curbs, path of travel from Accessible Parking to Accessible spaces, existing changes in level that may require a ramp or an elevator.
- Parking—This can be determined from the site plan.
- Building orientation with respect to *compass direction* and *sun path* to predict potential heat gain, glare, and how shadows will be cast. You can obtain this information by looking at satellite imagery

with a *north arrow* or *compass rose* and then tracking the sun's movement using a solar chart. Many computer modeling software programs simulate the sun's movement by entering the location's latitude, calendar date, and time. This is commonly called a *solar or shadow study*. A shareware software program that creates sun path diagrams can be downloaded from: http://solardat.uoregon.edu/PolarSunChartProgram.html.

- Views.
- Maintenance considerations/trash removal/deliveries.
- Use and abuse considerations—All buildings are subject to deterioration, whether by natural causes or man-made ones.
- Flexibility considerations including the amount of open space on the property that can be used for expansion of/additions to the existing building. This includes collecting data on required setbacks, easements, and elements on the property.

Usually, a set of plans for a building have been prepared according to prescribed professional standards upheld by design practitioners, but not always. As a conscientious designer, you must conduct a **field survey** to document the existing building conditions visually and with a tape measure, to determine the accuracy of the as-built drawings. But generally, the as-built plans are essential to include in your data-gathering and for your preliminary analysis of the site. Ideally, in terms of a base building plan, what you want is an editable CAD file that can be immediately opened and used. You may be able to obtain a native design document from its original source, the design firm that created it. With a little research, you may be able to locate the architect or designer and obtain the firm's written permission to use the file in your school project. Even if you can obtain this kind of file, you may want to ascertain the accuracy of the drawings by conducting a field survey and taking your own accurate measurements of the building.

Oftentimes, buildings are not built exactly as called for in the plan. Other times, a design firm will issue "as-built" plans that reflect how the building was eventually built. Keep in mind that the design firm may not want to release the file to you due to cost and liability. These CAD files are protected by copyright law, which prohibits their use without the express written permission of the author of the original document. Be respectful when requesting this type of document and

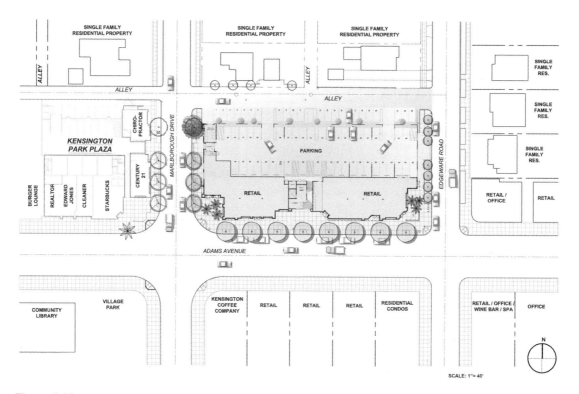

Figure 5.12
Site plan shows property boundaries, access to site, and surrounding buildings as well as site amenities such as parking, landscape, hardscape, usually drawn to an engineering scale, such as 1"=10' or smaller. A north symbol is typically included as well.

emphasize that you are using the file only for a school project and not for profit.

If you cannot obtain the editable CAD file, the next best thing would be the blueprints or copies of the construction documents. For most commercial sites, these documents would be part of the public record, kept by the local building or planning department in their records department. These documents can be located by their address or block/lot number and can be viewed via microfiche. Sometimes you can get printed copies. Again, the copyright laws protect the original designer, so in many cases you will be asked to fill out a form requesting the original designer's permission to copy the files. Allow time for this process to occur, as it can take up to thirty days. If these documents are not available through the city's records department, brainstorm about who might have these documents. Contractors, consultants who worked on the project, the building's owner or property management company may have them. If the property is for sale or lease, the real estate agent or leasing agent may have floor plans. If none of these sources has the information you need, here are a few questions to ask yourself:

- Is the building historically significant? If it is, you may want to try your local historical society.
- Is the building part of the city's infrastructure of public services, such as a firehouse or a building within a city-operated park? Some city agencies maintain records of their own buildings and would be able to supply you with a copy.
- As a last resort, most public buildings are required to have an **emergency egress plan**, *fire escape plan*, *building exit plan*, or *evacuation plan* posted in public view. See Figure 5.13 for an example of an emergency egress plan that would give you an idea of the shape of the building and the location of elevators, stairs, and exits. If you can get access to this by taking a photo, you can use it as a starting point for creating your own documents, supplemented with field measurements.

Tips on Field Measurements

Even if you can get a complete set of construction documents, you should double-check the information in the documents against the actual field measurements to verify the accuracy of the as-built plans. Professional designers may refer to the information on the existing plans that were prepared by previous designers,

Figure 5.13
Emergency Egress Plan typically found in public view in all buildings of public accommodation which can serve as a starting point for your analysis of the existing building.

architects, and engineers, but they are legally responsible for generating their own drawings based on field measurements taken by themselves or their staff.

There is an industry-specific, prescribed way to document existing conditions on a field survey. First, have a team of at least two people, if not three, each with a designated job.

- One person will be responsible for notations.
- The other two will do the measurements with a tape measure.
  - One person will be responsible for holding the end of the tape measure and calling out what he is holding it next to ("to wall," "to door opening," "from sill to floor").
  - The person at the other end of the tape measure will be responsible for calling out the numerical value in a consistent format. Decide, in advance, whether it will be in units of inches or feet-and-inches (centimeters or meters-and-centimeters) and try not to mix the two.

The person responsible for recording the measurements should decide which will be easier to interpret or which will be easier to enter into the computer when drafting (note: inches tend to work better than feet-and-inches). Many professional firms have replaced the traditional tape measure with laser measuring devices that give precise lengths. Laser measuring tools are digital hand-held devices that enable the team to avoid errors due to measuring around obstacles. Many are under $50 and quickly pay for themselves with saved time on site.

Use a mechanical pencil with an eraser. A mechanical pencil needs no sharpening; just make sure you have enough lead. Use 8.5″ × 11″-inch or 11″ × 17″-inch graph paper to sketch out each floor plan to fit on its own sheet of paper. Even better would be to put a sheet of graph paper underneath a sheet of vellum on a large clipboard and do your sketching on that. Pick one spot as the origin and use that spot to originate all of the measurements for that wall. In a multiple-story building, the spot should be structurally consistent on all floors. The following are standard abbreviations:

- M.O.   Masonry Opening
- W.H.   Window Height
- S.H.   Sill Height
- C.L.   Centerline
- B.O.   Bottom Of
- O.A.   Over All
- C.H.   Ceiling Height
- A.F.F.   Above Finished Floor.

It is usual to measure to the centerline of a window and then measure the width of the window. Another industry standard is to put ceiling heights in an oval. List objects measured in a consistent order; first by length, then by width, and finally by height. Wear protective clothing and comfortable shoes or boots. (You never know the condition of the existing building. You may find yourself crawling into a dusty attic or wading through unexpected ponds on the roof.) Figure 5.14 is an example of a field measurements document you might create.

As an interior designer, you are looking to collect data on existing conditions of the physical aspects of the building as well as the subjective or experiential ones, to determine constraints, possibilities, and sources of inspiration for your design. For example, determining which walls are load-bearing and which walls are non-load-bearing will be essential for determining the ease of potential reconfiguration of the space at minimal cost or disruption. Determining the locations of existing plumbing fixtures as well as the sanitary drain locations will allow you to later make informed decisions about possible locations of new fixtures at a minimal cost. You'll want to consider *quantitative* information, such as the number of windows (quantity), the sill height of windows (numerical measurement), or an *area take-off*, an activity often performed as part of flooring estimation to determine square foot areas of materials, as shown in Figure 5.15. These are examples of physical constraints and useful sizes for the purpose of comparison. There are equally important *qualitative* information items to document, such as the quality of the light (natural and artificial), temperature, ventilation, humidity, acoustics, and ergonomics of the space.

Part of site documentation could include taking an inventory of existing furniture, fixtures, and equipment—including historic elements or materials to be preserved, relocated, and reused or to be removed for salvage. For a designer who had the opportunity to turn an old farmhouse in Maryland into a bed and breakfast, **FF&E Inventory** (catalog of the furnishing, fixtures, and equipment) constituted a bound book

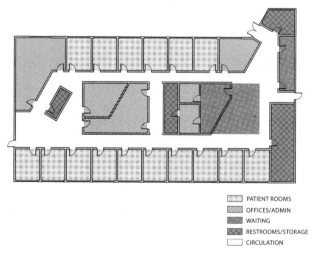

Figure 5.15
An example of an *area take-off* quantifying square foot areas designated for patient rooms, administrative offices, waiting area, restroom/storage, and circulation in a health clinic floor plan.

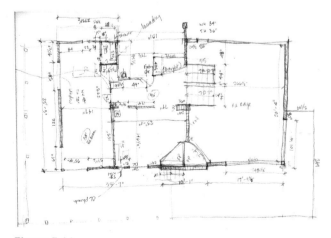

Figure 5.14
Example of building measurements recorded on a physical site survey (image by author).

of all the existing furnishings. Each furnishing had a separate page dedicated to it. The page included a photograph, a text description, dimensions (length × width × height), and an evaluation of the condition of the piece. Each piece of furniture was assigned a key number. Later, during the design process, the designer was able to incorporate the pieces into the furniture layout, labeled with the corresponding key code. She was also able to use the inventory document to determine the budget, basing estimates on how many pieces needed to be refinished and the extent of the refurbishment. Having this level of detail available helped the designer when she had to determine yardage for those pieces that needed to be reupholstered, and also helped her determine whether the remaining unused pieces could be sold to local antique shops.

A building is not just a structure; it is a collection of building systems. **Building systems** can be visualized like various systems in the human body. As in the human body, the systems are usually dependent on each other to perform their assigned functions. Imagine the building as a living thing—say, a very large animal. The **structural system** is like the animal's skeleton, holding the building up and giving it its underlying form. The skeleton or framework may be apparent on the exterior, as for a crab or a starfish, or hidden, as in a human being. The bones of the building may be steel, concrete, or wood members connected in such a way as to transfer the loads all the way to the earth. The fundamental (and often hidden) structural system of a building is the foundation. Foundation systems can be shallow, composed of a slab on grade, a crawl space, or a basement. Deep foundations include piles and caissons.

Structural framing systems are usually made of steel, wood, concrete, or masonry units, which utilize a series of load-bearing walls or columns. How do you determine the existing structural system? The easiest way is to sit down with an architect or an engineer and review the as-built plans and sections to identify the structural system. Is a particular building's structural system a steel frame with glass curtain walls? Or is it composed of cast-in-place concrete load-bearing walls? Perhaps it has large overhead trusses or deep beams that span long distances and rest on columns. About those columns: Regardless of the material the columns are made of, it is important to identify the column grid. You may be able to look at existing floor plans and sections to determine the column grid. Measure the

distance between columns to determine the **column bays**. Why would the column bays or column-spacing be important? Column-spacing establishes a rhythm in the building. A good interior designer understands this rhythm and plans the new walls or furniture systems to fit within this grid. The existence of columns also limits what kinds of functions can take place in the room. For example, a building that has a column every 20 feet will not be able to accommodate an indoor soccer field. If the column grid is not clearly identifiable, you may need to consult a structural engineer to determine which walls are load-bearing and which ones are non-load-bearing interior partitions.

Structural systems have a meaning that is not only functional but also historical and cultural. While it is important to understand the physical limitations of the structure, it is also a good idea to collect data on the cultural associations or historical origins of the structural system or spatial configuration. For example, a hacienda-style house has its roots in a Mexican traditional way of life, and the materials used—wood and plaster—have been selected because they are readily available in the region and they respond well to the climate. Islamic architecture utilizes towers—iconic "minarets"—as well as wind scoops as part of the natural ventilation system. Columns and arches in Islamic architecture also have cultural meanings that go well beyond the physical properties of holding up the structure.

Once you have identified all the structural components, you must analyze the building for possibilities and constraints. Measure the usable floor area. Usable floor area excludes the thickness of walls or uninhabitable shafts for plumbing. Measure the size of the windows and the width of the window mullions. Would you be able to put an interior partition between two existing windows? Identify stair and elevator locations and the existing corridors leading to building exits. Look at the section of the building to determine the existing ceiling heights and any structural elements that are not visible on the floor plan.

The other systems operate within the structural framework. A building breathes: it takes in outside air and gives off exhaust air. The respiratory system of a building is its form of ventilation, which is natural (through open windows, louvers, and vents) or mechanically operated (through ducts and HVAC equipment). A building also has a circulatory system, to keep it warm or cool, and a plumbing system, to carry hot and cold water in and out. It has muscles that allow it to move goods or people through it via conveyance systems such as stairs and elevators. A building's nervous system is its electrical system, as well as its security system or fire alarm system that alerts the building to potential danger. A final analogy is that the building has a skin: a cladding system that encloses the structure to make the spaces truly interior and to regulate the temperature, mitigate the effects of weather, and protect the inhabitants from rain, wind, unwanted intruders, and other environmental factors. A designer must consider each of these systems when evaluating the building for a potential use, as in a feasibility study.

Site Analysis

In landscape design, "the end product of the site analysis phase of the design process is a composite analysis map (sometimes referred to as an opportunities and constraints sheet). This is developed through an overlay process … delineating the most suitable and least suitable areas of the site for each analysis factor" (McBride, 2006). Beyond the functional aspects of a site, both physical and social, there are arguably intangible qualities of a site that may be explored by a design researcher within the creative paradigm. Unseen, immaterial qualities have been felt, explored, and analyzed by a variety of past and present cultures such as the practice of *feng shui*, *genius loci*, or *Vastu*. Trying Activity 5.2 will help you capture some of these palpable qualities using methods proposed by contemporary theorists' perspectives. You may want to explore others as well.

In *A Place of my Own: The Architecture of Daydreams*, author Michael Pollan documented in poetic prose his process of designing and building a place for himself. Trying to find the exact location for a small writing hut in the natural setting of his backyard, Pollan wrote about using multiple site analysis practices, and looking at the landscape from various perspectives. After his review of the existing literature on the subject (secondary sources) in the first couple of chapters, three main categories (domain areas) emerged. He realized he could choose the best location using the perspective of *scientist*, *artist*, or *mystic*. He tried all of them and recognized that all three perspectives arrived on a single location.

Pollan (2008) reflected, "At first it seemed uncanny to me that the three different perspectives I'd tried out on my site could have overlapped so closely" (p. 51). As the act of building unfolds, Pollan described his firsthand engagement with the process (primary sources) as well social interaction with the other characters: the architect, the framer, his wife, and the building itself (original data collection methods of interview and observation). We can understand, from this example, that knowledge can come to us from many sources and in many forms in the creative paradigm of research. If you enjoy Activity 5.2, consider trying the strategies offered by theorist Jane Rendell on her interactive website entitled *Site Writings* (https://www.janerendell.co.uk/), read Tim Ingold's book *The Perception of the Environment* published in 2000, and consider exercises outlined in Mark Allen Hewitt's book, *Draw in Order to See*, published in 2020.

Activity 5.2
Analyzing a Place Through Sensory Awareness

Purpose: This activity enables you to better understand a setting by adopting perspectives of "user-experts" to foster a sense of empathy, broadening awareness through movement, and engaging your senses.

Landscape architect Lawrence Halprin and choreographer Anna Halprin used an organizing tool for site familiarization with origins in dance notation (Halprin, 1970). Applying the concept of a musical "score" to the movement of individuals within and through a built environment, they found, opened

the investigator to observations and experiences that could easily be overlooked in a traditional *reconnaissance* (site survey). This, in turn, can lead to new questions, or nuanced sub-questions enhancing one's understanding of the design context.

This activity, adapted from Halprin's "City Map" score (Halprin, 1970, p. 81), enables you to heighten your awareness of all sensory inputs (not just sights, but sounds, smells, textures, the weather, your own sense of movement, and the rhythm of others' comings and goings) as you complete each step. It includes role-playing (you can use the roles suggested below or invent your own); approach it in a spirit of playfulness and discovery. Proceed on foot, sketchbook in hand. Record notes and drawings (no photos on this trip) of your activities and feelings.

Step One: Starting Point: The nearest public transit facility or car park. Imagine you are in a theme park. What narrative is this environment communicating? Record each feature around you that supports the themed "story."

Step Two: Find the nearest convenience store or supermarket to locate and purchase a portable lunch (including a light dessert). Imagine you are in a wheelchair or using another type of mobility device. How do you envision the difficulties faced by someone in this situation? Make a note of your interaction with the clerk, your check-out procedure, and how those may be impacted by a disability or impairment.

Step Three: Walk to the site, imagining the trip as a ritual procession. Sketch the features of your starting point, any "edges" that define your route, and "landmarks" or "districts" that you encounter along the way (see the discussion of Lynch's elements of Wayfinding in Chapter 2).

Step Four: When the site comes into view, stop, find a place to sit, and eat the lunch you purchased. Close your eyes for a few minutes simulating a visual impairment. What are your senses (other than vision) telling you about the place? Sketch your experience of place from the sensations of smell, sound, and touch. From which direction can you sense the warmth of the sun? What sounds of traffic indicate the position of streets and sidewalk? What scents indicate site amenities such as a coffee shop or flower market?

Step Five: Stand and face the sun. Note time of day, season, and position of the sun in terms of compass direction. Walk the rest of the way to the site entrance in silence. Now, imagine you are a job applicant on your way to the site for an employment interview. How does the approach, façade, and entry appear to someone who is seeking to work there? Sketch these elements.

Step Six: Enter and greet the first person you encounter. Do they speak your language or share similar cultural traits? Make a note of how they respond. Find a window from which you can see outside. Sketch the view. What does the view tell you about the neighborhood or locale?

Step Seven: After a walkthrough of the interior, depart the building as if you are the owner. Take your leave of, or otherwise say goodbye to others with this in your mind. Find a place to stop and enjoy your dessert. Reflect on your trip before returning to the transit stop or your car.

This activity uses role-playing to disassociate you from your role as "designer" and see the setting from different perspectives. Your hand-sketches may carry traces of your emotional response to the experience in a way that a photograph would not. Were you able to get into the attitudes suggested in each step? How did these roles influence your perceptions of the site? Share your experiences and record of the site visit with your colleagues in class.

Interior design has a few diagramming techniques especially for helping with the analytic process that precedes schematic design. It is dangerous to jump from data collection to schematic design without an intermediate step of analysis. That intermediate, analytic step is the interpretation of the data collected, which sometimes involves multiple overlays of diagrams. Using an overlay technique, begin your *site analysis diagrams* with what you know; then continue to add layers of information. These layers of information will eventually become more speculative than factual. There is a moment when documentation becomes interpretation, and the diagramming will help you reach a design solution during the schematic phase.

It is important to document your findings in a visual form, through diagrams. Figure 5.16 presents a layered diagram highlighting the structural constraints, circulation pattern, plumbing locations, natural light and views in the design process as a transition from information documentation to analysis. Start by identifying the structural elements (columns and walls) that would be difficult, or even structurally infeasible, to remove. You can begin to develop your own "language" through color, hatch patterns, and symbols. For example, you could mark the structural elements with a red marker. Then, identify existing plumbing locations, perhaps using a blue hatch to indicate plumbing walls and areas around piping, including the shafts and vents that contain the unseen piping. If the interior has other physical aspects that you want to document—such as condition of finishes, the feeling of the space, the view from the space—you can use color, hatch patterns, or text to communicate the site condition. The goal of these analyses is to identify the constraints or limitations of the site as well as its potential or possibilities.

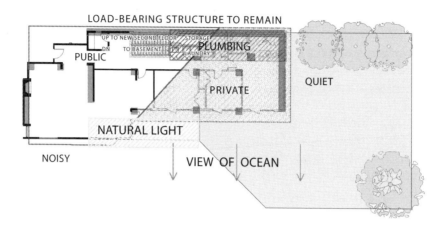

Figure 5.16
Example of a layered analytical diagram over an existing floor plan showing load-bearing elements, plumbing walls, natural light and views, as well as dividing the plan functionally into public and private areas.

Activity 5.3
Analyzing the Site for Constraints and Possibilities

Purpose: To practice analyzing an existing site condition graphically (through a series of overlay diagrams) and a text summary of possibilities and constraints.

Visit a local public space connected in some way with your research question or topic. It could be a restaurant, reception area or lobby, a museum, shopping mall, school, theater, religious institution, or someone's home. Sketch the floor plan. Document the space with additional photographs or video. On the sketched floor plan show:

1. Components of the structural systems (columns and load-bearing walls) using a *red* marker.

2. "Wet" areas (existing sinks, toilets, walls containing plumbing system elements) of the building using a *blue* marker.

3. Areas that receive natural sunlight/daylight with a *yellow* highlighter.

4. "Quiet" versus "noisy" (based on perceived sound levels) with two different *gray* hatch patterns.

5. "Active" versus "passive" area based on kind of activity with two different *green* hatch patterns. For example, activities such as reading, writing, studying, sleeping, or listening to lectures would be passive, while activities using gross motor movements, such as running, playing, or exercising, would be active.

6. Public, semi-public, and private areas regarding the existing traffic patterns (visitors and staff) or identified program areas. Use three different *purple* hatch patterns to differentiate.

7. Provide a legend to identify all hatch patterns and colors.

8. Pedestrian and/or vehicular traffic patterns. Mark all entry points with *bold arrows*.

9. Identify the view(s). In what direction are the views? And what do you see (for example, a park, an eye-catching wall mural, a distant mountain …).

10. Write a summary of what the site analysis diagrams revealed to you about the possibilities and constraints of the site:
    - *Feeling of the site*, inside and out (qualities of the space, including sounds, smells, safety issues, emotion)
    - *Neighborhood* and regional context (demographics, adjacent uses)
    - *Exterior and site conditions* (the style or character of the building, location of parking or pedestrian walkways)
    - *Interior configuration* (structural system and other interior building systems).

Create an existing conditions report focusing on the feeling of the site, the neighborhood, the exterior and site conditions, or the interior configuration. When you have finished, create a PowerPoint or other presentation that documents your findings. Present it to the class.

RESEARCH IN ACTION 5.2
A Sample Existing Conditions Report By Student

By Sara Plaisted

The document a student of interior design would be asked to produce is a written research paper that includes a textual summary of the information gathered about the site, along with visuals including photos, maps, and other research data. The following is one student's existing conditions report for her thesis project:

After researching three possible locations for a mixed-use project in Barrio Logan, I have concluded that the building is best facing west on a corner for maximum sun and prospect exposure. Two of the three possible sites either had a commercial coffee house or housing. The site I chose is located a little further east than I originally wanted, but the limitations the site presents are inspiring. There are options for parking if the empty lots are developed or the site is structurally sound to construct underground parking. I had originally planned to include a market in one of the three retail spaces; however, by surveying the neighborhood I found a very large market within walking distance down the street.

Absorbing the texture of the neighborhood, I found much inspiration for my design: metal, rust, concrete, wood, steel, chain link fencing, shipping containers in the nearby port, cars (headlights, tires, mirrors, grill, exhaust pipes, etc.), the railroad tracks, the Coronado Bridge floating just above eye level, local art.

- The site is located on the Northeast corner of Beardsley and National in Barrio Logan in what some may consider a run-down poor area, south of downtown.
- The site faces directly West with other corner views South.
- The site is currently occupied by what appears to be a place for car detailing, with a small "office" structure in the back of the site and a small Mexican food take-out restaurant [about 25 ft. wide by 100 ft. deep].
    - Sign for the car detailer says "Ye Olde Towne Pump."
- The site is about 100 ft. wide by 100 ft. deep, with an additional section in the back left behind the Mexican food place, at about 25 ft. wide by 50 ft. deep, totaling 11,250 sq. ft. for the lot.
- An alley is located directly behind the site.
- A house is located just behind the site in the upper right corner and takes up 50 additional ft. deep and 100 ft. wide.
    - 2 large oak trees are in the back right corner of the site.
- A bus stop is located directly in front of the site.
- The site is located 2 blocks West from the off-ramp of the 5 Fwy. South.
- East of the site [directly behind and across the alley] is an open lot with construction pending.
- South of the site [across the street] is a parking lot.
- Diagonally across the street [South-West] is the fairly new Family Health Clinic.

- Directly across [West] is a small market and juice stop, along with what appear to be office spaces.

- Adjacent to the left [North] is an open lot with junk cars. Beyond that are houses and a new apartment/condo building.

Most of the housing and buildings are old and somewhat run-down. There are many produce outlets, junk yards, and old housing with bars on the windows. Some parts of the area are starting to develop and new construction, businesses, and residencies are springing up.

- Down the block [South] is a large market with fresh fruits and vegetables and delicious tamales.

- Down the block [West] is a new hip bar/restaurant called The Guild that many artists frequent.

- Across from The Guild is an elementary school.

- On Cesar Chavez Blvd., 2 large lots are being prepared for the development of the Mercado del Barrio. Currently 2 bids are underway to develop multi-level affordable housing, a large market, theatre, street venues, retail space, park, and art space directly under the bridge, further expanding Chicano Park.

- A Fire Station is located on the corner of National and Cesar Chavez.

- On the corner of Cesar Chavez and Main, there is a large, open-air café with a local coffee roaster in the back.

- Catty-corner from there is the famous Chewy's Restaurant.

- Next to Chewy's on Cesar Chavez and Harbor is the Trolley Stop.

- Chicano Park is directly under the bridge and is known for the murals on the columns supporting the bridge, and for the outdoor space. Much of the artwork reflects the Hispanic point of view of those living in the area for almost a century. Such notable pieces include the comment on the toxins that the industrial companies release into the air, contaminating those who live in the area.

- The bridge is massive and very much a part of the everyday view of the people who live in and frequent this neighborhood.

- Views north are directly into downtown, with a view from Main Street right into Petco Park.

- Graham Downes' *Blokhaus* is located down the street with a cool hair salon and restaurant nearby.

Barrio Logan does have a reputation for being a little unsavory and dangerous, as it is on the poorer socioeconomic side north of the bridge. Closer to downtown is a bit nicer and more ideal for this project. The City of San Diego has been working to create the re-development of the "City of Villages," and within the next few years the area will start to improve. For now, it is prime time to move in and invest and help to better the neighborhood and bring culture and the arts in and improve the quality of the area. See below for a composite photo showing the site.

Student's composite photo of her site for a mixed-use thesis project.

DEVELOPING A CLIENT AND END-USER PROFILE

The *client* is the person who would hire an interior designer and/or provides the funding for your project. In the professional world, the client typically comes to you. When you are developing an academic project, however, unless the instructor provides you with a client, it is up to you to decide who that person or group of people might be. When seeking out a client for your thesis, ask yourself, "Who would be willing to invest in what I am proposing?" For example, if you are creating a women's shelter, your client might be the *American Red Cross*. If you are designing a museum, your client might be the *Smithsonian Institution*. Your client could be an individual, such as Oprah Winfrey; a company, such as GAP; an organization; a government agency; an institution, such as a university; or a foundation, such as the Getty Foundation.

Regardless of size or visibility, the client is the ultimate decision-maker for the project, so you will most likely include them in your study. Interviews will be discussed in detail in Chapter 6. You will develop questions in order to understand what impact the potential client will have on the project. For example, a recreation center sponsored by Nike is going to have a different design direction (and budget) than one run by a city government or one started by a local businessperson.

The client and the end-user are sometimes the same person, as in the case of a residential project or when a CEO or university president hires you to design their personal office. Some of the most dynamic thesis projects are those in which the student has identified a real person to approach as a client and can interview and observe the person and then use this information to develop a very realistic client profile and/or user profile. Most commonly the client is one of many end-users in a project—such as a couple who hires you to design a home for themselves and their five children, in which case they are two of seven end-users. A partner in a law firm might hire you to redesign the firm's offices, in which case the partner would be one end-user while the staff and visitors would be the other end-users. Other times the client is not the end-user.

When you present your design project, critics might point out that, given your client, some furniture or finish selections would be unrealistic. As you select your client, take some time to analyze the resources the individual or organization might have. This does not mean you should automatically select a wealthy client so that you "don't have to worry about budget." Be true to the project and remember that budget is not a limitation but an opportunity to be creative. In today's world, some of the most provocative projects are made from recycled license plates and reclaimed barn wood.

At a minimum, your **client profile** should include:

1. Name of the individual or organization
2. Name of the decision-maker within the organization
3. Logo if applicable
4. Location
5. Company organization and background
6. Budget constraints
7. Previous involvement with similar projects
8. Statement discussing the client's reason for investing in this project
9. Summary of the client's goals, wants, and needs.

Developing a client profile is one task for which the Internet can be especially helpful. You can begin by searching online to brainstorm the options for a project client. Once you have identified a client, there is often a wealth of important information about the client on the Internet, as well as ideas for how and where you might dig deeper. For example, you may learn on a Web site that your client has had books or articles published, so you might track down her publications. Or you might discover that your client's place of business is very near you, so you can arrange a site visit or even an observation session. Many students interview their hypothetical project client to get feedback directly from the source. In this case, the client may even attend the student's final presentation, to offer feedback. If you are not able to get an interview with your client's leaders or other management, there is still a good chance you could talk with another representative of the company or organization. This can be just as valuable, especially if that representative is also part of your user group.

Within a single project you can have great diversity in who will use or visit your project. So how do you determine who they could be, especially when you may need to recruit some actual (or potential) end-users to participate in your study? The best way to start your **end-user profile** is with an attitude of empathy. Empathy goes beyond sympathy in that it is the ability to put yourself "in the other person's shoes" and see things through that person's "lens of experience." Thoughtfully interpret the information you gather about the end-users to help you feel what they feel, see what they see, and experience what they experience. The result of this will be a clear insight into your user's wants and needs. For example, while conducting a photo study of a local hospital, a researcher documented a large clock on the footwall of a patient's room. The researcher's immediate interpretation was that the clock must be very discouraging to the patient as it slowly ticked away the minutes of the day. But a follow-up interview with the patient revealed that the clock was comforting to the patient. If she were hungry, she could see when lunch would arrive; if she was in pain she could see when pain medication would be delivered; and most important, it let her know when her next visitor would arrive. Developing a sensitivity to the needs and wants of your end-user is the heart of human-centered design.

Activity 5.4
Seeking Out the Experts

Purpose: To identify ideal candidates for an interview or groups of people who could be participants in a survey. Considering your research topic, research question, project type, client (if you have one), and your end-user profile, identify three individuals who would be potential interviewees.

1. In one or two sentences, describe the ideal person. Would they be an expert in a particular field? Would they be someone who came up in your literature review? Or would they be a person who has certain experiences that you would like to know more about? For example, if your broad topic is "homelessness," and your research question is, "what do individuals need in the design of a homeless outreach center?" you could consider someone who works at a similar center as an expert, or you may want to interview someone who has experienced homelessness.

2. Find three individuals (or groups or organizations) who fit the description. You can use the Internet or the library, or you can make use of faculty contacts, colleagues where you work, or contacts provided by fellow students. For example, if you are interested in finding out more about the airline industry, you may want to interview an airline employee such as a pilot or a flight attendant. You may be surprised at how quickly you will find that one of your co-workers or classmates knows someone in that industry.

3. Provide the name, qualifications, and contact information (phone number, mailing address, email address, and/or Web site) of each person you may seek to interview.

Interviewee Name	Qualifications or Position	Contact Information
1.		
2.		
3.		

4. For groups of people to serve as potential respondents in a survey, provide the name of the group or organization, the attributes that make these individuals ideal candidates, and contact information for that organization (it could be a group on social media).

Group or Organization Name	Qualifications or Attributes	Contact Information
1.		
2.		
3.		

ETHICAL CONSIDERATIONS

As interior designers, we are familiar with asking people questions, or observing people interacting with their environment to design better spaces for them. However, when scientific research involves human beings, researchers must be careful to avoid inadvertently harming them and respect the rights of all involved in a particular study. According to Moon (2009), "The National Research Act of 1974, passed in response to growing concern about the ethics violations in research, created the National Commission for the Protection of Human Subjects of Biomedical and Behavioral Research" which had three foundational principles: (1) respect for persons, (2) maximize the benefit-to-harm ratio of a study, and (3) justice for all involved.

Our research involves people, but we must take every precaution to make sure that the rights of people we interview, survey, and observe are respected. This may mean maintaining anonymity or confidentiality of each participant, as people have a right to privacy. Some practical ways to implement anonymity in a study is to assign each participant a number or develop a pseudonym for them. Later when you write up your study findings you will let your readers know that these are not the participants' real names. These strategies will be discussed in more detail in future chapters. Always inform people you are interviewing or observing (if they know that they are being observed) that they have the right to stop participating in your study at any time.

At the beginning of an interview, survey, or experiment (or any research method in which people are actively participating), you must identify yourself as a researcher, your institutional affiliation, and the purpose of data collection. You also must get permission from all participants. As you are designing your study, you must be mindful not to put people in embarrassing, awkward, or potentially dangerous situations in which they could be physically, psychologically, or socially harmed. All actively engaging participants should be aware that they are part of a study and that they are valued members, are respected and confident they are contributing to your study. It is important to thank them. Sometimes researchers offer tokens such as a coffee-shop gift card or a chance to win a small prize from a random drawing of all participants. The purpose of these is not to compensate people for their time, but simply as an act of gratitude and appreciation. If you do offer a gift, include what it is and the method of offering in your explanation of your research procedure.

Words such as *subject*, *respondent*, *informant*, and *participant* may be used to describe people in your sample population. These words all have slightly different connotations and should be chosen to reflect your research approach and worldview. For example, the word "participant" is often used to describe someone in a qualitative study by a researcher who assumes a *Constructivist* perspective, as they view the person as a co-creator of knowledge. *Post-positivist* researchers often refer to people as "subjects" in quantitative studies. As a researcher, you have the choice to refer to people in your study as it aligns with your own research philosophy. How would a researcher following a *Creative Paradigm* of research refer to members of their sample population? It is up to you to decide!

Navigating the Institutional Review Board (IRB) Process

Under U.S. Food and Drug Administration (FDA) regulations, an **Institutional Review Board (IRB)** is an "appropriately constituted group that has been formally designated to review and monitor biomedical research involving human subjects" (www.fda.gov). In accordance with FDA regulations, an IRB has the authority to approve, require modifications in (to secure approval), or disapprove research. This group review serves an important role in the protection of the rights and welfare of human research subjects.

The purpose of an IRB review is to assure, both in advance and by periodic review, that appropriate steps are taken to protect the rights and welfare of humans participating as subjects in the research. To accomplish this purpose, IRBs use a group process to review research protocols and related materials (e.g., **informed consent** documents and investigator brochures) to ensure protection of the rights and welfare of human subjects of research. An IRB may be embedded in your institution (consisting of faculty, administration, and members of your local community) or may be an independent body that is hired by a school or researcher. According to Moon (2009), IRBs "must have at least five members including at least one member whose primary concern is scientific, one whose primary concern is nonscientific and one who is not affiliated with the academic institution" (n.p.). Does your school or institution have an IRB? If you are conducting original research for a degree requirement, it is your responsibility to gather the necessary forms, fill them out correctly, and submit them in a timely manner to obtain permission to conduct your study.

Typically, an IRB needs to understand and evaluate:

1. Your research project title
2. Your faculty advisor
3. Where your study is taking place
4. Estimated duration of the study
5. Aims and goals (approximately two paragraphs)
6. Literature review and background of the study
7. Research design and methods
8. Human subjects: how you recruit, compensate and document "informed consent"
9. Potential risks, benefits, and risk management practices
10. Your professional training and qualifications
11. Funding sources
12. Potential conflicts of interests.

Identifying and Protecting Vulnerable Populations

According to the *American Journal of Managed Care* (AJMC, 2006), **vulnerable populations** can be divided into three categories: *physical*, *psychological*, and *social*.

Those with *physical* disabilities or needs include "high-risk" groups such as infants and ageing, or elderly, people, those with chronic disease or reduced immune system, and people who use mobility devices such as a wheelchair, as well as people with visual and hearing impairments. In the *psychological* domain, vulnerable populations include those with chronic mental conditions, such as schizophrenia, bipolar disorder, depression, and attention-deficit/hyperactivity disorder, post-traumatic stress disorder (PTSD), as well as those with a history of alcohol and/or substance abuse and those who are suicidal or prone to homelessness. In the *social* realm, vulnerable populations include families experiencing low-income, people living in abusive families, racial and ethnic minorities, the uninsured, the unhoused, immigrants, and refugees, particularly people who often encounter barriers to accessing healthcare services. "The vulnerability of these individuals is enhanced by race, ethnicity, age, sex, and factors such as income, insurance coverage (or lack thereof), and absence of a usual source of care. Their health and healthcare problems intersect with social factors, including housing, poverty, and inadequate education" (AJMC, 2006, p. S348).

As you begin the research process, consider the disadvantages and risks associated with a person in one of these categories, and take the appropriate measures to ensure that their rights are not being violated. Many additional precautions, such as seeking permission from a child's guardian, need to be taken before including them in your sample population.

Getting Informed Consent

Because we are conscientious researchers, we need to document that people have agreed to participate in our study or allow their children (or other family members who are in their care), to participate. Your professor or institution may provide informed consent forms, legal documents that show this permission, or you may be tasked with composing them yourself. This section of the chapter shows an example of a short consent form and a template for a longer consent form that may be used as a starting point for developing your own. At minimum, they should show your name, position, affiliation, title of your study and your contact information. In addition, it may leave an area for participants to include their own contact information, so that you can follow up with additional questions at a later date.

Sample "Informed Consent" Form (Wheeler, 2008)

"I _____ [respondent's name] hereby give my permission for _____ [student's name] to interview me and quote my responses in a scholarly research paper. I understand that this research paper will be submitted to an instructor at _____ [school name]. I understand that I waive any claim to copyright to this material should the student ever publish it in a scholarly journal or in electronic format online. I understand that the author [will/will not] maintain my anonymity as a part of this interview. I hereby give my permission in the form of my signature below."

Signature _____

Date _____

Informed Consent Form Template (by author)

Consent to Act as a Research Subject for

Study Title: _____

Principal Investigator: _____ (your name)

Institution: _____

Purpose of the Study:
(two to three sentences.)

Procedures:
(one to two paragraphs.)

Potential Risks and Discomforts:
(Include how you will keep their information private)

Potential Benefits to Subjects and/or to Society:
(one to two sentences.)

Participation and Withdrawal:
Your contact information:

Payment for Participation
"As a thank you for your participation, you will be offered a $15 gift card in exchange for your time and participation in this study."

Rights of Research Subjects:

"You have received a copy of this consent document to keep.

You agree to participate."

Signature of Participant _____
Date _____

___ **YES, you allow the use of audio recordings** for the purposes described above.

___ **YES, you allow the use of quoted text comments** for the purposes described above.

Name of participant as you would like for it to appear in publications.

CONCLUSION

In summary, a research proposal is your first step in gathering original data. As you have seen, there are many sources of site-specific and end-user information that supplement the generalizable data obtained during your literature review. Although you have done these sequentially, both site-specific data gathering and exploring previously published data continues throughout the remainder of your research journey. And, the research strategies you have identified may change over the course of pilot testing and getting feedback. In the next three chapters we will explore, in detail, how to collect original data through traditional, time-tested methods, and offer ideas for innovative data collection through interviews, surveys, and observation.

Key Terms

Authority Having Jurisdiction (AHJ)	End-user profile	Photo journal/photo study
Autoethnography	Ethnography	Programming/pre-design phase
Building systems	Feasibility study	Project type
Bulk	Field survey	Psychographic variables
Client profile	FF&E Inventory	Research proposal
Column bays	Generalizable	Research strategy
Consent	Geographic	Sanborn map
Context-specific	Informed consent	Scale
Cross-sectional study	Infrastructure	Scope
Demographic data	Institutional Review Board (IRB)	Structural system
Density	Longitudinal study	Topographic
Emergency egress plan	Municipality	Vulnerable populations
	Occupancy/use classification	Zoning

Discussion Questions

1. What site-related documents have you obtained? Did you try any of the tips offered in the reading? Discuss the challenges and successes you have experienced in this process.

2. How do you plan to make your study participant feel included in the research process? Discuss innovative ways to recruit participants and any pitfalls you may see in this process.

References

AJMC. (November 2006). Vulnerable populations: Who are they? *American Journal of Managed Care, 12*(13), S348–S352.

Cherry, E. (1999). *Programming for design: From theory to practice*. New York: John Wiley.

Creswell, J., & Creswell, J. (2018). *Research design: Qualitative, quantitative, and mixed methods*, 5th ed. Los Angeles CA: Sage.

Fact Monster/Information Please® Database. (2007). Pearson Education. Retrieved 2008 from www.factmonster.com

Groat, L., & Wang, D. (2002). *Architectural research methods*. New York: John Wiley.

Halprin, L. (1970). *The RSVP cycles: Creative processes in the human environment*. New York: George Braziller.

Hill, C.E., & Knox, S. (2021). Series Foreword. In: *Essentials of autoethnography* by C. N. Poulos. Washington, DC: American Psychological Association. Retrieved January 19, 2022 from https://doi.org/10.1037/0000222-001

Kelsky, K. (2015). *The professor is in*. Penguin Random House.

McBride, S. B. (2006). *Site planning and design*, West Virginia University. Retrieved from http://www.rri.wvu.edu/WebBook/McBride/section3.html

Moon, M. R. (2009, April). The history and role of institutional review boards: A useful tension, *AMA Journal of Ethics, Virtual Mentor, 11*(4) 311–316.

New York City Department of City Planning (NYC DCP). (2009). Zoning. Retrieved 2008 from http://www.nyc.gov/html/dcp/html/subcats/zoning.shtml

Pollan, M. (2008). *A place of my own: The architecture of daydreams*. New York: Penguin Group.

Rengel, R. (2007). *Shaping interior space*. New York: Fairchild Publications.

Sanborn Fire Insurance Maps. (2003). The Regents of the University of California. Earth Sciences & Map Library. Retrieved 2008 from http://www.lib.berkeley.edu/EART/snb-intr.html.

Smithsonian Institution. (2007). *Design for the other 90%*. New York: Cooper Hewitt, National Design Museum.

Weisberg, R. (2006). *Creativity: Understanding innovation in problem solving, science, invention, and the arts*. New York: John Wiley.

Wheeler, L. K. (2008). Research Assignment #3. English Department. Carson-Newman College. Retrieved April 20, 2008 from http://web.cn.edu/kwheeler/researchassignment3.html.

Interviews

LEARNING OBJECTIVES

After you complete this chapter, you will be able to:

- Recognize when to use interviews to gather data.

- Select from a variety of interview types.

- Prepare a predetermined list of questions using a range of open- to closed-ended question types.

- Confidently conduct, record, and transcribe an interview.

- Incorporate innovative, image-based inquiry techniques as an alternative to traditional interviews to help interviewees express non-verbal concepts.

- Prepare interview transcripts for analysis by reducing qualitative information through coding and other methods.

CONDUCTING INTERVIEWS

An **interview** is a data collection method involving discussion of personal or professional matters in which one person, the interviewer, asks questions of the interviewee. For interior designers, interviews are often essential tools used to obtain information relevant to a design project. An interview can investigate six primary areas of inquiry, with questions formulated to ask about the past, present, or future. According to Patton (1990) interviews seek to know about:

1. *Behaviors*—About what a person has done or is doing or will do
2. *Opinions/Values*—About what a person thinks about a topic
3. *Feelings*—Note that respondents sometimes respond with "I think …"; therefore, you should take care to inform them that you are looking for feelings.
4. *Knowledge*—What someone knows factually about a topic (as conditioned by their epistemological framework).
5. *Sensory*—About what people perceive and experience through somatosensory receptors: sight, sound, touch, taste, smell, as well as *vestibular* (related to balance and position) and *proprioceptive* or *kinesthesia* (related to body movement of joints, muscles, and skin, and perception of weight, speed, and force) modalities of experience (Taylor,

2009). See Figure 6.1 for overview of sensory data sources that can be considered. In Chapter 8 we will discuss how they can be measured.

6. *Background/History/Demographics*—Standard descriptive or background questions, such as age, education, residence, income level, culture, and expertise. This area includes questions about someone's knowledge of the origins of an organization, or timeline of events as they perceived them happening. Inquiries into levels of expertise and specialized knowledge are often referred to as "qualifying" questions in interviews, as well as in legal matters.

As suggested in Figure 6.1, interview questions about sensory perception should address all seven sense systems (Seven Senses, n.d.). Sight or *vision* is the capacity of the eyes to focus and detect images of visible light and generate electrical nerve impulses for varying colors, hues, brightness. Visual perception is how the brain processes these neural impulses recognizing, differentiating, and interpreting visual stimuli through comparison with prior experiences and memories. Hearing or *audition* is the ability to perceive sound by detecting vibrations due to subtle changes in air pressure as it passes through the ear. As with vision, these stimuli are processed and interpreted in the brain.

Smell or *olfaction* is our ability to detect scent consisting of chemical odor particles in the air, as processed

Figure 6.1
Consider asking questions which relate to all seven senses, as in this example of possible questions to ask about apple-picking in an orchard.

through the nose and to the olfactory receptor which leads directly to the brain, making this our most primal or immediate sense. Taste or *gustation* refers to the tongue taste buds differentiating food from poison. There are five basic tastes: salty, sweet, sour, bitter, and umami (savory). The ability to differentiate flavors results from a combination of taste and smell.

Touch or true **somatosensory** perception results from activating neurons in hair follicles and skin for texture and heat. Below the surface of the skin tissue such as fat and muscle responds to pressure. The **vestibular** system helps form the body's perception of its relationship with gravity, motion, speed, balance, and position in space relative to objects around us. **Proprioception** is the sense of effort, strength, or exertion, assisting the body in planning movement related to navigation and balance.

Interviewing is a skill, a learned technique involving planning, preparing, attending to verbal and non-verbal cues, and methods of tactical guidance and intervention in the flow of a conversation. Because it is a form of conversation, it may be natural for you to think you have the talent to interview, given your life-long experience having conversations. The interview process, you may then discover, can be uncomfortable or intimidating. You may be afraid to ask questions, especially when dealing with people you do not know. However, the interview process is *essential* to the field of interior design. Because interviewing is a skill, rather than a talent, you can become more confident and adept at this process through continued practice and experience of what works and what does not work. Watching skilled interviewers such as Oprah Winfrey or Ellen DeGeneres can help you build confidence and pick up some of the non-verbal cues that help an interview succeed. Another resource might be the interview techniques developed during the 1950s by such pioneers as Dr. Alfred Kinsey, author of *The Kinsey Reports on Human Sexual Behavior* (1948–53), and Robert K. Merton, author of *The Focused Interview* published in 1951 (Merton et al., 1990). These books served historically as groundbreaking additions to the expanding exploration of interview techniques.

Interviews are concerned with gathering information to discover meanings and to test theories. As we have learned in Chapter 2, a *theory* is a description of reality, or a proposed view that seeks to make sense of the interrelation of phenomena, events, or behaviors.

You might use an interview to test a theory or to help discover a problem to solve. For example, if you have a theory that management's views about the open-office plan arrangement differ from employees' views about it, you could set up informational interviews to ask questions that target how staff members on both sides feel about their sense of privacy, control, and efficiency. Through your questions, you would seek to reveal the beliefs underlying the way the office is arranged and simultaneously reveal the feelings (intended or unintended) that result from the furniture arrangement in this office and from, notably, its lack of full-height walls. Your theory that management prefers easy visibility and control of the office while employees prefer more privacy may be supported or refuted by the data you collect in your interviews.

TYPES OF INTERVIEWS
Informational interviews

Informational interviews are most often focused (carried out one-on-one or in groups) in person, over the telephone, through e-mail or videoconferencing. Some subcategories include *exit interviews* (which happen at the end of an activity or experience), *oral histories, investigational* and *journalistic* interviews, *medical case histories, professional consultation,* or *diagnostic* interviews to determine the cause of a problem through inductive inquiry. Although any of these types of interviews could be part of the toolkit of an interior designer, this chapter emphasizes information-gathering for research, giving special attention to in-depth interviews to gain new knowledge about a topic, or test a theory. Such interviews are especially useful to interior designers during the pre-design or programming, and design development phases. What are the different types of interviews for interior design research? As you read about the following types of interviews, consider which ones would be most appropriate for your project.

Client Interviews

Interior designers interview *clients* to discover their goals, wants, and values. Sometimes designers use the term *client* to mean all possible users of the space. However, this textbook uses **client** to refer specifically to the owner, organization, corporation, company, or decision-making agent who would be responsible for hiring the designer, making the key design decisions, and/or funding the project. Your interior design project has a real client or an acting client, but your research project may not. If you do have a client organization, or stakeholder in mind, what would you want to know? Obvious question content will address budget, function, location, size, and expected number of end-users (staff, visitors, and key population served by their project type). In an interview, you must also ask questions to determine the client's background or history, underlying values, belief system, as well as the goals and the mission of the project.

An historical example of a good client/designer relationship is the interaction of architect Louis Kahn with his client Dr. Jonas Salk in 1960. Through extensive interviews and intimate discussions, Kahn was able to understand the client's values and goals. Salk told the architect that he wanted "a place where Picasso would feel welcome." Kahn translated this to mean, "that anyone with a mind in the humanities, in science, or in art could contribute to the mental environment of research leading to discoveries in science" (Ronner & Jhaveri, 1974). This information helped guide the architect in producing one of the greatest masterpieces of architecture for scientific inquiry, one that has stood the test of time, offering humanity a glimpse into a collective yet solitary architectural experience, especially when viewing the ocean and sky from the courtyard as shown in Figure 6.2, and strolling through the sunlit open-air walkways under the study towers (Figure 6.3)

The client often approaches an interview with budget and functional issues foremost in mind. Such an interview can be viewed by the interior designer as an opportunity to co-create, with the client, a more holistic view of the project. Humanistic from the end-users' perspective, and other programmatic concepts such as security, safety, flexibility, sustainability, health and well-being, aesthetics, and "sense of place" within the community are not only altruistic goals held by the designer, but they may ultimately be important to the financial and organizational goals of the client. Indeed, if you as the designer do not raise such issues at the beginning of the project, the client may ask later why you did not, since these factors often have the highest potential efficacy when integrated into the early conception of the project. While clients are not always able to articulate the interrelationships of function, people, and performance in an interior design project, they have a right to expect that you will be a source of wisdom and valuable resource to them in this regard. As your interviewing skills improve, you will learn to include these topics in the client interview as matter-of-fact parts of the pre-design investigation. You would not ask the client "do you want your project to comply with the building code?" because it is already a given, hopefully specified in your professional contract or written agreement.

Figure 6.2
View of the horizon from the courtyard of The Salk Institute for Biological Studies in La Jolla, California.

Figure 6.3
Strolling through the sunlit arcades designed for scientists to walk and talk at The Salk Institute for Biological Studies in La Jolla, California.

End-User Interviews

Interior designers interview people to uncover how they use (or intend to use) spaces in the built environment. There are ordinarily different kinds of **end-users** in a particular project. For example, in a daycare center there would be administrative staff, full-time and part-time care providers, volunteers, and mothers and fathers who drop off their children—as well as the children themselves. It is also necessary to consider the maintenance and security staff, who might also be interviewed for their experience and opinions.

In the case of The Salk Institute for Biological Studies, the end-users constituted scientists engaged in groundbreaking research at the cellular and molecular level of life. Because Dr. Salk did not know who would be coming to his new facility, architect Louis Kahn interviewed scientists engaged in research at the University of Pennsylvania for a project that Kahn had already completed, The Richards Medical Laboratory. There is an interesting distinction between wants and needs, almost a dichotomy in this instance, which Kahn eloquently describes. According to Kahn,

> The scientists said they are so dedicated to what they are doing that when lunchtime comes all they do is clear away the test tubes from the benches and eat their lunch on these benches. I asked them was it not a strain with all these noises? And they answered … everything was terrible including the noise of the air conditioning system. So I would not listen to them as to what should be done.
>
> (Ronner & Jhaveri, 1974, p. 138)

In this quote, we can see that Kahn realized that the *wants* of the scientists did not align with their *needs*. Kahn summarized the needs he gleaned from the interview as follows: "I realized that there should be 'a clean air and stainless steel' area, and 'a rug and oak table' area … The garden became the outdoor spaces where one can talk. Now one need not spend all the time in laboratories" (p. 138).

Two subgroups of end-users would be the **participant end-user**, the current or designated future user of the space, and the **potential end-user**, a person who possesses the characteristics of someone who would use the space. In a museum project, identifying a potential end-user may involve (1) asking questions of people who have visited a similar type of museum or (2) selecting potential end-users from among people who are interested in a particular type of art or who live in the neighborhood. As you will see defined in more detail later in this chapter, a **focus group** is a small group of potential users of a particular service, product, or space who have been prescreened for certain characteristics—for example, expectant mothers who plan to work (to inform the design of a daycare center). In the example of the Salk Institute, the architect Louis Kahn interviewed scientists from the Richards Medical Laboratory project to gather information to inform his next project, the Salk Institute project. The scientists were members of a target market. Kahn identified them as potential users of the new laboratory as their level of experience matched the level of experience of persons who might use the new laboratory in the future.

Consider a second example: An interior design student was charged with researching the homeless problem in San Diego, California, to design a facility that would meet the needs of the homeless population in that city. First, the student collected information on a variety of topics; her sources ranged from government Web sites to a guided tour of a local homeless shelter. Her research question: In the local services for the homeless, what gaps exist that prevent a homeless person from returning to a permanent home? Her next step was to understand—from the point of view of a homeless person, as a potential user of her facility—what services were needed. Her target audience could be sorted by a common characteristic: experiencing homelessness. But there was a variety of other factors: physical disabilities, mental health, age, gender, culture, and educational or professional background.

While on a guided tour of the homeless shelter, the student researcher learned that homeless persons who did not live at the shelter lined up for free breakfast in a certain location. There would be approximately two hundred people in line on any given morning. To try to find out what a homeless person thought, believed, expected, and wanted, the student decided to interview some of the people in this group directly. She came up with a list of eight questions. The first two questions were general "icebreaker" or "warm-up" questions, intended to put the interviewee at ease. Notice the use of broad, open-ended questions. Do you think this was a good strategy?

Hi, my name is Dalia. I am a student at a local design school. I am researching the problem of homelessness in San Diego for a school project, and I am trying to understand what it is like to be homeless. May I ask you a few questions about yourself? Anything you tell me will be strictly confidential. I will not share this with anyone else.

1. Can you tell me a little about your life?
2. Can you describe for me a typical day you may have?
3. Where do you eat?
4. Where do you sleep?
5. Have you ever stayed in a shelter?
6. Would you like to work?
7. If you could change one thing, what would it be?
8. What do you feel would truly help you?

Dalia described some of the pitfalls of her interviews. At one point, while waiting in a line for breakfast to be served, she decided to ask her questions to a woman next to her. As the woman began to answer, a man in line interjected, "Don't listen to her; she's lying." and a verbal argument ensued. Dalia quickly thanked the woman for her time and ended the interview. Steps were taken in the future to approach the subject in a more private location (not within earshot of other people) to encourage truthful answers and to avoid conflict. Roulston would categorize the kind of experience Dalia had as one of many possible unexpected participant behaviors. Beginning researchers should be aware that people will react differently when being interviewed and should reflect in advance on their own anticipated actions (e.g., "will note-taking or digital recording make the respondent uncomfortable?") and assumptions about the flow of conversation.

Advocacy Interviews: User-Experts

Investigation of unique end-user needs is increasingly seen as an important source of information for interior design. Your commitment as a designer to principles of Universal Design, for example, may lead you to seek out user-experts to interview, to understand the contextual experiences of users with physical, sensory, or brain-based disabilities. A designer who seeks this kind of input recognizes that reading a book or following a set of published guidelines is a poor substitute for learning from the lived experiences of users. The

Institute for Human Centered Design acknowledges the contributions of both "primary user-experts" who live with a functional limitation, and "secondary user-experts" who may be "friends, family members, service providers, therapists, teachers, or anyone who has extensive experience sharing life with primary user-experts" (Research, n.d.). You may wish to interview other advocate user-experts if your project addresses the needs of emergent user groups whose identities as end-users are inadequately understood; for example, information about the opinions and needs of transgender users of restroom facilities is beginning to be addressed in revisions to the model International Plumbing Code and will soon find its way into local and state adaptations; however, inclusivity of the needs of non-binary people in building design is still in its early stages (AIA Chicago, 2020).

Expert Interviews

Interior designers need to gain information on a topic or project type from relevant experts. For example, when designing a spiritual space, it may be important to ask questions of a member of the clergy, or when designing a dental office, it may be important to interview a dental hygienist. Experts in a particular field will have insights and knowledge that will be essential to the success of your design.

Interior designers often use interviews to gain information about a specific professional or technical skill related to the area of design. You could interview a structural engineer when designing a mezzanine in a retail space; a Leadership in Energy and Environmental Design (LEED) Accredited Professional when considering sustainable features in your project; or a woodworker about fabrication techniques, properties of wood, and joinery when designing wood furniture. Increasingly specialized project needs may require professional consultation for acoustics, lighting, and audio-visual and digital media.

There are five stages to a successful interview:

1. Preparation
2. Arranging
3. Conducting
4. Recording (digitally capturing the audio/visual, or by taking notes)
5. Post-Interview Documentation: *reconstruction* or *transcription*

Preparation involves collecting background information on your subject matter as well as your interviewee. It is essential to familiarize yourself with terminology and acronyms. In order to get people to open up to you, you must know their lingo. For example, when a student was interviewing postal workers for a post office redesign, it quickly became apparent that there were many acronyms that she had to be familiar with to communicate fluently with the workers. They used "case" as a verb, as in referring to the activity of "putting the unsorted mail in slots in a case," and referred to temporary workers as "casuals," referring not to their demeanor but to their classification in the language of the federal employment system. You must identify your interviewee and anticipate the type of information that person will bring to your project. Preparation also involves making a list of questions, putting the questions in a logical order, and orchestrating the format of the interview—formal or informal. The list of questions is called a **questionnaire**. You might administer these questions aloud and face-to-face. Alternatively, you could send the list of questions (along with expected timeline for a response) and expect the responses to be sent back.

Before you choose your interviewees, ask yourself the following questions:

- Why am I conducting this interview rather than gathering information from other sources?
- Who are ideal candidates to be interviewed? A professional who works in the field? An academic who studies the issue? A published author who has already written books on the topic? A person in the local community who has dealt with this issue in his or her personal life? (Wheeler, n.d.)
- Is the person available for an interview?
- Do I have a solid base of knowledge about the topic that will enhance my credibility with interviewees?

Arranging involves contacting the interviewee and communicating your intent and your passion for the project as well as your respect for the interviewee's knowledge and participation. Arranging also involves selecting an appropriate location and time for the interview to take place. Sometimes the interview will be face-to-face, but often it can be a conference call (at a prespecified time over the phone) or via Web-based telecommunication. The following is a checklist of questions to ask yourself as you arrange an interview:

- Am I able to approach the interviewee from a positive standpoint, assuming that she or he will have time to talk with me?—Keep in mind that most people are usually flattered by the attention and are willing to participate in an informational interview, particularly if they know you're a student.
- Can I choose a location that is comfortable for the interviewee? Generally, people are much more willing to participate in an information interview if the setting is a comfortable and familiar one. Many professional interviewers suggest choosing the interviewee's office or a public location near their office, as the interviewee may be more comfortable in familiar surroundings. Another locational consideration is the potential for noise or distraction. Will a sit-down in someone's home be interrupted by their dog or will your cozy coffeeshop environment include something you did not anticipate, like a jazz band playing music in the background? Will an interview in someone's office be subject to interruptions by other staff, the phone, or e-mail pings the interviewee is unable to ignore?
- Have I informed the interviewee of the expected length of the interview, and obtained his/her agreement that this length will be acceptable? Have I clearly explained the purpose of this interview to my research? Have I addressed issues of confidentiality? Have I gotten written permission to use the information I receive from the interview? — See the example of an "Informed Consent" form to be completed by the interviewee at the end of Chapter 5.

Conducting the interview involves arriving on time, dressed appropriately, and prepared with tools to record the interview. It also involves establishing a rapport with the interviewee (or the staff of the interviewee if you meet at the interviewee's office), remaining focused and attentive to your surroundings, and picking up nonverbal cues about the interviewee. Before starting the interview, ask yourself these questions:

- Can I get a site tour before the start of the interview? A tour may help inspire questions you hadn't thought of before and improve rapport as your interviewee becomes comfortable with you by providing helpful insights along the way.

- Have I established myself as a trustworthy and reliable person to the staff or receptionist (the "gatekeeper"), and have I instilled confidence in the interviewee?
- Am I wearing professional attire in keeping with the office environment? If I am interviewing someone who may be intimidated by professional attire (children, elderly, homeless), am I appropriately dressed? Does my attire match the cultural expectations of my interviewee?

Recording could be as simple as audio- or video-recording the interview in real time. But sometimes these methods can make the interviewee uncomfortable or can be prohibitively disruptive. If you are going to audio or videorecord the interview, it is imperative to get permission when you set up the interview, or at least prior to the interview beginning. Even if you have previously obtained consent, extend the courtesy of asking again before turning on the device. And then confirm their agreement once the recording has begun, as well as identifying yourself, your interviewee, the date, time, and place of the interview.

Other recording methods include making notes on paper, bringing along a friend to transcribe the exchange, or having interviewees write or type their answers. Depending on your typing skills, you could bring a laptop computer to the interview and type while the interviewee is speaking (you may want to practice this skill beforehand). Select a recording method that will enable you to focus on the interaction and flow of question and answer.

Below is a list of questions to ask yourself during the interview:

- Do I understand what the interviewee is saying? Don't be afraid to ask for clarification of terminology that you may be unfamiliar with.
- Do my body language and facial expressions remain open yet neutral to avoid intimidating the interviewee or influencing the responses? You may want to ask yourself your questions in front of a mirror to practice remaining neutral.
- Have I reacted with surprise or strong emotion to any of the interviewee's answers? Have you remained attentive and reacted appropriately, so that the interviewee knows you are still listening with a certain degree of detachment? A good

trick is to maintain an attitude of "I've heard it all before."
- Are the questions flowing in a logical way? If the interview is not going as planned, you may need to improvise the order or wording of the questions.
- Can I continue in a nonjudgmental and nonthreatening way when the interviewee is unable or unwilling to answer a question, or is upset by a question?
- Do I feel that the interviewee is being truthful? Am I getting the responses I need?
- Have I left my contact information with the interviewee for future questions or information?
- Have I expressed my appreciation? In addition to a simple spoken "Thank you so much for your time," you are strongly encouraged to send a handwritten thank-you note in the mail.
- Have I gotten the information I need? Check to make sure the tape recording was successful. If you are using handwritten notes as a recording method, you may want to reconstruct the interview by writing out the responses in full sentences immediately after the interview ends—while the comments are still fresh in your mind. One last thing: If you don't have it already, ask for a mailing address so you can send that thank-you note.

DEGREES OF FORMALITY

Interviews range in formality and structure, depending upon the situation. The most casual type of interview is *informal conversation*, in which no predetermined questions are asked, to remain as open and adaptable as possible to the interviewee's nature and priorities. A researcher happens upon the subject without prearrangement and asks a few warm-up questions; then, during the interview, the researcher "goes with the flow." For example, as you enter a building, you encounter a resident and ask how many people live in the building. In the elevator, you ask another resident her opinion about the building's current occupants. And as you are leaving, you ask a person living in the building next door to give you his opinion of the neighborhood. All of these interviews are chance occurrences that yield a cursory opinion from a singular subject. Keep your eyes open for opportunities that arise on guided tours or in public places.

The *generally guided* approach utilizes a list of topics to be covered. This approach is intended to ensure that the same general areas of information are collected from each interviewee, but it allows for a degree of freedom and adaptability in getting this information. For example, to determine the public's opinion about the navigational signage system currently used in a local hospital, you informally survey random staff members, patients, and visitors in the waiting room. You ask each person about (1) their ease in locating destinations; (2) their opinions of the signage, wording, graphics, mounting heights, and location; and (3) possible suggestions for improvement. You do not ask everyone the questions in exactly the same way; you vary them depending on whom you are asking.

In a formal interview, a **standardized questionnaire** (a prepared list of questions that can also be used in a survey design will be covered in Chapter 7) is presented to an interviewee at a prearranged time and place. The interviewee is prepared to answer the questions. The questionnaire can consist of all types of questions, as outlined in the following section. For additional question types see Chapter 7.

THE QUESTIONS YOU ASK [AND ASKING THE QUESTIONS]

Interviews are distinctly different from social conversation. Although we may make polite conversation in interviews and ask questions in social interactions, all interviews are purposive, and goal directed. Questions are the heart of any interview followed by careful listening without interrupting. Three points determine the structure of the interview:

- Types of questions
- Phrasing of questions
- Question order.

Types of Questions

There are different types of questions. Questions may be primary, used to introduce a topic, and secondary which attempts to elicit further information (see Table 6.1). Question types also range from **open-ended** which are broad allowing for unrestricted answers to **closed-ended** in which respondents are forced to choose from a predetermined list of answers (as in Table 6.2).

Table 6.1 Primary and Secondary Questions

Primary Question	Response	Secondary (Follow-Up) Question
"How did you first get interested in surfing?"	"My parents lived by the ocean and gave me a surfboard for my fourth birthday."	"What happened then?"
"Are you satisfied with your office space?"	"No. I can't seem to get much work done."	"Why do you feel that is?"

Table 6.2 Questions Ranging from Open-Ended to Closed-Ended

Highly Open-Ended	Moderately Open-Ended	Extended Bipolar	Moderately Closed-Ended	Highly Closed-Ended
Broad, without restriction	Restricted to topic	Purpose: Requires a yes or no answer with elaboration	Asks for specific information	Predetermined list of choices of answer
"What don't you like about your kitchen?"	"How do you prepare meals?"	"Will this stove meet your needs? Why or why not?"	"How many cooks use this kitchen?"	"Is this a one-cook or two-cook kitchen?"
"What is a typical day in the office?"	"What is your role in the office?"	"Do you have enough privacy for meetings?"	"What are the qualifications for your position?"	"Would you describe your workspace as (a) excellent, (b) good, or (c) poor?"

There are also certain types of questions to avoid, including *leading* or *loaded questions* and *compound questions* as well as adding *tag lines* to questions (also known as *tagged questions*). See Table 6.3. for definitions of these unhelpful question types (reasons not to use them) and examples.

Sometimes, the most effective type of follow-up question is not a question, but a **probe**. "A *probe* is the interviewer's prompting for further elaboration of an answer" (Zeisel, 1984). The most powerful probe is for the interviewer to remain silent after asking the question. Most people are uncomfortable with silence, so they will try to "fill" it by talking. As the interviewer, resist the inclination to talk. Instead, wait for the interviewee to continue. You can increase the effectiveness of the silence with nonverbal cues such as a slight nod or an attentive, expectant facial expression and eye contact.

Probes are not usually part of the list of questions. That is, they are not usually scripted. Experienced interviewers have developed a skill for using different probes "on the fly" to encourage more from the interviewee. However, a novice interviewer may want to proactively identify and preliminarily insert potential probes after certain questions. There are names for different types of probes. See Table 6.4 for a list

of probes from Coopman's Online Tutorial, *Conducting the Information Interview* (2006), along with examples to illustrate each type.

The final question type that you may use is "Why?" Use of this type of question should be limited, because too many "Why?" questions may make interviewees defensive as they seek to justify a claim they have made or because such questions may frustrate them when they cannot explain why they feel a particular way. Also, if you ask too many "Why?" questions, interviewees may start to speculate or fabricate information because they may not want to admit that they do not know the answer. If you were being interviewed, how would you feel if asked these questions?

- Why don't your coworkers like the design of your workplace?
- Why weren't you consulted on the color choice?
- Why aren't you more productive in this office?

Carefully worded questions can motivate interviewees to answer freely, accurately, and thoughtfully. There are three factors to consider when phrasing questions: Language, Information Level, and Complexity. Use words that interviewees will understand, but do not be overly simplistic. Be specific, precise, and concrete and always take care to avoid

Table 6.3 Types of Questions to Avoid

Question to Avoid	Reason not to use	Examples
Leading Question	Implies that you expect a certain answer that can skew your findings	"Would you agree that child safety is the first priority?" "Doesn't the office seem too small to you?" "Are you ever going to organize this place?"
Loaded Question	Implies a certain answer and an underlying negative belief	"Don't you think this color scheme seems dated?" "Are those no-good teenagers responsible for this damage?" "Do you think management is lacking leadership abilities?"
Tag Lines	Inserted at the end of a question, which tends to weaken, confuse, or coerce	"You are planning to remodel your kitchen, *right*?" "I feel this is the right decision, *don't you*?" "I am going to draw it this way, *okay*?"
Compound, Multiple, or Double-Barreled Questions	Two or more questions combined into one question, which does not allow each question to be answered separately	"What is the best part of this job and how often do you get to do it?" "Who usually visits the museum during the day and in the evening?" "Why did you choose this location? Is it because of the view, the access to the park, or the building's historic value?"

Table 6.4 Probes

Type of Probe	When to Use	Examples
Nudge or Addition	To encourage interviewee to continue talking, but not in any specific direction (enhanced by nod and/or raised eyebrows)	"I see." "Go on." "Really?"
Clearinghouse	To make sure you have gotten all of the information on that topic	"Is there anything else?" "Are there questions I should have asked but didn't?" "Was there something you would like to add?"
Depth	To elicit greater detail	"What happened after you found your old guitar in the attic?" "Tell me more about your experience as a bicycle messenger in New York." "Please explain the installation process in greater detail."
Clarity	To understand the use of a particular word or phrase	"What do you mean by 'incompetent'?" "How are you defining excellence?" "Is it the hue that you don't like or the intensity of the color?"
Feelings	To explore emotions	"Why do you think you feel that way?" "What were you feeling at the time?" "Why did it make you happy?"
Focus	To get back on track when the conversation is drifting	"Let's return to your years as an editor." "You began by talking about your lack of storage space."
Accuracy	To verify information	"Was that in 1988 or in 1998?" "How do you spell their name?" "Did you say the color was 'old' or 'bold'?"
Hypothetical	To propose something based on the interviewee's previous response	"What would you have done differently?" "What advice can you offer?" "What would have been a better alternative?"
Reactive	To give the interviewee another chance to elaborate or react	"How do you explain that?" "What do you think about that?" "What is your response to that statement?"
Self-Descriptive	To find an underlying cause	"Did growing up in the South influence your choice of house?" "Was there an influential person in your life?" "What do you think happened to make you feel that way?"
Echo	An active listening technique that involves literally repeating back exactly what was said	
Summary	Paraphrasing the response to make sure you understand it	"So what I'm hearing you say is that you like the first option." "Like you said, you need more privacy." "Let me check to see if I understand your points …"

language or terminology that will offend or insult interviewees. Do not ask questions for which interviewees do not have the information. Do not ask questions that insult interviewees' intelligence, or are beyond their area of knowledge. Phrase questions so that they are simple, clear requests for limited amounts of information.

Question Order

Like speeches, interviews have an opening, a body, and a closing. As the interviewer, you want to begin the interview in a way that facilitates the interview process, ask questions that assist all parties in achieving their goals, and end the interview on a positive note. The interview's opening, sometimes referred to as "breaking the ice," usually sets the tone for the remainder of the interview. Your goal is to establish a productive climate so both you and your interviewee will participate freely and communicate accurately. You may want to demonstrate your knowledge of the subject matter by summarizing your research up to this point. For example, "I have read your article entitled 'Legal Assistance for Victims of Domestic Violence' and I have visited a local shelter for victims of domestic violence. I would like to ask you a few questions so I can better understand the services available."

The body of the interview is the series of questions and responses that aim to collect the information. There are different "shapes" to an interview, as described below and made visual in Figure 6.4:

- Funnel—Use this question sequence when the interviewee knows the topic well and feels free to talk about it, or when the person wants to express strong feelings. This is the most common of all question sequences for all types of interviews. In this sequence, the interviewer begins with broad, open-ended questions and moves to narrower, closed-ended questions. The interviewer may also begin with more general questions and gradually ask more specific questions.

- Inverted Funnel—This question sequence is effective when an interviewee needs help remembering something or to motivate an interviewee to talk. In this sequence, the interviewer begins with narrow, closed-ended questions and moves to broader, open-ended questions. The interviewer may also begin with more specific questions and gradually ask more general questions, as the interviewee becomes more comfortable.

- Tunnel—In this sequence, all questions have the same degree of openness. Also called the "string of beads" question sequence, the tunnel sequence allows for little probing and variation in question structure. It can be useful for simple interviews seeking surface-level information, but not for in-depth interviews.

According to Carter McNamara (1999), question order is essential to getting the maximum benefit. He has a few additional tips:

1. *Ask about facts before asking about controversial matters (such as feelings or beliefs)*. With this approach, interviewees can more easily engage in the interview before warming up to more personal matters.

2. *Intersperse fact-based questions throughout the interview*. Long lists of fact-based questions tend to leave interviewees disengaged.

3. *Ask questions about the present before questions about the past or future*. It is usually easier for interviewees to talk about the present and then work into the past or future, especially if the topic is a sensitive or emotional one.

Upon conclusion of the interview, your goal is to leave the interviewee feeling positive and satisfied with the interview. The interviewer is responsible for signaling the upcoming conclusion, as with "My final question ...."

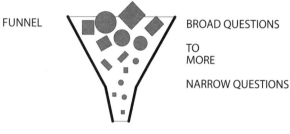

FUNNEL — BROAD QUESTIONS TO MORE NARROW QUESTIONS

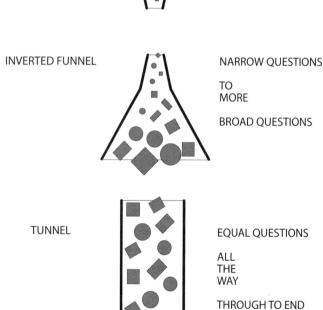

INVERTED FUNNEL — NARROW QUESTIONS TO MORE BROAD QUESTIONS

TUNNEL — EQUAL QUESTIONS ALL THE WAY THROUGH TO END

Figure 6.4
Diagram showing three different ways to organize an interview: Funnel, Inverted Funnel, and Tunnel. Larger shapes refer to broad or open-ended question while smaller shapes refer to detailed, follow-up, or closed-ended questions.

At the end of the interview, feel free to provide the interviewee with a summary of key points of your conversation. Not only does it provide a good indication that you gained knowledge from their answers, but it also serves as a test of your listening and note-taking skills. As your conversation with the interviewee ends, highlight key take-aways and overall conclusions or point out areas of agreement and disagreement. Ask the interviewee to verify the accuracy of your summary. Close your notebook or turn off the recording device to communicate that the question-and-answer phase of the interview is concluded. If necessary, restate the confidential nature of the interview—and the purpose and use of the information. Be alert to other bits and pieces of information, as the interviewee may relax and relay important information as part of an informal chat. A sincere farewell marks the end of a post-interview discussion.

To emphasize the importance of the interview, Dr. L. Kip Wheeler, an English professor at *Carson–Newman College*, had this message for students:

> Congratulations. You have engaged in firsthand research and found information that may never have been recorded before in any publication. You are one step closer to becoming an authoritative writer on this topic. Other writers may end up quoting you and your publications on this matter.
>
> (Wheeler, n.d.)

Transcription and Interview Data Reduction

There are several ways to compose a post-interview record. If the interview was audio-recorded, you may want to type a written **transcription**. There are computer programs designed to help you with this task. For example, the program *InqScribe* (free download at https://www.inqscribe.com/) used along with headphones (to block out background noise) and a foot pedal (that assists you in stopping, slowing down, or rewinding the audio file) provides a solid platform to conduct this process. There are talk-to-text programs as well, that help speed up what is typically a time-consuming process. However, engaging the act of listening to the audio and transcribing what you hear can be an eye-opening experience in and of

itself. You may start to see patterns emerging in the interviewee's speech that were not noticeable at the time, or you may find yourself seeking to transcribe the voice tone, or emphasis of the speaker and put those words in bold, capitalized, or underlined. You can also note long pauses, laughter, or sarcasm as the need arises by putting square brackets around such side notations.

If you took hand-written notes during the interview, you may want to write out the responses in full sentences (as soon as possible) while the conversation is still fresh in your mind. You may also summarize the interview in a report using direct quotes from the interviewee or paraphrasing what the interviewee said. All these methods correspond to a **reconstruction**. Make sure to note the technical information necessary to cite the interview in your working bibliography, including the proper spelling of the interviewee's name, appellations, affiliations, and the date, time, and place of the interview.

In addition to documenting the interview, you may want to do a post-interview assessment. Your objective in this assessment is to evaluate the information you have just obtained for accuracy, relevance, and completeness. Can you verify the facts you have collected? Do you have any follow-up questions or concerns? And, finally, it is customary to thank your interviewee with a follow-up card or a handwritten note.

The resulting transcript is very useful. We can take the words of the transcript and do all sorts of **data reduction** methods to transform the qualitative data (verbal answers expressing thoughts and feelings) into quantitative data (numbers and percentages). For example, identifying recurring patterns of language or noting how many times an interviewee used a certain word or phrase can give you evidence you need that the word or phrase is important data to consider. Determining how to partition responses into categories or groups is called **coding** (Zeisel, 1984, p. 164). An example of a student coding an interview transcript for emergent codes to reduce the qualitative data to quantitative data is in the Research in Action 6.1 box: "A Mental Vacation." More on how qualitative data may be reduced, presented, and interpreted to reveal statistical data or metaphors will be explored in Chapter 9.

RESEARCH IN ACTION 6.1
A Mental Vacation

Interior design student Amanda Dowell discussed how she gathered information to answer, "How can the environment foster creativity?" Amanda stated, "Initially I posted a survey on social media, asking participants to define creativity. Some people responded:

- ' … doing something that excites you, challenges you and helps you to see the world in a new way.'

- 'Creating new worlds based on inspiration, environment and your imagination.'

- '… creating or doing something in a way that is outside of the realm of how things are usually done.'

- '… having the ability to express your ideas, thoughts, and emotions in various forms.'

- 'Being in touch with your inner state.'

- 'Connection, Flow, Creation … Joy!'"

Amanda then conducted one-on-one interviews to ask how the environment played a role in their mental state to help their ability to be creative. To summarize the results, Amanda drew a visual representation of a key contributing factor to a creative environment—which she called "a mental vacation". People, she noted, reported feeling the most creative when they periodically take breaks, go for a walk, move their body, and get in touch with nature. Her image consists of cool, soothing tones and a pathway along a pool of water, with glimpses of trees and sky in the distance. Curved lines represent an organic quality, as well as mystery, providing a motivating factor to discover what may be hidden around the corner, out of view.

Drawing of a "Mental Vacation," a visual which attempts to summarize and illustrate the interview data linking creativity to the environment.

Activity 6.1
Testing a List of Questions to Ask

Purpose: To practice putting together a list of questions to ask in an interview.

1. Generate a list of five or six questions for each interviewee you listed in Activity 5.3 *Seeking Out the Experts*. Apply the wording techniques and question order discussed in this chapter.

2. Break into teams of two and conduct mock interviews in class with your fellow students. Use probes during your session.

3. Record the mock interview using the note-taking and reconstruction method.

4. When you have concluded the interview, ask for feedback from your interviewee. Did he or she feel your questions were appropriate? Can your interviewee offer any insight into improving the content or format of the questions?

Activity 6.2
Distinguishing Truth from Falsehood

Purpose: To practice reading body language to determine whether an interviewee is being truthful.

1. Create a list of questions regarding personal experience in the past. Examples: Have you ever been involved in a car accident? Have you ever lied to someone to get them to do something? What is your most vivid memory from elementary school? Did you use public transportation to come to school today? Or the interviewer can ask the interviewee to recount a story or an anecdote based on a suggested topic.

2. Break into teams of two and conduct informal interviews. The interviewee will attempt to answer the question with either a truth or a falsehood. The interviewer should observe the body language of the interviewee to help determine whether the interviewee is telling the truth or is lying.

EXPLORING ALTERNATIVE INTERVIEW TECHNIQUES

Sometimes conducting a conventional one-on-one interview cannot yield the information we are looking for. For example, you and the interviewee might not speak the same language. Or the interviewee might not be able to communicate verbally, as with young children, people with dementia, or those with learning disabilities. Many times, an individual may not have the vocabulary, like designers do, to describe their wants and needs regarding the built environment. In all these cases, finding and trying alternative interviewing techniques can be very rewarding.

Focus Group

As previously mentioned in this chapter, if you have already identified your target market and you know the user profile, you might use a *focus group* to gather opinions from potential end-users of the space. A **focus group** is an alternative approach to interviewing as it combines more than one perspective in a single conversation.

Even though it may take place in a controlled setting, the goal is to foster natural conversation on a broad or controversial topic. Focus groups take a user-generated approach to discovering new information, as members of the group may bring up things you may not have thought to ask about. The primary endeavor of the researcher is to be a facilitator of the focus group. That is, the researcher should introduce a question or topic and then allow the members of the groups to have a conversation or dialogue. The best way to conduct this research method is to have an audio recording device strategically placed in the middle of a table and position the members of the group sitting around the table equidistant from the recording device. The researcher can then take notes about who is speaking, to make sure they can identify the various voices that will be present on the recording, and to moderate or redirect the group if one person seems to dominate the conversation. It is essential to make sure that all voices are heard. A strength of the focus group method is that the conversation may head in unexpected directions, to the surprise of the researcher. This differing direction could be useful data.

Non-Verbal or Image-Based Interactions

Swiss psychologist Hermann Rorschach pioneered the use of graphic representations in an interview setting beginning in 1921, using respondents' interpretations of ambiguously shaped "ink blots" to assess their projections of thoughts, emotions, and beliefs onto the images. During the 1940s and 1950s, the sociologist Robert Merton often used images and photos in "focused interviews" to help elicit feelings about war from war veterans, with the belief that people are sometimes moved more by an image than a word. Since then, it is common understanding that people tend to assign meaning to images, and for designers to use imagery to focus attention or gain understanding from an interviewee without using traditional language. In his book *Inquiry by Design*, John Zeisel (1984) also mentions using photos or drawings as a non-verbal probe—for example, to assist in getting a respondent to more clearly visualize something that happened in the past (such as showing a victim in a police interrogation a photo of the crime scene), or to get office workers to think more spatially about a room or an environment (for example, showing a photo of a doorway or a lock on the door). For example, to get a clearer picture of a client's mental images of style, a kitchen designer may ask the client to collect clippings from design magazines. The word *modern* may mean something different to a designer than it means to a client, so images tend to help clarify discrepancies in historical styles and overcome cultural differences related to use of language or concepts in general. Similarly, design-researchers may use images in the interview process to get interviewees to go deeper, into regions to which words cannot take us, to memories, subconscious beliefs, and unconscious (or nonconscious) needs.

In non-verbal or image-based inquiries, the researcher has a choice whether to provide the images to bring to the interaction, or to ask the interviewee to supply the images. If the researcher supplies the images, the interviewee could be asked to respond to the images. Henry Sanoff (1991), in his book *Visual Research Methods in Design* talked about extracting cognitive information by asking the subject to record **self-reports** in response to viewing phenomena in the built environment which could be views of rooms, engagement with exteriors, photos of buildings, or video. The form of these self-reports may be verbal, written (in a diary format), or visual (through the interviewee supplying photographs or artwork in response). In addition, a researcher can ask the interviewee to bring photos, drawings, art objects, or other artifacts to help start the conversation, or to explain a feeling, thought, or desire. In this way we can see that the interview process could incorporate *user-generated imagery*, when an interviewee provides visual documentation in some format which becomes part of the raw data of the study.

Another example of a self-report is the practice at many weddings of inviting guests to take photos with their smartphones and uploading them to a common folder which becomes the end-users' contribution to the wedding album. This practice enhances understanding of the multiple perspectives enjoyed on that significant event. In other words, this is a good way for the wedding party to get an insight into the subjective experience of their guests. Instead of relying solely on the professional photographer to capture the day, the wedding party seeks alternative perspectives from the point of view of their guests. The wedded couple or their family may then establish a social media page where the guests can upload images. We can use similar techniques to gather information from our subjects, by having them photograph what is important to them about their environments.

The architect Jennifer Luce gave disposable cameras to employees of a furniture showroom and asked them to photograph what was most important or inspiring to them about the products they sold and about their work environment. She collected more than 500 photographs that included details of the furniture, views of nature, and artistic interpretations of the existing workplace. She posted many of them on a tackable wall surface in her office for a meeting with the client, the owner of the showroom, to give the client a sense of what the employees envisioned for the new showroom, as well as to provide a jumping-off point for her own ideas. "When you look at it all on the wall, all the info—there is the kernel of a really strong innovative and new idea" (J. Luce, personal communication, January 3, 2008). This method works equally well with photographs originally captured digitally, and today's designer may want to consider the palpable advantages of a physical display over a web-based post.

Architect Gives Her Clients "Homework"

In her initial meetings with a client, Jennifer Luce spends much of the time using creative techniques to try to determine the client's needs. For Luce, an interview is an interactive effort in which she tries to get at the client's underlying values or needs, ones that the client may not be able to articulate. "We give our clients assignments to express themselves. This exercise immediately breaks down barriers and opens doors … During this unique interview process with residential projects, we have a very important goal: to discover the deep-seated desires and personality of the client" (J. Luce, personal communication, January 3, 2008). The following excerpt is taken from a story in the *New York Times* about working with Luce's client, Greg Lemke, a scientist in La Jolla, California.

After their first meeting, Ms. Luce asked Dr. Lemke to create a work, in any medium, that would reveal his sensibility. "The idea was to really get to know how he thinks," said Ms. Luce. As Dr. Lemke recalls it, "Jennifer auditioned me as a client." Dr. Lemke, a lover of classical music (and an amateur composer), made a tape of several of his favorite fugues, including one by Shostakovich. The fugue, Ms. Luce realized, is about variation on a theme. With a basic structure in place, the composer can go off in unexpected, sometimes even whimsical, directions. With that realization, Ms. Luce came up with the idea of building a spine down the middle of the house, as a kind of structure from which she could explore architectural variations. The spine contains storage for everything from clothes to music to Dr. Lemke's research notes. Its doors are a mosaic of weathered zinc, hot rolled steel and lacquered wood. (Bernstein, 2007)

The architectural researcher Edith Cherry pioneered the concept of participant end-user involvement. She writes extensively about involving end-users (schoolchildren) in the design process by having them participate in creative drawing exercises to envision their ideal school (see Figure 6.5).

"The measure of the exercise is not so much in whether the ideas make their way into the final design, but did we have a good time? And did the kids feel that they had contributed? Did they get excited about their new school? Did we as designers form a commitment to do a good project for them?" (Cherry, personal communication, June 4, 2008).

Sorting Techniques

Edith Cherry advises you to orchestrate participants' activities by providing categories or headings in organized group interview situations. "Adults usually do not like to draw. Instead, we use idea cards. Give the group a ten-minute deadline and have them put them up on the wall" (Cherry, personal communication, June 4, 2008). For projects that have multiple points of view, many different staff types, or complex issues, this kind of communal, unrestricted session is a great idea. Headings on the wall, for a school project, might include "Activities," "Operation," "Aesthetics," "Recreational," and "Educational." As school administrators, faculty,

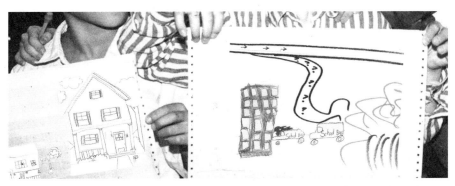

Figure 6.5 Photo of children's drawings of their school to gain insight into how they envisioned their ideal school (adapted from Edith Cherry).

and staff fill out the cards, you can pin up the cards under the appropriate heading. Always include a category called "Other" to welcome ideas or issues that do not fall under any identified category. Once cards have accumulated in this temporary "parking lot," you can revisit them to determine, with their originators, whether they comprise a new category or continue as outliers to the main headings. This activity allows user groups of all sorts to see what ideas or issues are faced by other users of the space. For a complex project such as designing a detention center, there are all kinds of staff members who may be able to provide valuable input. Workers on the night shift may face different problems than those on the day shift. The corrections officers would see things differently than would the cooks. This kind of session could help you—as well as the entire staff—examine the design challenges from multiple points of view.

RESEARCH IN ACTION 6.3
How Can a Nine-Year-Old Girl Design a $400 Million Hospital?

A patented process for uncovering hidden concepts and distilling information into an emerging **metaphor** called **Zaltman Metaphor Elicitation Technique (ZMET)** was used to come up with a strong design concept for a children's hospital in Pittsburgh. Architect Lou Astorino and his staff at his architecture and engineering firm turned to ZMET to conduct ninety-minute interviews with representative end-users (patients, staff, and administration) that included sharing thoughts and feelings about a topic. The interviews with ZMET result in composite images (collages) that represent the subconscious needs and wants of the interviewees. Based on metaphors that evolved out of the extensive interview process, Astorino takes the information and filters it to extract design concepts and solutions that respond to the deep-seated wants and needs of the hospital end-users. In this case the strongest metaphor identified was "*Transformation.*" Everyone interviewed in the hospital experience wanted to feel transformed in some way, not only from sick to well but also from unbalanced to balanced, and from feeling a lack of control to empowerment or the ability to manage. Astorino created a report explaining how this goal could translate to design solutions.

One of the design solutions involved the creation of a "Transformation Corridor" that begins at the garage where the family parks and carries through to ambulatory care where they check into the hospital. The corridor literally transforms as the child and family walk through it. A mural that begins with very geometric graphics changes into a cocoon, then to a butterfly as the family reaches registration, where the three-story atrium contains butterflies hanging as artwork in the space. The corridor transformation also includes other design elements such as the lighting, textures, and the floor tiles which change to express a changing of seasons. Furthermore, research revealed that the hospital experience begins on the car ride heading to the hospital. Thus, the exterior of the hospital needed to be welcoming to children. Astorino performed a color study with kids resulting in a sophisticated palette implemented on the exterior. Because the site is on a hillside it became an iconic landmark seen by the patient from far away as they approach the hospital.

For every project, *fathom* brings together a variety of experts, specialists, and consultants such as industrial designers, graphic designers, interior designers, color specialists, anthropologists, psychologists, and neuroscientists. This dynamic team reviews all the complex information gathered and interprets it with a variety of unique perspectives to best determine the

The composite graphic images resulting from the interview process, and the resulting design, a "transformation corridor."

programming and design criteria that will respond to create that feeling.

When *fathom* was developing the program for a *Veterans Administration* hospital called *Veterans' Recovery Center*, they asked this question: "How can we allow our nation's veterans to help change the face of the VA?" The answer was to let the veterans tell their own stories. For example, one of the end-users was a homeless veteran who was suffering from a mental illness. At one time he had been a special agent in the armed forces and had earned several medals for serving his country. As a designer, you have an opportunity to recognize that this end-user is not simply a homeless person. This is not how he started out, and in fact he has done amazing things in his life. So, knowing this, can you let him help you design his space?

Activity 6.3

Employing an Innovative Interview Technique

Purpose: Engage in an image-based inquiry to practice using images in an interview.

1. Select one of the many image-based interview techniques discussed in this chapter. Design and conduct an innovative interview using images with one of the interviewee types below.

2. Select an interviewee from one of the following categories:

   a. Group of people

   b. Young child (with permission from caregiver)

   c. Non-verbal adult (someone who speaks a different language, someone who is hearing impaired, or otherwise cannot communicate with you in a traditional verbal exchange)

3. Present your raw data to the class. Data may consist of user-generated drawings, photos, or images sorted by category, or collages composed using a ZMET technique.

4. Discuss the possibilities and challenges of your selected technique and what you learned while conducting it.

CONCLUSION

As a professional interior designer and design-informed researcher, you are going to be expected to interview potential clients, end-users, and experts on a regular basis. It is important to become a confident interviewer. Knowing when an interview needs to take place, identifying candidates for the interview, and then convincing the potential interviewee to give you the information is the first task. The second task is to properly prepare a list of pertinent questions, meet the person in an appropriate manner, and accurately record the information. Not only will acquiring this series of skills allow you to gather usable information, it will also instill in you a sense of confidence about interacting with clients and design professionals in the future.

Look for potential interviews everywhere. If you simply talk to people whom you know, it is remarkable how quickly you will find that a friend, a neighbor, an instructor, or a family member knows someone who may have information about your topic. Interviews are the perfect opportunity for meeting new people, understanding another person's perspective, establishing a professional contact, and setting the stage for a future relationship. View the interview not as an isolated event but as the beginning of a relationship. The interviewee could serve as a jury member at your final presentation, could be a future employer, or could be a future client when you enter the professional arena.

Key Terms

Client
Closed-ended question
Coding/codify
Data reduction
End-user
Focus group
Interview

Metaphor
Open-ended question
Participant end-user
Potential end-user
Probe
Proprioceptive
Questionnaire

Reconstruction
Self-report
Somatosensory
Standardized questionnaire
Transcription
Vestibular
Zaltman Metaphor Elicitation
Technique (ZMET)

Discussion Questions

1. What makes interviewing an attractive data-gathering method for your research? How would interviews help answer your research questions?
2. What are potential downsides to using interviews as a data-gathering technique?
3. Have you seen an interview broadcast in the media that stood out to you? Show a video clip, play an audio clip, or share an excerpt of the interview transcript with the class. Discuss what made this interview successful or impactful.
4. How do you plan to minimize your influence as a researcher on the interviewee?
5. How would you be able to tell if the interviewee is being truthful? What additional steps could you take to verify the information?
6. What other questions (if any) do you have about the interview process?

References

AIA Chicago (2020). Conference: Gender Neutral Design: Restrooms and Beyond, June 16, 2020, Chicago, IL.

Bernstein, F. A. (2007, August 23). From modest to modernist. *New York Times*. Retrieved May 9, 2009 from http://www.nytimes.com/2007/08/23/garden/23luce.html

Coopman, S. J. (2006). *Conducting the information interview*. Online tutorial, San José State University. Retrieved May 9, 2009 from http://www.roguecom.com/interview

Kinsey, A. (1948–1953). *The Kinsey Reports on human sexual behavior*. New York: Signet.

McNamara, C. (1999). *General guidelines for conducting interviews*. Minneapolis, MN: Authenticity Consulting.

Merton, R., Fiske, M., & Kendall, P. (1990). *The focused interview: A manual of problems and procedures* (2nd ed.). New York: Free Press.

Patton, M. (1990). *Qualitative evaluation and research methods*. Thousand Oaks, CA: Sage.

Research. (n.d.). Retrieved from Institute for Human Centered Design: https://www.humancentereddesign.org/services/research

Ronner, H., & Jhaveri, S. (1974). *Louis I Kahn complete works 1935–1974*. Boston, MA: Birkhäuser Basel.

Roulston, K., DeMarrais, K., & Lewis, J. B. (2003). Learning to interview in the social sciences. *Qualitative inquiry*, 9(4), 643–668.

Sanoff, H. (1991). *Visual research methods in design*. New York: John Wiley.

Seven senses (n.d.). Retrieved from http://www.7senses.org.au/what-are-the-7-senses/

Taylor, J. L. (2009). Reference module in neuroscience and biobehavioral psychology. *Encyclopedia of Neuroscience* (pp. 1143–1149). New York: Academic Press. Retrieved March 15, 2021 from https://doi.org/10.1016/B978-008045046-9.01907-0

Wheeler, L. K. (n.d.). Research Assignment #3. English Department, Carson–Newman College. Retrieved April 20, 2008, from http://web.cn.edu/kwheeler/researchassignment3.html

Zeisel, J. (1984). *Inquiry by design: Tools for environment–behaviour research*. Cambridge, UK: Cambridge University Press.

Surveys

CHAPTER 7

LEARNING OBJECTIVES

After you complete this chapter, you will be able to:

- Recognize when to use surveys as a data-collection method.

- Choose statistical scales of measurement to align your variables, data categories, and desired comparative outcomes.

- Compose multiple question types and know when to use various open-ended and closed-ended options.

- Design your questionnaire in terms of layout and sequence.

- Pilot test and refine your survey.

- Practice online and in-person distribution methods for surveying using standardized questionnaires.

- Prepare your survey data for analysis in both graphic and written forms.

In this chapter, we explore methods that seek to query multiple people to generate statistical data. For example, if school administrators asked you to recommend paint colors for their classrooms, there are several ways to inform your decision. You could, first, read about scientific experiments conducted which sought to make a causal connection between wall color and learning from a biological, cognitive, or neuroscience perspective. Next, you could read about studies performed in classrooms from educational, behavioral, or other social science research. You could look at an anthropological or cultural study which related color to learning within a particular end-user population such as an age range (elementary school age children) or culture (Southern California school district). You could supplement these study results with original data by interviewing several end-users such as teachers and students to get their opinions and preferences (as discussed in Chapter 6). But if you wanted to know what the *majority* of students preferred in this particular school, and you wanted to have current, local, and context-specific statistical evidence to back up your claim to the school board, you would want to conduct a *survey*.

ADMINISTERING SURVEYS

In general, to **survey** means to query (someone) in order to collect data for the analysis of some aspect of a group or an area. In a more technical sense, a **survey design** refers to that act of formulating and conducting a statistical study of a sample population by asking questions about knowledge, opinions, preferences, and other aspects of people's lives. For the purposes of interior design research, *survey design* means to reach out to clients or potential end-users to obtain information essential to informing the program or programmatic requirements, the problems to solve, as well as data for solving the problems. Like interviews, surveys attempt to get information from people using a topic-related list of questions referred to as a *questionnaire*. Surveys, like interviews (explored in Chapter 6), are a type of personal report in which people report information about themselves which may, or may not, be truthful. It is our hope that by getting a large quantity of responses, truthfulness overall will emerge, as we feel that most people will tell the truth, especially when

they can take a survey anonymously. In addition, when there are simply too many people to interview individually, an appropriate interior design research method will be a survey design. In this chapter, we will be asking people questions in order to generate statistical data for *descriptive*, *predictive*, or *comparative* purposes.

Continuing our example of a school board seeking advice on paint colors, a *descriptive* survey may show that 90% of the students preferred a distinct shade of blue. A *comparative* survey might reveal that, while 90% of students chose this blue, only 60% of the faculty selected the same color. If the survey is done as part of a longitudinal study, it may compare data over time, such as "sixty percent of the faculty chose blue as the most appropriate color for a classroom this year, as opposed to only 40% last year." A *predictive* survey might try to link the concept of being a student or teacher (an independent variable) with the dependent variable of color preference for the purpose of proving or disproving a hypothesis that color preferences depend on how the respondents view the function of color in the classroom. For example, maybe after reviewing results from the first survey, your research question becomes, "why are students choosing blue more often than teachers for the color of their classroom walls?" You speculate that students chose a soothing and relaxing color to reduce anxiety, while faculty preferred a more stimulating color to help keep students alert. You could then design a carefully worded series of questions to help determine whether your hypothesis is supported by the data.

As mentioned earlier, one of the main reasons for selecting survey design over interviews as a data collection method is when you need to gather the opinions of a large sample of a group and are unable to interview each of them. Additionally, you would choose to prepare and conduct a survey when your task is to turn the opinions or self-reported behaviors of a group (qualitative information) into quantitative information. To do this, you must design a standardized questionnaire consisting of questions that can turn responses into numbers or percentages. It is not an easy task, but when it is done correctly it can yield very useful data for your project.

Figure 7.1 shows a famous, yet simple survey design conducted within the *Bauhaus* in 1923. Kandinsky circulated this graphic question requesting respondents

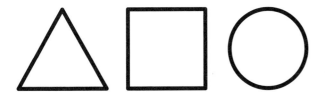

For the purposes of investigation the wall painting workshop requests solutions to the following problems:

1. Fill in these three forms with the colors yellow, red, and blue. The coloring is to fill the form entirely in each case.
2. If possible, provide an explanation for your choice of color.

Figure 7.1
Kandinsky's "psychological test," distributed as an informal survey to members of the Bauhaus in 1923 (from Lupton & Abbott Miller, 2019, p. 56).

to fill in the triangle, square, and circle with their choice of red, yellow, and blue. He then asked them to provide an explanation indicting how they thought their selected color related to the shape.

According to Lupton and Abbott Miller (2019), Kandinsky "hoped to discover a universal correspondence between form and color" and that the informal inquiry was "an attempt to identify the grammar and elements of a 'language of vision'" which, since then, has been embedded as part of modernist design education (p. 56). They go on to say, "Kandinsky achieved a remarkable consensus with his questionnaire—in part, perhaps, because others at the school supported his theoretical ideal" (p. 56). In 1990, Lupton and Abbott Miller readministered Kandinsky's "psychological test" to contemporaneous designers, educators, and art critics to see if they could replicate the results. Would respondents answer in much the same way, or would their color choices differ? In other words, after 67 years since the results showed a relationship between color and shape, was this theory still valid? If you are curious about their findings, they have published some of the survey responses in their book, *The ABC's of the Bauhaus*. In Activity 7.1 you are encouraged to try and test this out on your own.

Activity 7.1
Testing Your Survey Skills

Purpose: To replicate a famous survey and compare your data with their findings.

Distribute the questionnaire with the blank shapes (Figure 7.1), and have your friends, family, or colleagues assign the three colors to the three shapes and see how they respond. You can distribute the simple graphic question via e-mail, or on paper, leaving a stack of copies, colored markers or pencils, and a box with a slot in the top (clearly marked) for people to drop completed questions, or you can conduct the data collection in person at your school or neighborhood with random passers-by. Collect a minimum of thirty responses. Then organize them in stacks (or digital folders) by patterns or trends which seem to emerge from the collected data. Present your findings to the class.

What did you learn by doing this activity?

The reasons for using a **standardized questionnaire**, an identical series of questions distributed to a group of people, are (1) to survey as many people as possible with the most timely and efficient means and then (2) to be able to turn those people's responses (raw data/qualitative data) into quantities such as percentages or majorities. This numerical statistical data has a variety of uses, but primarily it is used to form a substantial basis for future design decisions. This chapter will help you design questions, and organize and sequence those questions, to create a survey instrument. Then we will explore methods of *surveying* or distributing those questionnaires to a sample population. After collecting the raw data there will be some guidance on representing the data through graphic or visual means such as graphs, charts, and tables. In Chapter 9 we will explore the process of analyzing the results and the different ways of interpreting the statistical data.

TYPES OF SURVEYS AND QUESTIONNAIRES

As interior design researchers, we can survey clients to understand needs, values, goals, industry trends, business perspective on value of design, organizational culture, institutional norms, and potential obstacles to accepting our design ideas. We can survey end-users about experiences, expectations, preferences, and opinions. In addition, we can survey potential end-users to help determine the future direction of a proposed program or to help inform a type of space that has not existed before. This section of the chapter explores the different audiences you might want to reach and the tool you would design for that purpose.

Client (or Potential Client)

Before an initial client meeting, interior designers may use a survey to find out basic information such as company history, organization and values, project goals, project scope, and budget. If the client, or the decision-making agency, involves more than one person, a survey allows the individual members of the group to anonymously voice their opinions about their personal goals or priorities. The designer can then share the findings with the rest of the group as part of a quest to ascertain the priorities or establish the goals of the collective stakeholders. One goal might be to uncover which key personnel the group believes the designer should interview to gather more in-depth information.

RESEARCH IN ACTION 7.1
An Exhibit Makeover Start-Up Agenda

The exhibit planner Alice Parman calls this questionnaire her "*Start-Up Agenda*." She asks a series of mainly *open-ended questions* which allow for unlimited responses but then narrows the questions to have the respondents delineate "the most important facts about the subject matter" and "most frequent questions asked about the exhibit" to help outline a clear agenda for the museum project. By the end of the survey, she asks the stakeholders to rank how they think the current museumgoers perceive their museum. Alice outlines the purpose of having the whole group participate in the survey:

> These concepts and values will guide me as I design and fulfill a planning process that is customized to your situation, resources, and project goals. Interpretive planning is grounded in the mission, vision, and identity of your institution. One of my most important responsibilities as a facilitator and planner is to continually advocate for actual and potential audience members. [My goal is to] create a plan that is energizing and inspiring, yet realistic and doable within the institution's capacity and your community context.
>
> (Parman, 2008)

Below is a sample survey, adapted from a document titled "*Exhibit Makeover Worksheets*," that Alice might ask her clients to complete to help her get a design project under way.

Main Facts

What are some of the most interesting things, juiciest tidbits, or compelling details about the subject matter?

_____

_____

_____

What are the top two most important facts about the subject matter?

_____

_____

What are the most frequent questions people ask about this exhibit?

_____

_____

_____

Community Role of _____
(your museum)

Review each description as it might apply to your museum today. Check the descriptions that you think best match how your community *currently* views your museum.

Rank order each description on a scale of 1 to 5 (1 = perfect match; 5 = not at all like us).

▶

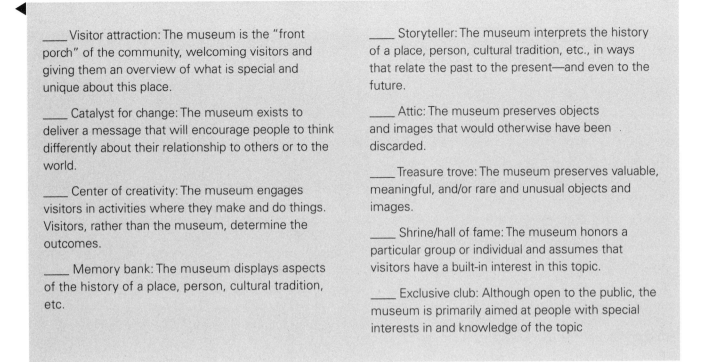

____ Visitor attraction: The museum is the "front porch" of the community, welcoming visitors and giving them an overview of what is special and unique about this place.

____ Catalyst for change: The museum exists to deliver a message that will encourage people to think differently about their relationship to others or to the world.

____ Center of creativity: The museum engages visitors in activities where they make and do things. Visitors, rather than the museum, determine the outcomes.

____ Memory bank: The museum displays aspects of the history of a place, person, cultural tradition, etc.

____ Storyteller: The museum interprets the history of a place, person, cultural tradition, etc., in ways that relate the past to the present—and even to the future.

____ Attic: The museum preserves objects and images that would otherwise have been discarded.

____ Treasure trove: The museum preserves valuable, meaningful, and/or rare and unusual objects and images.

____ Shrine/hall of fame: The museum honors a particular group or individual and assumes that visitors have a built-in interest in this topic.

____ Exclusive club: Although open to the public, the museum is primarily aimed at people with special interests in and knowledge of the topic

To evaluate client satisfaction, we can also set up a list of questions to be answered at the completion of a project. Usually, this list of questions is referred to as a **Satisfaction Survey** or **Exit Poll**. This information could be used to improve customer service or collect references for future projects. In interior design projects, a **Post Occupancy Evaluation (POE)** can also be conducted which may include a survey to clients about the design of their new facility, but often includes a survey of end-users (staff and other visitors or occupants of the space), along with *observations* (discussed in Chapter 8).

End-User

Are the employees of the company satisfied with their work environment? Can they offer any suggestions for improvement? An end-user questionnaire is aimed at uncovering data that would support or refute any preconceived notion or theory the client has about the experience of the users of the space. This kind of questionnaire must guarantee absolute anonymity so that the respondents can answer the questions honestly and without fear that giving a negative response would affect their job security or otherwise put them at risk. Many times, an end-user has valuable information or feedback about the current space that would then require more in-depth study through one-on-one interviews (discussed in Chapter 6) or direct *observation* (discussed in Chapter 8).

An example of an end-user questionnaire used to survey faculty members for a redesign of their faculty workspace is in the Research in Action 7.2 box titled Faculty Workspace Questionnaire. Notice how this survey mainly uses a series of choices in a **ranking question** to establish priorities, a blank area for open-ended comments, and then offers a **clearinghouse question**, which you may also use in interviews, which is a type of follow-up question or probe used to make sure you have elicited all the information a respondent wants to provide on a topic. Also, since this questionnaire was printed on paper and left in the faculty workspace, it includes instructions at the end indicating what the respondent should do with the completed form as well as the deadline for submitting a survey.

Target Market

A target market questionnaire might be used to help you identify your end-user group when the group is not known. Who would be most likely to use your new facility? This kind of questionnaire enables you to generate a *user profile*—or to elaborate on a user profile if a vague notion of who would use the space has already been determined. For example, if your client would like to open an alternative birthing clinic, what are the characteristics of the target audience? Obviously, the target audience would be pregnant women or women who are planning to become pregnant, but how can you more fully detail your user profile to design a space that would cater to this user group's specific needs and closely align with their sense of aesthetics?

The first couple of questions in this type of questionnaire would be **qualifier questions**; that is, these questions would focus on whether the respondent fits the overall target audience. Is the respondent a woman? Is she of child-bearing age? Is she married or in a committed relationship? Is she planning to have a child or additional children? And would she consider using the alternative birthing methods your client is planning to offer at the facility?

Once the respondent's applicability is determined, the next part of the questionnaire would focus on the respondent's demographic information, such as where she lives, what her income level is, and what her cultural background may be—to give substance to the user profile. In the remainder of the questions, you would be asking about her expectations and desires for the ideal alternative birthing clinic, from functional qualities to aesthetic ones. This last kind of question may include many descriptive words (often referred to as **semantic differentials**) and images to help inform a research-based design concept.

Popular Opinion

Sometimes it is necessary to get a sense of what people think about a proposal or an existing condition, even if these people will not be clients or end-users of a space. These people are neighbors, or anyone else who could be affected by the proposed design—including those people who may perceive your project as competition. Acknowledging and understanding the opposition to your project may be just as important to the project's success as rallying those who favor the project. This group may also include those who have expert opinions that could help improve your design. Expanding on the example of the alternative birthing clinic, respondents to a popular opinion questionnaire may include midwives at other alternative birthing clinics or doctors who favor traditional medical practices (so that you can at least understand the concerns of a divergent opinion). Questions in this type of survey include qualifiers that establish the person's education level or areas of expertise, followed by opinion questions. Sometimes, incorporating these people into the planning process will open doors that seem to have been closed, or it will establish a dialog that will allow your project to proceed more easily.

COMPOSING A QUESTIONNAIRE
Types of Questions

Survey question types should be mostly closed-ended, because many people are being consulted and it is easier to quantify number of responses when there is a limited number of choices. You must know *exactly* what you are trying to find out and what your goals for the questionnaire are, so that you ask questions that are specific, and you quickly get to the point of what you are trying to accomplish. You may want to use different types of questions to verify an answer. Asking a question in more than one way will help limit the chance that your results will be skewed because your audience was confused by a particular question. Your questionnaire not only needs to present your questions, but it also needs to identify the

characteristics of the subject so that you can more easily see whether you are reaching your end-user or target market. To achieve this, make sure you integrate the following kinds of identifying questions in your questionnaire.

Types of questions:

- Qualifiers
- Open-ended or nonstructured questions
- Multiple-choice questions
  - Forced-choice
  - Check-all-that-apply
- Nominal categories
- Interval categories
- Ratings scale
- Likert Attitude Scale
- Ranking
- Sentence completion questions
- Visual interpretation questions
- Contingency questions.

Qualifiers are questions that test whether the respondent fits a list of certain predetermined qualifications. You may want to ask these questions up-front, because they will determine whether the respondent fits the user profile of the population. You will need to collect simple *demographic data* (as discussed in Chapter 5) such as age, gender, education level, occupation, and mobility/ability levels and so forth, that would qualify the subject as a member of your defined population. These human characteristics help you to build a demographic profile, which is a collection of attributes assigned to a particular population. Qualifiers can also be questions about the person's lifestyle, habits, and preferences. For example, if you are looking for people who frequent hair salons more than once a month, you may have to compose two questions: one that asks whether respondents have ever been to a salon, then a follow-up question regarding intervals of frequency— less than once a month, once a month, and more than once a month.

Open-ended or *nonstructured questions* should be used only (1) when the sample population is small or (2) as a follow-up to a series of closed-ended questions as an opportunity to gather clarification for answers. It is generally too difficult to translate the many answers generated by open-ended questions into statistics that would identify trends. Imagine tallying election results if all the candidates were write-ins!

RESEARCH IN ACTION 7.3
An Earth-Friendly Spiritual Experience

For initial information-gathering, you may not know enough about the subject to develop other types of questions, so a *preliminary* survey may include only *open-ended questions*. Interior design student Jennifer Kautz was interested in gathering general information on a sensitive subject: people's experience with contemporary funeral services in the United States. To accommodate a variety of possible answers, Jennifer put together the following questionnaire. Notice how the questions are subdivided, and how the intent of the questions is stated to help ensure clarity.

For questions 1 through 3, I would like for you to consider what you know and have experienced for funerary services in general.

1. In your experience, what has been the most helpful aspect of funerary services in dealing with your grief over the loss of a loved one?

2. What has been the least helpful aspect?

3. If you could change anything about the funeral service industry, what would it be?

Questions 4 through 6 are more specific to one particular loss that has affected you.

4. What was your relation to the deceased?

5. What kind of ceremony, if any, accompanied the funeral services?

6. Did you participate in the ceremony? If so, in what capacity did you participate?

Lastly, in questions 7 through 9, I would like to know what you might have considered for your own funeral arrangements.

7. Would you prefer cremation, burial, or some other way of caring for your remains at the end of your life?

8. What kind of services and/or ceremonies would you like for your own funeral? Why?

9. Is there a special place you would prefer to have your remains scattered, buried, enclosed, or memorialized? If so, where and why?

The results of this open-ended questionnaire identified many issues, including the respondents' desire to participate more in preparing the body for burial, their desire for funerals to be more spiritual and connected to the earth than religious and formal, and the surprising number of respondents who wished to be cremated rather than buried. Responses to questions 7 through 9 allowed the student to project what the funeral of the future would look like, and the responses influenced her decision to create a more sustainable and earth-friendly project situated in a nondenominational, parklike setting.

Multiple-choice questions can come in two varieties: *forced-choice* and *check-all-that-apply*. When giving a person a multiple-choice question with only one response required, you want to make sure that the categories are mutually exclusive—that is, that your categories do not overlap. This can be a simple yes/no question. Or it can have different categories, as in age ranges. For example, the age categories "under 11, 11 to 20, 21 to 40, 41 and over" are mutually exclusive (Zeisel, 1984, p. 164). When a question contains a list, you want to make sure it is *exhaustive*. An **exhaustive list** includes *all* the possible responses to the question. It is very difficult (and sometimes impossible) to think of all of the possible responses to a question. And you run the risk of bad data because a key response may be missing. You also run the risk of your respondent becoming annoyed or frustrated that their answer is not listed as a choice. In summary, provide an exhaustive list in your question, or your resulting data may not be accurate. It is very simple to do so. To make an incomplete list exhaustive, researchers add an "other" category (Zeisel, 1984, p. 164).

According to education technology website byjus.com, "in statistics, the variables or numbers are defined using different scales of measurement. Each level has specific properties that determine its use in statistical analysis" (2022, n.p.). Refer to Figure 7.2 to see how the levels build on each other in terms of the relationship of categories to each other. There is an art to dividing up possible answers on your survey question.

LEVELS OF MEASUREMENT

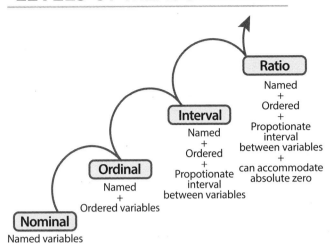

Figure 7.2
Levels of measurement in statistical scales: nominal, ordinal, interval, and ratio (https://byjus.com/maths/scales-of-measurement/).

First consider whether your categories are nominal, interval, ordinal, or ratio.

With the root of word derived from *nom*, Latin for name, **nominal categories** are different possible answers based on *names* of things, such as kinds of furniture (*chair*, *table*, or *desk*); or *descriptive* words, such as *curved*, *active*, or *busy*; or *adjectives* to describe the way a space feels, such as *intimidating*, *powerful*, or *comforting*. If you wanted to know the types of activities that a person does in a room, you could generate a list for the respondent to choose from, such as sleep, eat, study, entertain, relax, play, work, and so forth. Thinking about your research question jot down a list of options that you might ask your respondent to choose from. Would you like to know their favorite from a list of colors? Or places they have visited? Or amenities they would like to have access to in their work environment? A brainstorming session with others to create a comprehensive list is the best way to start composing a question using nominal categories. You will then narrow down the number of choices to align with your overarching research question and questionnaire design. Make sure not to overwhelm the respondent with too many choices.

When there is some sort of order to the variables, such as low to high (magnitude), hours of the day, order of tasks, or some other sequencing, you will create categories along an **ordinal scale**. Like the nominal scale, the ordinal scale is considered qualitative data since

it is descriptive in nature. When you want responses that indicate frequency (number of times per week, for example), intensity of feeling, or degree to which respondents agree or disagree with a statement, you will want to use a **ratings scale**. This question type most often involves ranges from "low to high," "least to most," or "agree to disagree." If you have posted a review to a restaurant of have responded to a customer satisfaction survey at the end of a retail transaction, you have experienced an ordinal scale.

Another type of question that uses an ordinal scale is *ranking* in order of importance or priority. These types of questions are often difficult for people to answer. And there may be many unknowns from the researcher perspective in why the respondent ranked the items the way they did. A follow-up method may be necessary to find out details behind the ranking. Example: Rank in order of importance the following aspects of your work environment:

_____ Privacy
_____ Storage
_____ Low Noise Level
_____ View
_____ Temperature
_____ Work Surface

To make ranking questions conceptually easier, you could vary them by allocating a percentage or a fixed amount to each category.

Example: What percentage of your total budget do you envision spending on each of the following kitchen components? Must total 100 percent.

_____ Cabinets
_____ Appliances
_____ Flooring
_____ Countertops
_____ Backsplash
_____ Fixtures/Hardware

Another variation on this type of question would be to have respondents select a few of the choices without ranking. Sometimes just knowing the top three categories, for example, may be all you need to know. It may be less intimidating, and far less math involved, for a respondent to just choose a few items from the list.

One very popular example of a ratings scale is the ***Likert Attitude Scale***. This is a widely used scale in which respondents are given a list of statements and asked whether they "strongly agree," "agree," are "undecided," are "neutral," "disagree," or "strongly disagree." These are used to measure attitudes (Fraenkel, Wallen, & Sawin, 1999). It is a good idea to group all of these questions together under a single heading so that the respondent becomes familiar with the scale and can move more quickly through the questions (Zeisel, 1984). A central question is whether there should there be an odd or even number of divisions. An odd number of divisions gives a "neutral" center value, while an even number of divisions forces respondents to take a non-neutral position.

Interval categories involve numbers that have consistent or proportional values in between such as hours, sizes, ages, or income level in dollars. These are considered quantitative data since you can use the numbers generated from your survey to find the average, or you can subtract one category from another mathematically. You can also create intervals using ranges such as age ranges commonly used in qualifier questions or comparing sizes such as small (100–200 square feet), medium (201–399 square feet) and large (400+). In this case you decide what the interval will be. Divide the items into increments that make sense to the user. In statistics, interval categories are preferred since it enables you to measure things quantitatively that are not necessarily measurable absolutely. For example, an interval scale which allows patients to indicate their pain level from 1 (very little pain) to 10 (excruciating pain) is useful to doctors in assessing the amount of medication to administer. It also allows doctors to compare pain levels in a single patient over time. **Ratio scale** compares quantitative data across different units of measure such as the conversion of pounds to kilograms or square footage to meters. It is very similar to interval scale with an added feature of having an absolute zero value.

Beyond these standard closed-ended qualitative and quantitative question types are more structured open-ended questions. **Sentence completion questions** give the respondent an opportunity to answer in a creative way. These questions can be used to spark an unexpected response (one you may never have thought of) that might influence your research project and subsequent design projects immensely. They can be used at the beginning of a questionnaire, as an icebreaker, to get respondents warmed up. They can be used to get end-users to think outside the box or

placed after a series of questions designed to influence or guide the open-ended response. Or they can be used as a fun, light-hearted way to establish a rapport with an unknown respondent—to humanize the anonymous responses.

Examples of sentence completion questions:

- My dream kitchen would have _____.
- If I could meet someone famous (living or passed away), it would be _____ _____.
- My favorite time of day is _____ because _____.
- If they made a film about my life, _____ (insert actor's name) would play me.
- If I were a food, I would be _____.
- When I was growing up, _____ had a big impact on my life.
- If I had a choice of "superpower" it would be the ability to _____.
- I never understand why most people seem to care so much about _____.
- If I won a million dollars, I would _____.
- I recently solved a difficult problem through _____.
- My greatest fear is _____.
- One thing I would like people to know about me is _____.

You can also turn creative sentence completion questions into multiple choice:

- I believe people are/are not (choose one) responsible for their actions.
- If I had a choice of a superpower I would choose to fly/to be invisible (choose one).
- When I was younger, I played a lot of football/chess (choose one).

As you can see from the last question, sometimes you have forced your respondent to decide between two choices, neither of which applies. For example, perhaps when you were younger you did not play football or chess. In that case, you would want to include a choice of "none of these" or a fill-in the blank marked "other."

Visual interpretation questions allow respondents to respond to an image (a photograph, drawing, or diagram) or to compare a series of photographs. For example, one student wanted to explore what types of space were most conducive to studying. Using her knowledge of environmental psychology, she selected photos of spaces, each with one variable: size of room, ceiling height, amount of sunlight. She posed questions that had a choice of three photographs each, and she asked the respondent to select the photograph whose content was most conducive to studying. She then increased the complexity by showing photographs of furniture pieces and asking which would accommodate the respondent's needs for studying. She found that most students preferred to use a bed rather than a chair or a desk for studying.

Another team of students asked their teachers and classmates to provide a drawing, sketch, or photograph of their ideal work space in order to gather information about supportive furnishings for designers. Figure 7.3 shows a selection of their raw data.

You may find yourself using all question types in your survey as in Figure 7.4. You can explore an issue through a series of questions or overlapping questions to test the same concept.

Figure 7.3
Student presents a collection of drawings by participants in response to a question asking them to draw supportive workspace furnishings.

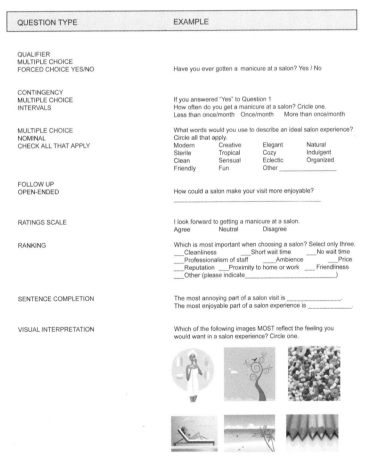

Figure 7.4
Sample questionnaire using multiple question types.

There are, of course, some question types that you probably should avoid. The first type is simply *weak questions*. For example, "What is your favorite color?" is a weak question because there are too many ways to interpret or apply the question. It is not specific enough to yield a valid answer. Are you asking a person about her favorite color for a wall in an office or her favorite color for a cocktail dress? This example illustrates an important part of composing a survey: Specificity! Answers would differ depending on the context and the object that is to be colored.

Another type of question to avoid is one that *assumes there is a universal meaning to subjective words*, like design terms and adjectives. A good example would be the use of the word *comfortable* in a question. For some people,

a "comfortable" space is open, free of clutter, streamlined. Other people would describe "comfortable" as plush, cozy, and full of personal items. You may not be able to use answers that come from *questions about general likes and dislikes*. Questions like "Do you like your job; why or why not?" and "Do you like to drink wine?" leave too much room for misinterpretation, because they combine feeling, thoughts, beliefs, and actions. Rework these questions to ask about *behavior*. For example, you can ask, "Do you drink wine?" followed by a **contingency question** about how often or in what situations the respondent drinks wine. Then you can ask specifically about a feeling or belief about alcohol consumption. The final question type to avoid is *questions that make assumptions* or lead respondents

---

Activity 7.2

Composing a Questionnaire Using Multiple Question Types

Purpose: To practice writing different kinds of survey questions for the purpose of redesigning an interior space.

In this Activity, you will design a questionnaire to collect data for a cafeteria redesign for your school. The task is to query past, current, or future students (anticipated end-users) for the purpose of understanding which cafeteria amenities are used most, liked most, used least, and liked least. Use Table 7.1 to compose a simple survey of nine

questions. The first two questions should be qualifier questions, making sure that the respondent fits the end-user profile. The remaining questions should range from broad to specific, investigating the respondent's interaction with existing cafeteria furniture, fixtures, and equipment (FF&E) and allowing them to voice their opinions and preferences. The last two questions can be any type of question. Feel free to create two questions that help you gather innovative ideas for future redesign of the cafeteria. If your school does not have a cafeteria, feel free to modify the subject matter to reflect a space your school does have such as a reception area, student lounge, reading room, or library.

Table 7.1 Write Your Own Survey Questions for a Nine-Question Survey

Question Type	Purpose	Write your questions here:
Qualifier	To determine the respondent's experience with the space.	
Qualifier	To determine the age, gender, or education level of the respondent, or any other demographic information you would like to know.	
Open-Ended	To determine cafeteria behavior or preferences	
Multiple-Choice	To determine behavior or preferences	
Ranking/Scale	To determine preferences	
Sentence Completion	To collect innovative ideas	
Visual Interpretation	To find deeply rooted or subconscious desires	
Other	To collect additional data	
Other	To collect additional data	

to take an obvious side on an issue. An example would be "Wouldn't you recycle more often if bins were provided in the cafeteria?" Who would answer "no" to that kind of question?

The graphic layout of a questionnaire is very important. The questionnaire should not appear long, intimidating, or confusing. It should be clear, concise, and inviting to the respondent. Several items must be stated clearly at the outset. Make it clear:

1. *why* people are being surveyed
2. *how long* the questionnaire should take
3. *how* to fill it out (for example, with pencil or pen)
4. *what to do with it* when completed.

DISTRIBUTING A QUESTIONNAIRE (THE ACT OF SURVEYING)

Implementing the survey can be done in-person face-to-face, in-person as a leave-behind, or online. A questionnaire can be written, oral (the researcher can ask the respondent the questions and record the respondent's answers), or electronic (distributed via the Internet or through e-mail). Written surveys can be mailed to the respondents, or distributed via mailboxes at work, or they can be left in a public area along with a drop box for returning completed surveys. It is important to get permission when distributing a survey in this last manner. You cannot simply go into a classroom or wait outside a business without securing permission. In fact, it is important to understand the difference between private property and public spaces. While free speech is protected under the U.S. Constitution, interfering with business could be a complicated issue; it is important to obtain written permission from the businesses you may affect when you're attempting to collect information from subjects in a survey.

The most popular and promising method of distribution is through the Internet. Web sites such as *SurveyMonkey.com* and *Wufoo.com* offer students a way to customize a questionnaire and distribute it to a list of e-mail addresses. The respondents are assured anonymity and can respond at their own convenience. The *limitation* to this method is that you can collect data only from persons who have an e-mail address or access to a computer.

How can you reach your intended audience? Distributing or conducting a survey involves a certain degree of salesmanship and optimism, as well as an abundance of energy and courage. Doing a survey in person requires a great deal of time and legwork. For example, if you are trying to collect information about shopping habits in a grocery store, you may need to stand outside as people are entering or exiting to ask your questions. If you are planning to survey students in the student lounge, you must prepare a sign and a drop box and plan to be there to answer questions when the lounge is full of students.

It is often difficult to overcome people's suspicions about how you are going to use their information. So, you must establish a rapport with your survey subjects. Whether by speaking to potential subjects personally or by writing a clear and compelling introduction to the survey, you need to (1) establish that you are a student, (2) assure their anonymity and confidentiality, and (3) pinpoint your project goals. You might offer incentives for completing the survey, such as a free coffee, snack, gift certificate, or the promise to be entered into a raffle for a prize. Professional survey companies often have respondents earn points, coupons, or discounts in exchange for completing surveys.

As we discussed in Chapter 2, a *population* includes all the members of a particular group of individuals that you have decided to study or to describe. It is usually very difficult or impossible to study an entire population (Fraenkel et al., 1999). Consider these examples of *entire* populations:

- All persons who have a family member who has been diagnosed with autism
- All women who are experiencing or have experienced infertility
- All preteens in the United States who play video games
- All teachers, staff, and students at a particular school
- All persons who live or work in a certain part of town.

A *sample* (as discussed in Chapter 2) is a subgroup of a population that is thought or meant to be representative of the population (Fraenkel et al., 1999). An individual member of the sample group would be called a *subject* or *respondent*. The most common method of selecting a sample group of subjects is a **random sample**: selecting people by chance. The idea is that each member of the population has an equal probability of being selected, which reduces the likelihood of a sample being biased (Fraenkel et al., 1999). A few things to consider are:

- Who are your subjects/participants? Perhaps produce a mental image of your ideal group.
- How will you choose them?
- What would you say is a **limitation** of your sample? Limitations are potential weaknesses that exist and are typically present in any study.
  - Is the size of your sample too small?
  - Are you reaching people from a narrow area?
  - Are there inherent biases to your sample, such as people who share your point of view?

According to *Wordvice*, an academic editing and proof-reading company, there are two main categories of limitations to a survey design research method: "those that result from the methodology and those that result from issues with the researcher(s)" (Wordvice, 2021). A methodological limitation is built into the design. For example, perhaps your online survey method limited your respondents to those who had access to a computer, and who could read English. A limitation arising from the researcher might be that you only surveyed people in your neighborhood, or people who you knew. In addition, "when you conduct *quantitative* research, a lack of probability sampling is an important issue that you should mention. On the other hand, when you conduct *qualitative* research, the inability to generalize the research findings could be an issue that deserves mention" (Wordvice, 2021).

Pretesting Your Questionnaire

Once you have completed the first draft of your questionnaire, it is advisable to test the questionnaire (1) for the length of time it takes to complete and (2) for clarity. "Make a few copies of your first-draft questionnaire, and then ask at least three readers to complete it. Time them as they respond … Discuss with them any confusion or problems they experience" (Axelrod & Cooper, 2008, p. 699).

Consider assembling a focus group just for the purpose of pretesting the questionnaire. Did you get the kind of responses you were seeking? Did the group misunderstand any of the questions? Review the group's answers with them to determine whether the intent of each question was clear. Keep in mind that you may have to revise the wording of a question, the order of the questions, or the type of question. You may have to add further instructions. For example, a questionnaire recently distributed at a school failed to tell respondents what to do with the survey after they completed it! Believe it or not, this kind of error occurs quite often because the researcher is so caught up in the content that simple logistical tactics often go overlooked.

Activity 7.3
Implementing Your Survey

Purpose: To distribute your nine-question survey composed in Activity 7.2 and collect a minimum of 30 completed surveys.

1. Obtain permission from the administration at your school to survey students.

2. Your target population in this activity will be all the students who have attended, currently attend, and will attend your school. Your minimum sample of thirty students will be drawn from this larger population. How do you plan on obtaining your sample? Consult Chapter 2 to recall the variety of methods for obtaining your sample.

3. Distribute the survey that you composed in Activity 7.2 in person, as a leave-behind, or online.

4. Provide incentives, such as candy or stickers, and see if you can motivate the students to respond freely and honestly.

5. Make notes about the decisions you had to make to reach your target audience, the challenges you faced, the successes you experienced, and tips you would give other design researchers about this process.

6. Did you get the responses you expected? Were there any surprises? How would you modify your survey design?

7. Share your completed surveys and notes with the class.

SUMMARIZING SURVEY DATA

The way that interior designers most often summarize their survey results is in a text format called a *summary statement*. A typical summary statement might be "survey results showed the majority of workers ranked personal storage space as their highest priority and lounge seating as the lowest priority." When you prepare a summary statement, be specific, and acknowledge inherent weakness in your findings, if necessary. Let readers draw their own conclusions about the possible causes or, at the very least remain neutral about the possible cause or solution at this point. Another sample summary statement might be "out of 250 faculty, only 36 responded to the online survey. Of those surveyed, only three people, less than 10 percent, were satisfied with their workspace. One could infer that the remaining staff members were satisfied, but the few who were asked informally why they didn't take the online survey most often said they were just too busy."

RESEARCH IN ACTION 7.4
A Sample Summary Statement

The following summary statement was made by an interior designer to the administration of a school. The statement summarized the findings of an informal survey that had been distributed via faculty mailboxes at the school. The questionnaire presented a list of areas of concern, and the faculty members were asked (1) to rank the areas in order of priority to them and (2) to make suggestions for improving the faculty workspace. Included in the designer's report was a floor plan that served to reflect, graphically and spatially, the findings of the survey. This floor plan was not intended to be the final design; rather, it was included to provide clarity in terms of physical relationships, quantities, lengths, constraints of the space, and clearances.

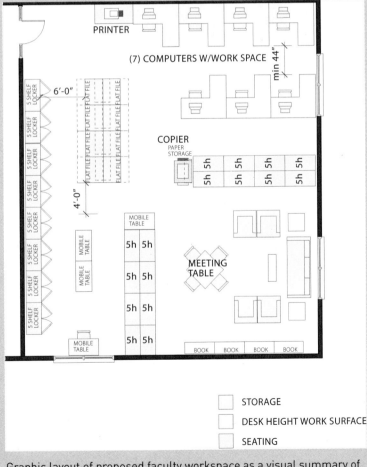

Graphic layout of proposed faculty workspace as a visual summary of survey results.

Out of 60 possible respondents, 35 feedback forms were returned by email, which represents 58 percent of the total user population. Below is a summary of their comments listed in order of priority from highest to lowest. The floor plan provides a visual representation of the areas described in Table 7.2.

Table 7.2 Sample Summary of Survey Data in Text Form

Area of Concern (List in highest to lowest priority)	Summary of Data
Individual Storage Units	This was the highest priority. Responses indicated there seemed to be a variety of storage types. Respondents recommended a combination of lockers, flat files, and locked shelving, as well as file cabinets. Tall faculty members were worried that they would be assigned to a drawer that would be too low for them. I was inspired by the way the faculty mailroom is set up with flat files below and shelving at eye height. In the scheme provided, a faculty member could elect to have a combination of locker, flat file, and shelving. Interior design faculty members wanted there to be desk-height table space near the lockers on which to lay stuff down as they load or unload their binders. Also, to make sure that all the aisles are accessible, there was concern for a minimum width. This has been adjusted in the new plan.
Computer Workstations	Additional computer workstations were the next highest priority. Faculty seemed to like the placement of the computers near the door so they could look through the glazing to see if there were any computers available before entering the workspace. Many faculty members only make use of the room when they need to use a computer. Faculty requested that wi-fi always be available. They also wanted to see an additional photocopy machine with paper storage placed near the printer, which was not originally thought of as an area of concern.
Layout Area for Grading	Most faculty reported that they grade student work in the classrooms, but that they valued a work surface for other work. I provided a few mobile tables that can be used, as well as additional workspace at each computer for paper/book/project layout. The current computer carrels do not provide any clear desk space adjacent to the computer. One faculty member was vehemently opposed to sharing workspace with any other faculty member. I think this must be addressed for the room to work.
Informal Conversation Area	Although this was not high priority, most faculty agreed that a place to sit and relax was a good idea, especially because there is no nurse's office. There was a suggestion for more than two comfortable lounge chairs (I have provided four) and for increasing the length of the sofa (instead of a love seat), so that two people would feel more comfortable sitting there, or someone could lie down if they had a headache.
Meeting Area	This was also not high priority, but it could serve as an informal meeting space or additional layout space. Someone suggested meeting with students there, but this room is just for faculty.

Choosing Graphic Representations of Data

In this section, we will review the standard ways researchers represent the raw data received using surveys. These standard graphics should be selected based on question type and type of data. Representation of data is the first step in preparing the data for analysis, interpretation, and discussion. Many times, if a researcher chooses an inappropriate graphic, the future analysis of the data will not be correct. In Chapter 9 we will explore data analysis and representation in more depth.

Consider using graphs, charts, tables, and other graphical materials to help you organize and summarize your data. Visuals can be very compelling and informative when properly done. To help you build a graph, explore online tools such as the one available at the National Center for Education Statistics (NCES, 2008) Web site: http://nces.ed.gov/nceskids/createagraph. When using Web sites such as SurveyMonkey to conduct your survey, you can choose graphic styles to represent the data, using color and shapes which visually communicate your results.

Line graphs can be used to show how something changes over time, indicating peaks and valleys (highs and lows) in the data. A line chart distributes category data evenly along a horizontal (category) axis and distributes all numerical value data along a vertical (value) axis. Line graphs can also be used to compare changes over the same period of time for more than one group by color-coding or using distinct line types to visually differentiate the groups. As shown in Figure 7.5, a line graph needs to have a title which clearly explains the purpose and data source, a legend, as well as indicate the unit of measure along each axis. Note the different shape of individual data points (round for Building A and square for Building B) as well as the two different line colors. This is done so that if the graph is printed in black and white or grayscale, the two different categories can still be distinguished visually. This graph compares the quantity of electricity (measured in kilowatts) used in two different buildings over the course of a year by showing each month's use as a single data point. Connecting the points to create lines gives the impact of continuity and the feeling of rising and falling quantities. Full descriptions and clear labeling allow the viewer to understand what the graph is showing.

Pie charts (as in Figure 7.6) do not show changes over time. They are used to compare the parts of a whole. Use pie charts when you are trying to show percentages or subcategories of a larger group such as age ranges, gender identities, languages spoken, and other demographic data. Pie charts use color or patterns to produce a powerful graphic which direct the viewer's attention to variations within a sample population. Pie charts can also break down the costs involved in a project, time spent on different tasks associated with a project, representing both continuous and discreet types of quantitative data. The overall effect of the pie chart is that it yields a visual snapshot of simultaneous occurrences or expresses a diversity of conditions at a fixed point in time. Note that the pie chart in Figure 7.6 uses both color and hatch patterns to differentiate categories. Choose color and patterns that are neutral or correspond to other colors in your presentation to minimize visual distraction or give false impressions of the various categories.

Use **bar graphs** (as in Figure 7.7) to compare items across different groups, comparing different items in related categories, or to track significantly larger changes over time. When you are trying to measure changes over time, bar graphs are best used when changes are larger, as small changes do not show up well graphically. Once again, the title of your bar graph

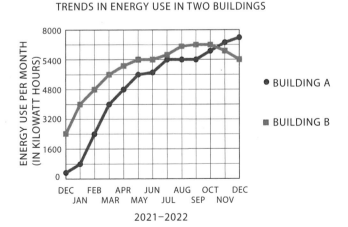

Figure 7.5
This line graph compares two buildings by showing the use of energy (each month) over the course of a year.

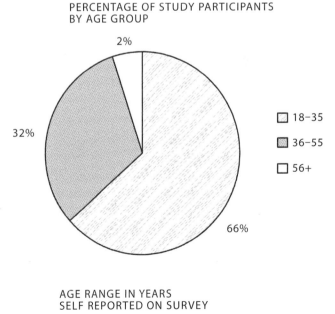

Figure 7.6
This pie chart shows the breakdown of age ranges in a sample population.

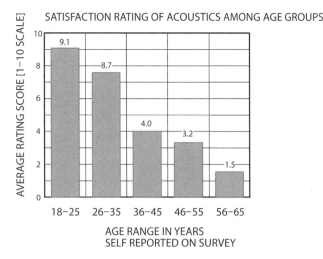

Figure 7.7
Bar chart example showing satisfaction rating among age groups.

needs to explain what is being shown or compared. In Figure 7.7, the bars represent the average score on a ratings scale for each age group surveyed. In this chart we see that the average satisfaction rating for the acoustics of a place is higher among the younger people surveyed.

Another type of chart is an *X–Y plot*, also referred to as *scatter* plots, to determine relationships between two numerical values. Scatter plots may look like line graphs; however, the main difference between scatter plots and line charts is the way they plot data on the horizontal axis—a scatter chart never displays categories on the horizontal axis. A scatter chart always has two value axes to show one set of numerical data along a horizontal (value) axis and another set of numerical values along a vertical (value) axis. The x-axis is used to measure one event (or variable), and the y-axis is

used to measure the other. If both variables increase at the same time, the variables have a positive relationship or correlation. If one variable increases while the other decreases, the variables are said to have a negative relationship. Sometimes the variables follow no pattern and are said to be unrelated. Recall the discussion in Chapter 2 about Figure 2.12 about a scatter plot used to show correlation and causation. Be cautious about assuming that a correlation is a causal relationship. That is, just because two variables have a relationship with each other, one variable did not necessarily cause the other. Simply because the age of the respondent had a positive correlation to the income level of the respondent, do not conclude that aging *causes* income level to rise. The data indicated only that these two characteristics were related in *some* way.

CONCLUSION

When there are too many people for you to be able to interview each one personally, or when you need to convert the opinions of many people into a quantity or a statistic, surveys are an effective way to collect that information. In the interview process (covered in Chapter 6), you gather introductory information that can help you create a survey. In a survey, you are trying to accomplish only a few focused goals or trying to get an answer to a very specific question. The interview helps you to understand what your question is, then your survey targets getting that question answered. As you will see in Chapter 8, sometimes your survey must be followed up with direct observation, as people's actions often speak louder than their words.

Key Terms

Bar graph	Multiple-choice question	Ratings scale
Clearinghouse question	Nominal categories	Ratio scale
Contingency question	Open-ended question	Satisfaction survey
Exhaustive	Ordinal scale	Semantic differential question
Exit poll	Pie chart	Sentence completion question
Interval categories	Post occupancy evaluation (POE)	Standardized questionnaire
Likert Attitude Scale	Qualifier question	Survey
Limitation	Random sample	Survey design
Line graph	Ranking question	Visual interpretation question

Discussion Questions

1. What are the strengths and weaknesses of the survey design data-gathering method?
2. What are the different kinds of surveys, and how can you envision using one of the many survey types in your research project?
3. Have you ever taken a poorly worded or badly designed survey? Do you recall the purpose of the survey or who distributed it? Do you recall any questions that stood out as awkward or confusing? Discuss how the survey could have been reworded or redesigned to better serve the respondent.
4. Considering the types of graphic representations discussed in the chapter, when would you use a pie chart, a line graph, a bar chart, or a scatter plot? What could be the danger in choosing the wrong type of graphic to display your data?
5. How do you think representation of survey data affects interpretation of data? Can you think of ways that people may be misled due to the graphic chosen to represent data?

References

Axelrod, R. B., & Cooper, C. R. (2008). *The St. Martin's guide to writing* (8th ed.). Boston, MA: Bedford/St. Martin's.

byjus.com (2022). https://byjus.com/maths/scales-of-measurement/

Fraenkel, J., Wallen, N., & Sawin, E. I. (1999). *Visual statistics: A conceptual primer*. Needham Heights, MA: Allyn & Bacon.

Lupton, E. and Abbott Miller, J. (2019). *The abc's of the Bauhaus and design theory*. (First published in 1993 The Cooper Union for the Advancement of Science and Art; 1991 to accompany the exhibition). Princeton, NJ: Princeton Architectural Press.

National Center for Education Statistics (NCES). (2008). *Graphing tutorial*. U.S. Department of Education. Retrieved June 2008 from http://nces.ed.gov/nceskids/createagraph/default.aspx

Parman, A. (2008). *Museum consultant and organizational coach*. Retrieved from www.aparman.com/

Wordvice (2021). Retrieved March 20, 2021 from https://wordvice.com/how-to-present-study-limitations-and-alternatives/

Zeisel, J. (1984). *Inquiry by design: Tools for Environment-Behavior research*. Cambridge: Cambridge University Press.

CHAPTER 8

Observation

LEARNING OBJECTIVES

After you complete this chapter, you will be able to:

- Use casual and systematic observation in interior design research.

- Employ appropriate Environment-Behavior (E-B) techniques for observation in naturalistic settings.

- Record observational data through notes, sketches, behavioral mapping, photo journaling, videorecording, and virtual methods.

- Incorporate experiential and quasi-experimental observations in controlled environments into your research plan.

- Develop, test, and refine your observational study instruments.

As interior designers, we know the act of looking carefully at the natural and built environment as an integral part of the design process. Award-winning architect and designer Jennifer Luce observed,

> I once took a seminar in landscape design in which students spent the first week measuring things: the width of a street, height of a tree, the number of people that cross the street in one hour. It was put on by a company called *West 8* in Rotterdam, the Netherlands (http://www.west8. nl). I asked myself, "What is this method, this process, going to do for the student?" Basically, it lays the cards on the table. Once you understand the elements which seem almost mundane, they become the building blocks, the basis for understanding. Without a foundation of information, you don't have the right to create something new.
>
> (J. Luce, personal communication,
> January 3, 2008)

UNDERTAKING OBSERVATIONS

We are constantly gathering information about our environment. When you take a dog for a walk, for example, he uses his senses of smell, touch, sight, and hearing to gather important information about his environment. This is also true of humans. As a child, you may know your grandmother's kitchen from the smell of cookies baking or you might know your school by the color and texture of the brick. For people with limited vision, the senses of hearing, touch, and smell become elevated in importance. To locate a bus stop, many people may rely on the sound of the traffic, the texture of the pavement (feeling for **detectable warnings**, ground textures which warn pedestrians they are stepping into traffic), and the smell of engine exhaust.

Like a dog sniffing to see who has passed, we use our senses to obtain information about the current situation as well as events that may have happened in the past. This chapter will focus on **observation**: the use of one or more of the senses to obtain and record information on individuals, objects, or events, as a method of gathering information for interior design (Fraenkel, Wallen, & Sawin, 1999). As we have seen, in research for interior design, it is important

to investigate previously completed projects that are similar in scope, program, or project type, known as *case studies*, as well as to examine project-related documents such as maps and construction plans (as discussed in Chapter 4). In addition, some essential contextual information can only be gathered by directly observing the environment (for example, site analysis discussed in Chapter 5).

TYPES OF OBSERVATION

As suggested in Figure 8.1, five main types of observation for interior design research, organized from the least to the most amount of prior preparation required, are: *casual, systematic, participant, simulation,* and *experiment*. Forms of observation for interior design come from other disciplines such as anthropology, sociology, biology, natural, and physical sciences, and can incorporate qualitative and quantitative data gathering methods. We can observe people casually, tuning our informal people-watching skills to a higher purpose, or we can systematize our observation, using *behavior mapping or shadowing* techniques. We can construct *models, mock-ups,* or *prototypes* that create *simulations* of reality. We can go further by setting up controlled environments to conduct *experiments* to observe how people act under given conditions.

Merriam and Tisdell (2016) remind us that regardless of the type of observation, *validity* and *reliability* (both aspects of *trustworthiness*), need to be considered in the conceptualization of your study as well as in the act of data collection. According to Sommer and Sommer (2002), "*Validity* is the degree to which a procedure produces genuine and credible information … *Internal validity* is the degree to which a procedure measures what it is supposed to measure … *External validity* refers to the generalizability of the findings" (p. 4). Are the qualitative data credible, confirmable, and transferable? In addition to being valid, research should also be *reliable*; that is, another scientist, using your procedure, should be able to replicate similar results. Are the quantitative data internally and externally valid, reliable, and objective, to the extent possible? Documenting the procedures and providing enough detail so that the findings will make sense to consumers of your research are your highest priorities.

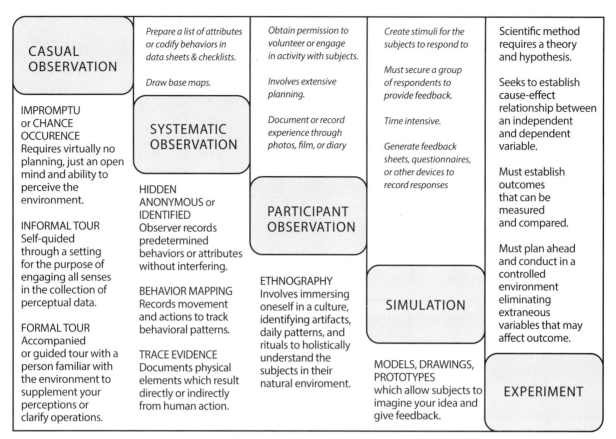

CASUAL OBSERVATION	Prepare a list of attributes or codify behaviors in data sheets & checklists. Draw base maps.	Obtain permission to volunteer or engage in activity with subjects. Involves extensive planning. Document or record experience through photos, film, or diary	Create stimuli for the subjects to respond to Must secure a group of respondents to provide feedback. Time intensive. Generate feedback sheets, questionnaires, or other devices to record responses	Scientific method requires a theory and hypothesis. Seeks to establish cause-effect relationship between an independent and dependent variable.

IMPROMPTU or CHANCE OCCURENCE Requires virtually no planning, just an open mind and ability to perceive the environment.

SYSTEMATIC OBSERVATION

INFORMAL TOUR Self-guided through a setting for the purpose of engaging all senses in the collection of perceptual data.

HIDDEN ANONYMOUS or IDENTIFIED Observer records predetermined behaviors or attributes without interfering.

PARTICIPANT OBSERVATION

Must establish outcomes that can be measured and compared.

FORMAL TOUR Accompanied or guided tour with a person familiar with the environment to supplement your perceptions or clarify operations.

BEHAVIOR MAPPING Records movement and actions to track behavioral patterns.

TRACE EVIDENCE Documents physical elements which result directly or indirectly from human action.

ETHNOGRAPHY Involves immersing oneself in a culture, identifying artifacts, daily patterns, and rituals to holistically understand the subjects in their natural enviroment.

SIMULATION

Must plan ahead and conduct in a controlled environment eliminating extraneous variables that may affect outcome.

MODELS, DRAWINGS, PROTOTYPES which allow subjects to imagine your idea and give feedback.

EXPERIMENT

TYPES/LIMITATIONS

TYPES OF OBSERVATION FOR INTERIOR DESIGN

Figure 8.1
Five basic categories of observation for interior design with preparation tasks involved for each method.

Casual

Casual observation may occur when something in the environment catches your attention and warrants further investigation. It is a way to collect information that may not likely be gathered from an interview or a survey alone. These impromptu or informal observations may occur anytime and anywhere you find yourself. You can cultivate the ability to identify problems in common situations: waiting in line at the bank, dropping your child off at daycare, or shopping in a mall. Casual observation allows researchers to experience a building from an end-user perspective, and later to help identify the design problem, and propose a solution. For example, you may notice that the pedestrian entry into a supermarket dangerously conflicts with vehicular traffic, or that you get lost in a hotel casino, or you wonder why the line at the bank is so long. This kind of casual observation occurs when your situation focuses your intention on some aspect of the built environment that is irritating, or it may be exceptionally noteworthy and well designed. It may happen while wandering through a neighborhood, park, garden, or building; impromptu instances of being aware, alert, and observant. For example, one interior designer had to take a friend to the emergency room for a dislocated shoulder. She was shocked to see that the only entry was up a ramp placed very far from the parking lot, which meant she had to drop off her friend (who was in agonizing pain) to hunt for a parking space. This led her to do further research on the condition of emergency room entrances, and ultimately to suggest "valet parking" for emergency rooms. If they have it for restaurants, why not emergency rooms?

The combination of experiences from your senses results in what landscape architects call the ***genius loci***, the spirit of the place. The roots of this term lie in Roman mythology. In contemporary usage, *genius loci* refers to a location's distinctive atmosphere; it infers that designs should always be adapted to the context, to support the essence of the place (Norberg-Schulz, 1980). Pay attention to your senses of sight, sound, smell, and touch (for this last one, think of textures, temperature, etc.). You can even incorporate the fifth sense, taste, in your observations, when appropriate. Consider the taste of local cuisine versus the back of a postage stamp! Because taste often depends on smell, it can be very relevant, for example, in waiting room design for a healthcare site. Envision the effect the scent of coffee, or a "tea experience," has in a waiting room. When patients walk into the office, they could be smelling chai rather than antiseptic cleaners.

It can be impossible to capture or comprehend the essence of a place solely from the photographs, maps, or textual accounts you find in your literature review. Would you be able to understand how it feels to be on a cliff overlooking the ocean if you have not been there? To record a casual observation, you might make a mental note, written notes, a video, or still photography. Later you can organize the photos and notes in a sequence that corresponds to what you observed, to help you recall the experience, and communicate it to others.

Consider this example of a casual, yet focused, observation. When her mother asked her to redesign an outdoor space that the boys would use when they stayed over, interior designer Annahi Barce observed the behavior of her nephews at her mother's house over the course of several visits. Figure 8.2 shows a photograph of what she observed. She discovered that the boys did not sit still to play with their toys as she had assumed. They were very active, and their activities included rearranging their large toys, playing with gardening equipment, jumping, and fighting with each other.

Analyzing her observations led her to conclude that the existing, undifferentiated play space did not encourage focused activities such as reading, writing, or making art. As shown in Figure 8.3 Annahi designed a semi-enclosed space that diffused the light. Taking cues from traditional "school" design, she provided seating and tables, a roll-up, storage garage for toys, and colorful art objects for inspiration. The transformed space which encouraged focused play was warmly received by the client, and happily used by the boys.

Casual observation can also take the form of an unobtrusive, informal, self-guided tour of a place. Taking note of the maps or signage available to visitors can be a first step in seeking to understand the space. If you are able, photograph publicly posted items designed for navigation or informational purposes. They will be helpful for future analysis. Many times an institution open to the public will have brochures

Figure 8.3
The redesigned space articulated a more structured play space for the boys which included environmental cues for focused activities such as making artwork.

Figure 8.2
An interior designer takes a photo to document her observation of boys playing in their grandmother's courtyard.

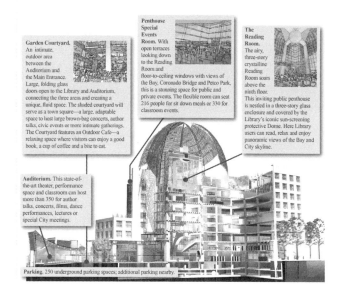

Garden Courtyard. An intimate, outdoor area between the Auditorium and the Main Entrance. Large, folding glass doors open to the Library and Auditorium, connecting the three areas and creating a unique, fluid space. The shaded courtyard will serve as a large, adaptable space to host large brown-bag concerts, author talks, civic events or more intimate gatherings. The Courtyard features an Outdoor Cafe—a relaxing space where visitors can enjoy a good book, a cup of coffee and a bite to eat.

Penthouse Special Events Room. With open terraces looking down to the Reading Room and floor-to-ceiling windows with views of the Bay, Coronado Bridge and Petco Park, this is a stunning space for public and private events. The flexible room can seat 216 people for sit down meals or 330 for classroom events.

The Reading Room. The airy, three-story crystalline Reading Room soars above the ninth floor. This inviting public penthouse is nestled in a three-story glass enclosure and covered by the Library's iconic sun-screening protective Dome. Here Library users can read, relax and enjoy panoramic views of the Bay and City skyline.

Auditorium. This state-of-the-art theater, performance space and classroom can host more than 350 for author talks, concerts, films, dance performances, lectures or special City meetings.

Parking. 250 underground parking spaces; additional parking nearby.

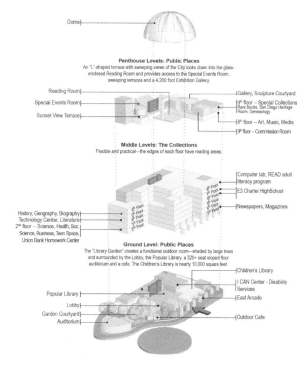

Figure 8. 4a and 8.4b
A self-guided tour can also be a form of casual observation. Maps for self-guided tours supplied by institutions such as public libraries as shown in this figure can also be used for *document analysis*.

containing floor plans, or three-dimension maps dedicated to assisting you in gathering information on a self-guided tour. See Figure 8.4 for a good example.

According to Frey (2018), **document analysis** is a form of "qualitative research that uses a systematic procedure to analyze documentary evidence and answer specific research questions … When used in triangulation, documents can corroborate or refute, elucidate, or expand on findings across other data sources, which helps to guard against bias" (p. 1) This means that a written artifact such as meeting minutes, training documents, records, diaries, and so forth obtained from the client, end-user, case study, or printed item discovered posted on walls gleaned from an observational site visit can help support your other data-gathering methods. Posted signage can also serve as an artifact to be analyzed in terms of content and graphics. We will discuss this in more detail in Chapter 9.

If you are taken on a guided tour, the behaviors you see may be modified because the subjects know that they are being watched. You may encounter the Hawthorne effect, a tendency for people to change their behavior when they know they are being watched (recall the Hawthorne effect discussed in Chapter 2). The purpose of your observations on a tour would be to get a firsthand, direct experience of the space and subjects in question. The presence of a **docent**, or tour guide (illustrated in Figure 8.5), provides additional factual data, and enables you to ask questions of a knowledgeable source.

Systematic

Systematic observation usually occurs *after* casual observation, when a situation needs more in-depth observation and you have already compiled lists of

Figure 8.5
A knowledgeable tour guide can help you get valuable information about a place. Keep in mind that when observing a place on a guided tour you may be perceived as an outsider by those being observed.

predetermined attributes or behaviors. There are many different systematic observation techniques, each designed to focus the researcher's attention on certain aspects of the people or the environment. Sommer and Sommer (2002) suggested a "multimethod approach for flexibility in dealing with obstacles encountered" during a behavioral research project (p. 7). The choice of methods, they emphasized, should be guided by the questions to be answered.

The first step is to determine the *unit of analysis* (discussed in Chapter 2), and to *codify* the process—that is, to come up with a series of symbols or words, a kind of shorthand—to represent both the attributes and the activities of the subjects. Are you interested in observing a single person, a small group, or a larger section of society? Are you looking at an interaction between an end-user's ergonomic relationship with their workspace, a family's experience in a kitchen, or groups of children interacting in a classroom? Concerning attributes, for example, if you wanted to divide a group of children by gender, you could use symbols on your map, such as a triangle to represent a boy and a circle to represent a girl. **Visual notation** is the shorthand technique that you will use to codify the attributes and activities of the subjects. It could be as simple as color-coding the activity. If you were observing people in a gym, in your notation you might use a red pen to represent people who are running, a blue marker for those lifting weights, and a green marker for people who are resting between exercises. Or the notation could use descriptive abbreviations: "run," "wts," and "rest." Once you have established a list of what you are looking for, you will want to show how these behaviors occur in the room or space. *In Studies in the Anthropology of Visual Communication, Handbook for Proxemic Research*, Edward T. Hall (1974) described a detailed *coding index* which included eighty codes that helped him, and his fellow researchers, transcribe "transactional data for proxemic analysis" (p. 41) This document can also be referred to as a *codebook*. By coding interactions between **dyads** (or pairs of subjects interacting), he was able to perform statistical quantitative analysis to support his qualitative data.

Looking for Physical Traces

As interior designers, we are very interested in the physical environment itself: the spaces, the objects, and the relationships between them. We can observe what exists, or how things change over time. And we can also take note of what is missing in an environment, something designers often refer to as "the presence of absence." In addition to the observing behavior in progress, "observation methods can include studying the physical evidence left by the interaction of people and the environment" (Sanoff, 1991). This **trace evidence**—the objects manipulated, left behind, or taken away—gives an indication of patterns of behavior or attitudes toward the environment. Like the forensic approach taken by detectives investigating a crime scene, this method demands you look for indications of activity and then interpret those findings. For example, in a school library, what does the lack of dust, a worn path in the flooring tile, or the chipped edges of desks mean to an interior designer? What does the presence of graffiti on a schoolyard wall, security bars on windows, or an abundance of trash indicate?

Sommer and Sommer (2002) define trace measures as "the physical remains of interaction" (p. 75). According to Guerin & Dohr (2007, p. 5),

> this type of research is critical to the designer because it gives you an opportunity to know what often goes unsaid by clients and users. There are two types of traces that are measured, erosion and accretion. **Erosion traces** are shown by deterioration or wear that provides a look at the usage pattern. **Accretion traces** are a build-up of a residue or an interaction. These traces are added to the environment and show how the user has changed an environment.

Sommer and Sommer (2002) noted that trace measures are also used in the study of animal migration. Researchers count the number of bird's nests to track breeding and density or look at contents of droppings for information about eating habits (p. 77). For human behavior, researchers such as Zeisel (1997) have further divided accretion evidence into *legitimate* and *illegitimate*. Sanctioned additions such as signage installed by property owners may be considered legitimate, while acts of vandalism, graffiti, or litter would be considered illegitimate. Sommer and Sommer (2002) also pointed out the use of *latrinalia*, the technical name given to illegitimate writing on a restroom wall. Some designers and their clients have embraced these kinds of acts, transforming them into sanctioned ones by installing chalkboards or whiteboards in public areas, and encouraging the addition of artwork by the people using the space.

Trace evidence could also show up as manipulation of the built environment by the occupants or an **adaptation**. For example, noticing chairs arranged in a circle may indicate a group discussion occurred, both confirming and underscoring need for flexibility in seating furniture. Studying adaptations can greatly contribute to an interior designer's knowledge about how the environment needs to be redesigned. For example, cardboard taped over glazing in doors may indicate the occupant's need for privacy, and a handwritten sign stuck to an entry door with an arrow telling people to enter elsewhere indicates a need to address wayfinding and place legibility.

Artifacts are useful objects which have meaning within a culture. For ritual—both public and private—in daily life, an artifact is any object made or modified by a culture. These objects include tools, weapons, clothing, furniture, items used for ritual, artwork, useful crafts, and decorative items that may also reflect a culture, practice, or preference. Meanings assigned to artifacts are usually emotional as well as reflecting a set of values or beliefs. For example, a tombstone, a wristwatch, and a flag all have meaning beyond their physical appearance. The tombstone marks the passing of a loved one and denotes the physical presence of that person's remains. The wristwatch may have been given to someone by his grandfather, who has passed away. A flag symbolizes a nation, a culture, or an ideology that a person may be willing to die for.

The significance of an artifact goes far beyond the item's material value or worth and may have a significance that may not be apparent at first. What the observer may view as a rag could be a remnant of a baby blanket, or a piece of a woman's wedding dress. Memories, which are intangible, become more real to a person in the presence of such an object. Your notes about an object should go beyond describing its physical appearance. You should also explore how the object is used, stored, and cared for. In addition, consider the impact of the object in the room in terms of its placement among other objects. Is it prominent or relatively obscure among similar objects? A description of a candle means nothing without mention of its placement on an altar, whether it is symmetrically balanced with a similar candle, its height in the room, and when it is lit.

Regardless of which type of *systematic* observation technique you use, you need to decide how to record the data. One method is to construct prepared (digital or printed) **data sheets** with editable areas for the date, time, and setting, as well as checklists for behaviors to be identified or quantities to be indicated (Sanoff, 1991). These sheets could have different symbols or words to abbreviate types of users and activities observed. There could be blank spaces on which to record details, such as the number of people, the type of activity, and the duration of the activity. Also, there should be predetermined categories that focus your observation. For example, if you are observing people waiting in a birthing clinic, you may identify subcategories of users as (a) pregnant women, (b) children, and (c) other adults (clearly not pregnant); or as (a) couples, (b) single women, and (c) families; or as (a) first-time visitors, (b) return visitors, and (c) emergency visitors (in labor). These categories could be listed on preprinted sheets so that you can simply enter check marks during the observation period. Essential to have a column or area for notes that may occur to you on the fly, such as "Expectant mother observed panicking when her child was out of sight" or "Noticed there was always someone waiting outside the single restroom."

Observing Behavior

In the field of interior design, we not only observe the physical environment, but the inhabitants, occupants, or end-users interacting with their surroundings. **Environment-Behavior (E-B) research** is one way to study how people interact with their environment. This branch of study is also referred to as *Human-Environment*, or *Person-Environment-Behavior Research*. "E-B Studies can be useful, not only in defining design problems, understanding existing phenomena, formulating design objectives, and preparing an architectural program, but also in actual design, by integrating E-B concepts and research into design studio teaching: into design thinking" (Shehayeb & Sherif, 2009, p. 272). According to Shehayeb and Sherif (2009), such "skills involve … unobtrusive observation techniques … descriptive statistical analysis … annotated behavior mapping and analysis; and … development of space program sheets for an activity setting" (p. 272).

In the *hidden observer* method, subjects are unaware that they are being watched. The researcher might use

Table 8.1 Four Common Types of Environment-Behavior (E-B) Observation Methods

Observation Type	Example
Hidden/ Anonymous	Sitting on a park bench, watching park-goers interact around a public fountain.
Identified Outsider	A tour of a workplace in which an employee introduces you to her coworkers and their current office layout.
Participant	Serving food in a restaurant to find out how to improve efficiency between the kitchen and dining room.
Action Research	Conducting a study in an Alzheimer's daycare facility which results in proposed interior design improvements shared with the patients and staff.

a one-way mirror or a hidden camera, both of which raise some ethical questions (since the subjects are not aware they are being observed, it is not possible to obtain informed consent). This technique is often used by toy manufacturers to observe a focus group of children testing out a manufacturer's products. It is also employed in police interrogations. In interior design applications, the observer may also be slightly removed from the action—for example, on a mezzanine looking down on an interior mall space, or on a rooftop observing the playground below. In any of these cases, the hidden observer may not be close enough to the subjects to be able to observe details or may not be able to use all of her senses (hearing, smelling, touching) to fully record all of the nonvisual details. But it can provide a sufficient overview.

An **anonymous (hidden) observer** is one who blends in with the other subjects in an environment: like another patient in a waiting room, another subway passenger, or another art student in the park (Zeisel, 1997). Zeisel refers to this kind of observer as a "marginal participant," and includes deliberate choice of clothing, posture, and the objects you are carrying such as a camera for a tourist, a notebook for a student, and a sketchpad for an artist. This kind of observation can be very successful, as long as the observer is self-aware and sensitive to the environment.

An **identified outsider** is one who is clearly observing yet has the potential to remain neutral and not interfere with the natural behavior. An example would

be a college student observing a classroom at a grade school. The teacher introduces the observer to the children and briefly explains that the observer is interested in observing the class. Although the subjects are aware that they are being observed, it is assumed that, over time, they will resume their normal activity and allow the observer to view natural environment behavior. Remaining unobtrusive may require some skill on the observer's part. With older subjects, the risk is that the observer may be viewed negatively as a spy; steps should be taken to make clear that the observer is not going to relay information to management, law enforcement, or any agency the subjects may perceive as threatening. As introduced in Chapter 2, and mentioned earlier in this chapter, the act of observing may affect the observed. The Hawthorne effect is a tendency for subjects in an experiment or other type of study to change their behavior as a result of being studied (Fraenkel et al., 1999).

Participant observation occurs when the observer interacts with the subjects of the study in some way. There are varying degrees of interaction, and each level involves the risk of observer effect (the observer somehow influencing the observed) and subjective interpretation by the observer. Some researchers believe that *any* act of measuring influences the objects being measured. A researcher or designer engaged in *participant observation* is aware that his or her behavior will have an effect—but the subjective nature of the study will not be compromised, as the intent is to understand through activity.

An innovative technique for gathering, interpreting, and communicating qualitative information is to use an anthropological approach. As introduced in Chapter 5 an *ethnographic study*, a descriptive anthropological technique, involves the study and documentation of a culture. In other words, ethnography tells the story of a people. As we will explore in Chapter 9, descriptive studies can be communicated through narrative or by telling a story using a cast of characters derived from observation. As interior designers, we can apply the same storytelling techniques to understand and communicate information about our end-users. An ethnography study can help you go beyond mere statistics to accomplish the following:

- Identify patterns in behavior.
- See "backstage."

- Capture emotional expression.
- Tell a story.
- Pay attention to detail.
- See from a new perspective.

Ethnography uses many of the same techniques we have already discussed, such as interviews and observation, but it also uses interpretivist documentation of cultural immersion, a term known as **thick description**, coined by Geertz (1973) to communicate details of the observations while simultaneously extracting or constructing the meaning of the information gathered. According to Glesne (2011), the term *"ethnography comes from the Greek ethnos, meaning a people of cultural group, and graphic meaning to describe"* (p. 17). Using culture as a theoretical framework for studying and describing a group, ethnographic research forms the basis of cultural anthropology, the intensive study of a particular culture, society, or community through **fieldwork**, which usually involves living or working with the people being studied to learn about their way of life. Ethnography examines, in a holistic, comprehensive, and interactive way, the daily rituals and patterns that make up a culture. Ethnographers serve to exemplify participant observers; they may take part in the activities with the sample population to increase understanding of the observed behavior. Cultural anthropologist, Dr. LiAnne Yu, summarized this concept perfectly:

> If you want to understand what motivates a guy to pick up skateboarding, you could bring him into a sterile laboratory and interrogate him … or you could spend a week in a skatepark observing him interacting with his friends, practicing new skills and having fun. Ethnography is observing people's behavior in their own environment so you can get a holistic understanding of their world—one that you can intuit on a deeply personal level.
>
> (AIGA, 2009, p. 4)

Examples of ethnography that pertain to interior design would be to participate in a drum circle for several weeks in a local park to understand the culture of the park-goers, as part of redesigning the park; to volunteer at an animal shelter to understand the process of rescuing animals, as part of planning a rescue facility; or to serve meals in a local shelter in order to understand the complexity of planning spaces to serve people experiencing homelessness. Ethnography is not just about observing. It is also about immersing oneself in a **cultural milieu**, a sociological term which refers to the immediate physical setting and social environment. A person's behaviors, operating in a specific venue with social norms, customs, and beliefs should not be recorded solely as a series of sterile actions, but as operating within a system, imbued with meaning particular to that place and time. As discussed earlier, one of the ways ethnographers discover meaning is by examining artifacts, to learn what people value and hold dear (AIGA, 2009, p. 7). Artifacts have spiritual, emotional, or historical meaning to a person or a group of people. A collective may assign significance to architectural elements, such as the columns and arches in an Islamic Mosque, or how Mexican culture assigns meaning to photos, skulls, and fruit in a *Day of the Dead* altar.

As introduced in Chapter 5, *autoethnography*—a qualitative approach in which the researcher crafts a creative narrative as the central character—emerged out of a need (driven by researchers' intuition of something missing) to capture deeper, richer, fuller evocations of cultural scenes (Poulos, 2021). An *autoethnographic study* therefore employs observational, data-driven, phenomenological methods of research and writing that "aims to offer tales of human social and cultural life that are compelling, striking, and evocative (showing or bringing forth strong images, memories, or feelings)" (Poulos, 2021, p. 5).

Action Research

To Merriam and Tisdell (2016), **action research** is a form of "practitioner research" which not only pursues an understanding of a phenomenon but also "seeks to engage participants at some level in the process in order to solve a practical problem" (p. 49). According to Glesne (2011), action research "grew out of the work of Kurt Lewin in the mid-1900s … grounded in the positivist paradigm … with cycles of discovery, intervention, and evaluation … used particularly in industry research as ways to make businesses more efficient" (p. 23). **Participatory Action Research (PAR)**, as it is currently known, is prevalent in education research to improve the practice of teaching and learning, as well as foster "social transformation through active involvement of marginalized or disenfranchised groups" (Glesne, 2011, p. 23).

The "action" part of action research is a collaborative phase in which researchers and stakeholders positively contribute to the social, economic, or political context under observation. "Grassroots efforts," according to Kaplan, Kaplan, and Ryan (1998), "have often served to coalesce community resources and to challenge bureaucratic assumptions" (p. 124). Results of your study may help raise awareness or suggest a way to organize groups to enact legislation to address a problem. Ideally, this approach complements a creative paradigm of research, envisioning interior design as an agent for positive social change and research to develop meaningful relationships. As Glesne (2011) states, observation can be "a radical action when you use your inquiry to witness the stories and lives of those whose voices are ignored or silenced" (p. 24).

DOCUMENTING OBSERVATIONS IN NATURALISTIC SETTINGS

There are many techniques for documenting sensory data, that which is seen, heard, smelled, tasted, and felt by the study participants. From scientists to *sommeliers* (wine experts), from chemists to choreographers, and from medical doctors to musicians, each highly specialized discipline has developed a way to describe, evaluate, document, and compare what they see, taste, feel, or hear. Experts in these areas hone their skills far beyond those who are not familiar with the subtle differences in flavors or tones. Using these notations and languages, they can not only document and compare, but can also create elaborate and complicated dance moves, string notes together to compose a song, or configure chemicals to produce a medicine. Each discipline has diagram techniques, labeling and categorizing systems to communicate this data to others. Design researchers also share a common language of notation through some of the following methods.

Field Notes and Data Sheets

Time is accelerated in most field observation experiences. Assuming you are committed to make the most of the opportunity, you may find it impossible to do justice in your notes to the richness of the phenomena you are observing in real time. As a field researcher, you will strive to become an efficient note-taker simply because you don't want to miss anything. Writing on the field of anthropology, from which discipline the concept of field notes is drawn, Roger Sanjek differentiates between "*scratch notes*" and field notes (Sanjek, 2019). **Scratch notes** are the quick jottings to capture things to be expanded immediately thereafter, in typed field notes. Scratch notes protect the observer from forgetting, they are *aides-mémoire* (literally, "memory aids") which usually make sense only to the observer.

Field notes, written up as soon as you have left the observational setting, are the notes on which you will draw for later analysis. Field notes are primarily for the use of the observer and require still more modification to make sense to others. They are the raw material to which you will return again and again as you meditate on the meaning of your observations and eventually craft the written insights that will be read by others.

Wolfinger (2002) identifies two strategies for writing your field notes shortly after an observation. The first is very simple: chronologically—what happened first, what happened next, and so on, until the end. The second is more systematic, as Wolfinger relates in an example from James Spradley (1980, p. 80) that establishes each observed phenomenon within a framework of nine attributes:

1. Space: the physical place or places
2. Actor: the people involved
3. Activity: a set of related acts people do
4. Object: the physical things that are present
5. Act: single actions that people do
6. Event: a set of related activities that people carry out
7. Time: the sequencing that takes place over time
8. Goal: the things people are trying to accomplish
9. Feeling: the emotions felt and expressed

One can foresee the usefulness of such early categorization in cases where the researcher seeks to establish patterns within large volumes of observational data. Especially when used in combination with digital tools such as a relational database, or even the rows and columns of a spreadsheet, such a framework offers a powerful tool for the management of transcribed observations.

Montgomery and Bailey introduce another written artifact, the theoretical *memo* (2007, p. 68). The **theoretical memo** is a thinking tool for the researcher. It is the first attempt to connect an observation to a theoretical explanation. As such, it is preliminary, but it gives the researcher the benefit of an artifact produced by her mental processing of the things she has recorded from the field. Since the memo is a tool for documenting a researcher's developing thoughts, and not intended for publication, it allows for some freedom to try out new ideas, or propositions answering the question "why?"

Behavior mapping, or *behavioral mapping* is a graphic technique used to document and represent actions, interactions between people, or between people and their environment. If you wanted to study the behavior of children on a public playground or in a classroom, or worshippers in a church, you may want to go out into the field, do some direct observation, and diagram or map your observations. You may also want to study a given space over time—for example, the different interactions of people in a hotel lobby or in an airport waiting area—or compare inhabitants of a local park during the day to the inhabitants and activities in the evening. There are two types of behavior maps: *place-centered* and *person-centered*.

Place-centered mapping involves making a base drawing of the space prior to the observation period, showing physical objects: barriers (full-height walls, partial-height walls, glass, or translucent partitions), furniture, ceiling height changes, material changes, lighting levels, and so on. Then you would map a subject's behaviors within or through the space. This type of map indicates flow patterns of certain types of user, reveals major circulation paths, and could expose conflicts between types of users. For example, in a restaurant, you may want to observe the way different users—wait staff, patrons, and kitchen staff—use the front lobby. Does the path of the wait person ever intersect the path of a patron, or does the path the kitchen staff takes to the dumpster interfere with the delivery of food by the wait staff?

RESEARCH IN ACTION 8.1
A Day in the Life …

Jorge Rodriguez's 88-year-old mother had been staying at his home in a temporary situation, so the family had set up a bed for her in the recreation room. Jorge wanted to make this space a permanent residence for her, and he sought a solution from an interior designer. When the designer got to the house, she was expecting to interview the woman to find out her preferences. However, the woman did not speak English and was too shy to have her son translate. So, with her permission, the designer observed her for the remainder of the day. This experience allowed the designer to see, firsthand, how the woman used the existing space. Observing her gave insights that the designer never would have gleaned from simply interviewing her or her son. The designer observed how the woman used furniture to support herself while moving around the room. She observed how she used the arms of her sturdy armchair to slowly lower herself to a seated position and how she retrieved her knitting supplies hidden in the cushions.

The designer realized that the placement of the chair allowed the woman the best view of the home's long driveway so that she could see when family members were returning home, and she saw that the chair's high back and pillows allowed the woman to take a nap while seated in her watching post.

Jorge had pointed out that games and puzzles were an important part of his mother's day. But observation allowed the designer to understand how the round game table offered no dangerous corners, how the woman chose a seating position diagonally opposite the entry door so that she could easily see entering family members, and how the table allowed her to leave a puzzle partially completed and then return to it later. Multiple chairs enabled her to interact with her grandson through board and card games. The designer also observed the woman at her daily prayers at the foot of the bed: how she carefully lowered herself to a kneeling position and used the bed to rest her elbows. The placement of the bed allowed her to look up at the sky through the existing skylight, which, her son confirmed, was essential to

▶

her daily ritual. While she was lying in bed, she often looked at the many photos, which were all visible to her from that position. Jorge offered the possible explanation that she said "goodnight" to all the photos.

To analyze the use of space, the designer used *behavior mapping*, translating the woman's observed activities into a graphic form and codifying the behavior. Thus, the designer recorded the woman's main paths of travel, using a red dot to mark the places where she stood or sat for more than 15 minutes and using a yellow line to indicate the direction she was looking in. It became possible to see aspects of the room that were most important: the parts providing (1) visual access to the driveway to see when family members were coming home, (2) physical access to the window to open and close the drapery, and (3) visual access to photos from a sleeping position. During the designer's visit, the woman made one spoken request: privacy "*curtinas*" to be made by her son-in-law, which would mean more to her than anything purchased at a store. The designer made note of this on the map as well.

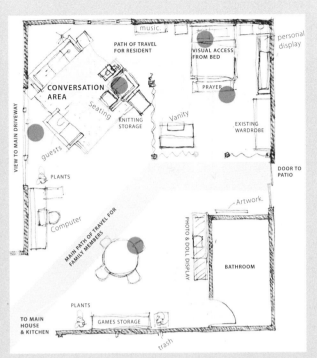

A behavioral map reflecting a designer's observation of her client's mother using a temporary living space. The map uses colors and shapes to indicate path of travel, most-used locations, and direction of the occupant's gaze.

Person-centered mapping involves selecting an individual to follow for a given period to obtain information about how that person uses or interacts with a space. Basically, this kind of mapping involves tracking your subject and making notes about *location*, *movement*, and *observed behavior or activities*, and considering the *length of time* for each activity. **Shadowing** is a type of person-centered tracking in which you observe naturally occurring behavior in a natural environment over several days. For example, this technique could be used to identify the tasks that a typical office employee performs, the amount of time required to do the tasks, and the way the employee uses the space. At the same time, it could help identify problems that may be interfering with office efficiency and productivity. The observer follows an employee through the workday and records every movement to gain a clear picture of how that employee uses the space.

Consider this example: A company was preparing for a redesign. The interior design firm performed its initial research, which included shadowing an employee for a day. To minimize the potential observer effect (discussed in Chapter 2), the shadower maintained a considerable distance so as not to influence the employee's behavior. The shadower did such a great job, in fact, that the employee forgot he was being observed until he went into a small supply closet to get a ream of paper, turned around to leave, and was startled to find himself nose to nose with his shadower. The shadower had been able to watch from a distance throughout the day, but to be thorough and not take his eyes off of his subject, he had inadvertently stepped into the supply closet, startling his subject!

Activity 8.1

Defining the Public and Developing a Data Sheet

Purpose: To generate many ways of categorizing people and prepare a form that will allow you to record what you are looking for (observational data) and other field notes while you are observing participants in a naturalistic setting.

1. Visit a public place—such as a museum, zoo, park, airport, plaza, or store—in which there are many different types of people.

    a. As you watch the people engaged in various activities, list as many different categories as possible. At first, your categories may be based on apparent *inherent* physical characteristics such as age or height. But as you observe the people in this space, see how many other categories you can think of. You can sort your subjects based on other *applied* physical characteristics, such as whether they are wearing a hat, and *activity-based* categories, such as whether they are carrying, or chasing after, a small child.

    b. Can you observe physical details that would allow you to sort people into *inferred* categories, such as whether they are tourists or live locally, are married, or perhaps have a certain job or occupation? Use the table below as your starting point. Name at least ten additional categories not already listed and indicate the kind of category for each one.

2. Using the categories developed in step one compose a matrix or sheet on which you can record the number of people in each category quickly and easily. Options:

    a. Design a separate page for each category in which you would make a check mark for each person you observed who belongs in that category.

    b. List categories in a column on the left and provide space to record in a column on the right.

    c. Limit your categories to just a few (three or four) and arrange categorical boxes graphically on a page.

3. How do you plan to represent individuals who fall into more than one category?

4. Share your preliminary data sheet with your class. Note the different kinds of forms that have been generated.

Table 8.2 Developing Descriptive Categories of People

Category	Inherent	Applied	Activity-Based	Inferred
Age	X			
Height	X			
Wearing a hat?		X		
Carrying a child?			X	
Tourist				X
Local Resident				X
Married				X
Occupation				X
1				
2				
3				
4				
5				
6				
7				
8				
9				
10				

Activity 8.2
Drawing Behavioral Maps

Purpose: to practice performing a behavioral mapping exercise in a public setting as a hidden observer, and then as an identified observer.

1. Select an environment in which you can observe the actions of people in the space without noticeably altering their behavior. Your objective is to map your observations on a sketch of the place under observation. One way to observe possible seating preferences is place-based mapping: your unit of measure is occupancy/non-occupancy of each seat. Noting this dependent variable at regular intervals of time (try every five minutes) will yield a log of occupancy over time (come prepared with multiple paper copies of the layout you can mark quickly, or a digital drawing on a tablet device you can mark and save at every interval). A dry run of the note-taking will tell you what conditions may affect your ability to gather good data.

   a. Select a seat in the observation area or an adjacent space with a view of the observed area. What effect might your own position have on the behavior of your subjects?

   b. Make a mark at each time interval on each occupied seat in your sketch. Work quickly to fully document conditions at each five-minute mark before things change.

   c. If possible, note persistence of the same individual in a seat over the course of multiple intervals. If this is too much to do, don't worry, you still have a great record of simple occupancy.

   d. Note external and adjacent features (the embarkation point, the direction where "people-watching" is best, location of trash cans or other aspects of the setting) which may influence behavior.

   e. After ninety minutes to an hour, you will have a data set that can be shown on a composite map using a representation of density for each seat over time. You can also enter the data in a spreadsheet and generate various graphs of occupancy over time or total usage. Sort and graph the data in the spreadsheet by variables that make sense for your setting, such as orientation, sun direction, or entry/exit point.

What did you discover? Was your hypothesis about the most popular seats confirmed? During high traffic times, which seats were the last to be occupied? During low traffic, which seats were the first? What happened that you didn't expect? What do you speculate might have influenced the behaviors you observed? Would you expect different outcomes at different times of day and different days of the week?

2. Person-centered observation is a good method for collecting qualitative evidence in a designed environment. As opposed to the previous task, now you will follow the actions of one or two individuals over time as they move from place to place and interact with others. In this case, you may be an *identified observer* and it may be useful to inform your subjects they are being observed, explaining to them the purpose of your observations. As noted, this method works well for understanding how someone in a work setting interacts with their environment, or how the participants in instructional or entertainment environment achieve their purpose. This activity is based on the example of a teacher in a classroom, but it can be adapted for a wide variety of subjects.

   a. Ask your subject(s) for permission to observe them at work. If other people are part of your subject's work milieu, ask her to announce your presence and reason for being there.

   b. Prepare for yourself a list of conditions, expected behaviors and environmental interactions, such as the subject being in, or moving in and out of, "zones" in the setting, engagement with whiteboards, digital equipment, people, clothing, and accessories that may play a role. Being prepared with a shorthand method of notation for each of these anticipated phenomena will free up your time to note unanticipated phenomena.

   c. Station yourself in an agreed location from which you can take notes with a sketchbook (note: the collection of evidence using photography or videorecording, for download and subsequent analysis, is a corollary method—it allows for the possibility of detached analysis following the in-person experience;

however, the presence of the camera in the behavior setting may influence behavior more than a person with a sketchbook; it requires a higher level of consent from the subjects, and relies on participants' comfort with the method).

d. At the beginning, note the anticipated conditions from Step 2 so you can turn your attention to more careful observation of your subject's behavior. While it is not time-based

in the way of Activity 8.1, your notes may say "returns to whiteboard again" or "strolls in front of window" or the like.

e. This kind of observation allows you to note gestures, expressions, and draw inferences about personal affect: "looks to the clock" or "leans on lectern thoughtfully" are qualitative observations that paint a picture of the subject in her work environment.

Thank your subject and other participants at the conclusion of the observation. For qualitative observation, it is key to transcribe and expand on your real-time notes as soon as possible afterwards. The written narrative of actions, behavior, and affect becomes a primary source for future analysis and reference.

Photo journaling, or a *photo study*, involves the researcher documenting the subject matter in a series of photographic images to create a story or narrative. This creative documentation technique can be a standalone method or used to supplement other forms of data. A photo study for interior design typically documents the interaction between people and their environment, or physical trace evidence. You can either take the photos yourself or offer the user or ask stakeholders to take pictures of "a day in their life." Sometimes this second option works better since you will see the experience directly through the eyes of the end user. You can focus a photo study in various ways: take images of the space itself, objects in the space, people in the space, activities in the space, or a combination of all of these. The key is to remain open-minded. Photograph whatever seems significant at the time,

free of interpretation. You can extract meaning and draw conclusions later. A combination of field notes, a sketched map, and a photo shown in Figure 8.6 shows the author's attempt to capture the behaviors of families observed in a Japanese garden in Southern California.

Figure 8.6
Field notes and photo journaling records behavior at a bridge of stepping stones crossing a water feature in a public park. Photo on left; field notes categorizing and counting participants and sketched map on right.

Activity 8.3
Documenting Points of View

Purpose: To add a layer of empathy to your observation process by performing your observation technique through the eyes of a camera attempting to represent a particular end-user's point of view.

Choose a public or private space that you have access to such as a park, beach, museum, zoo, shopping center, playground, school, restaurant, theme park, or someone's home.

1. Select one of the following perspectives:

- An infant, toddler, or small child

- A teenager

- An athlete such as a surfer, skateboarder, or biker

- A cat, dog, or other family pet

- A person with a mobility device such as a wheelchair or crutches.

- Other _____

2. Using a digital camera, take photos from your adopted perspective. What is their eye-height? What do things look like from their point of view? What might catch their attention? What would be meaningful or significant to them?

Rule for this photo study: Do not take pictures of the person or animal you are portraying. Only take pictures of the *artifacts or objects* in the environment that would stand out, be important, or have meaning to your adopted perspective. Document how you imagine your adopted perspective would interact with the environment. (Recall the discussion of trace evidence earlier in this chapter.) Keep in mind that an object you photograph, such as a shoe, could be connected to a person, but the subject of the photo must be what is significant about the shoe, not what is significant about the person.

3. Digitally assemble your images, arranging them in groups or attempting to tell a story through the images, or create other meaningful relationships by juxtaposition.

4. Share your montage with the class and have them guess whose perspective you have adopted. Did they guess correctly? Also ask for them to look carefully at your photo collage. Do they see something that you did not?

5. Discuss and summarize what you have learned by doing this activity.

Activity 8.4
Looking Deeply and Describing a Phenomenon

Purpose: To spend time exploring layers of detail in human–environment observation and to practice qualitative "thick description" in a narrative or conversational format.

Visit a public or private space in which people are interacting with their environment for an extended period of time. Choose one of the following scenarios:

- Vendors interacting with shoppers in a farmer's market or mall.

- A family preparing dinner or celebrating an occasion.

- A formal cultural event such as a religious gathering or ceremony.

- People using a park, attending a sports event, or visiting a museum exhibit.

- People finding their way in a transportation hub such as a train station or airport.

- Other: _____.

1. Spend at least thirty minutes observing your chosen location from one vantage point. Write down as many notes as possible about what you notice. Create a list of physical *trace evidence* including *accretion* traces, objects (litter, graffiti, items left behind), *erosion* traces (worn paths in the grass, items that are missing), and indications of *adaption* (a blanket spread out for a picnic, an open umbrella creating shade, temporary barriers such as construction cones or signage). After each item, list implications, behavior, or beliefs that could have caused the trace evidence.

2. Spend another half hour in the same location making notes about interactions that you observe visually, as well as sounds, scents, and textures around you. What is the main purpose of the gathering? Are there instances of interactions that occur off to the side? What is the atmosphere? What is the mood of the people in general?

3. Choose one person to focus on for at least fifteen minutes. Describe them physically, what they are doing, and how they are interacting with other people. Give your character a name. What is their role in the story of the events going on?

4. Present your qualitative "thick description" to the class. What do they find interesting about your study? What questions do they have? Do they think any important data is missing?

Videorecording

Merriam and Tisdell (2016) warn behavioral researchers that the act of videorecording is too intrusive an advocate for note-taking (p. 149). However, if you choose to record human behavior, you must consider the ethics behind such an endeavor (addressed in Chapter 5) and must obtain permission from those who are videorecorded. Whether you use a video camera or your own observation, Merriam and Tisdell (2016) suggest that you "shift from a 'wide angle' to a 'narrow angle' lens – focusing on a specific person, interaction, or activity, while mentally blocking out all the others" (p. 150).

A memorable and successful landmark study headed by Joseph Tobin in 1989 entitled, *Preschool in Three Cultures*, utilized video in a comparative, "multivocal," ethnography study. The researchers describe how they came to their research methods:

> Early in this project we were struggling to find an appropriate approach for studying Japanese, Chinese, and American preschools ... The use Asch, Conner, and Asch made of ethnographic film to stimulate a second, reflexive level of discourse gave us the idea of using videotapes of preschool to stimulate a multivocal text.
>
> (Tobin, Wu, & Davidson,1989, p. 4)

They began each chapter of the study with a twenty-minute videotape of a typical day in one sample preschool from each country. Then, they introduced the voices of preschool teachers, parents, and administrators who each tell their own story about what is going on in the video, as narrated overlay. In a third layer of inquiry, they showed the videos of the other schools to the teachers, parents, and administrators and recorded their reactions as they "discuss, deconstruct, and criticize" the videorecording of the other schools. The researchers focused on two or three children in each class as characters in a story, and exposed the subjective limitations of the study, by stating that "we unconsciously tended to focus on misbehaving, aggressive, and highly verbal children" (p. 7). In their own words, "the result is three videotapes that are very subjective, idiosyncratic, culture-bound ... emotional and dramatic ... visual ethnographies" (p. 7). Video recordings may seem like objective, accurate representations of human–environment behavior;

however, the viewpoint will always be a subjective one. Even if the camera is a surveillance camera mounted on a building, it still only produces one vantage point.

Video recordings may be a good way to capture interaction and act as raw data that later can be coded, much like a transcript of an interview as discussed in Chapter 6. Tobin et al. remind us that when we videotape people, *place*, *time*, and *social class* matter. The videographer researcher must document, and explicitly state the circumstances, to give meaningful context to the video content.

Virtual Methods of Observation

Merriam and Tisdell (2016) noted that "ethnographic methods need to be combined with an understanding of virtual worlds, since the online or virtual world is a culture in and of itself" (p. 158). As we discussed in the beginning of Chapter 1, technological advances often cause a shift in humanity's experience which may usher in a new technological age. New technological ages require that we adjust our scientific inquiry to accommodate the new reality that humans experience. Real-time maps available on our smartphones show traffic patterns, weather, climate change and other information that is useful to study in relation to the built environment, as well as perceiving communities through social media.

Merriam and Tisdell (2016) cite a researcher in 2013 who conducted her study entirely through "computer mediated communication through Skype interviews and online observations which they call 'cyber ethnography'" (p. 158). Online participant observations include discussions and postings via social media which include "subcultures of larger communities made up of people with a particular interest." Platforms such as Reddit, Facebook, Instagram, YouTube, and many others offer the ability to observe conversations, posted images, and video.

One student, interested in observing interactions of people who go to theme parks, accessed this community by joining social media groups dedicated to this purpose, and was able to conduct interviews and surveys. In addition, despite the pandemic, she was able to virtually observe the wait times for rides using the *My Disney Experience* mobile app. She operationalized the construct of theme park ride *popularity* by equating popularity with *longer wait times*. She then compared wait times over the course of a typical Sunday in November. She organized the wait times for identified rides into an Excel spreadsheet, and then compared wait times with type of ride. Results showed that the most popular ride was a screen-based ride, which was also the newest ride. Figure 8.7 shows how she documented her data in a table format.

CONDUCTING EXPERIENTIAL STUDIES IN CONTROLLED ENVIRONMENTS

According to Amedeo, Golledge, and Stimson (2009), the term *experience* is used in a variety of ways: the act of "acquiring information," "something felt or accumulated" over time, or "the content found in a mental state" (p. 225). As you may recall from Chapter 3, *phenomenology* is a twentieth-century philosophy associated with an approach to research emphasizing the experience of the individual as the quintessential area to study. This philosophy underlies qualitative research as well as some quantitative methods, especially in neuroscience, cognition, and psychology. Merriam and Tisdell (2016) stated that phenomenological research focuses on the lived experience and "how experiencing something is transformed into consciousness" (p. 26).

For interior design research, **experiential studies** can take extensive pre-study preparations, as you must figure out how to create a controlled or manipulated environment, how you operationalize your constructs, how an experience or treatment is measured, and how you control for outside or mitigating factors that could influence the results. What do you want to measure and how will you measure it? "Generally, a scientist uses an *operational definition*; that is, defining something by the means used to measure it. For example, hunger might be defined as hours since last eating, or attitudes by a score on an attitude scale" (Sommer & Sommer, 2002, p. 3). In Chapter 9 we will discuss how to represent, interpret, and communicate those measurements. But for now, let's explore our options and face those operational and logistical challenges.

Experiments and Quasi-Experimental Studies

An **experiment** involves conducting an observation in a controlled environment using the scientific method. "An experiment is a type of study in which a researcher deliberately manipulates an independent variable … to observe what changes occur in one or more dependent variables" (Fraenkel et al., 1999). This kind of study typically attempts to produce and defend a cause-and-effect relationship. For example, if the *independent variable* is "furniture arrangement" and the *dependent*

	SET-BASED RIDES		SCREEN-BASED RIDES		BLENDED RIDES							

Sunday, November 22, 2020

ATTRACTIONS	9:30 AM	10:30 AM	11:30 AM	12:30 PM	1:30 PM	2:30 PM	3:30 PM	4:30 PM	5:30 PM	6:30 PM	7:30 PM	8:30 PM	9:30 PM
Animal Kingdom													
Na'vi river Journey		45	55	45	55	40	55	55	60	60	45	36	
Avatar Flight of Passage		75	75	90	90	105	105	115	115	120	120	105	
Kilamanjaro Safari		30	30	25	20	35	20	25	30 N/A	N/A	N/A		
It's Tough to be a Bug!		10	10	20	25	25	25	35	15	10	15	10	
Kali River Rapids		10	10	10	40	30	25	20	25	10	10	10	
Expedition Everest		35	45	35	55	40	50	50	50	50	50	25	
TriceraTop Spin	N/A		5	5	5	10	10	5	5	5	5	5	
DINOSAUR		10	45	50	45	50	65	55	40	40	35	10	
Hollywood Studios													
Star Tours - The Adventures Continue			20	25	20	25	20	25	15	15	10		
Muppet Vision 3D			10	25	25	25	15	30	15	15 N/A			
Millennium Falcon: Smugglers Run			90	75	65	65	60	70	45	45	35		
Alien Swirling Saucers			30	60	30	15	20	20	20	10	10		
Slinky Dog Dash			80	80	70	70	65	80	70	60	0		
Toy Story Mania			35	35	25	20	20	25	20	15	15		
Mickey and Minnie's Runaway Railroad		N/A		85	60	60	50	45	40	30	25		
The Twilight Zone Tower of Terror			60	45	40	40	50	40	40	40	25		
Rock 'n' Roller Coaster Starring Aerosmith			60	60	40	50	50	60	60	45	55		
Lightning McQueen's Racing Academy			15	30	30	15	15	15	15	15 N/A			
Epcot													
Spaceship Earth				35	45	10	25	25	15	15	35	20	5 TBD
The Seas with Nemo and Friends				40	35	10	5	10	10	5 N/A		5	5	5
Living with the Land				10	30	20	10	10	10	10 N/A		10	10	10
Soarin' Around the World				60	60	60	60	50	50	50 N/A		30	30	30
Journey Into Imagination with Figment				10	45 N/A		20	35	45 N/A	N/A	35	15 N/A	
Frozen Ever After			N/A	65	90	90	90	105	105	120	95	80	80
Gran Fiesta Tour Starring The Three Caballeros				5	10	20	20	20	20	20	15	10	10	10
Test Track			N/A	95	75	80	75	65	85	105	40	70	45
Mission: SPACE				65	50	45	55	30	15	50	15	20	15	10

Figure 8.7
Spreadsheet showing hourly wait times for theme park rides over the course of a day, color coded by set-based, screen-based, and blended rides for ease of comparison.

variable is "socializing," you can control the arrangement of furniture in a room with human subjects and record their degree or level of social interaction. In this example, you may also need a *control group* and to account for the *extraneous variables*—that is, the variables you have not accounted for that may affect your outcomes, such as the degree to which the subjects know one another. If the subjects are friends, they may socialize regardless of furniture arrangement.

An experiment also documents a change that results from an intervention or treatment. In the experimental study design, the researcher tries to isolate the dependent variable and attribute the change to the manipulation of the independent variable, in a correlational or causal relationship. Physiological, emotional, and cognitive processing (learning) data can be measured using a pre- and post-test method, which would gather baseline, or pre-test data, and compare it with post-test data. For example, interior designer Amanda Dowell wanted to see how Emotional Freedom Technique (EFT) affected a person's capacity for creativity. She first defined "creativity" through her literature review and a survey, and then operationalized the construct of creativity. In this case, she determined that a drawing produced by the subject would serve as a document that she could later "mine" for data. She predicted that a pre-treatment drawing would be less creative than a post-treatment drawing.

An experiment starts with a *hypothesis*, which is what the researcher thinks is true. For example, a student thinks that the reason many students are not using the library to study is that the library is too noisy. Her experiment is to temporarily reduce the noise in the library by putting up acoustic treatment. If the number of students who study in the library increases because of her intervention, her hypothesis is supported. The trick is to make sure there are no other variables that may have been the cause of the increase—for example, that the time of year is closer to finals or that the student lounge, where most of the students usually study, is closed.

In an experiment, there is an inherent need to measure and compare. In the example just mentioned, the *number* of people is being measured. But you could also measure *length of time* spent in the library. For the socializing experiment, you could have measured the *distance* between people. Other measurements in interior design experiments could be *temperature*, *cost*, or *weight*.

Simulations and Models

As interior designers, we represent our ideas through simulations and models which allow the viewer to imagine our space as a potential reality. Every time we construct a virtual model using Sketch Up or Revit, export images from it, or create animated virtual walkthroughs, we ask our viewers to imagine that our design is reality and to respond accordingly. **Simulation** is defined as the imitative representation of the functioning of one system or process by means of the functioning of another. Simulation also refers to the examination of a problem often not subject to direct experimentation by means of an intermediary device made to look, feel, or behave like what is to be studied. Simulated scenarios are often used to train people. A **scale model** is a type of artifact used in simulation as a miniature, but proportionally correct, representation as in Figure 8.8.

In a simulation, the subject or participant knows that the model or scenario is not reality. A simulated client meeting, for example, would mean that someone acts as a client to replicate an actual client meeting to help a student designer develop presentation skills (in a low-risk setting) or role-playing in a *mock interview*, playing the role of a prospective employer to help a student develop interview skills. Traditionally, the simulation is the act of re-creating a condition that occurs, perhaps daily, for the purpose of recording responses, yet the subject is aware that this occurrence is not reality. With scale models, the viewer must imagine themselves as tiny figures inhabiting the space, and actively use their imagination to construct that imagined reality.

In *Simulacra and Simulation*, Jean Baudrillard (2006) lamented that, in recent history, simulation has displaced reality to become a **hyperreality** (a state in which the real is supplanted by the imagined for the

Figure 8.8
Interior design student demonstrates how to attach a wood-framed treehouse to a tree using a physical scale model.

viewer and supersedes or allows us to transcend real time and space). He alleged that production of spatial configurations via computer modeling software is "the map that precedes the territory ... produced from a radiating synthesis of combinatory models in a hyperspace without atmosphere" (pp. 1–2). He further noted that the difference between the real and the imaginary has become blurred or, especially for the newer generation who have grown up with immersive simulation technology since birth, no difference at all. Have simulated experiences such as those found in video games replaced "real" experiences? For example, can technology allow children to accept a digital or representation of an animal as a substitute for interacting with a real animal at a petting zoo? Will simulated zoos ultimately replace live zoos?

In the education and practice of interior design, we are familiar with generating a variety of scale models which range in size, detail, materials, level of craft, and focus. From crude study models, roughly constructed to act as a three-dimensional extension of a diagram or sketch, to a finished model would include furnishings and photo-realistic rendering of walls, floors, and entourage (human figures and other accessory objects) to help showcase functionality and use of space, or further ignite imagination of possibilities of the space by the viewer to help "sell" the design. The process of construction can also be explored using a physical scale, with a performative flair as you can assemble the components as part of the presentation. For the purpose of research, simulation of space can help us gather data about what is going on in the human body, show the effect of daylight through windows or other

openings, explore artificial lighting effects through colors and patterns, and simulate the interior finishes and textures to evoke a visceral response in the viewer. Figure 8.9 shows a physical finish model, and Figure 8.10 shows a virtual model that does all of these.

Figure 8.9
Three views of a student's scale model to study filtering daylight to reduce damage to artwork while still providing the benefits of natural light to museum occupants.

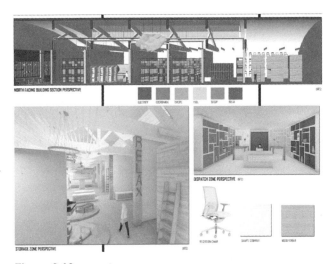

Figure 8.10
Three views of a student's virtual model to illustrate color coding and wayfinding ideas for a company's storage system.

RESEARCH IN ACTION 8.2
A Model for Librarians

The Albuquerque Main Library needed a make-over. Much had changed in library service, especially with digital book checkout and other electronic services. Part of the remodeling project included a new circulation and information desk. From previous work experience, the design team knew that stakeholders and end-users sometimes

encounter difficulty understanding floor plans and other drawings. To address this communication problem, the team drew up a plan, interior elevation, and exterior elevation of their best guess at the program for these major desks. They then cut out these images and taped them together into a three-dimensional study model of the desks. As shown in the photo, the librarians used the model to imagine themselves using the desk which helped them to decide where they needed computers, drawers and shelves for storage, and size and shape of worksurface area. The design team introduced complex concepts of accessibility, sight lines for security, and ergonomics in an interactive, user-friendly experience which was documented and used to inform design decisions (E. Cherry, personal communication, June 4, 2008).

Librarians interact with a study model of their future reception desk, giving valuable feedback to the design team.

Sometimes, however, an experiment involves a simulation. A research team of architects and neuroscientists, Djebbara, Fich, Petrini, and Gramann (2019), conducted an experiment using *virtual reality (VR)* technology to simulate a person walking through a doorway. Subjects wore specialized headgear and backpacks which recorded neurological data as the subjects experienced passing through the virtual doorways. Researchers recorded electronic impulses in the brain and nervous system, before, during, and after the experience, and compared the data, to gain insight into how the brain coded environmental affordances such as the apparent width of the passageway. Figures 8.11a, 8.11b and 8.12 show the experiment's research procedure and data collection methods.

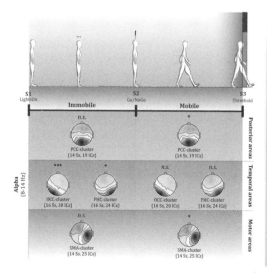

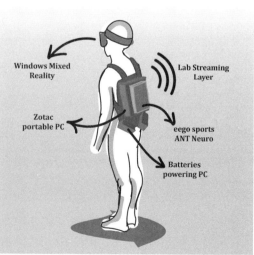

Figure 8.11a and 8.11b
Virtual reality simulation in an experiment in *Body, Brain, Architecture Research* at Aalborg University in Denmark by Djebbara et al. (2019).

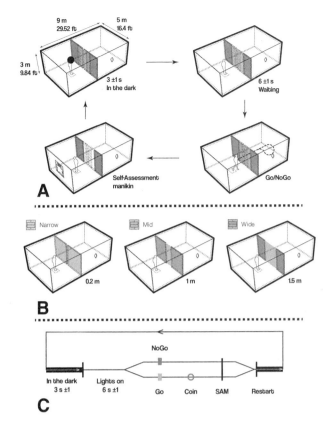

Figure 8.12
Illustration depicting subjects walking through a narrow, mid-sized, and wide virtual doorway in an experiment in *Body, Brain, Architecture Research* at Aalborg University in Denmark by Djebbara et al. (2019).

What More Can You Measure?

When taking a phenomenological approach to your research you may want to measure an individual's physiological reaction or behavioral response to an interior space. Or you may want to gather data on a person's sensory or emotional experience of an environmental condition such as patterns, colors, light levels, or furniture configuration. The *Society for Neuroscience* (SfN) asks you to

> Think about what happens in your body and mind when you speak in front of a crowd—your brain state is very different from when you are asleep. Perhaps you notice changes in your breathing, heart rate, or stomach. Maybe your thoughts are racing or panicked. Or maybe you are energized and excited to perform for your audience. These are examples of the complex brain state called arousal.

(2018, p. 9)

Measuring an environment's effect on a person's level of arousal involves setting up controlled experiments, defining and controlling for variables while gathering physiological data types from heart-rate to brain waves. Environmental factors can raise the brain state of arousal through high levels of sensory input or *stimuli* such as noise (auditory), and clutter (visual), creating an unwarranted, negative side of arousal commonly known as *stress*. How can we identify these **environmental stressors** using research strategies to understand how we might mitigate or eliminate them?

Nowadays we have so many portable physical activity monitoring devices and corresponding apps on our phones. We can map our route taken, distance traveled, number of steps walked, heart rate, blood pressure, and even how much sunlight we received. We can track these individual data points over time to see trends or patterns to study how aspects of the environment positively or negatively affect our physical health and emotional well-being. Refer to *Research-Based Programming for Interior Design* (Robinson, 2020) or Salk Institute of Biological Studies (www.salk.edu) for contemporary scientists studying **circadian rhythm**, the daily cycle of natural light and darkness, and its effect on health and well-being, including metabolism (which influences a person's weight), the nervous system (which affects a person's mental health), and other common chronic conditions at the cellular and organ level.

Kinesiology is the scientific study of body movement addressing physiological, biomechanical, and psychological mechanisms of movement. Using research methods adapted from physical and occupational therapy, interior design researchers can study an individual's movement through a space or interaction with a feature such as a door, window, or chair to gather data. A central question to interior design research is whether to measure **conscious** (acting with critical awareness associated with frontal brain activity) or *nonconscious* responses to the physical environment. The term **nonconscious** describes any activity which occurs without cognitive awareness such as reflexes, instincts, as well as learned habits. Interior design research often involves studying what psychologists call **schemas**, pre-existing knowledge structures involving memory and behavior. An example of a schema might be how someone gets ready for work in the morning or how children behave in a classroom.

In addition, interior designers might be interested in studying **scripts**, pre-existing knowledge structure involving event sequences, typically in social or transactional situations. For example, you may want to study the way someone typically orders food in a restaurant to inform a new idea for a hospitality project, or how people behave at weddings for the redesign of an event space. **Kinesthetics** is the study of body motion and perception involving the development of awareness of movement (both conscious and nonconscious). Studies of human motion include measures from motion tracking systems, electrophysiology of muscle and brain activity, and other behavioral and cognitive research techniques.

There are numerous ways for design researchers to incorporate physiological data-gathering methods into your research project. According to Society for Neuroscience's (SfN) comprehensive publication *Brain Facts* (2018) **electroencephalography (EEG)** technology used to record electrical activity of the human brain in response to a variety of stimuli and activities can be paired with **functional Magnetic Resonance Imaging (fMRI)**, a technology that uses magnetic fields to detect activity in the brain by monitoring blood flow.

> fMRI provides an indirect view of neuron activity, but **magnetoencephalography (MEG)** detects actual electrical currents coursing through groups of neurons. Studies using electrical recordings from inside the human brain can be paired with fMRI to tell us more about the brain activity patterns of the default mode network and how brain regions coordinate their activity during tasks that utilize the functions of this network.
>
> (pp. 64–65)

These studies help identify which brain regions "are involved in emotion, personality, introspection, and memory" in order to ultimately understand "how brain function drives behaviors in humans … [and] uncover many principles of learning and memory" (p. 108).

The Society for Neuroscience (SfN) concludes, "As new techniques and technologies emerge, scientists will add them to their repertoire of techniques that can deepen our understanding of the brain and suggest new ways to help people whose lives are affected by brain disorders" (p. 110–111). Interior designers can add to the conversation by proposing ways to use this information and co-direct studies which collect this kind of information. Interior designers can partner with neuroscientists, behavioral psychologists, and physiologists to continually seek the answer to the questions: what more can we measure (in both the physical environment and in humans), and what does it mean (in relation to the environment's effect on living beings)?

In support of a creative research paradigm, Gray and Malins (2016) state, "the development of technology has led us to a point where we are inundated with instruments and devices that allow us to sense, experience, collect, store, analyse and communicate far more information than ever before. The vast range of 'tools' for investigation has expanded the range of existing research methodologies and methods and made possible new ones" (p. 94). They urge designers to use creativity when approaching scientific instruments, to move knowledge forward in art and design.

Mock-ups, Prototypes, and Usability Testing

Research in interior design can borrow some methods from studies testing the efficacy and usability of *user-interface* (UI) or *user experience* (UX) design by cognitive scientists such as Don Norman. On the surface, both testing professions adopt a human-centered way of analyzing and re-designing products and delivery systems. Don Norman, a cognitive scientist, is credited with coining the term "user experience" in the late 1990s which comprehensively addresses all aspects of an end-user's interaction with a company, a service, or a product, or the combination of all three. It is a scientific process that evaluates the functionality and aesthetic value of a piece of furniture, to the showroom it is placed in, the website its image is placed on, to the company's delivery and return policy. User experience had grown out of user-interface, as that area of specialty centered around the aesthetics and legibility of products that someone would interact with such as a control panel on an airplane or computer screen. Involving the end-user in evaluations is the key here. Testing a product, a room, or a series of spaces that involve the participation of actual or potential end-users can be designed to reach beyond just observation in data collection, to gather data about the thoughts, feelings, and emotions of those interacting. In a paper by cognitive scientist David Kirsh (2012) called "Running It Through the Body" he explained:

There is a tacit assumption in situated cognition that performing an action yields a type of knowledge—*participant knowledge*—that is irreducible to knowledge acquired by observing someone else performing the same action—*observer knowledge*. A violinist acquires more knowledge by playing a piece than by listening to someone else. He is embedded more profoundly in the situation. A dancer is able to understand something qualitatively different about a dance phrase by dancing it. Just watching leaves something out.

(p. 593)

According to Lee, Wickens, Liu, and Ng Boyle (2017), a **mock-up** is a very crude approximation of the final product or space, often made in foam core or cardboard. Mock-ups differ from scale models in that they are typically built to 1:1 scale or "actual size." Setting up observations involving participants interacting with full-scale mock-ups will yield important information about its intended functionality, its anthropometric or ergonomic relationship to potential end-users, and to catch any errors or make corrections before producing it using expensive materials. Sometimes in the process of construction, mock-ups will instantly reveal unforeseen design flaws that other methods will fail to yield such as the incorrect height, limited visual access, undesirable overall aesthetic effects, how adjustability or flexibility needs to be built in to fixed items, glare, and other sensory and perceptual cues. For example using a full-scale cardboard mock-up of a reception desk, an accessible kitchen, or a work station is common practice in healthcare, education, and other institutions or organizations before implementing a proposed design on a large scale. Researchers conduct **usability tests**, using a checklist or series of activities to gauge the efficiency or appropriateness. Beyond that, interior design researchers may want to include other metrics to understand how a person felt, how they made choices about which way to proceed, or which object to interact with.

After preliminary issues have been identified through usability testing of mock-ups, a design researcher might want to create a **prototype** of a product or space. Prototypes frequently have more of the look and feel of the final product without full functionality. Like a mock-up, a prototype will give users and designers something to react to and use in testing design criteria. In a recent study, interior design student, Meli Apone,

orchestrated a room with a variety of affordances such as a bowl of candy, a series of mysterious doors, and curious objects in a bookshelf such as candlesticks and mirrors to gather data on which of the items would appeal to her end user population. She used the resulting quantitative data (how often an object was touched or interacted with), and qualitative data (what the person did with the objects, as well as interview responses as to why they chose the items) to inform her thesis project, a choose-your-own adventure theme park ride.

Mock-ups and prototypes are commonly used to conduct **usability tests** which evaluate whether a design or space is easy to use or "user friendly." As it applies to interior design research, usability is based on the following factors (Wickens et al., 2004, p. 59):

1. *Learnability*—The design should be easy to familiarize oneself with, so the user can rapidly begin getting work done.
2. *Efficiency*—The system should be efficient to use, so that a high level of productivity is possible.
3. *Memorability*—Everything should be logically placed, so that the user will easily relocate items.
4. *Errors*—The system should have a low error rate, in that the user can operate all systems or amenities without mistakes.
5. *Satisfaction*—The design should be pleasant to use, live in, work in, or look at. The user should "like it."

Interior design research can also borrow *user interface design* **heuristic** evaluation developed by Nielsen and Molich in the 1990s. According to the Interaction Design Foundation, the guidelines include: clear visibility, match real-world expectations, prevent error, promote flexibility of use, be consistent with graphics, minimize cognitive load and avoid clutter (only essential amount of information presented), and overall, strive to empower the user. While a heuristic evaluation identifies problems and narrows down the potential design solutions, *usability testing* evaluates those design solutions as they involve interaction with a user (Lee et al., 2017). To prepare the usability test, you must clearly establish what "usability" is in this situation and identify the **task scenario**, or describe the *representative tasks* to help you establish whether the criteria for usability have been accomplished. For an in-depth look at basic usability testing protocols, including preparing a test schedule, checklists, and data gathering sheets, consult chapter 8 in *Research-Based Programming for Interior Design* (2020).

CONCLUSION

Observation requires patience, commitment, and focused attention. Like interviewing, it is a skill that can be improved through practice. To be a good observer and to learn from your observation, you must call on available resources such as your immediate surroundings, your sensory perceptions, and your documentation skills (videography, sketching, counting, and map-making to note a few). Observation requires looking from multiple perspectives as well as noting changes over time.

Key differences in research methodologies exist when a researcher chooses to conduct their study in naturalistic settings in which you observe humans in their everyday environment, as opposed to crafting a controlled environment in which you intentionally manipulate variables to influence outcome. As you evolve as a designer, observation techniques will expand and develop. Just be sure to keep a fresh, open perspective and never take anything for granted.

Key Terms

Accretion traces
Action research
Adaptation
Anonymous (hidden) observer
Artifacts
Behavioral mapping
Circadian rhythm
Conscious
Cultural milieu
Data sheets
Detectable warnings
Docent
Document analysis
Dyads

Electroencephalography (EEG)
Environment-Behavior (E-B) research
Environmental stressors
Erosion traces
Experiential studies
Field notes
Fieldwork
functional Magnetic Resonance Imaging (fMRI)
Genius loci
Heuristic
Hidden observer
Hyperreality

Identified outsider
Kinesiology
Kinesthetics
Magnetoencephalography (MEG)
Mock-up
Nonconscious
Observation
Participant observation
Participatory Action Research (PAR)
Person-centered mapping
Photo journaling
Place-centered mapping
Prototype

Scale models	Shadowing	Thick description
Schema	Simulation	Trace evidence
Scratch notes	Systematic observation	Usability test
Script	Task scenario	Visual notation
	Theoretical memo	

Discussion Questions

1. Since reading this chapter about observations as a research method, have you become more attuned to your surroundings? What have you become aware of in the built environment?

2. What do you find challenging about observation as a research method? What makes planning and executing an experiment so difficult and time consuming?

3. What is the difference between an *instrument* and an *artifact* in an observational study?

4. How does *ethnography* differ from other types of observational studies?

5. How does *Participatory Action Research (PAR)* differ from other observational studies?

6. Find an example of a study which relies on observation. Did they collect quantitative or qualitative data? Was the observation part of a mixed methods study design?

7. Describe some typical limitations of a study incorporating observation research methods. What questions do you still have about limitations of a study?

8. What phenomena, do you think, would be some of the most important to observe? What phenomena would be most difficult to observe?

References

Amedeo, D., Golledge, R. G., & Stimson, R. J. (2009). *Person-environment-behavior research: Investigating activities and experiences in spaces and environments.* New York: The Guilford Press.

American Institute of Graphic Arts (AIGA). (2009). *An ethnography primer.* Retrieved January 30, 2009, from http://www.aiga.org/resources/content/3/7/4/5/documents/ethnography_primer.pdf

Baudrillard, J. (2006 [1981]). *Simulacra and simulation.* Originally published in French by Éditions Galilée [1981], translated by S. F. Glaser. Michigan: University of Michigan Press.

Djebbara, Z., Fich, L. B., Petrini, L., & Gramann, K. (2019). Sensorimotor brain dynamics reflect architectural affordances. *PNAS Proceedings of the National Academy of Sciences of the United States of America, 116*(29), 14769–14778.

Fraenkel, J., Wallen, N., & Sawin, E. I. (1999). *Visual statistics: A conceptual primer.* Boston, MA: Allyn & Bacon.

Frey, B. (2018). *The SAGE encyclopedia of educational research, measurement, and evaluation* (Vols. 1–4). Thousand Oaks, CA: Sage.

Geertz, C. (1973). Thick description: Toward an interpretive theory of culture. *The interpretation of cultures: Selected essays* (pp. 3–30). New York: Basic Books, A Member of the Perseus Book Group.

Glesne, C. (2011). *Becoming qualitative researchers: An introduction* (4th ed.). Boston, MA: Pearson Higher Education.

Gray, C., & Malins, J. (2016). *Visualizing research: A guide to the research process in art and design.* New York, NY: Routledge.

Guerin, D., & Dohr, J. (2007). *Research 101 tutorial: Part III, research methods.* InformeDesign, University of Minnesota. Retrieved December 25, 2007, from http://www.informedesign.umn.edu

Hall, E. T. (1974). *Handbook for proxemic research.* Washington D.C.: Society for the Anthropology of Visual Communication (SAVICOM).

Kaplan, R., Kaplan, S., & Ryan, R. L. (1998). *With people in mind: Design and management of everyday nature*. New York: Island Press.

Kirsh, D. (2012)., *Proceedings of the 34th Annual Cognitive Science Society*. Eds. Miyake, N., Peebles, D., Cooper, R. P. Sapporo, Japan, August 1–4, 2012, pp. 593–598.

Lee, J., Wickens, C. D., Liu, Y., & Boyle, L. N. (2017). *Designing for people: An introduction to human factors engineering*, 3rd ed. Charleston, SC: CreateSpace.

Merriam, S. B., & Tisdell, E. J. (2016). *Qualitative research: A guide to design and implementation* (4th ed.). San Francisco, CA: Jossey-Bass, A Wiley Brand.

Montgomery, P., & Bailey, P. H. (2007). Field notes and theoretical memos in grounded theory. *Western Journal of Nursing Research*, *29*(1), 65–79.

Norberg-Schulz, C. (1980). *Genius loci: Towards a phenomenology of architecture*. New York: Rizzoli.

Poulos, C. N. (2021) *Essentials of autoethnography*. Washington, D.C.: American Psychological Association. Retrieved January 19, 2022, from https://doi.org/10.1037/0000222-001

Robinson, L. B. (2020). *Research-based programming for interior design*. New York, NY: Fairchild Books/Bloomsbury.

Sanjek, R. (Ed.). (2019). *Fieldnotes: The makings of anthropology*. New York: Cornell University Press.

Sanoff, H. (1991). *Visual research methods in design*. New York: Van Nostrand Reinhold.

Shehayeb, D. K., & Sherif, N. H. (2009). Cities, cultural diversity, and design pedagogy: Enhancing people environments paradigm in education. *International Journal of Architectural Research*, *3*(1). Retrieved from https://www.researchgate.net/publication/26597712_Cities_Cultural_Diversity_and_Design_Pedagogy_Enhancing_People_Environments_Paradigm_in_Education

Society for Neuroscience (2018). *Brain facts*. Washington, D.C.: Society for Neuroscience. Retrieved from https://www.brainfacts.org/the-brain-facts-book?gclid=CjwKCAjwwo-WBhAMEiwAV4dybSrTri2RTXr_gCq9KxjOf9d-d66TvXcFqlqmZBK_gzGGyaqnp-mS_dRoCex-gQAvD_BwE

Sommer, R., & Sommer, B. (2002). *A practical guide to behavioral research: Tools and techniques*, (5th ed.). New York: Oxford University Press.

Spradley, J. P. (1980) *Participant observation*. New York: Holt, Rinehart & Winston.

Tobin, J., Wu, D., & Davidson, D. H. (1989). *Preschool in three cultures: Japan, China, and the United States*. New Haven, CT: Yale University Press.

Wickens, C. D., Lee J. D., Liu, Y., & Gordon-Becker, S. E. (2004). *An introduction to human factors engineering*. Upper Saddle River, NJ: Prentice Hall.

Wolfinger, N. H. (2002). On writing fieldnotes: collection strategies and background expectancies. *Qualitative research*, *2*(1), 85–93.

Zeisel, J. (1997). *Inquiry by design: Tools for Environment-Behavior research*. Cambridge: Cambridge University Press.

Data Analysis and Representation

LEARNING OBJECTIVES

After you complete this chapter, you will be able to:

- Integrate persuasive argument, theory, and perspective into your results and findings.

- Analyze and represent your study's quantitative results.

- Uncover and communicate your study's qualitative findings.

- Form meaningful interpretations in your mixed methods study.

- Use data visualization, knowledge visualization, and visual metaphors to communicate results, findings, and interpretations.

- Employ ethnographic methods of narrative and data storytelling.

When you finally start to collect data, the experience can be very rewarding, and you may think you are finally getting some answers to your research questions. But do not jump to conclusions. There are still two more layers to scientific inquiry. One involves decisions about (1) *methods of analysis*, and the other involves choices about how to (2) *represent your results*. Both tasks are critical to the research process before you can confidently report your findings and discuss what they mean. Typically, **findings** are the end product of data analysis in qualitative research but can also follow the reporting of *results* (previously defined in Chapter 2) in quantitative studies.

After you collect your study data, you will need to assemble them in some usable format which allows comparison within the subject group, between groups, or both. You will have **raw data** (a mixture of different types of source or primary data which includes completed questionnaires, interview transcripts, photos, and so forth) and *prepared, reduced, or processed* data. It is important to keep careful records of all your data. Most research institutions require that researchers keep their digital data securely backed up on a drive that is only accessible to the researcher, and hard copies of the data (original handwritten, drawn, or printed surveys, interview transcripts, photos, analog video or audiotapes, and field notes) locked in a physical safe. This practice protects the privacy of information related to your study participants, as well as retrievability if someone asks to see your data in the future. All originals or copies of documents analyzed should also be kept if other interested parties request to examine them. Your reputation as a design researcher begins with your attention to detail, documentation skills, and ethical treatment of study data and participants. Your ability to build *ethos* in the scientific community lies in the transparency of your procedures and accessibility of other researchers to your contribution to the body of knowledge.

This chapter revisits and integrates many of the concepts introduced in previous chapters. We first reconsider *what constitutes evidence* and how to build a logical argument from the data you have collected. In addition, we circle back to the role *theory* plays as a filter through which we label, sort, categorize, reduce, and make meaning of data. We examine the data analysis process; how to construct, compare, and interpret the results of our inquiry. The chapter concludes with ways to compose a research **narrative**, a spoken or written account connecting study events or telling an evidence-based story, to help you link your audience to your results, and explore cumulative or **summative** concepts within the creative paradigm of research. These methods and approaches help us identify, clarify, and communicate implications for practice, build evidence for a new design approach or theory, and/or promote future research in interior design. Concepts in this chapter contribute toward realizing a conclusive research project or study that you can write about, publish, or communicate through an interior design project, or other creative endeavor, as explored in Chapter 10.

REVISITING CONCEPTS OF ARGUMENT, THEORY, AND PERSPECTIVE

What constitutes evidence? As in a court of law, the burden of proof is on those making claims or allegations. In this case, that person is you! As we discussed in Chapter 2, evidence consists of sound quantitative and credible qualitative data that are logically connected to the problem being studied in a causal or correlational relationship. As presented in Chapter 4, the researcher appeals to *logos* (logic) and *pathos* (empathy or emotion) of their audience. In addition, as introduced in Chapter 3, people will use the researcher's diligence, reliability, and credibility to determine a sense of *ethos* (character). Your research study should seek to build and support all of these. Empirical evidence or data gathered through the scientific method can be used to promote logic, and your rich qualitative descriptions can promote a passionate or emotional response, indicating or underscoring the importance of the work, and your highly transparent, detailed procedures can instill confidence in the reader that your study has been professionally, responsibly, and ethically conducted, making your results or findings interesting and applicable to practice and further research.

> Good, useful data should always be part of an argument. Thus, data needs to be organized and delivered within a coherent story. However, what makes a good data story? … [D]ata stories should

surprise, should provide a new, more convincing explanation for time-worn ideas, and should propose a course of action.

(Matei, n.d.)

Historically, empirical evidence discovered through the scientific method was considered objective. However, any product of humans can be considered mind mediated. That is, while the scientific method aims at reducing the likelihood that the study results happened by chance and limiting the influence of the researcher's subjectivity, the act of discovering and communicating information has inherent cultural and personal biases.

From a *constructivist* perspective, the body of knowledge about a particular subject is a form of social construction. Researchers tell a compelling story about the results of their study. Other people believe them until a subsequent study successfully refutes the results. In this way, knowledge is continually being produced, revised, and constructed. Researchers make *claims* supported by *evidence*. Evidence takes many forms, but it is only relevant if it answers or addresses the research questions posed.

As identified in Chapters 3 and 4, researchers can take advantage of their personal and professional capital by integrating powerful *anecdotal* evidence, or vivid descriptions of what the researcher has experienced related to the study topic and methods. We understand the inherent power of telling information in the form of a story and can extend this idea to communicate our entire research process. According to Schank (1990), a *story* used for teaching contains a theme or topic, characters who engage in a plot or series of actions, a result or outcome and an underlying lesson or message for the listener to learn. A story might have a greater effect on the listener than simply stating facts. Schank (1990) used the word "indexing" to describe how listeners tend to file stories they have heard with previously heard stories that they consider similar, or memories they believe are linked in some way. So, stories can be memorable. People use stories to understand new concepts relative to their lived experience. In fact, Schank (1990) claimed "human memory is story-based" (p. 12). Stories help us understand context. Events and experiences become stories when we retell them to others. Overall, listening to a story is an enjoyable way to learn.

An illustration of the power of inductive reasoning is portrayed in the Research in Action 9.1 box "I realized I was asking the wrong question." After reading, consider the following questions: What do you think is the central message of the anecdote? Why do you think this example was included in our discussion of types of evidence? Do you think the qualitative anecdotal evidence, in this case, has been a successful way of communicating a concept?

RESEARCH IN ACTION 9.1
"I Realized I was Asking the Wrong Question"

At the Salk Institute for Biological Studies, Amy Rommel studied cancerous tumor cells in the brain. Her laboratory experiments involved trying different ways to kill the tumor, or at least to reduce its size. She discovered that the more aggressive her methods trying to destroy the tumor, the more earnestly the tumor would seem to figure out ways to circumvent her efforts and keep growing. At one point she tried cutting off its blood supply, only to discover that the tumor grew its own blood vessels! She found herself frustrated and confused. This got her to thinking, what was she missing? She took a walk on the Salk courtyard (shown in Chapter 6 Figure 6.2) and tried to think of another way to approach the problem. She began with the basics: what was cancer? The definition of cancer, Amy knew, was a cell that did not subdivide to produce copies of itself. It contained damaged DNA that did not instruct it how to replicate to produce a healthy functioning cell. Instead, she thought, it was like a stem cell without direction. Stem cells are found in fertilized ova (or eggs) that then turn into zygotes and, eventually, embryos. At some point the stem cell's DNA "turns on" so that it becomes a specialized cell, like a skin cell or a brain cell. Visualizing the cancer cell as a stem cell without good information, whose only

▶

message was to survive, she realized maybe she was asking the wrong question! Rather than trying to kill it, perhaps that question was: how can we "tell" the cancer cell to become a healthy functioning cell in the body? This realization changed the way she approached her research and has led to many breakthroughs in treatments for brain cancer at the cellular level.

ANALYZING DATA

Data analysis can be understood as a series of decisions made based on types of data, types of comparisons, and questions asked. Figure 9.1 illustrates this process as a linear one in which we seek to refine raw data into a form we can use to compare, contrast, or from which we can identify categories and/or patterns. Recall *coding* to transform qualitative data (such as an interview transcript) into *nominal* categories, counting the number of times each instance appeared. The idea that we uncover patterns in our processed data, which allows us to propose a theory or to tentatively confirm or refute a causal occurrence, is called **predictive analytics**. This kind of data analysis is prevalent in many marketing strategies and other business-related research. According to Agost (2016) processing data relies on "hindsight," sorting and noticing patterns requires "insight," and the ability to make predictions constitutes "foresight" (n.p.).

But data analysis is not always a linear process. In fact, it is best represented in a flow chart (see Figures 9.2a and b). Sometimes the act of reducing, cleaning, and poring over our data reveals a need to communicate intermediate visuals (charts, graphs, and diagrams) to help express emerging concepts, or whatever appears to be emerging from the data, that will help answer our research questions.

The basis for *validity* and *reliability* may align with the pre-set standards of the scientific method, or diverge, as in a creative paradigm of research. For quantitative data to be valid, you must rule out bias, fraud, or incompleteness. As discussed in Chapter 2, *explanatory* quantitative studies seek to show *correlation* or *causality* prove a *hypothesis* or test a *theory* using *descriptive* or *inferential* statistics. To state that something has *statistical significance* means you must rule out a chance occurrence through establishing a *P-value*. This process is what researchers refer to as *processing* or *cleaning* the data. For both quantitative and qualitative data, you will want to make each step in the process *explicit*, and always try to overcome *assumptions* and minimize errors, and eliminate *cognitive* or *confirmation bias*, as explored in Chapter 3.

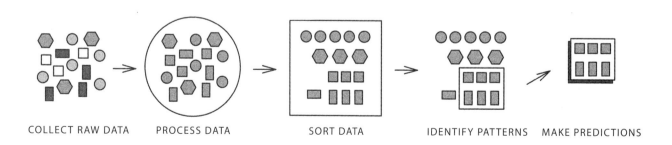

COLLECT RAW DATA   PROCESS DATA   SORT DATA   IDENTIFY PATTERNS   MAKE PREDICTIONS

Figure 9.1

Processing data from collection to predictive analysis. Modified and adapted from Agost (2016) https://bigdata-madesimple.com/5-examples-predictive-analytics-travel-industry.

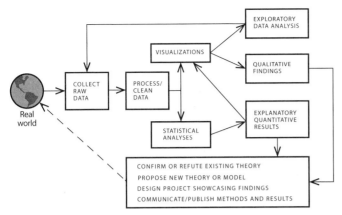

Figure 9.2a
Data analysis flow chart.

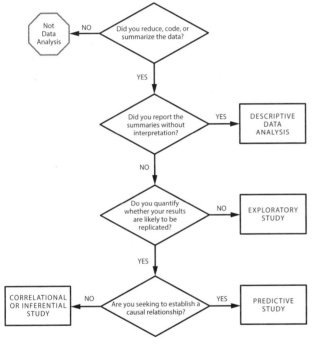

Figure 9.2b
Data analysis flow chart.

VISUALIZING INFORMATION

Our lives are driven by data and facts and so is the world. Doctors ponder over lab results while patients nervously await their conclusions; politicians worry about polls and unemployment rates; scientists warn of rising global temperatures; managers obsess about performance indicators; students about grades; instructors about their evaluations. We even find ourselves addicted to the metrics of social media, looking at our site usage, public reach, and success measured in number of "likes," clicks, or comments on our posts.

Data communication is the lubricant of everyday life (Matei, n.d.). In a quantitative study, the data will support or refute the theory that was tested. In qualitative studies, the data may also support a theory, build on a theory, or we may use an inductive approach to arrive at a new theory.

Representing Results

According to Creswell and Creswell (2018) **results** are the end product of quantitative data analysis. Interpretation in quantitative research is how "the researcher draws conclusions from the results of the research question, hypotheses, and the larger meaning of the study" (p. 248). It is a mistake to assume that numbers speak for themselves. Part of the researcher's duty is to explain the *statistics*, or numerical percentages derived from the data. For example, you may write "ninety percent of those surveyed had been to a museum." Or you could write, "nearly ten percent of those surveyed had never been to a museum." Both statements are true, according to your survey data, but the way you write them indicates how you approach the data, and what meaning(s) you ascribe to them. Drawing conclusions depends on your interpretation of statistics.

A *statistic* (covered in Chapter 2) is a numerical characteristic of the sample that measures relationships, such as percentages, averages, and tendencies. "*Descriptive statistics* refers to a variety of methods that are used to simplify, summarize, organize, and identify relationships among quantitative data and sometimes to visually display such data" (Fraenkel et al., 1999, p. 20). As William Trochim (2006) explains, *inferential statistics* are used "to reach conclusions that extend beyond the immediate data alone." He continues:

> For instance, we use inferential statistics to try to infer from the sample data what the population might think. Or we use inferential statistics to make judgments of the probability that an observed difference between groups is a dependable one or one that might have happened by chance in this study. Thus, we use inferential statistics to make inferences from our data to more general conditions; we use descriptive statistics simply to describe what's going on in our data.
>
> (Trochim, 2006)

Your results will consist of the relevant descriptive data of your sample; that is, how many were men or women (if relevant), their age ranges, abilities, and other demographic data. These data should be presented in a *summative table* format, pie chart or bar chart, which aggregates all the accumulated data into one visual. "A **table** is a data structure that organizes information into rows and columns. It can be used to both store and display data in a structured format" Christensson (2011). Tables include a set of **fields** or cells to input data points based on what data the table needs to store in vertical columns and horizontal rows. *Databases* store data in tables where specific values can be accessed by requesting data from an individual column and row. **Spreadsheets** combine both purposes of a table by storing and displaying data in a structured format, with the added value of formulas, an interactive expression that calculates values within or across cells, and functions, which are predefined formulas. Computer programs like *Microsoft Excel* and *Apple Numbers* provide a grid, or matrix of cells in which users can enter data. By formatting data in tables, spreadsheet applications provide a convenient way to enter, store, sort, analyze, and share data with others.

After descriptive statistics, Harkiolakis (2018) stated, "this presentation should be followed by inferential statistics and the acceptance or rejection of the study's hypotheses along with an account of potential violations of assumptions that can affect the interpretations of the findings" (p. 249). The *statistical significance*, results of tests that were run on the data (such as *P-value, ANOVA, or Chi Square* results discussed in Chapter 2), will form the core upon which the discussion is built. Harkiolakis cautioned that "pointing out aspects of the results … should be as blunt as possible to eliminate any influence that might bias the reader" (p. 249).

According to the American Psychological Association (APA) *Online Dictionary* (2020) a **figure** is a "graph, drawing, or other depiction used to convey the essential findings from a research study." Common figures used in physical and social sciences are diagrams, photos, or illustrations that build on what is written in the body of the paper, and often capture what cannot be fully described in words. A figure can also be stylized or manipulated text, as in a **word cloud** (also known as a *tag cloud, wordle,* or *weighted list*), which illustrates

hierarchically how often a word appears in a transcript by assigning greater size or color (see Figure 9.3 for an example). Or it can be a quote that is set apart from the main text and used for expressive purposes. In general, both tables and figures supplement the text. Chapter 10 will offer advice and examples of how and when to reference these features in a written thesis, article, paper, or poster. A discussion of typical charts and graphs used for quantitative data is found in Chapter 2.

In addition to using text, we can develop, communicate, or reinforce our ideas, concepts, and findings effectively through images, a technique of **data visualization** sometimes referred to as *knowledge visualization.* This tool is especially useful when you are trying to capture the essence of insight, experience, attitudes, values, perspectives, opinions, and predictions. Similar to using concept imagery to reinforce and communicate your interior design concepts to clients, images such as a chart, diagram, or illustration to present information in a visually striking way, called an **infographic**, can help sell your research ideas as well, sometimes more effectively than words alone. Consider the adage, "an image is worth a thousand words."

Figure 9.3

A word cloud generated from the transcript of this chapter showing relative sizes of words based on how often they appear in the text. We can see the most common words in this chapter are "data," "research," "can," "study," and "story." What can we learn from this word cloud? (Generated by author using https://www.wordclouds.com/).

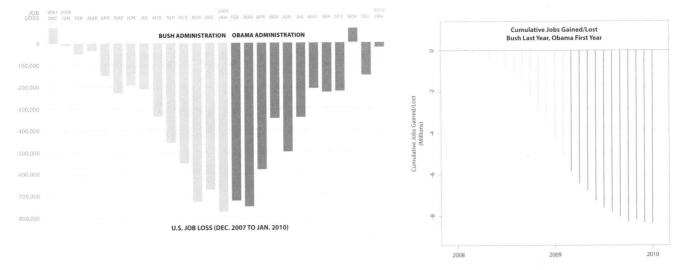

Figure 9.4
Two bar graphs which claim to show the same data but illustrate different conclusions.

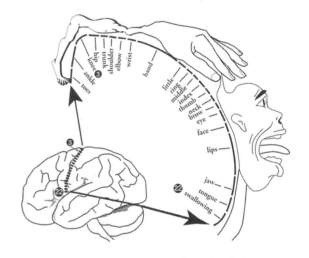

One of the masters of knowledge visualization is American statistician, Edward Tufte, who was referred to as the "da Vinci of data" by the *New York Times* and the "Galileo of graphics" by Bloomberg news. Figure 9.4 shows a data bar graph from 2010 that President Obama used to illustrate his claim that he had "inherited this mess" alongside a subsequent graphic which claimed to show that Obama's influence merely accelerated a trend towards recovery. "Taken together, these two charts, each with the same data but different biases in presenting that data, serve as a testament to the slipperiness and persuasive power of the infographic" (Ashlock, 2010). Shortly after these graphics appeared, the Obama administration hired Tufte to lead their infographics team. Consult Tufte's books and website for inspiring ways to represent data. https://www.edwardtufte.com/tufte/

Figures 9.5a and b show a very famous two-dimensional graphic representation of the brain called the cortical homunculus, and the resulting three-dimensional model referred to as the **homunculus man**. In the 1930s, brain surgeon Wilder Penfield performed studies which sought to match parts of the cerebral cortex with the corresponding voluntary body functions and feeling they controlled. What he discovered and brilliantly described in these visuals was a "vastly distorted view of the human body: the cortical homunculus ... [which] represents the importance of various parts of your body as seen by your brain" (Inglis-Arkell, 2010).

Figure 9.5a and 9.5b
Brain surgeon and researcher, Penfield's famous two-dimensional graphic representation of the brain called the cortical homunculus, and the resulting three-dimensional model referred to as the homunculus man, which mapped number of sensory neurons in brain to size of body parts.

As you can see in the model, the hands, genitals, and facial features comprise a vast number of neurons giving sensory information to large amounts of brain space. According to Inglis-Arkell (2010) "although the cortical homunculus is a curiosity, Penfield's work in mapping the brain's relationship to the body was invaluable." The power of medical illustrations on the public is still prevalent today, impacting the way many people view science, health, and disease. For example, did you realize that the now-famous "spiky blob" known as the coronavirus was designed by two young medical researchers, Alissa Eckert and Dan Higgins? See Figure 9.6.

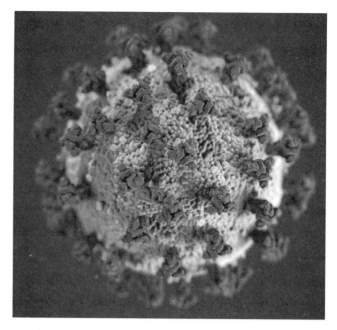

Figure 9.6
The CDC's official medical illustration of SARS-CoV-2, the now-famous cause of Covid-19, designed by Alissa Eckert and Dan Higgins.

Activity 9.1
Graphically Summarizing Your Study

Purpose: To practice communicating your research question, theory, and result in a graphic format.

1. Collect three images to present.

   ❑ *A Found Photograph (to illustrate the problem)*—Find a photo that is a visual representation of your design problem or issue. Be creative. What would express the essence of the problem? Look at the list of inspirations at the end of Chapter 3 for ideas on where to look for this image.

   ❑ *An Image of a Hand (to illustrate your theory)*—To graphically represent your theory, produce a photograph of a hand. In this image, document a hand engaged in a way that reflects your theory about the problem and/or the solution to the problem. You can photograph the image yourself or have a friend take the photo. The important thing is that the hand is the subject of the image. The hand embodies action, and your theory is essentially a call for action to solve the problem. Remember this: Your solution is what you will do, but the theory embodies how you will do it.

   ❑ *A Line Drawing, Diagram, or Object (to illustrate a result)*—Find a line drawing, a diagram, or an object that is an expression of your quantitative result or finding. This could be something you make or something you find. Again, just let it be an expression of your vision of how your research question appears to have been answered at this point in analyzing the data. This is not meant to be a design drawing for an interior design solution or project. It is an expression of the meaning behind the apparent result.

2. Present your three images to the class along with your thesis statement. Get feedback on the clarity of your ideas. Do the images you selected support the nature and goals of the project? Figure below presents an example of knowledge visualization applied to a thesis question: How do parents feel about their child's safety at school?

Knowledge visualization example consisting of a photo illustrating concept of child safety, the researcher's hand holding an egg symbolizing the underlying theory of protection, and a composite drawing representing parents' report of wanting a "bubble of safety" around their child.

Uncovering and Communicating Findings

According to Harkiolakis (2018), evaluation of "findings mean considering the theoretical framework of the research … in accordance with the purpose and research questions of the study" (p. 249). **Interpretation** in qualitative research means "the researcher draws conclusions from the *findings* of data analysis" (Creswell & Creswell, 2018, p. 248). Findings may refer to lessons learned, or new information. Researchers then compare the new information with what they found during the literature review or compare with their own prior experiences.

Continuing from our discussion in Chapter 6, raw qualitative data from an interview can be in the form of notes or an interview transcript which has been reconstructed from notes or transcribed verbatim from an audio recording. *Transcription* (as discussed in Chapter 6) is the formal process of converting an audio (or video) recording into text. Oftentimes this may be a verbatim, word-for-word written document of the spoken word from interview responses, and other naturalistic recordings such as stories, songs, chants, and poems (Clifford, 1990). This kind of data can be further processed for analysis by reducing the data through *coding*, or chunking like information, such as identifying recurring words, or data segments such as phrases or concepts. Codes, as defined in Chapter 6, are *operational*, have names (discrete categorical names rather than numbers), low level of inference or judgment, and can be branched hierarchically (to include subcategories) (LeCompte &

Schensul, 1999). Codes can be taken from a previous study or theory. Or you can make them up for your study. Pre-coded data are in forms such as numbers that can be counted such as test scores, attendance, ratings from a scale, or nominal data (names of things) that were items on a list or survey that your respondents chose from (LeCompte & Schensul, 1999, p. 61).

A researcher facilitates this process by creating an index of codes used, or **codebook**, "a list of the codes used for the analysis of a particular collection of data, the names of the variables that the codes represent, and a list of the kinds of items that are to be coded for each variable" (LeCompte & Schensul, 1999, p. 85). The codebook finalizes codes that either have emerged from the data (using an inductive approach) or have been imposed on the data (using preexisting constructs of a theory). According to LeCompte and Schensul (1999) codebooks always include a complete list of all options available for closed-ended questions, examples of *units of analysis* (behaviors, actions, beliefs, ideas, etc.) the researcher will be looking for, and "a set of criteria spelling out characteristics that should be present in the data before it is coded with a particular code" (p. 85). "Before researchers can produce scientifically supportable interpretations of their data, they have to isolate specific items or elements called units, which are similar to codes" (p. 68). According to LeCompte and Schensul (1999), a researcher *perceives*, *compares*, and *speculates* on the relationship of these units. Following an inductive process, a researcher builds these units into **formative theories**, ones that arise from the data.

Different software applications allow the researcher to set up codes using color, abbreviations, and even emojis! Use of computers in analyzing coded data also enables researchers to sort and group similar codes, count the frequency of codes in a particular transcript or across many coded transcripts, and create digital graphic displays of "hierarchical or temporal relationships between and among categories of data" (LeCompte & Schensul, 1999, p. 91). Figure 9.7 shows excerpts of coded transcripts of interviews. This document was produced using *HyperRESEARCH* software program (study by author).

In the spreadsheet in Figure 9.7, we see a list of individual interviewees (given numeric pseudonyms to maintain anonymity of participants) who have mentioned a word or phrase associated with a particular code. We also see the line number showing where this instance of our code appeared in the transcript of the interview. On the right-hand column, quoted phrases reveal the actual words of the participant. It provides a way for peers to evaluate the reliability of your coding system. In addition, this process allows for a researcher to review the reduced data to find patterns, see things in ways that were not apparent at first glance, and generate other insights.

This study also serves as an example of *emergent coding*, that is, a code which became apparent after collecting the data. In this study, the researcher noticed the word "story" coming up in interview transcripts. This process led to transforming qualitative data into quantitative by highlighting the single word "story" and counting the number of times people in her study said it. This study serves as an example of the value of seeking the unexpected and the creative aspect of research—which may emerge as a theme, theory, or *metaphor*. In this study, the researcher identified that *storytelling* (an extension of the word *story*) was an important feature of the tour for the visitors. Poetic similarities to the experience of a child being read to from a picture book while in a rocking chair, this newly minted "storytime for adults" metaphor unites some of the researcher's insights into the visitor experience of the visual and auditory sensory experience guided by a person of authority. Visitors were able to interact with a trusted expert at a slow and steady pace. The researcher then found an image, "storytime rocking chair" which visually summarized how soothing movement and words seem to groups of learners while also serving as a form of entertainment.

Figure 9.8a and 9.8b shows this emergent **visual metaphor**, a figural representation of an idea that uses analogy or association without relying on text. We saw an example of this in Chapter 6, in the boxed feature "A Mental Vacation." The interior design student summarized her findings through a drawing which showed the sky, a tree, and a meandering path around a pool of water. In this way, the student linked elements that we have experienced, engaging our memory, and allowing us to link that prior knowledge to new knowledge. Recall from Chapter 6 that a *metaphor* is a literary device that describes something familiar to yield a transfer of knowledge to something unfamiliar. As defined by Lakoff and Johnson (1980), "the essence of a metaphor lies in understanding and experiencing one kind of thing in terms of another" (p. 5). In this way, a visual that we may be familiar with, such as a family sitting in a rocking chair, allows us to compare with a situation we may not have experienced, such as a small group of people in a trusting relationship with a tour guide.

Becker (1998) identified the power of imagery in telling scientific stories:

Generally speaking, professional imagery has to do with the kind of causality we think might be

S_3a Visitor initial transcript	22	S_3a_09_EA_NL_PC_M: And the story of the mayor.
S_3a Visitor initial transcript	24	S_3a_11_EA_NL_PC_F: And I think near the end of the tour, talking about the film and the son, and the story of Kahn.
S_3a Visitor initial transcript	24	And for all of us who are architects you know the story of Kahn.
S_3a Visitor initial transcript	40	Telling us just enough about the history and its relationship to why this building came to be.
S_3a Visitor initial transcript	45	It was a description of a history of the product and how the evolution of the product gave life to this place.
S_3a Visitor initial transcript	47	S_3a_12_EA_NL_PC_M: There's an interesting economic part of the story.
S_3a Visitor initial transcript	72	I go to places I always like to try and find somebody else to tell me a little bit more of the story of the place.
S_3a Visitor initial transcript	75	S_3a_12_EA_NL_PC_M: She had a story too.
S_3a_10_EA_NL_PC_M Follow up	16	So that was a nice bit of information, architectural history of the project.
S_3a_10_EA_NL_PC_M Follow up	42	00:13:30.13] S_3a_10_EA_NL_PC_M: I think for the non-architect, maybe the back story would be really interesting and important.
S_3a_11_EA_NL_PC_F Follow Up	4	We think that it was nice to hear the story about those two architects who had originally worked on the first building and worked with Kahn.
S_3a_11_EA_NL_PC_F Follow Up	14	To introduce us to the ongoing story of the Salk was just wonderful.
S_3a_11_EA_NL_PC_F Follow Up	20	And that has to do with the story.
S_3a_11_EA_NL_PC_F Follow Up	20	What a great story, the story of the Johnson family, the story of Frank Lloyd Wright.
S_3a_11_EA_NL_PC_F Follow Up	24	Just that sort of story that every building has about how the building has changed over the years.
S_3a_11_EA_NL_PC_F Follow Up	24	And the story once again, sort of getting to that because there were big problems with that at Richards Medical center.

Figure 9.7
Excerpts of "coded" transcripts in spreadsheet output from HyperRESEARCH software.

operating. Do we think the phenomenon we're studying is totally governed by chance, so that a model of random activity is appropriate? Do we think it is partly chance and partly something more deterministic? Do we think it is best described as a narrative, told as a story? In other words, in thinking about the phenomenon, we include in the picture we build up some notions about the kind of conclusion we will draw about it, the kind of paradigmatic thinking we will assimilate it to. These paradigms come to us out of our participation in a world of social scientists.

(pp. 19–20)

As he stated, we have "many images of the way the social world in general works … a world governed by random activity; the social world as coincidence; the social world as machine; the social world as organism; the social world as story" (p. 34). Becker then goes on to address concepts: "We define concepts and our definitions are shaped by the collection of cases we have on hand" (p. 120). He described using an inductive process to reach a conclusion: "The immediate consequence," Becker realized, "is that every study can make a theoretical contribution, by contributing something new that needs to be thought about" (p. 127). For example, one can explore the concept of "culture," "family," or "bureaucracy" by amassing a number of individual cases, grouping them by similarities or sorting by differences, and make a summarized judgment. The conclusion will have more impact if there are visuals to accompany the summary, mainly to help ground the findings in the reader's everyday experience or build on their prior knowledge. In interior design, abstract, programmatic concepts such as "privacy," "accessibility," or "place-legibility" can also be made more concrete and palpable through imagery. What conceptual imagery can we create that will tell the story of what we sought and what we found through conducting our study? For this kind of inquiry, we turn back to ethnography as an apt methodology.

Exploring Ethnography Further

One of the most impactful qualitative methodologies is *ethnography*, revisited from Chapter 8. Ethnographic studies are typically qualitative studies that incorporate interview, survey, and observation methods. Data from

Figure 9.8a and 9.8b
"Storytime Rocking Chair" used as visual metaphor to express the findings in a qualitative study about narrative and learning.

each of these methods can be reduced, analyzed, and interpreted. LeCompte and Schensul (1999) articulated that "ethnographers have only three basic kinds of data: information about what people say, what they do, and what they leave behind in the form of manufactured artifacts and documents" (p. 1). The method used to collect this kind of data ranges from "very unobtrusive to very obvious, and from very undirected to highly directed" (p. 1). Regardless of the way data was collected, "ethnographers create ethnography in a sometimes tedious and often exhilarating two-step process of analysis and interpretation" (p. 2).

> Analysis of data reduced them to a more manageable form that permits ethnographers to tell a story about the people of group that is the focus of their research; *interpretation* of that story permits ethnographers to describe to a reader what that story means.
>
> (p. 2)

"Raw data" are coded, counted, tallied, and summarized to "crunch the data" or create "chunks of data." This process permits the ethnographer to discover patterns and themes to produce "cooked data" (p. 3). From raw data to cooked data sounds very much like making a soup or stew! In essence, the analogy is perfect for research for interior design, as raw data may not be digestible to practitioners, as a meal served to them would be. We need to show how this data can be useful to interior design professionals and future interior design researchers.

According to LeCompte and Schensul (1999), "Results are descriptions of what happened in a study and are a critical step leading to the end product ... but they are not the final step" (p. 5). The final step typically involves a call to action for future researchers to build on what your study found, or a way the study informs those who would implement an intervention or modify the built environment to improve life of the occupants and end-users. Interpretation goes beyond results to dissect, reassemble, or explain what you have discovered, and to say something important that no one yet has said.

"Qualitative data are descriptive; they pertain to the qualities or characteristics of people, places, events, phenomena, and organizations" (Le Compte & Schensul, 1999, p. 6). *Inscription* is the "act of making mental notes prior to writing things down" (p. 13). In other words, it involves learning to notice what is important to the people you are studying, and what no one else may noticed or have been trained to see. *Description* occurs after inscription. It is the act of

writing things down in jottings, logs, journal entries, sketches, and field notes. Then you may go one step further in that your descriptions may extend to narratives of events, behaviors, conversations, activities, and explanations, ending up, or leading to, interpretation.

LeCompte and Schensul define *vignettes* as one way to begin organizing data. A **vignette** is "a short dramatic description" which serves as an example (p. 181). Vignettes are "snapshots or short descriptions of events or people that evoke the overall picture," like memorable short stories, because they construct, in dramatic form, notable and reportable data (p. 181). Vignettes and summaries, though, are not the end product of ethnography. They merely serve as "advance cognitive organizers" or salient descriptive evidence which, combined with empirical facts gained through scientific methods, can flesh out the write-up of an ethnographic study. We can learn from the variety of ways ethnographic studies organize their findings to construct meaning. Renowned American anthropologist Harry F. Wolcott (1994) expounds on three ways ethnographers approach communicating their data:

- ❑ *Thick Description*: *"What is going on here?"* Provide long, detailed passages from field notes using participant's own words to stay as close as possible to what you observed. Let the data speak for itself. Provide a lens through which readers experience what you have found from your participants' perspective (p. 12).
- ❑ *Narrative/Analytic Account*: *How do things work?* Organize, expand, or extend beyond pure description to identify key factors and relationships. Provide a lens through which readers experience what you have found from your perspective.
- ❑ *Interpretation/Interpretive Analysis*: *What does it mean?* use data to support a theory, speculate on possible reasons or expand well beyond what was observed (Wolcott, 1994, pp. 18–22).

Wolcott (1994) further encourages ethnographic researchers to explore many ways to write about their research, which applies to research for interior design. Consider these ways to organize a narrative or tell a story:

1. *Chronological order*—relate the events in the order they occurred.
2. *Researcher or narrator order*—relate the events in the way the researcher experienced them.

3. *Progressive focusing*—cinematically zooming from a broad to a close-up view, and then gradually backing away to include more context.

4. *"Day-in-the-life"*—take the reader immediately to the scene of the action to communicate the setting as it is experienced on a typical day.

5. *Critical or key event*—create "a story within a story" by highlighting a celebratory or revolutionary event significant to the end-users.

6. *Plot and characters*—when you want to focus on a sociological perspective, or interaction between individuals, you can create a scenario using characters, plot, and outcome.

7. *Groups interacting*—rather than using individuals as characters, you can create a sociological viewpoint from describing groups such as gangs in a region, or families in a neighborhood, or groups such as students, faculty, and administration in a school.

8. *Follow an analytical framework*—you can use a theory (as described in Chapters 3, 4, and 5 such as Affordances, Prospect-Refuge, Wayfinding, etc.) as a framework to describe the behaviors or reports involved in your study.

9. *The Rashoman Effect*—derived from the Japanese director Akira Kurosawa's 1950 film classic, this social science narrative strategy tells the same event from multiple points of view. The story unfolds as seen through the eyes of different participants.

10. *Write a mystery*—this technique employs an inherent problem-solving capacity in the reader of the research. Begin the narrative stating a problem to be solved, and the researcher as detective (recall Ingrid Fetell Lee's TED talk discussed in Chapter 1, "*Where Joy Hides and How to Find It.*")

Overall, Wolcott's (1994) advice to us, as interior design ethnographers, is to highlight, display, and identify patterns, compare what we find with other cases, and connect our findings to a theory or theories. Then we should critique the research process; that is, acknowledge the limitations of your study and offer other explanations that may be plausible for your conclusions. "The sheer accumulation of data carries no accompanying guarantee that anything of importance will be learned" (p. 38). However, interpretation marks a "threshold in thinking and writing at which

the researcher transcends factual data ... and begins to probe into what is to be made of them" (p. 36). In finalizing our discussion of analysis in qualitative design, consider this quote (Krippendorff, 1989):

> *Content analysis* is ... potentially one of the most important research techniques in the social sciences. It seeks to analyze data within a specific context in view of the meanings someone – a group or a culture – attributes to them. Communications, messages, and symbols differ from observable events, things, properties, or people in that they inform about something other than themselves; they reveal some properties of their distant producers or carriers, and they have cognitive consequences for their senders, their receivers, and the institutions in which their exchange is embedded. Whereas most social research techniques are concerned with observing stimuli and responses, describing manifest behaviors, differentiating individual characteristics, quantifying social conditions and testing hypotheses relating these, content analysis goes outside the immediately observable physical vehicles of communication and relies on their symbolic qualities to trace the antecedents, correlates, or consequences of communications, thus rendering the (unobserved) context of data analyzable.
>
> (p. 403)

Content analysis begins with choosing a sample of documents, photos, videos, or other qualitative data items and going through a process of selective reduction. As illustrated by Krippendorff (1989) in Figure 9.9, the dark blob on the left represents real life phenomena or raw data. The content analysis research process then proceeds from left to right. You must determine your target analytical constructs as established by a theoretical lens. For example, are you taking a *linguistic* (dealing with words or phrases) or a *cognitive* approach (looking at the way someone thinks or makes a decision)? Are you looking at physical elements such as wayfinding elements in a hospital or types of artwork found in a person's home? Or perhaps you are interested in exploring other sorts of patterns found in individuals, collective human behavior, relationships, or environments. With content analysis the sky is the limit in terms of what you can look for, how

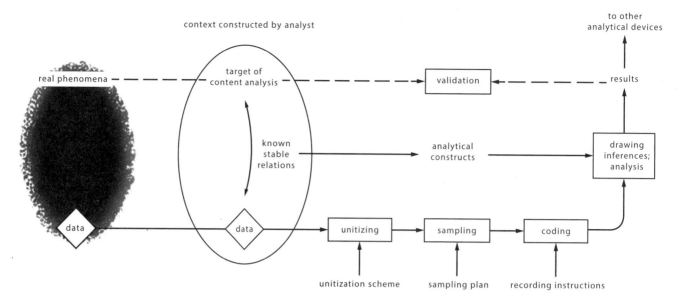

Figure 9.9
Content analysis research process diagrammed by Krippendorff, 1989, p. 406.

you implement your plan, and how you draw your inferences.

According to Columbia University (2019) two general types of content analysis are *conceptual* analysis and *relational* analysis. A conceptual analysis could be at the level of word, phrase, sentence, or theme, and can be quantified by counting how many of the instances occur within a transcript or other source of qualitative data such as a video or audio recording. Recall the coding process discussed earlier in the chapter. A relational content analysis looks for evidence of *affect* (emotion or tone) such as negativity or joyfulness, or *proximity* across time, people, or space within a written or graphic document, such as neighborhoods on a map or clusters of emotional outbursts noted in the crowd at a public gathering. Carley (1990) offered the idea adding three

more methodological approaches: *procedural analysis* (how something operates or is intended to operate), *emotional analysis*, and in-depth discussion as other means to analyze content data.

Together, the research methods of *document analysis* (discussed in Chapter 8) and content analysis are advantageous on several fronts. They allow for both qualitative and quantitative analysis. In fact, the strength of these methods is the ability to translate qualitative data into quantitative and vice versa. Analyzing documents provides valuable historical and cultural insights and the methods associated with document analysis are relatively unobtrusive and inexpensive. Document and content analysis can also yield compelling graphics and other creative visuals in their reduced form to help us communicate our findings. We will explore this idea further at the end of this chapter.

Activity 9.2

Creating a Visual Metaphor from Data

Purpose: This in-class activity is designed to help you creatively illustrate your findings as well as scientifically interpret qualitative and quantitative data to create a compelling visual representation that clearly communicates analysis of the data.

1. You will be paired randomly with another member of the cohort or class. Each pair will meet (or be placed into their own break-out room via Zoom if virtual) to privately share their data with each other. You will have thirty minutes to look at your partner's raw and/or processed data, and another thirty minutes to offer some way to visually represent and interpret this data into a compelling graphic using lines, color, hatches, and/or other image manipulations such as a *ZMET* collage (described in Chapter 6) or similar technique.

2. Quickly skim the data. Using any of the methods discussed in class, begin to creatively represent and analyze the data. Use any tools necessary such as freehand sketches, images, or photos found online, modified images using Photoshop, or three-dimensional forms using SketchUp, CAD, or other app. Be prepared to explain your completed image with the whole class.

Prepare to discuss:

   a. What did you find interesting about the data?

   b. What were the representation method(s) you used and why?

   c. Detailed description of what your graphics represent.

   d. Ask for feedback from your partner—did you inspire them in some way?

What did you learn by doing this activity?

MAKING SENSE OF THE DATA

As discussed in earlier chapters, your study can mix quantitative and qualitative data collection methods to see if each method yields findings that *converge* on a single conclusion or offer further explanation to that conclusion. For example, did survey data match interview or observational data on exercise routines during the COVID pandemic? Your study may take the form of an *explanatory sequential* mixed method. For example, survey or experiment data led to the design and implementation of interviews or observation method. Or you may have designed and implemented an *exploratory sequential* mixed methods study; for example, interview(s) or observation led to the design of a survey or an experiment. In mixed methods studies, you are either answering a question, testing a theory, or making claims and must match the appropriate analysis with the data concerned.

The example in the following Research in Action box is an approach by a student who used a survey method which had both quantitative and qualitative data, as well as analysis of a case study. He sought to use both to converge on a result to inform his interior design capstone project. He called his study "Political Will to Design" and the resulting project, "The Blok." He first looked at a case study of a theme park which sought to create a sense of community, a radial design centered on a playground which could be observed and monitored by parents and caregivers. But then his research question emerged, "What creates a sense of community in a public park?"

RESEARCH IN ACTION 9.2
Political Will to Design

By Jesse Mitchell

During the process of formulating my ideas, our professor brought in a previous student to present a project she thought would give us some inspiration. The student's project was a safe-injection site for people with drug addictions. The presentation was powerful and showed this student's willingness to go the lengths to get the answers they wanted to design something that is sometimes considered taboo in our society: the safe oversight and use of illegal substances like heroin. Around this time, other events began to unfold. The year was 2020 and we had all been put on lockdown due to the coronavirus and a man named George Floyd had just been killed by a police officer. The riots and explosion of police violence that followed were traumatizing. I spent weeks stuck on Twitter, locked in my home watching the world unfold. The murder of George Floyd became an echo for millions around the world. It became a call to every culture or subculture that has felt minimized or persecuted.

▶

I wanted to know how these events might affect public opinion on public space and how we could design in response to it. I informed the professor that I wanted my project to contribute to the dialogue in relation to the protests. She suggested I form my survey around what people in the neighborhood of the site wanted and not just what I wanted. I compiled a short survey of seven questions: question one was to establish age groups—"What age group are you in?" providing them with choices like "18–24, 25–34, etc."

The bar chart to the right shows the demographic breakdown of age range of my sample population. Question two was a qualifier: "Do you go to the park?" My project involved designing a community center in a public park and I was looking for information from people who go to the park. Question three was a check list of different activities that can be done at the park like dog walking, picnicking, and fishing. Because it was an election year, I included options such as rallies, demonstrations, and protests. The idea was to give them real options with a few plausible outliers. I found a gap in my data when I looked at my results and saw that no one had attended rallies, protests, or demonstrations at the park. I saw the absence of data as data. I intended to fill that gap.

Question four was out of curiosity because the riots and heavy police presence had created a sense of insecurity and fear: "___ makes a community feel safe." I was letting survey takers solve the problem for me and allowing them to interpret it how they wanted. Fill in the blank. There were no right or wrong answers. Responses I collected were both encouraging and depressing. Some wrote "security and curfews," while others wrote, "family" and "respect." The word "nothing" was a recurring answer. Questions five and six presented two sets of pictures of protests, anti-lockdown protests in Michigan and BLM protests in Minneapolis and Georgia, with a simple question for each. "How do these images make you feel?" Responses ranged from, "uncomfortable" to "infuriated" and "sad but necessary." The final question was open-ended, "How do you think these events will affect public spaces?" Answers were coded for frequency and displayed as a graphic shown below.

What I uncovered was that there were young people who had never participated in rallies or protests

What is your age range?

Answered: 13   Skipped: 0

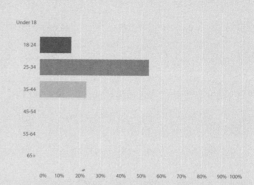

Descriptive demographic data, a bar chart used to represent the age range distribution of those who responded to the survey.

What activities or facilities do you do or use at the park?

Answered: 13   Skipped: 0

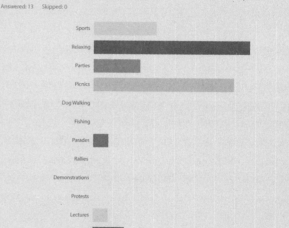

A bar chart used to represent the activities reported by respondents. Lack of responses in rallies, demonstrations, and protests indicated meaning to the researcher.

at the park and when asked about current events, sounded worried and upset and wanted a place to organize safely and voice their opinions. The violence in the news and on social media was unavoidable. The information I compiled and the things I witnessed led me to develop a design for a community center that offered legal representation, first aid training, community outreach, food banking, voter registration, polling, and a café bookstore. I called it "The Blok."

How do you think this will effect public spaces?

Because people feel unsafe in their public spaces this feeling should generate positive progression the protestors are fighting for

I'm honestly unsure. Between this and the virus I'm not certain we'll be seeing any public spaces any time soon.

People need places where they can organize safely. Present or future

Will continue to be gathering spaces because people need to be social regardless of the reason.

More security

Qualitative data organized hierarchically to show open-ended responses.

Drawing Conclusions

This chapter addresses how to think about research—from data collection to data analysis to reporting results—as a narrative process. As shown in Figure 9.10, the underlying mechanics of a study involve data collection, data reduction, display of data at varying levels of reduction, and forming a conclusion. Can you literally draw your conclusion? Using basic numerical literacy in the form of statistics, and employing a compelling textual narrative, you can build a clear and direct path for advancing your reportable results which seek to demonstrate causality, correlation, or some other theoretical relationship. At minimum, you need to show how your research question was answered by the data and offer a reasonable explanation for how the hypotheses were tested. You need to tell your audience, whether they are your thesis committee members, your peer reviewers, or your family, why you reach the conclusion you have reached.

We conclude this chapter by delving into the rich field of *data storytelling*. Drawing a conclusion here has a double meaning. As we saw earlier in the chapter under the section of data visualization, as

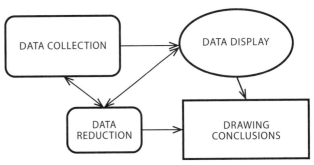

Figure 9.10
Conceptual diagram underlying the research process. (Adapted from LeCompte and Schensul, 1999, p. 196 citing Miles and Huberman, 1984).

designer–researchers we can literally draw something as a result from our study. Recall also the graphic used by Amanda Dowell in "A Mental Vacation" in Chapter 6. **Data storytelling**, according to Dykes (2019) goes beyond data visuals to harness the power of the story, to make your argument engaging, persuasive and memorable. He described "marry[ing] the science of data with the art of storytelling" through the "three core pillars of data storytelling: data, narrative, and visuals" (p. 16). He offered good advice for novice researchers: don't assume that potential merit of an insight will ensure its acceptance by your intended audience! People may not be open to new findings which contradict their beliefs due to cognitive biases (discussed in Chapter 3). So, we need to construct a compelling story using our data in creative ways to help sell our new ideas.

Dykes (2019) defined an **insight**, derived from Middle English for "inner sight," as "an unexpected shift in the way we see things … uncover[ing] a new relationship, pattern, trend or anomaly" (p. 8). He points to the success of TED Talks which helps us to assimilate new information by listening to stories and looking at visuals. Dykes highlights how a combination of these elements helps explain, enlighten, and engage as shown in Figure 9.11. Dykes also adds two more Greek terms to our ability to persuade our audience. In addition to *ethos* (credibility), *logos* (appeal to logic or reason), and *pathos* (appeal to emotion) previously explored in this textbook, Dykes (2019) added "*telos*—an appeal to purpose and *kairos* (an opportune moment)" in order to enact change (p. 32). In other words, your presentation must be designed to get your audience's attention, have them understand the importance or relevance of what you are telling them, make it memorable, and then have them take action. And timing, as they say, is everything!

There are many free data analysis software programs and apps for data entry, data management, and data analysis that go beyond the scope of this book. There are also many graphics programs available to designers to create presentations (which are also outside the scope of this book). Whatever software you use, the goal is the same: to produce reduced data in a form that is timely for its purpose and aligned with the capacities and expectations of your readers, critics, or viewing audience.

This chapter ends with two examples of data storytelling which include a clear visual along with an accompanying story of what the data meant in the context of each study. Figure 9.12 shows a culmination of a research study involving guided tours of an architectural landmark. Through observation and interviews, the researcher determined that learning on a guided tour was greatly influenced by the guide at the beginning of the tour (who acted as an authority on the subject matter) and then the gradual increase in social interaction during the tour. Learning (measured as the ability to recall facts from the tour) increased when visitors were encouraged to talk about what they had seen directly following the tour activity. This graphic, which was woven into a story presented at a tour guide training session, helped tour guides facilitate visitor learning. Docents were able to understand how to use social interaction to gauge visitor expectations in the beginning of the tour, how to introduce questions during the tour for visitor engagement, and then to hold a summary session at the end to encourage visitors to express themselves and ask additional questions.

Journalist, educator, and multidisciplinary artist Jaime Serra Palou (2005) collected objects from the pocket of his seven-year-old son over a six-month period. He then arranged them in four concentric conceptual circles with the overarching themes of: play, candy, nature, and magic (from inside to outside). Entitled, "Data in Pockets," this piece becomes not only a representation of inquiry, but a work of art to be pondered by the viewer (Figure 9.13). As stated on his website, his approach

Figure 9.11
Dykes (2019) diagrams showing how data, narrative, and visuals complement each other in different ways (p. 31)

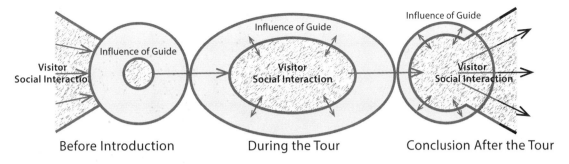

Figure 9.12
Diagram showing the findings from a qualitative study: social interaction before the tour helps gauge visitor expectation, during the tour helps promote engagement, and after the tour helps visitors "rehearse" memories to enhance learning.

Figure 9.13
A data visualization which also functions as art, Palou (2005) created an arrangement of objects collected over six months from the pockets of his seven-year-old son arranged in four concentric conceptual circles: play, candy, nature, and magic (from inside to outside).

is a "paradox in content and form, as he focuses on the singular subject, using data as his raw material and infographics as his logical representational tool." Telling a story with data can be an artistic endeavor, especially when accompanied by the explanation of how the data was collected and an insight into what it may mean.

CONCLUSION

In the creative paradigm of research, all methodologies and methods are on the table, so to speak. Our goal as design-informed researchers is to satisfy the requirements of the scientific community, and to operate within the framework of scientific paradigms that we clearly articulate and set out for ourselves. We use our design and communication skills to create a credible data story that ultimately links our claims to evidence, and our research questions to findings.

Key Terms

Codebook

Content analysis

Data storytelling

Data visualization

Fields

Figure

Findings

Formative theories

Homunculus man

Infographic

Insight

Interpretation

Kairos

Narrative

Predictive analytics

Raw data

Spreadsheets

Summative

Table

Telos

Vignette

Visual metaphor

Word cloud

Discussion Questions

1. How does the *creative paradigm* play a role in data analysis and representation?
2. This chapter offered some examples of information visualization and visual metaphor. Many other examples exist in our everyday life. What additional examples can you think of to share with the class?
3. How does the methodology of ethnography enhance interior design research? When would an ethnographic study be inappropriate as a research methodology for interior design?
4. What concept in this chapter caught your attention and warrants further understanding? What outside resources have you found to help you explore data analysis and representation?

References

Agost, R. A. (2016, September 6). Top 5 examples of predictive analytics in the travel industry. *Big data made simple*. Retrieved February 3, 2022 from https://bigdata-madesimple.com/5-examples-predictive-analytics-travel-industry

American Psychological Association (APA) (2020). *Online Dictionary*. Retrieved from https://dictionary.apa.org/

Ashlock, J. (2010, February 17–19). Infographic of the Day: Obama Says "I Inherited This Mess" with a Chart. *Upswing*. Fast Company. Retrieved from https://www.fastcompany.com/1552319/infographic-day-obama-says-i-inherited-mess-chart-war-infographics-update

Becker, H. S. (1998). *Tricks of the trade: How to think about your research while you're doing it*. Chicago, IL: The University of Chicago Press.

Carley, K. (1990). Content analysis. In R. E. Asher (Ed.), *The encyclopedia of language and linguistics*. Edinburgh: Pergamon Press.

Christensson, P. (2011, June 6). *Table definition*. Retrieved March 28, 2021 from https://techterms.com

Clifford, J. (1990). Notes on (field) notes. *Fieldnotes: The makings of anthropology* (pp. 47–70). New York: Cornell University Press.

Columbia University (2019). *Content analysis*. Retrieved from https://www.publichealth.columbia.edu/research/population-health-methods/content-analysis

Creswell, J., & Creswell, J.D. (2018). *Research design: Qualitative, quantitative, and mixed methods approaches*, 5th ed. Los Angeles, CA: Sage.

Dykes, B. (2019). Effective data storytelling: How to drive change with data, narrative and visuals. Hoboken, NJ: John Wiley & Sons.

Fraenkel, J., Wallen, N., & Sawin, E. I. (1999). *Visual statistics*. Columbus, OH: Allyn & Bacon.

Harkiolakis, N. (2018). *Quantitative research methods: From theory to publication*. Lexington, KY: Nicholas Harkiolakis.

Inglis-Arkell, E. (2010, October 21). *How your brain sees your body: Meet the cortical homunculus*. Retrieved March 30, 2021 from https://io9.gizmodo.com/how-your-brain-sees-your-body-meet-the-cortical-homunc–5670064

Krippendorff, K. (1989). Content analysis. In E. Barnouw, G. Gerbner, W. Schramm, T. T. L. Worth, & L. Gross (Eds.), *International encyclopedia of communication* (pp. 403–407). New York: Oxford University Press. Retrieved from https://repository.upenn.edu/asc_papers/226/

Lakoff, G., & Johnson, M. (1980). The metaphorical structure of the human conceptual system. *Cognitive science, 4*(2), 195–208.

LeCompte, M. D., & Schensul, J. J. (1999). *Analyzing and interpreting ethnographic data.* Walnut Creek, CA: Alta Mira Press.

Matei, S. A. (n.d.) *Data storytelling.* Retrieved March 27, 2021 from https://eventreg.purdue.edu/info/data-storytelling/

Palou, J.S. (2005). Data in Pockets. Retrieved from https://www.archivosjaimeserra.com/archivos/tp2jegw97rntm35m2shjbd472kznl8

Schank, R. (1990). *Tell me a story: Narrative and intelligence.* Evanston, IL: Northwestern University Press.

Trochim, W. M. (2006). *Survey research. Research methods knowledge base.* Retrieved from: http://www.socialresearchmethods.net/kb/intrview.php.

Wolcott, H. F. (1994). *Transforming qualitative data: Description, analysis, and interpretation.* Thousand Oaks, CA: Sage.

CHAPTER 10

Implications for Practice and Future Research

LEARNING OBJECTIVES

After you complete this chapter, you will be able to:

- Conclude your study and discuss the implications of your research.

- Outline your written thesis, abstract, or research summary in an academic format to fit your instructor's or institution's guidelines.

- Choose the project type and scope of a studio component of your focused inquiry which showcases your findings.

- Inform other design practitioners and future design-researchers about your research through professional and academic venues.

- Brainstorm ways to share your research with an even wider audience through popular writing, trade conferences, educational workshops, and business ventures.

How should we write our research? Who is our audience? The rhetorical, ethical, and methodological issues implicit in that question are neither few nor trivial. Rather, the question reflects a central contemporary realization: all knowledge is constructed. Writing is not simply a true representation of an objective reality ... Instead, through literary and rhetorical structures, writing creates a particular view of reality.

(RICHARDSON, 1990, P. 9)

Your research will lead you to speculate, assign meaning, and reach *conclusions*. How you assemble and present your information will determine whether others will get on board with your conclusions and find your study's results useful. As we have acknowledged and illustrated throughout this textbook, knowledge is constructed through respectful dialogue, open-minded exchanges, and consistent levels of curiosity on the part of dedicated and focused researchers and practitioners, gaining multiple perspectives on our observations and conclusions. Given the right tools and guidance, everyone can conduct scientific inquiry and contribute to understanding aspects of the built environment, and their effect on human well-being.

This chapter walks you through the process of translating and incorporating aspects of your study into a cohesive body of work. Research work often culminates in a thesis, a journal article, or a conference presentation. Sometimes research informs a single design project, in school or in practice. But often-times the findings of a study are applicable to many projects. It is the responsibility of the researcher to disseminate knowledge to the intended audience in an appropriate format. Conversations with colleagues, presentations (both formal and informal), and contributing to publications form our fundamental way to collaborate and move knowledge forward. Building the body of knowledge for our profession involves the work of artists, scholars, and practitioners in the fields of material science, social science, and design science. Think of your research project as contributing to this endeavor. Research of the built environment has an extensive history and long way to go in the future, in an ongoing process of inquiry, testing, analysis, and communication.

In Chapter 4 we discussed the purpose and structure of a written thesis, as expounded by Umberto Eco. Building on this timeless advice, we will explore how a correctly formatted and properly developed thesis, when required, can help you make a strong argument for your conclusions. Ultimately the goal of your thesis is to enrich the knowledge available to all research-informed interior designers, as well as to inform and inspire future design-informed researchers. A thesis-level interior design project typically includes a studio component consisting of two- and three-dimensional representations of a design solution. Your course description may refer to a *final presentation* or a *capstone project*. And you will likely be developing a written component as a supplemental or stand-alone document.

Toward the end of the chapter, we will touch on the many avenues which provide opportunities to extend your work to *consumers of research* (design educators, practitioners, students, potential employers, clients, institutional policymakers, end-users, and the general public). Some of these venues include attending and presenting at conferences, publishing articles or books, creating curriculum, giving academic talks and lectures, conducting seminars or professional workshops, curating exhibits, and producing ideas for documentary films or instructional television shows. Other opportunities exist in designing prototypes or built work which exemplifies, reflects, or seeks to further test your findings. Many research-informed designers can develop and implement business models, and other professional products and ventures, inspired by your research. How can you get your valuable information to where it can create the most benefit?

COMMUNICATING RESEARCH

Most research endeavors generate a written component or authored artifact. As introduced in Chapter 2, if research informs more research (or provides for general knowledge) it is called *basic research*, as opposed to information used to solve an immediate problem or inform a practical issue at hand which is called *applied research*. Results from research in interior design are typically applied or integrated into a thesis-level studio design or conclude with speculation indicating how to apply the findings to the built environment. As explored in Chapter 4, this kind of *summary*, *discussion*, or *interpretation* may be found within a larger section of a paper or study write-up called a *conclusion*. According to Barnet, Bedau, and O'Hara (2020) a **conclusion**, "from the Latin claudere, 'to shut'—ought to provide a sense of closure, but it can be much more than a restatement of the writer's thesis" (p. 227). It can also add a sense of meaning, an emotional appeal for action that you urge the reader to take. Barnet et al. (2020) pointed out items, paraphrased and expanded here, that provide a sense of closure:

- A return to something stated in the introduction.
- A recap of major points, either set chronologically according to the order in which they were

discovered, or put hierarchically, in relative importance of the findings, from the most to least valuable, or most to least surprising.

- A peek at what might happen if the study's findings were implemented in a useful form.
- Stating a few of the remaining unanswered questions.
- Pondering a few unasked questions, or ones that arose during, or at the conclusion of, the study.
- A suggestion of specific actions the reader can take after reading the paper or viewing the research project.
- An anecdote, brief account, or illustration that summarizes the findings in an engaging and memorable way.

Depending on the nature of your research, you may find yourself agreeing with someone while adding a new thought or disagreeing with an accepted idea without seeming disrespectful. Barnet et al. (2020) ask you to ask yourself "how can I make clear in my writing which ideas are mine and which ideas are someone else's?" (p. 415). Some sentence starters, they suggest, for presenting what is known or assumed are "As we know from history … " and "According to _____ (researcher or respected author), _____ (actual percentage or statistic) of those surveyed agreed that … " (p. 416). You can also cite authors who have argued a point, emphasized a need, or developed a theory. In your discussion, include actual quotes with the year of the publication and page number, or **paraphrase** (restate in your own words) and attribute the origin

of the idea to that author. In academic writing, there is a logical progression that seeks to build on the work of others, extend or refute the findings of others, and present alternative views in an ongoing dialogue. When you are writing, especially in American Psychiatric Association (APA) style, try to construct your sentence using action verbs, typically in the past tense, such as "observed," "reported," "suggested," and so forth, rather than using passive verbs such as "was" or any other forms of "to be."

In addition, as we discussed in Chapter 2, interior design research runs the gamut of the research spectrum, from the tradition of the physical sciences which typically uses deductive reasoning to test theory in a *positivist–empiricism* to the *phenomenal* realm of individual sensation and experiences which may use inductive reasoning to generate theory, to the *creative paradigm*, which uses abductive thinking, as demonstrated in Figure 10.1. This figure attempts to capture the diverse methods of science-writing associated with different research perspectives and methodologies, to remind you that you have choices in how you write about your research. The diagram may show these as categorically separate, but they may overlap, intersect, or be inconsistently represented across boundaries.

Many times "inductively accomplished research is to be reported deductively" (Richardson, 1990, p. 17). Richardson (1990) also noted that "narrative is both a mode of reasoning and a mode of representation" (p. 21). Underlying each writing style is a way of knowing about something, through *empirical scientific inquiry, speculation, revelation* (recall the *Aha moment*

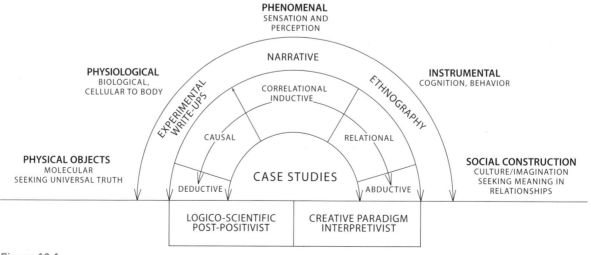

Figure 10.1
Spectrum of perspectives, reasoning methods, and methodologies for science writing for interior design research.

from Chapter 1), and *anecdote*. In addition, these writing styles change over time. Writing about research for interior design draws from a diverse range of science writing techniques used in observational studies, such as descriptive ethnographic case studies, detailing a simulation using models or virtual environments, or documenting end-user interaction with mock-ups and prototypes in usability studies.

Confusion within an academic or scientific community often arises when one form of writing is not accepted by a researcher taking a different perspective. For example, you would not want anecdotal evidence or speculation to be used in a scientific paper about the effectiveness of a vaccine! On the other hand, you would learn a great deal about how to design a kitchen for a family if a researcher used anecdotal evidence to describe how they observed a similar family prepare a traditional holiday feast as a reflection of their culture. While the author of this textbook subscribes to an *interpretivist* or *constructivist* perspective and views interior design research as situated within a *social science*, she also acknowledges the importance of incorporating empirical evidence garnered from a *post-positivist* perspective using the scientific method to conduct experiments and quasi-experimental studies.

As we have seen in Chapter 9, science writing includes many **rhetorical devices** used in literature or prose writing such as *metaphor*, and *narrative*, to effectively inform, persuade, and motivate readers. Richardson (1990) explained that qualitative writing in social science differs from writing for positivist–empiricism "which looks for universal truth conditions, the narrative mode is contextually embedded and looks for particular connections between events. The *connections* between the *events* is the *meaning*" (p. 13). Richardson noted that data storytelling (explored in Chapter 9) occurs in all science, whether it is made explicit or not. "Whenever we write science, we are telling some kind of story, or some part of a larger narrative. Some of our stories are more complex, more densely described … others are more abstract, distanced from lived experience" (p. 13).

When design-informed researchers conduct qualitative research, learning about people through interview or participant observation, their knowledge "is always historically and temporally grounded … [and most] are keenly aware that knowledge of the world they entered is partial, situated, and subjective knowledge" (Richardson, 1990, p. 28). However, if interior design research is performed from within a positivist/empiricist paradigm, one must still be aware that "because knowledge is always partial, limited, and contextual, there is no escape from subjectivity" (Richardson, 1990, p. 28).

Discussing Implications for Design

A discussion of the study's **implications** provides suggestions for how the findings can be used in everyday practice or how the researcher imagines and foresees this information serving to inform future research. How can practitioners of interior design and related fields incorporate your findings into their own evidence-based design practice, or research-based design solution? How can they use your information for strategic planning to inform their client's home, office, institution, business, related findings to health, wellness, efficiency, alignment with a business model or organizational values and goals? How do your study results benefit the client, end-users, or bottom line? Figure 10.2 represents how results and

Figure 10.2
Researchers interpret quantitative results and qualitative findings to synthesize implications for practice (practical applications) as well as to inspire other design-researchers.

findings (explained in Chapter 9) are synthesized by the researcher to create meaning and connection to the research questions. The researcher then speculates about possible implications the findings have in practice and future research. Beyond implications, in a qualitative study there may be *reflections* or *final thoughts*, offering and embedding advice to future researchers considering broaching the same subject.

WRITING A PAPER, THESIS, OR DISSERTATION

As we discussed in Chapter 4, an interior design *thesis* is an argument or a position that a designer develops and supports through a provocative and complex interior design project. There are three organizational parts to an interior design thesis:

- The *thesis statement*—the identification of a problem and proposed solution,
- The *thesis proposal*, or statement of intent, which clarifies the details of the proposed thesis solution and outlines the project proposal,
- The **thesis project**, where you apply the findings through a proposed solution in a real-world design scenario or use the studio component of the project to further expand your research.

A thesis includes the identification of a problem and a proposed solution to the problem which has been tested through the thesis project (Hodge & Pollak, 1996). Your thesis project should be a synthesis of everything you have taken from your education thus far, allowing you to draw upon your skills in a complex and challenging application. "A wise student recognizes relationships between one semester's studio project and the last and predicts issues and interests for exploration in the next; each project stands on its own as well as within a body of work" (Hodge & Pollak, 1996, p. 8).

An analogy may be drawn between a *hypothesis* and a *thesis*. They are very similar, with each of them involving the testing of an idea. A thesis, however, exists on a larger scale with a hypothesis acting as one of the many tools used to direct, develop, and strengthen the thesis. The thesis is not just the solution; it also includes all the research and influences that came together to provide an explanation for the solution to the problem.

As you prepare to conclude your interior design thesis, keep in mind these five basic principles:

1. *Your thesis is a claim supported by evidence.* It is not a statement of fact or an observation, but rather an *assertion* about the facts you have gathered and observations you have conducted. For example, to say that people use many toxic cleaning supplies is to state a fact. A thesis about this topic would first identify a problem: people are poisoning the environment with chemicals to keep their homes and buildings clean. Then it would present a solution: the specification of materials that are durable, stain-resistant, and easy to clean—materials that will reduce the excessive use of toxic cleaners (LEO, 2003).

2. *A thesis is research-based.* It uses outside sources, including all of those discussed thus far—literature reviews, personal reports, observation, case studies, experimentation, and the development of hypotheses. Also, the direction your research takes was influenced by your adopted philosophies and theories.

3. *You are an authority.* The depth of research supporting your thesis project should make you an authority or expert on some focused element of the design field. Thus, you want to take on a topic and project for which you have some kind of personal and professional interest, such as lighting design, exhibit design, or green design.

4. *Your findings are useful and can be applied.* The thesis project should have a current and relevant purpose and use that can be applied as a contribution to the expanding body of knowledge in the field.

5. The thesis project *followed an organized procedure*, including a literature review, research question or hypothesis, use of theory, data collection, analysis, findings and implication for practice and future researcher. You have a well-documented record of your research process and data gathered and can supply curious consumers of your research who want to substantiate claims made in your study or interior design project.

Most often, the *thesis statement* is a two- or three-sentence declarative statement—positioned near the end of the first paragraph of the thesis proposal or statement of intent—that explicitly outlines the purpose or overall point of your project and makes a claim that you will support and defend with your research. A good analogy is that a thesis statement is to a thesis project as a topic sentence is to a paragraph. Usually, the thesis statement comprises three parts: problem, theory, and solution. You state the problem or issue you have identified, then your theory about this problem, and finally your proposed solution to the problem. The problem is *why* you have chosen this thesis. The solution is *what* will solve the problem. The theory connects the two by telling *how* the solution will solve the problem. Your research will either support this model or weaken it.

The basis of your thesis inquiry can also be posed as a question. The question "Is this the right solution to the problem?" would be answered through a series of unfolding revelations that progress toward a conclusion that finally answers the question. If you want to try this format, don't lose sight of your content in the process of rewording it. Try turning some practice statements into questions before tackling your thesis statement. For some, the thesis is a series of statements, followed by thought-provoking questions to reinforce the research direction. As we explored in Chapter 1, your thesis statement is a response to an open-ended *research question* that motivated your research process.

Your thesis statement will present your knowledge in a well-written, coherent format, and it will establish the foundation of your thesis project. It must include the following elements: (1) the identification of a current and relevant design problem and (2) a proposed design solution to the problem. Often it is bracketed by an opening explanation of what inspired the project or by clarification of the context of the problem, as well as a clear closing statement of the designer's goals for the project. By solving the problem, what do you hope to accomplish? Finally, your thesis statement must also take a stand, declaring that this one solution over all others is the correct one.

An alternative to a stand-alone written thesis in interior design is an **exegesis**, which is a piece of writing that typically accompanies a creative thesis-level project. According to Crouch and Pearce (2012), the exegesis "has a history of association with the creative disciplines, where it is understood as a critical and analytical document submitted alongside a creative project ... The function of an exegesis in design research is to inform and expand upon the finished design solution" (p. 166). "The thesis," they expounded, "is based on a research question and is self-contained.

It includes a detailed literature review and a methodology section" (p. 166). In contrast, they continued, an "exegesis should be thought of as integrated into the practice component. Just as the practice of design is a mixture of doing and thinking" (p. 166). This type of writing facilitates *praxis*, a Greek term for "the interrelationship between thinking and acting and reflecting on the results of our actions" (Crouch & Pearce, 2012, p. 14). In this way Crouch and Pearce view the *exegesis* as a reflexive engagement with the act of designing. In an exegesis, they explained "the literature review is often incorporated into the main discussion rather than treated as a separate section" (p. 166).

Similar to both a thesis and exegesis, a **dissertation** would be presented as part of a doctoral program of study or PhD (Doctor of Philosophy degree). A dissertation is typically much lengthier, perhaps two to three times longer, which emphasizes original research conducted by the author as its primary focus.

Formatting a Thesis

According to Eco (2015), "A thesis is a typewritten manuscript, usually 100 to 400 pages in length, in which the student addresses a particular problem in his chosen field" (p. 1). He goes on to say that it is "a piece of original research, in which one must not only know the work of other scholars but also 'discover' something that other scholars have not yet said" (p. 2). He advises students to create a work plan which includes "the title, the table of contents, and the introduction" as well as a "'secret title' of your thesis, the one that usually appears as the subtitle ... the formulation of this point constitutes a sort of *question*" (p. 108). After this, he advises the student to "subdivide your topic into logical sections that will correspond to chapters in the table of contents" (p. 109). He offers multiple ways to organize a table of contents, and how to add "branches" or subtopics. "Whatever method you use, a hypothetical table of contents should contain the following (*author has added in italics*):

1. The state of the issue (*introduction and contextualization*)
2. The previous research (*literature review*)
3. Your hypothesis (*or research questions*)
4. Your data collection methods
5. Your supporting data *or results*
6. Your analysis of the data *or findings*

7. The demonstration of your hypothesis
8. Conclusion and suggestions for further research" (Eco, 2015, p. 110)

One good way of understanding the many ways of formatting a thesis is to go on a "thesis treasure hunt," to explore what previous design researchers have produced to communicate their study. Conference proceedings from Interior Design Educators Council (IDEC), as well as studies showcased in other professional organizations are helpful places to start, as well as individual schools, universities, and programs which post examples of student theses (for example https:// digitalcommons.risd.edu/interiorarchitecture_master-stheses/). Although the formats vary widely, theses typically follow an order to include: an abstract, introduction, methods, findings, discussion, and conclusion. Table 10.1 expands on this basic format to show the goals and questions to answer in each section, an idea of what that section may include, and helpful tips.

Table 10.1 The Thesis Outline and Tips for Each Section		
Section or Chapter Title	**Goals, Suggested Content, & Questions to Answer**	**Tips**
Title Page	What is the name of your project? What is your name? What month and year was it completed? What university, school, institution, and department fostered your work? Is it part of a larger study or does it fulfill a requirement for a degree? Who were the advisors or or members of the reviewing committee?	Typically, five to fifteen words, including a title and subtitle (clarifying specifics of the study after a colon). Succinctly describe the research project in as few words as possible, in a way that provokes interest in a potential reader. Many times, the title is the last thing to be crafted, although you may have a "working title" which is subject to editing at the end of the study.
Abstract	What was the purpose of the study? What conceptual frameworks or theories were used to design the study, look at the data, or analyze the results? Briefly describe the methods, how the data was reduced, and the results or findings.	Depending on the format the abstract can be from 150–300 words. The abstract is most often read (after the title) so it is important to show relevance to potential readers.
Introduction	What is your background, your interest in the subject matter, and the purpose of the research? What are the research questions or problem statements?	Show your passion for your topic, your personal and professional capital and outline the main points of the problems or issues. May introduce key terms, especially the words that show up in your title.
Review of Literature	What is the history of the field or main viewpoints of the domain areas surrounding this subject? Are there terms that need to be defined or further explored?	May be organized into subsections of each domain area of your annotated bibliography. May include conceptual frameworks and theories used, Identify the founders or original authors or well-respected authorities in those theoretical areas, and give background information on current state of the theory.
Methods	Clearly state the research questions, research paradigm, type, how subjects were selected, and data collected and recorded. How were data reduced and analyzed? Provide table and figures as necessary to organize and communicate formative and summative data.	There are many ways to organize this section, depending on your type of study.
Results/ Findings	Present quantitative result and qualitative findings.	Keep it simple and as clear as possible, although the nature of your work may lend itself to complexity.

Discussion/ Implications/ Limitations	What did the data reveal to you in relation to your research questions? What meaning do you derive? What did you learn when you compared to literature review or your prior experience? Acknowledge limitations of the study that would limit the generalizability or possibly bias results. Small sample size, or type of study participants that were not represented in the sample are limitations.	This section could be combined with other sections. All studies have some sort of limitation which needs to be acknowledged.
Conclusion	Place the study within a larger context. How did you answer the research questions with this project? What were the main take-aways?	Summarize your research and include final reflections, implications, and recommendations for implementation, or suggest ways future researchers could build on your research.
Appendix or Appendices	Examples of documents too large to include in the body of the text. Include research instruments such as blank surveys, interview questions, maps, plans, and templates used.	A use of the appendix to showcase study instruments facilitates future researchers in replicating your study.
References, Works Cited	Show the depth and breadth of your research sources. Include books, articles, websites, video segments, and image sources. Give credit to the sources that built your argument. Avoid plagiarism.	Your choice of format should align with your instructor's preference, or institutional guidelines with regard to standards such as APA, MLA, and Chicago Manual of Style.

Activity 10.1
Outlining Your Thesis Paper

Purpose: To turn your research project into an organized thesis outline.

1. Go on a thesis treasure hunt, either in your school library or look online for an example of a written thesis paper that is similar in subject matter, scope, or type of research. Look particularly at the Table of Contents. Assess the way it aligns with or differs from the broad outline illustrated in Table 10.1. Note what you learned from examining this particular version of thesis organization and format.

2. Use the center aligned format below to create your title page. Fill in the underlined words with your information, and then remove the underline.

Five- to 15- Word Title
Your Name
Your Institution/Department
Class Name, Number or Section
Your Professor or Advisor's Name and Credentials
Date submitted

3. Using the multilevel list format below as a starting point, fill in your section or chapter titles. Modify the outline to accommodate your needs. Feel free to move subheadings to different chapters or sections. Continue to add more sublevel headings to construct an outline of your own thesis. Remove all underlines before printing or submitting for feedback.

Table of Contents
Abstract

1. Introduction
    1.1 Purpose of Study
    1.2 Background

2. Review of Literature
    2.1 Theoretical Frameworks
        2.1.1 _____
        2.1.2 _____
    2.2 Definitions_____
        2.2.1 _____
        2.2.2 _____
        2.2.3 _____
    2.3 _____

3. Methodology
   3.1 Research Questions
   3.2 Procedure
   3.3 Instruments
   3.4 Data Collection
   3.5 Data Analysis
   3.6 Limitations
   3.7 Ethical Considerations

4. Findings
   4.1 Pre-Treatment and Post-Treatment Results
   4.2 _____
   4.3 _____
   4.4 _____

5. Discussion and Conclusion
   5.1 Implications for Practice
       5.1.1 _____
       5.1.2 _____
   5.2 Recommendations for Future Research
   5.3 Final Reflections
   5.4 Conclusion

Appendix A
Appendix B
References

4. Share your outline with the class for feedback.

The content of your thesis must be written with careful deliberation, reviewed by your advisors, and polished until it finally accurately encompasses the complexity of your thesis project. One major part of the thesis content is found in the *abstract* or *research summary* which explains your research in five to ten concise sentences, or one to three paragraphs, as defined in Chapter 4. The following are some principles to follow when writing a summary of research. Your thesis is not a fact or casual observation; it must beg to be proved. Someone should be able to theoretically argue against it. How successfully they argue will depend, of course, on how persuasive you are. Your thesis takes a position on a topic rather than simply announcing that the project is about a topic. Clearly taking a stand may encourage controversy or inspire other points of view. Discussion of your thesis studio component should call attention to the innovation in your project. Your thesis argues one main point, which may be followed by a few specific supporting points that will also be addressed. Most importantly, the paper passes the "So What?" test. It tells us something new about something we care about. As you develop your thesis outline, use the following questions to test your statement:

- *Complexity:* Did my thesis study answer or explore a challenging design question?
- *Relevance:* Is the point I am making one that would generate interest in those associated with the field? Would it promote thought-provoking discussion or argument?
- *Scope:* Is my thesis too vague? Too general? Should I focus on a more specific aspect of my topic?
- *Objectivity:* Does my thesis deal objectively with the topic at hand, or is it an emotional declaration of my personal feelings?
- *Professional Context:* Does my introduction place my thesis within the larger, ongoing scholarly discussion about my topic?

Communicate your research procedures so that they are capable of being used by others, independently of you. Your conclusions will add to the body of interior design knowledge, and another researcher should be able to pick up where you left off and build upon your conclusions (Groat & Wang, 2002, p. 46).

Activity 10.2
Composing an Abstract and Research Summary

Purpose: To describe your research in an abstract and summary format.

1. Compose an abstract to summarize your research project. The summary should begin with the logic you used in creating your hypothesis and close with a brief discussion of your results. Only a few references should be in the abstract. Your abstract should be between 250 and 300 words, be double-spaced and typed, be free of spelling and grammatical errors, and not possess any plagiarized material.

Refer to the (comical) sample abstract below for word usage and flow:

Sample Abstract

This study investigated the relationship between kitchen design and its potential influence on nutritional intake by asking the research question, "Can kitchen design influence college students to choose healthy snacks over junk food?" I developed a survey instrument which integrated the *Berkley Nutrition Scale* by Block and Jackson (2000) to rate the level of nutrition in the snack choices of the participants and the *Crisco Kitchen-Design Scale* (Rosenberg, 2015) to measure kitchen efficiency and aesthetic in the participants' homes. Two hundred college students from the Southern California area took a ten-question online survey to determine if a positive correlation existed between high ratings of kitchen design and self-reported low number of instances of eating junk food in a typical week. Results indicated overall relatively low-rated kitchen designs and extremely high levels of poor nutrition choices among the participants. A second research method was used to determine if a kitchen designed to showcase healthy food would influence snack choices. Interior design students constructed a full-scale prototype which incorporated low shelves holding fruit and difficult-to-reach high shelving for bags of *Flamin' Hot Cheetos*®. Once again, the findings revealed kitchen design did not deter students from overwhelmingly choosing the less healthy option. Students were observed using multiple methods to reach the high shelves, while ignoring the lower shelves. I suggest further research to determine implications of kitchen design on food choices and health, particularly in dorm-style or communal living, and eating habits in young adults living abroad or in other parts of the United States.

2. Use the following fill-in-the-blank, sentence-starter activity to create a research summary (adapted from Crouch and Pearce, 2012).

   a. The aim or goal or purpose of _____ (insert thesis title) is to _____ (choose one of the following words or find a more appropriate one: analyze, characterize, compare, examine, illustrate, present, survey, design, reconstruct, understand, test ...) ...

   b. The thesis is composed of five chapters, each of them dealing with a different aspect of _____ (insert your topic)

   c. Chapter 1 is introductory and _____ (choose one of the following words or find a more appropriate one: defines, describes, reviews, deals with ...) _____ (insert another aspect of your topic). The chapter is subdivided into two parts. Part 1 describes _____ and explains _____. Part 2 deals with ... Chapter 2 examines .... The chapter consists of three parts. Part 1 focuses on .... Part 2 investigates .... Part 3 addresses the issue of .... Chapter 3 is subdivided into two parts and provides an outline of relevant ... Part 1 illustrates ....Part 2 looks at .... Chapter 4 concentrates on problems resulting from ... Part 1 describes .... Part 2 recommends ... changes to be made in ... Conclusions are drawn in Chapter 5. The main aim of the study showed _____has been reached. The author suggests that _____ should be changed/introduced/applied.

3. Share the abstract and research summary with the class to get feedback. Keep in mind that abstracts and research summaries are works-in-progress and will continually be revised throughout your writing process.

IMPLEMENTING FINDINGS

A traditional interior design thesis project includes a practical application of research into a studio-based project, which seeks to supplement, incorporate, or result from, a study. Many books have been written which focus on the integration of research findings into the design of the built environment. For an example, the author of this textbook has also published *Research-Based Programming for Interior Design* (2020) which begins with the premise that truly innovative human-centered interior design starts with gathering relevant data to inform the programmatic requirements. It is suggested to consult that text to assist you with your research-informed design process for the studio component of your thesis-level project.

Informing the Project Program

Embedded somewhere in the thesis proposal will be the identification of your *project type*, which usually defines the primary function of the space. It is important to develop your research, identify the problem, and propose the solution before selecting your project type. Although you may have an idea of where the project type is headed, simply by the focus of your research, the identity of the project should emerge out of a response to the problem. Otherwise, you may end up with a "square peg in a round hole" situation, where you limit the potential of what your project type could be by forcing it to be something you are already familiar with.

Once you have identified your project type, you will need to familiarize yourself with the terminology, controversy, and innovation. "Every project type has a history of development and its own vocabulary. There are theories or philosophies associated with each building type that you need to understand … [In the real world], your client already knows many of these things, and in order for you to communicate, you have to speak the language" (Cherry, 1999, p. 87). You should also have an understanding of the context of the project: political, social, geographical, or historical (Cherry, 1999). When designing a restaurant, for example, you might want to know about the dramatic origins of the restaurant in France after the French Revolution—as a place that served *essences*, broths made primarily from chicken and beef and served to restore strength to the sick. Knowing this historical reference might help to enrich your programming and design process and add meaning to your design decisions. Use the case studies (discussed in Chapter 4) and observation techniques (discussed in Chapter 8) to familiarize yourself with your project type and to help you identify issues common to the project type. In the book *Programming for Design*, Edith Cherry uses the example of a museum. Regardless of the uniqueness of a particular museum project, the museum project type always addresses issues of flow and how museum patrons will circulate through the building and the exhibits. Your project research should alert you to this issue, so that the issue can inform your thesis proposal and programming process (Cherry, 1999).

In addition, your creative exploration may include the programming and design issues associated with the **project program**, a document that assimilates and organizes information gathered by the programmer into a form that is usable by the designer as the basis for their schematic design. Also called *programming document* or *design brief*, it varies in terms of format, length, and type of detail. But generally includes such performance requirements as sustainability, budgets, social responsibility, and prescriptive needs such as size of spaces, furnishings, proximities, and so forth. For a comprehensive look at this process, we encourage you to read the companion textbook, *Research-based Programming for Interior Design* (2020).

A question that students often ask is, "How big does my project have to be?" This is a valid question, but at this point the project is not concerned with scale, or *relative size*. During the thesis development, there may or may not be a requirement for how many square feet the project must be. What matters may be how in-depth you go. In a thesis project, scope, or the *depth and detail of the project*, is everything. For example, an industrial designer could be given the task of designing a backpack, a seemingly small design project. However, the industrial designer could spend months designing the backpack if he integrates innovations such as a solar panel that collects energy to power a small reading light, or a waterproofing technique to allow the pack to be submerged in water (Smithsonian Institution, 2007). As mentioned earlier in this book, after the Columbine school shooting in April 1999, some backpacks were designed with Kevlar to be bulletproof in the case of another shooting, and after the attacks on the World Trade Center in New York City you could find an executive backpack that included a parachute! More recent is the development of a backpack with an ergonomic shape, and a bungee cord suspension system to reduce the impact of the backpack's weight on the body (Ball, 2006).

Rather than focusing on the size of the project, focus on the scope and on what you can accomplish in the time frame allotted with your classes. If you select a small single-family dwelling, the small size could prompt you to increase the level of detail to increase the scope of the project. If you are designing an airport, the large size means you would need to focus on carefully chosen areas to reduce the scope of the project.

SHARING YOUR RESEARCH WITH A WIDER AUDIENCE

According to Crouch and Pearce (2012) "the form that your research reporting takes is dependent upon the purpose of the research, for whom the research was undertaken, and who will be reading the report" (p. 161). They remind us that, "as in all acts of communication, it is important to match the message to the audience for which it is intended … Academic research requires a careful description and justification of the ways in which the research has been conducted" (p. 161). But when reporting research to a potential client, end-user, or other stakeholder, a more informal discussion of the study may follow a focused description of what the findings mean to the built environment to solve an immediate problem.

There is a common misconception that the thesis project is the culmination of your research efforts. Nothing could be further from the truth! Your research journey and thesis project towards earning a degree in academia represents your ability to produce entry-level or minimum requirements into the design-informed research profession. It can be seen as a first step in a lifetime of research-informed practice in interior design. From this point of view, design research manifests as an ongoing process, in which each completed or built project becomes the basis for new research. For example, a common practice in evaluating the effectiveness of a project is a Post Occupancy Evaluation (POE). Introduced in Chapter 7, this process uses carefully crafted observational studies along with corresponding end-user satisfaction surveys and/or in-depth interviews to garner important data about how features of the built environment worked (or failed) in practice. Imagine each research-informed project building on the next for the remainder of your career.

Due to the enormous impact of interior design in many aspects of our lives, sharing information to improve interior design is not limited to academic or professional publications but can help people in many aspects of their lives. For example, the practice of interior design encompasses retail, entertainment, travel, healthcare, wellness, workplaces, and public spaces, as well as home design, real estate, business, education, cultural, recreational, and religious places. At the conclusion of this section is a brainstorming activity which challenges you to research and explore many previously untapped venues to share your findings creating value in the real world.

Publishing in Academia and Beyond

The academic arena of interior design includes educational institutions in which research and learning are conducted. These venues offer students of interior design an opportunity to engage in academic conversations, present their work in a variety of ways such as speaking engagements, sitting on panels, and poster presentations. Submit your well-written *abstract* to a conference for a paper presentation or format your thesis defense presentation to a peer-reviewed periodical for publication. Good examples of academic platforms for publishing are the *Journal of Interior Design* (*JID*) which is sponsored by **Interior Design Educators Council (IDEC).** IDEC hosts annual regional and international conferences which accept student submittals. Past conference proceedings and future conference themes can be found at idec.org.

One way of transitioning from your thesis project presentation to a wider audience is to create and submit your work to be shown as part of a *conference poster* session. According to Alley (2013), "The purpose of scientific posters is to present work to an audience who is walking through a hallway or exhibit. At a conference, the presenter usually stands next to the poster, thus allowing for passers-by to engage in one-on-one discussions with the presenter. In a hallway, posters are stand-alone presentations for passers-by." Alley's website, craftofscientificposters.com offers free

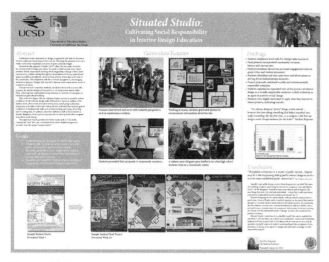

Figure 10.3
Example of a conference poster.

templates for you to easily create your own scientific poster. The site also shows other examples and offers advice. See Figure 10.3 for a good example of a research poster.

In summary, to be effective, the poster first must attract someone who is walking by and may have limited time or be distracted. The title should be catchy or memorable, and clearly align with the research content so that the audience can easily recognize the subject matter and purpose. Other graphic design advice includes:

- Use upper- and lower-case text in place of all caps since it will be easier to read.

- Differentiate areas on the poster to make them fun to read with accompanying photographs, drawings, and graphs with captions, bullet points, or short sentence text descriptions.

Professional organizations such as American Society of Interior Designers (ASID), **International Interior Design Association (IIDA)**, and **American Institute of Architects (AIA)** also host conferences. There are many trade organizations which also have conferences, conventions, and research-related publications to reach designers and those in related trades who practice Evidence-Based Design (EBD). If you look again at your literature review, you will see that you have now come full circle—all information sources you have consulted are now places you may use to seek out ways to publish your newly minted thesis project. Many professional and trade organizations offer membership

opportunities, host conferences, and publish periodicals and research journals to keep both members and the public up to date on current topics, issues, and trends related to their area of interest.

Many large companies offer to publish white papers, authoritative research to promote a product, service, or technology as described in Chapter 4. If your research involves a marketable product or serves to influence consumers and other potential customers of an existing furnishing, finish, or design strategy, this may be an appropriate outlet for you. Through many of these organizations, you can enter design competitions and apply for research grants. In addition, local colleges, universities, libraries, and museums may also host a lecture series, workshops, exhibitions, or their own form of conferences, that offer opportunities for you to present your work to people who may be interested. At first, you can sign up to attend these events. When you feel confident that your research fits their venue, you can submit your work.

In the more public forum, you may want to write a book. Most publishers require an aspiring author to write a **prospectus**, which describes the rationale, outstanding features, intended audience, and comparison to existing books on the same subject matter (the competition!) for marketing considerations. Publishers also frequently require a table of contents (TOC) or extended table of contents (ETOC), a sample written chapter, as well as a ***curriculum vitae*** (**CV**) or summary of credentials including education, certifications, research experience, teaching positions, previously published writings, and professional affiliations.

When writing a book for a particular trade (interior designers), a textbook (design students), or popular reading (homeowners, families, business owners, etc.) consider the **tone**, the way you express your attitude towards the research and the participants, with either a sense of authority, level of formality, or casualness in language. Richardson (1990) stated that "tone is revealed in many different ways such as choice of metaphors, organization of material, how a quotation or a person's experience is framed and treated by the narrator" (p. 39). You can use the same research with different tones to produce work that frames the findings in a way that appeals to different audiences.

Consider more rhetorical devices on which to build a book or business: *continuum* and *typology*. A **continuum** is "an imaginary construction" along which objects, or levels of some design construct, can be arrayed (Richardson, 1990, p. 51). For example, if your research revealed **typology** or a classification system for something in the field of interior design, this can be an excellent rhetorical device on which to base a "how to" book for novice designers. The Research in Action 10.2 box "On the Origins of *Joyful*," recounts one designer's journey from inductive speculation to reach a research-based conclusion about what environmental aspects can contribute to a feeling of joy. Her resulting book, blog, and website promote this sort of typology which is interesting to ordinary people, as well as students and design professionals.

Activity 10.3
Brainstorming Publishing Venues

Purpose: A brainstorming activity that challenges you to think of as many different venues to share your research and thesis project.

1. List all the different key terms that may be associated with your thesis project and research. For example, if your research centered around children on the Autism spectrum in a water park, key terms might be: Children, Autism, Water Park.

2. Look up these key terms online to search for government agencies, professional, educational, cultural, out-reach, and community-based organizations which would offer information to members (or the public) interested in these areas.

3. List at least ten organizations, research hubs, or educational institutions you have found. Also note what kind of publications they offer and types of competitions, exhibits, lectures, or conferences they sponsor.

4. Narrow down the list to three or four which stand out to you as viable. Perhaps they are local or seem like they would be interested in your work.

5. Share your ideas with the class.

Research-Inspired Examples: A Blog, a Book, and a Business Model

Sometimes informing a vast amount of people, such as the public, means you have to think outside of the box. Your research project may lead to a product such as a marketable furnishing, a new way to organize or construct a home office, or an innovative product, toy, or game to teach others about the power of design. Creating lectures, talks, seminars, and curricula for peers is a good idea. How about a research-inspired after-school program for children, a workshop for your neighbors at a home-improvement center, or an exhibit of your work at a local museum?

This chapter ends with a look at three design researchers who took research seriously, but then transcended the academic environment to reach more people. The examples included here are intended to provoke new ways of looking at how to apply research of the built environment and how to reach popular audiences.

In the first example, interior design student, Meli Apone, started a blog which focused on her research in theme park design. Three blog posts are included here to give some idea of the range of research topics that can be featured. The first blog post talks about the history of Disneyland from a designer's perspective. The second one delves into the technology behind Disney's most beloved attraction: *The Haunted House*. The third post celebrates the life of a designer who made enormous creative contributions to Disney rides in terms of color, art, and culture and who may serve as a mentor for young women interested in entering a creative field such as design.

In the next example, industrial designer Ingrid Fetell Lee speaks about her research journey in a TED-talk "Where Joy Hides and How to Find It" (May, 2018) which began at the end of her final studio critique in school. From her interest in what elements in the built and natural environment make people feel joy, she wrote "Joyful" a book, and an interactive website and *newsletter* which inform people about the ongoing discoveries about the power of design to increase well-being in our everyday environments.

In the final example, interior designer Emily Corless speaks about a business model which was born through an informal yet rigorous action-research project that has successfully filled a gap in services for a group of people who were in dire need of interior design services. *Humble Design* serves formerly homeless families who have recently acquired housing and helps them make the new living space their well-designed home. This psychological and emotional connection to home reduces their likelihood of returning to homelessness.

RESEARCH IN ACTION 10.1
Disney Knows Best!

By Meli Apone

Come along for the ride as we dive into the *Imagineers'* design of the world of yesterday, tomorrow, and the land of fantasy! Since 1928, Disney has inspired each generation through cartoons, merchandise, television programs, and theme parks. This blog follows my research interests in design aspects of the Disney theme parks and resorts. Along with following specific designers, I will also explore the process of design from concepts to completion, along with the mechanics and aesthetics of built attractions. I am excited to share these posts as I discover more about my favorite place and the professionals responsible for creating such a happy space for all.

Blog post #1: Welcome Foolish Mortals, to the Haunted Mansion

Today, we will be discussing the iconic attraction, the *Haunted Mansion.* The original *Haunted Mansion* resides in New Orleans Square at the Disneyland Resort. Let us learn the history and then next week we will discuss the gags and tricks that bring the Victorian Manor to life.

The idea for a haunted house began with the early stages of the park. The first ever concept drawing for the *Haunted Mansion* was by Harper Groff, located just off Main Street, overlooking the town church (Surrel, 2015). This idea, along with the church, was quickly scrapped. The concept reappeared in 1957, with Art Director Ken Anderson, who drew up a sketch inspired by multiple structures, including the Shipley Lydecker house, in Baltimore, Maryland. Along with the look of the building, Ken Anderson also conceptualized various story lines for the walk-through experience inspiring a sign for the front gates to welcome ghostly inhabitants to "enjoy active retirement" (Surrel, 2015, p. 20). Disney wanted to make sure the ride would be a "people eater," meaning it could entertain thousands of guests per hour (Surrel, 2015, p. 22). Marc Davis and Claude Coats were appointed to finalize the mansion. Davis viewed the attraction as humorous, while Coats envisioned it being scary. They both got their way in some areas of the attraction. Bob Gurr enhanced a newly developed track system that moves on a continuous loop by suggesting the ride vehicles rotate so the guests' viewpoint will be where the Imagineers want it (Surrel, 2015). The *Haunted Mansion* opened its doors to the living on August 9, 1969. The attraction was so highly anticipated by guests over the years that it became an instant classic.

Blog Post #2: Haunted Mansion: A Bag Full of Tricks

Last week, we discussed the history of the *Haunted Mansion* and this week we will dive into how the illusions are created. The Walt Disney Company is founded on the film industry which is known for their special effects. The *Imagineers'* call the special effects they create in Disney theme parks "illusioneering."

In the *Haunted Mansion,* illusions begin before you board the ride itself. As guests enter the foyer, the archway slowly encloses into a room with no visible means of escape. Then the walls begin to stretch upward. The trick performed is simply an elevator moving downward to the "Doom Buggy" loading station which is the official ride. Guests hear "*please don't pull down on the safety bar. Your Ghost Host will lower it for you.*"

One of the most effective illusions is the "endless hallway" filled with antiques, doorways, and a coffin with a corpse yelling "let me out." This illusion is created by forced perspective (Surrel, 2015, p. 91). The end of the surprisingly short hallway is a mirror elongating the space. To make it spookier, the designers placed a

▶

"floating" candelabra in front of the mirror to embellish the gag. The Doom Buggies continue past doors knocking on their own to a room where a floating head in a crystal ball speaks. Madam Leota, modeled after Leota Tombs, a former *Imagineer*, is one of the earliest shown examples of projection mapping in the parks (Iwerks & Tang, 2019). A mold of her face was taken and placed inside the crystal ball that hangs by wire and is carefully manipulated to create a floating illusion. Completing the illusion, a recording of Tombs projects onto the sculpture—this is the art of projection mapping.

As the guests approach the exit, the Ghost Host heeds a final warning to "*beware of hitch-hiking ghosts.*" This leaves us with our final illusion as guests look into a mirror to a see a ghost sitting beside them. Surrel (2015) mentions that the hitchhiking ghosts were an afterthought but thankfully they were included to complete the ride. The mechanics behind this feature are depicted below.

Technology has grown immensely since the attraction opened in 1969. *Imagineers* have updated and enhanced scenes over the years including the HatBox Ghost, adding lightning to the foyer, and allowing Jack Skellington from *The Nightmare Before Christmas* to move in for the holidays. However, the overall design and concept persists. The *Haunted Mansion* remains a staple to any Disneyland visit.

Blog Post #3: Mary Blair: Master of Color

Mary Blair is recognized for her impeccable use of color and introducing modernism to Disney (Iwerks & Tang, 2019). Some say it's hard to remember the times before her revolutionizing color combinations, as they were not yet a part of the company's narrative. Why was she so important to the Disney company? I welcome you to fall down the rabbit hole with me!

Mary Blair fancied art since she was a child, winning many awards in her youth. She was first hired to sketch a little dog named Lady, which eventually would be made into the feature film *Lady and the Tramp*. A little over a year later, Mary quit to pursue painting at home. Walt Disney was more than upset when he heard the news of her departure and, in result, proposed a South American getaway. Together they traveled to Brazil, Argentina, Bolivia, Peru, Ecuador, Guatemala, and Mexico City, in which Mary found herself absorbing the colorful variations found in different cultures. Her most renowned works, *Alice in Wonderland* "Falling Down the Rabbit Hole," "March of the Cards," and "*it's a small world*" project were greatly influenced by the South America voyage. Officially, Rolly Crump is credited for designing the façade of "*it's a small world,*" but he notes that it is inspired by the stylings of Mary Blair (Iwerks & Tang, 2019).

Although Mary Blair died in 1978, her work lives on and continues to influence new projects. Pete Doctor, Chief Creative Officer of Pixar, stated, "In every production, there's a phase where we say, 'Let's look at Mary Blair stuff!'"

These two graphics display how the hitchhiker ghost illusion works. Graphic "A" shows a dark room while graphic "B" shows the "ghost" illuminated and in result is materialized into the scene (adapted from www.hauntedhouse.com).

Rolly Crumps' Mary Blair-inspired "it's a small world" façade lit up at night during the holiday season.

RESEARCH IN ACTION 10.2
On the Origins of *Joyful*

It's 2008, and I'm just finishing my first year of design school. I'm at my first year-end review, which is a form of ritual torture for design students, where they make you take everything you made over the course of the year and lay it out on a table and stand next to it while a bunch of professors, most of whom you've never seen before, give you their unfiltered opinions of it. So, it's my turn and I'm standing next to my table, everything neatly lined up, and I'm just hoping that my professors can see how much effort I've put into making my designs practical and ergonomic and sustainable. I'm starting to get really nervous, because for a long time, no one says anything. It's just completely silent. And then one of the professors starts to speak, and he says, "Your work gives me a feeling of joy."

(Fetell Lee, 2018)

The quote above opens a TED Talk by Ingrid Fetell Lee "Where Joy Hides and How to Find It" (May, 2018). Dressed in pink and orange with each fingernail polished in a different bright color, Lee goes on to explain how the comment by her professor sparked a research journey: a quest to find out what joy was, and how to find it.

She began with a simple open-ended research question, "How do *tangible* things make us feel *intangible* joy?" She delved into previously published research studies to discover "broadly speaking, when psychologists use the word 'joy,' what they mean is an intense, momentary experience of positive emotion … That feeling of wanting to jump up and down is one of the ways that scientists measure joy."

Over the next few months, she asked everyone she met, "what brings you joy?" Systematically collecting their responses, patterns began to emerge. What do flowers, bubbles, rainbows, swimming pools and tree houses have in common? What about ice cream cones with sprinkles? Or confetti, which she noted, is "one of the most joyful substances on the planet." She also collected images and pinned them up on her wall, like a detective looking for clues.

"One day," she remarked, "something just clicked," and she became conscious of sensational and perceptual common qualities such as playfulness, abundance, multiplicity, and surprise. In this "Aha moment" she coined the phrase: "Aesthetics of Joy." She found that findings in neuroscience showed that love of color can be traced to our evolutionary ancestors' need to find nourishing fruit, and that round shapes did not activate the parts of the brain associated with fear or anxiety, as sharp or angular objects did.

Now, over the past few years, Lee sees her mission as designer to implement these elements and principles into everyday life, especially in spaces for the most vulnerable among us, such as children and the elderly. The implications for her research are far reaching as it relates to the built environment, prompting her to build an interactive website which showcases the concepts and a book, *Joyful: The Surprising Power of Ordinary Things to Create Extraordinary Joy*, which enables her to reach a broader audience.

Image captured from the *Aesthetics of Joy* website and the cover of *Joyful: The Surprising Power of Ordinary Things to Create Extraordinary Joy* by Ingrid Fetell Lee (2018).

RESEARCH IN ACTION 10.3
Humble Design: A Business Model Which Filled a Gap

By Emily Corless

In 2009, Treger Strasberg was working in Detroit when she discovered that one of her coworkers, a single mom with several young children, was homeless and living in her car. Treger immediately helped her find an apartment, but she soon realized that her coworker had no budget for furniture. Treger and her friend Ana started collecting items to furnish the home. They called on friends, neighbors, people they didn't know—asking for beds, linen, furniture, and kitchen items. After they finished, the furniture donations kept coming so Treger called nine different shelters and said, "We have all this stuff, and we want our donations to go directly to families who are in need." The shelters all responded, "That's really a great idea, but nobody does that." Treger had identified a hole in the system, and *Humble Design* was born.

Not only did Treger use observation and personal experience to determine the need for her business, she also put together teams of dedicated designers who extensively interview the formerly homeless families that *Humble Design* now serves. Partnered with over twenty agencies in five cities across the country, social workers and case managers refer their clients to receive design services. The "week of service" process begins as *Humble Design* designers record measurements and other pertinent field data about the existing space.

Designers then meet with the clients on Monday (typically in their home, but sometimes virtually).

They talk with the clients about their background, their needs, design style, and favorite colors. If the client has children, the designers will interview them and ask them about their interests and preferences as well. Designers at Humble have discovered that personalizing a bedroom or homework area for the children, using their favorite colors, images, as well as their names on pillows or artwork, encourages the youth to feel their own sense of ownership of the space. They hope it will lead then to be empowered to take care of their rooms and study more. See images below.

As Treger says, "We don't ask them for their social security or medical forms. We ask them to tell us about their journey and what things they love. The biggest thing we emphasize here at *Humble* is that we provide dignity to clients." *Humble Design* serves as a great example of a research-informed business model embedded with an ongoing research component to continuously collect data which serves to inform future design solutions.

I felt like I was a failure

Still from Humble Design. Interviewing people led to discovery that what they really needed was some dignity.

but what I've seen is single moms

Still from Humble Design data collection. Designer records field data.

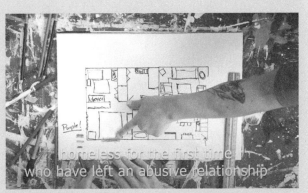

homeless for the first time who have left an abusive relationship

Still from Humble Design. Interior designers work to help formerly homeless families feel more at home.

CONCLUSION

To add to the body of knowledge in interior design, your research procedures and findings must be communicated. Building a strong argument for your conclusions involves attention to detail from the beginning. As you conclude your study, write your paper, design a studio component, and defend your thesis, keep in mind that the entire process relies on your open-minded ability to incorporate feedback from your instructors, advisors, and peers. This responsive inclusion will help to ensure that the knowledge presented to the rest of the world has been based in the scientific method, uses appropriate methods to collect and analyze data, and is valid, reliable, and credible.

Background information discovered during your literature review allowed you to confidently build a case for the gap in knowledge, or area upon which you could expand. Consistently applying deliberate, reflective practices throughout the research process led to data that was gathered ethically and responsibly, eventually analyzed for meaningful conclusions. Upon successful completion of your research project, continue to explore the many ways you can communicate your findings. Ask further questions which seek to enrich the built environment, inform interior design practitioners, and inspire future design researchers.

Key Terms

American Institute of Architects (AIA)
Conclusion
Continuum
Curriculum vitae (CV)
Dissertation
Exegesis

Implications
Interior Design Educators Council (IDEC)
International Interior Design Association (IIDA)
Paraphrase
Praxis

Project program
Prospectus
Rhetorical devices
Thesis project
Tone
Typology

Discussion Questions

1. How important is communication in the field of research? Can you think of any examples of how communication fosters the research process? What other ways do you think would foster greater communication in the current age?

2. What rhetorical literary devices were discussed in this chapter? Which ones do you feel would be most useful or appropriate for your research?

3. What are ways you envision your research adding to the body of knowledge in the field of interior design?

4. Can writing about research be completely objective? What aspects of research are subjective? How can you balance objectivity and subjectivity in research?

5. How were you inspired by the research-inspired examples at the end of the chapter? What are some other ways that research informed a product, space, or other creative design endeavor?

References

Alley, M. (2013). *The craft of scientific presentations: Critical steps to succeed and critical errors to avoid*, 2nd ed. New York: Springer. Retrieved June 27, 2022 from http://www.craftofscientificposters.com/design.html.

Ball, P. (2006, December 20). The backpack that's easier to carry. *Nature* https://doi.org/10.1038/news061218-8.

Barnet, S. Bedau, H., & O'Hara, J. (2020). *From critical thinking to argument: A portable guide*, 6th ed. Boston, MA: Bedford's/St. Martin's.

Cherry, E. (1999). *Programming for design: From theory to practice*. New York: John Wiley.

Crouch, C., & Pearce, J. (2012). *Doing research in design*. London: Bloomsbury.

Eco, U. (2015). *How to write a thesis*. Translated from the original Italian *Come si fa una testi laurea: le materie umanistiche*. (1977/2012) Bompani/RCS Libri S.p.A. Cambridge, MA: MIT Press.

Fetell Lee, I. (2018) *Joyful: The surprising power of ordinary things to create extraordinary happiness*. New York: Little, Brown Spark, a division of Hachette Book Group.

Groat, L., & Wang, D. (2002). *Architectural research methods*. New York: John Wiley.

Hodge, B., & Pollak, L. (Eds.). (1996). *Studio works 4: Harvard University Graduate School of Design (No. 4)*. New York: Princeton Architectural Press.

Iwerks, L., & Tang, M. E. (Directors & Producers). (2019) *The Imagineering story: Episode 1* [Disney+]. Los Angeles, CA: Walt Disney Company.

Literary Education Online (LEO). (2003, October 14). Literacy Education Online. "Thesis statement." Retrieved 2008 from http://leo.stcloudstate.edu/acadwrite/thesistatement.html.

Richardson, L. (1990). Writing strategies: Reaching diverse audiences. *Qualitative Research Methods*, Vol. 21. Sage.

Robinson, L. B. (2020). *Research-based programming for interior design*. New York: Fairchild Books/Bloomsbury.

Smithsonian Institution. (2007). *Design for the other 90%*. New York: Cooper Hewitt, National Design Museum.

Surrell, J. (2015). *The haunted mansion: Imagineering a Disney classic* (Illustrated ed.). Disney Editions.

glossary

A priori relating to or denoting reasoning or knowledge arising from theoretical deduction rather than from observation or empirical evidence. Also referred to as *Nativist*.

Abductive reasoning pragmatic approach to problem-solving, design, and artistic endeavors, making a probable or tentative conclusion from what you have experienced.

Abstract a brief (typically 250 words) descriptive summary of a research project describing what was studied, why it is important, and how the research was conducted including an overview of the results, findings, or implications.

Academy of Neuroscience for Architecture (ANFA) promotes and advances knowledge that links neuroscience research to a growing understanding of human responses to the built environment offering lectures, collaborative sessions, and conferences for students and professionals.

Accretion traces physical evidence that indicates a behavior or interaction, a build-up of a residue, or something added to the environment as a result of a behavior or an interaction. May be legitimate (legally placed) such as a sign prohibiting parking, or illegitimate (not legally place) like graffiti on a building or litter in a park.

Acronym a word formed from the initial letter or letters of each of the successive parts or major parts of a compound term such as NATO or LEED.

Action research a form of applied research conducted in a localized or practical setting (such as a classroom, workplace, or facility) which mutually benefits the researcher and those being studied.

Adaptation a type of trace evidence that shows a manipulation of the built environment by the occupants which could yield insight into an issue or indicate a design problem to solve.

Aesthetics a branch of philosophy dealing with the nature, purpose, creation, understanding, and appreciation of beauty.

Affordance term coined by cognitive psychologist James J. Gibson to describe how features of the environment offer opportunities for interaction and how perception of those features enable us to understand how to use them.

"Aha" moment a sudden moment of clarity which yields a new understanding, connection, or solution; a memorable insight.

American Institute of Architects (AIA) a collective voice of professional architects and policymakers working to advance quality of life in the built environment and protect the public's health, safety, and welfare.

American Psychological Association (APA) the leading scientific and professional organization representing psychology in the United States, consisting of researchers, educators, clinicians, consultants, and students. Publishes and maintains standards for scientific writing (www.apa.org).

American Society for Interior Designers (ASID) professional organization dedicated to generating and disseminating applied knowledge among members and to promoting the value of interior design to the public.

Analysis of Variance (ANOVA) a statistical tool created by Ronald Fisher in the early 1900s used to compare data from two sets or populations to differentiate between factors which have statistical influence and random factors; a one-way ANOVA compares three or more groups.

Anecdotal evidence a personal account or story used to garner attention, emotionally engage, humanize research statistics, and/or build trust with listener or reader.

Annotated bibliography a flexible, compilation of study citations, explanatory notes, and summaries organized by student for future use in a literature review or other original paper.

Anonymous (hidden) observer one who blends in with the other subjects in an environment to yield a study method that minimizes the Hawthorne effect. Also known as a marginal participant.

Anthropometrics the study of comparative sizes and ranges of ability in human bodies.

Applied research scientific inquiry conducted for practical purposes, to improve the quality of something or solve an identified problem.

Argument a term used in logic which refers to an attempt to persuade someone to adopt our point of view while elevating the cognitive or intellectual capacity for reason.

Artifacts useful objects, made or modified by humans, which have meaning within a culture. Common examples include tools, clothing, furnishings, and items used for rituals.

Assumption a fact, statement, or belief taken for granted; fundamental perspective, agreement, or position that allows use of a theory by multiple people.

Augmented reality the use of virtual effects such as filters and digital overlays to enhance real world experience.

Authority Having Jurisdiction (AHJ) the local governing agency, offices, or individuals responsible for enforcing codes in the project's location.

Autoethnography a qualitative approach in which a researcher studies and expounds upon a topic of personal experience.

Bar graph a graphic means of quantitative comparison by rectangles with lengths proportional to the measure of the data or things being compared.

Basic research scientific inquiry conducted to understand a phenomenon for general knowledge.

Behavioral mapping the act of recording participant movement and interaction with the physical environment during observation as part of Environmental-Behavior research; it can be person-centered (also known as shadowing) which follows a particular person, or place-centered in which the focus of the map is the place with people moving through it.

Bias a systematic mistake based on prejudice or assumption.

Biophilia/Biophilic design a comprehensive system which supports human's biological affinity for natural elements in the built environment.

Block quote a sentence or paragraph of text longer than forty words used from another source, formatted separately from the running text.

Body-Conscious Design (BCD) a method or perspective within human-centered design that simultaneously includes physiological, psychological, and cultural perspectives in research and design of the built environment, focusing on the health benefits of good ergonomics aligning with yoga practices and neuroscience.

Boundary object a concept in social and technological sciences used to identify items which cross or serve to inform multiple research disciplines. Examples include specimens, field notes, and maps.

Brainstorming a method for generating multiple ideas as quickly as possible emphasizing spontaneity and withholding judgment.

Building systems various operational entities consisting of assemblies of components that make up a typical facility including structural, mechanical, electrical, plumbing, security, lighting, and life safety.

Bulk term used to describe municipal codes regulation of number of square feet, height, or lot coverage allowed to be built on a particular area or lot.

Case study an in-depth examination of a previously completed, or proposed, project that has conditions related to your own project, which serves as a prototype or an example of either a successful or an unsuccessful design solution.

Categorical data discrete or disconnected sets of names or numbers.

Cathedral effect the theory that perception of a high ceiling height contributes to greater cognitive flexibility, generation of ideas, and creativity.

Causal/causation measure that shows how one action is directly responsible for or related to an outcome.

Chicago Manual of Style (CMS) an authoritative reference organization for scientific writing used by authors, editors, proofreaders, indexers, copywriters, designers, and publishers.

Circadian rhythm the daily cycle of natural light and darkness, and its effect on health and well-being.

Citation formal reference in an act of quoting.

Claim an assertion or statement open to challenge that typically requires evidence for others to agree with and endorse.

Clearinghouse question a type of follow-up question or probe used to make sure you have elicited all the information a respondent wants to provide on a topic.

Client the owner, organization, corporation, company, or decision-making agent who would be responsible for hiring the designer, making the key design decisions, and/or funding the project.

Client profile part of the project program which is a detailed description of the sponsoring agency or owner which typically identifies key personnel or stakeholders and their areas of expertise, background, and values.

Closed-ended question respondents choose from a predetermined list of answers.

Codebook a list of the codes used for the analysis of a particular collection of data, the names of the variables that the codes represent, and a list of the kinds of items that are to be coded for each variable.

Coding/codify partitioning qualitative responses or data into groups to transform to quantitative, or numerical data.

Cognitive bias systematic errors in thinking that occur when processing or interpreting information which may be as a result of a neurological disorder or an overwhelming amount of information; a nonconscious bias due to brain processing.

Column bays a term used to describe the rhythm and spacing of structural elements in the building.

Comparative case study the research activity of contrasting two similar projects to discern and note interesting differences.

Concept map a tool for brainstorming by using words to link thoughts and ideas throughout the research process.

Conceptual blockbusting overcoming preconceived notions and mental walls that prevent idea generation during problem-solving.

Conclusion from the Latin *claudere*, "to shut," a recap of major points, a return to statements made in the introduction, and suggestions of meaning at the end of a written paper, study, or thesis.

Confirmation bias a cognitive tendency to seek out and employ information that aligns with our pre-existing beliefs, which tends to be very powerful and often difficult to overcome.

Confounding variable intervening or mediating variables that may be the cause rather than the independent and dependent variables you are trying to isolate to discern a causal relationship.

Conscious acting with critical awareness associated with frontal brain activity.

Consilience a convergence of knowledge from the diverse fields of science originally sought by E. O. Wilson (1984).

Constructivism/interpretivist a worldview based on the idea that knowledge is constructed by relative consensus; an approach to social science and related disciplines which align with a constructivist understanding of reality.

Constructs components of a theory, mental abstractions, which can be empirically measured such as hue, intensity, age, height, or intelligence, or subjectively distinguished such as comfort, motivation, anxiety, satisfaction, or convenience.

Content analysis a process of selective reduction, decision-making, and interpretation of a sample of documents, photos, videos, or other qualitative data items.

Context-specific knowledge garnered from or identified as only occurring in a particular place, circumstance, or state.

Contextualize the act of placing a study within the framework of past, current, or related studies, providing the background, origins, or factors contributing to a situation, practice, or an issue under study.

Contingency question a follow-up question as a result of a respondent answering a previous question on a questionnaire, during an interview or survey.

Continuous data expressed as a rational number, unit of measure on an infinite scale, or any value between two numbers along an uninterrupted extension in time, space, range, or sequence.

Continuum an imaginary construction along which objects, or levels of a construct, can be arrayed.

Control variables variables that are measured and statistically "controlled" to further show that the causal relationship did not happen by chance or accident.

Convergent thinking detail-oriented and focused cognitive process; see vertical thinking.

Correlation measures the degree to which two variables move in relation to each other.

Creative paradigm an approach to research in arts and design which calls for realms of inquiry that extend both outward (to the physical environment) and inward (to the mind).

Creativity the act of developing novel, useful, or new combination of ideas characterized by or resulting from a combination of flexibility in thinking and focused concentration.

Cross-sectional study a type of observational research associated with social science that analyzes data of variables collected at one point in time, or over a short set period, across a sample population or predefined subset. Also known as a *transverse* or *prevalence* study.

Cultural capital refers to the unique combination of knowledge, experience, and connections of an individual seen as valuable assets.

Cultural milieu derived from French, a term used in sociology to mean the immediate physical and social environment surrounding observed behavior in a natural setting.

Curriculum vitae (CV) a summary of academic credentials listing education, certifications, research experience, teaching position, published writings, and related achievements and awards. Typically, longer than a résumé at three to ten pages.

Data facts and statistics collected for the purpose of reference, comparison, or analysis.

Data reduction refers to ways researchers process data including methods to transform qualitative data (verbal answers expressing thoughts and feelings) into quantitative data (numbers and percentages).

Data sheets prepared (digital or printed) pages with editable areas for the date, time, and setting, as well as checklists, symbols, or abbreviation for behaviors to be identified or other predetermined categories that focus your observation.

Data storytelling compelling infographics and other visuals representing data organized in a narrative sequence to construct an engaging, persuasive, and memorable presentation.

Data visualization using images to communicate or reinforce ideas, concepts, findings, as well as insight, experience, attitudes, values, perspectives, opinions, and predictions.

Database a large collection of data organized especially for rapid search and retrieval.

Deductive reasoning deriving logical conclusions by formulating a hypothesis, using a predetermined theory, and progressing from general to specific; seek to prove using a series of logical "if, then" statements.

Demographic data statistical, quantitative, or categorical information about people in a given area, sample, or population such as age, gender, income, ethnicity, education level, occupation, and so forth, used for descriptive purposes.

Density a measure of people per square foot in a municipality.

Dependent variable an object, event, idea, feeling, time period, or any other type of category you are trying to measure that changes or relies on other factors for change.

Descriptive statistics a set of brief representative amounts that summarize a given data set or sample commonly displayed in visual charts and graphs.

Descriptive study seeking to document and analyze existing relationships to gain a better understanding of a behavior, need, or condition.

Design a creative process that emphasizes making decisions with an overarching goal or intention to solve a problem or devise something for a specific function, purpose, or need. Can be a noun, verb, or adjective.

Design-informed researchers designers who use scientific research methods to actively gather data to inform their own projects or for others to use.

Design science an area of research concerned with the studying the design process itself, typically in the fields of engineering, human/computer interface, and social media/algorithms, but can also be applied to visual arts, music, education, or design.

Detectable warnings ground textures which warn pedestrians they are stepping into traffic, reaching the edge of a platform or the top of a flight of stairs.

Discrete data individual or disconnected; see categorical data.

Dissertation presented by a student in a doctorate program of study; similar to a thesis but typically lengthier and more focused on original research.

Divergent thinking cognitive processes which generate multiple ideas or solutions; see lateral thinking.

Docent tour guide.

Document analysis a form of qualitative research which studies a written artifact such as meeting minutes, training materials, patient records, and so forth obtained from an institution or person associated with the subject of the study. Can include posted signage, maps, and marketing materials as well.

Domain areas subcategories of a broader research topic. For example, when studying collaborative school design, you may have domain areas such as classroom layout, worksurface designs, and types of group projects as influences or aspects.

Dyads pairs of people interacting collected or analyzed as one unit of behavior in observation.

Electroencephalography (EEG) technology used to record electrical activity of the human brain in response to a variety of stimuli and activities.

Embodied cognition an emerging paradigm in neuroscience and architecture which links the health, development, and well-being of the brain and nervous system directly to the experience of the physical environment.

Emergency egress plan *fire escape plan*, *building exit plan*, or *evacuation plan* required to be posted in public view.

Empiricism a worldview or perspective based on the premise that knowledge must be observable and strives to make these observations as objective as possible.

End-user profile outlines the target population of the project typically including the age-range, abilities, and other demographic information such as special needs of the people who will be served by the project. Use statistical information from literature review and original data collection.

End-users various anticipated people who will be visiting, working, or living in the designed project. Participant end-users would be the current or actual user of a space who engages with the designer during the programming phase to give information. Potential end-users possess characteristics of someone who could use the space in the future.

Environment-Behavior (E-B) research a branch of study interested in learning how people interact with their environment

Environmental stressors identified factors that raise the brain state of arousal through high levels of sensory input or *stimuli* such as noise (auditory) and clutter (visual), creating an unwarranted, negative side of arousal commonly known as *stress*.

Epistemic frameworks/Epistemology ways of knowing the world/the study of how we know things; the nature and grounds of knowledge.

Ergonomics the study of interaction of the human body with tools and furnishings while engaged in activity or work.

Erosion traces deterioration, wear, or missing items in an environment caused by behavior or interaction that provides insight at the usage pattern or indicates a design problem to be solved.

Ethnography descriptive scholarly documentations of a culture, or a person as a representative of the culture.

Ethos Greek for ethical character and morals as related to an individual, group, or institution.

Evidence relevant, verifiable, representative body of facts, physical documents, artifacts, or testimony, used to support claims made in a logical argument, or instances to formulate or refute a theory.

Evidence-based design (EBD) a process for the conscientious, explicit, and judicious use of current best evidence from research (which uses the scientific method involving experiments or quasi-experimental methods) to make and justify critical design decisions.

Exegesis a piece of writing that typically accompanies a creative thesis-level project to inform and expand upon the finished design solution.

Exhaustive list includes all the possible responses to a question on a questionnaire. A list can be made exhaustive by simply adding an "other" category to allow for unanticipated responses.

Exit poll a questionnaire or survey at the end of a project or experience. A similar device is a Satisfaction Survey.

Experiential studies a controlled or manipulated environment designed to engage participants in order to observe them. Requires extensive preparation in how you operationalize your constructs, how an experience or treatment is measured, and how you control for outside or mitigating factors that could influence the results but not as rigorous as an experiment.

Experiment an operation or procedure carried out under controlled conditions to yield particular observations to discover or illustrate an effect or test a hypothesis; often conducted in a laboratory with specially designed instruments and other measuring tools.

Explicit clearly communicated; opposite of implied or implicit.

FF&E Inventory documentation of existing furnishing, fixtures, and equipment of a project.

Feasibility study a service provided by a designer which helps client to determine if a proposed site fits a project's program requirements.

Field notes written up as soon as you have left the observational setting, on which you will draw for analysis.

Field survey a site visit which involves measuring and visually documenting the building conditions.

Fields cells in a table or database to input data, typically organized as vertical columns and horizontal rows in a spreadsheet.

Fieldwork study of a particular culture, society, or community through active participation with the people being studied to learn about their way of life.

Figure graph, drawing, or other depiction used to convey the essential findings from a research study.

Findings end product of a quantitative study; similar to results.

Five Phases of Design a cross-disciplinary industry standard of the five billable stages of a design project for the built environment consisting of (1) Pre-Design/Programming, (2) Schematics, (3) Design Development, (4) Contract Documents, and (5) Contract Administration.

Focus group a method of qualitative research for social science and marketing which employs a small group of potential end-users and gathers information from their answers to questions, as well as the interactive discussions that naturally arise.

Formative theories Following an inductive process, a researcher perceives, compares, and speculates on relationships observed and builds suppositions that arise from the data.

functional Magnetic Resonance Imaging (fMRI) a technology that uses magnetic fields to detect activity in the brain by monitoring blood flow to provide an indirect view of neuron activity.

Gap in knowledge identified area or detail that has been missed, overlooked, or ignored by previous researchers or practitioners.

Generalizable data that apply universally or widely applicable to a majority; refers to the ability to accept or draw a conclusion from particulars.

Generational theory developed by German sociologist Karl Mannheim (1928) positing that people are significantly influenced by the socio-historical milieu they grow up in, creating a cohort shaped by their shared experiences of technology and world occurrences.

Genius loci translated from Roman mythology to mean the "spirit of the place" referring to a location's distinctive atmosphere.

Geographic information of or belonging to a region, typically of natural topographic features and boundaries related to mapping the earth.

Grounded theory refers to the idea of inductively deriving emerging patterns from collected data in a research study to form or propose a new theory.

Habits routine behaviors, often associated with emotion, memory, and pattern recognition, which form strong neural pathways in the individual performing the behaviors.

Hawthorne effect the effect on behavior of study participants who know they are being watched. Also known as *observer effect*.

Heuristic a mental shortcut that allows people to solve problems and make judgments quickly and efficiently; also referred to as rule-of-thumb strategy.

Homunculus man Penfield's famous three-dimensional representational model which mapped number of sensory neurons in brain to size of body parts.

Hyperreality a state in which the real is supplanted by the imagined for the viewer and supersedes or allows us to transcend real time and space.

Hypothesis a testable explanation, a tentative assumption, an interpretation of a situation or condition used as the ground for action, and/or an antecedent clause of a conditional statement.

Identified outsider one who is clearly observing yet has the potential to remain neutral and not interfere with the natural behavior. Most likely to trigger the Hawthorne effect.

Implications a section of a thesis or study that provides suggestions for practical applications of the study's findings or how the researcher imagines and foresees this information serving to inform future research.

Implicit unstated, unspoken, or underlying.

Independent variable an object, event, idea, feeling, time period, or any other type of category you are trying to measure that stands alone and is not changed by any other variables you are trying to measure such as a participant's age.

Inductive reasoning a method of drawing conclusions by first looking at a set of specific observations or instances; a process beginning with gathering data to identify patterns, pose a theory, or make a generalization in a bottom-up approach.

Inferential statistics comparative measurements taken from a sample which focus on relationships and associations between subjects or groups in order to test hypotheses.

Infographic accessible visual explanation which supports decision-making; using simplified images, words, and numbers to communicate a concept, statistic, or process.

Information Age technological era following the digital revolution in the mid-twentieth century which introduced personal computers.

Informed consent a process of disclosure of the risks, benefits, and voluntary nature of being a study participant in an attempt to garner permission from a participant, or guardian of the participant.

Infrastructure often hidden or unseen supporting services to a project such as mechanical, electrical, and plumbing systems.

Insight an unexpected shift in the way we see things which uncovers a new relationship, pattern, trend, or anomaly.

Institutional Review Board (IRB) a group that has been formally designated to review and monitor research involving human subjects with the authority to approve or disapprove submitted studies.

Instruments tools designed for the purpose of gathering information within a study. Examples include laboratory equipment used for experiments as well as questionnaires and checklists.

Interior design a distinct profession with specialized knowledge applied to the planning and design of interior environments that promote health, safety, and welfare while supporting and enhancing the human experience. Founded upon design and human behavior theories and research, interior designers apply evidence-based methodologies to identify, analyze, and synthesize information in generating holistic, technical, creative, and contextually appropriate, design solutions.

Interior Design Educators Council (IDEC) the leading organization and authority on interior design education seeking to advance scholarship and service open to members who teach interior design and related or allied professions. See www.idec.org

International Interior Design Association (IIDA) commercial interior design association which supports design professionals, educators, students, firms, and clients advocating for advancements in design education, legislation, and leadership. http://www.iida.org

Interpretation a term in qualitative research which means the researcher draws conclusions from the findings of data analysis and describes the lessons learned or new information.

Interval categories involve numbers that have consistent or proportional values in between such as hours, sizes, ages, or income level in dollars, considered quantitative data since you can use the numbers generated from your survey to find the average or perform other operations such as subtractions and additions.

Interview a data collection method which involves asking questions to get information; a type of personal report in which two or more people discuss personal or professional matters, in which one person asks questions of the other; a formal consultation at which information is obtained from a person typically by asking and answering of questions.

Kairos *Greek for* an opportune moment.

Keyword search term used by librarians to link a document to an information retrieval system in digital databases, and for search engines to identify content in websites.

Kinesiology the scientific study of body movement addressing physiological, biomechanical, and psychological mechanisms of movement, typically using research methods adapted from physical and occupational therapy.

Kinesthetics the study of body motion and perception involving the development of awareness of movement (both conscious and nonconscious). Studies of human motion include measures from motion tracking systems, electrophysiology of muscle and brain activity, and other behavioral and cognitive research techniques.

Lateral thinking cognitive exploration to generate multiple ideas, possibilities, or solutions.

Library catalog a searchable database of an institution's or organization's resources, typically a diverse range of books, periodicals, video and audio-recordings, maps, and other archived documents or works.

Likert **Attitude Scale** a widely used scale in which respondents are given a list of statements and asked whether they "strongly agree," "agree," are "undecided," are "neutral," "disagree," or "strongly disagree" used to measure attitudes.

Limitation potential weaknesses that exist and are typically present in any study. Common methodological limitations are a small sample size, convenience rather than true random sampling, and biases inherent in a sample.

Line graph a graph in which points representing values of a variable for suitable values of an independent variable are connected by a broken line used to show how something has changed over time indicating peaks and valleys. Can compare more than one group by color coding or graphically differentiating the multiple lines.

Literature map a diagrammatic representation or graphic tool which links sources to your research topic and domain areas helping to organize a literature review.

Literature review a comprehensive collection and synthesis of previously published studies, articles, books, lectures, and other high-quality sources that offers an overview about current knowledge relevant to a topic.

Logic the science of the formal principles of reasoning which entails the use of critical thinking as a means of testing ideas and in debate.

Logos the Greek root of the word logic (see logic).

Longitudinal studies measure or describe change that occurs over time.

Magnetoencephalography (MEG) detects electrical currents coursing through groups of neurons when studying the brain's response to stimuli.

Measure of central tendency (mean, median, mode) attempt to describe a whole set of data with a single value that represents the middle or center of its distribution; also known as an average.

Metaphor a literary device that describes something familiar to yield a transfer of knowledge to something unfamiliar.

Mixed methods using quantitative measures along with qualitative data collection techniques to conduct a research study.

Mock-up a crude approximation of the final product or space (at full scale), often made in foam core or cardboard, and often used to help understand functionality in furniture and product design.

Modern Language Association (MLA) an organization which promotes a style of documentation that may be applied to many different types of writing, mainly in the liberal arts and humanities.

Monograph a type of study focused on one example of a phenomenon.

Multiple-choice question question type that allows respondent to choose from a limited number of responses that are mutually exclusive, or do not overlap. Can be limited to one response or select all that apply.

Municipality local government agencies such as town, city, or county which typically regulate land use and zoning, and keep public records for access by community members and researchers.

Narrative a spoken or written account connecting study events or telling an evidence-based story, to help the audience to the study results, and explore cumulative or summative concepts.

Neuroplasticity a biological term for the brain's ability to alter its synaptic networks and continue to develop through reinforcing pathways or patterns of neurons (memory) and weakening or disregarding others.

Nominal categories choices based on names of things, action verbs, or adjectives.

Nonconscious describes any activity which occurs without cognitive awareness such as reflexes, instincts, as well as learned habits.

Objective free from bias, chance, individual human perception, and error.

Observation is the use of one or more of the senses to obtain and record information on individuals, objects, or events, as a method of gathering information for interior design; can be casual, systematic, participant, simulation, or experiment.

Occupancy/use classification the intended use of a building, floor or space as assessed by risk factors and defined by the International Building Code (IBC).

Ontology the study of being, what constitutes objective and subjective existence, and what it means to exist.

Open-ended question designed to allow for unrestricted answer by the interviewee. Also known as an nonstructured question.

Operationalize how constructs are put to use; how researchers define what they are trying to measure. For example, what components would you use to measure "happiness" in a study?

Ordinal scale categories organized along some sort of order to the variables, such as low to high (magnitude), hours of the day, order of tasks, or some other sequencing.

P-value a measure of the probability that an observed difference could have occurred just by random chance (0.05, 0.01, 0.001). The lower the p-value, the greater the statistical significance of the observed difference being outside of a chance occurrence. In social science research, we often select the 95 percent significance level which gives us the critical p-value of 0.05.

Paradigm see **worldview**.

Paraphrase restate in your own words.

Participant end-user a person who volunteers for your study who is a current or designated user of the space to be designed.

Participant observation occurs when the observer interacts with the subjects of the study in some way.

Participatory Action Research (PAR) similar to participant observation with the addition of action research, a collaborative phase in which researchers and stakeholders positively contribute to the social, economic, or political context under observation.

Pathos (empathy) Greek for "appealing to the heart."

Peer review process in which authored research is reviewed by other experts to determine relevancy and accuracy of published information in written work in academia.

Person-centered mapping involves selecting an individual to follow for a given period to obtain information about how that person uses or interacts with a space and making notes about *location, movement,* and *observed behavior or activities,* and considering the *length of time* for each activity. Also known as shadowing.

Philosophy literally translated from Greek as the love of wisdom, refers to underlying sphere of thought, general understanding, or system of core concepts related to disciplines of sciences and liberal arts.

Photo journal/photo study a research activity which combines taking photographs and written notes to produce captions or a narrative essay to document observation.

Pie chart used to compare parts of a whole such as demographic data of a sample population or costs involved in different aspects of a project.

Pilot study a small-scale preliminary investigation which aims to test an instrument (such as a questionnaire), assemble a sample pool, try out a distribution method, or explore the feasibility of an approach. It is a preliminary test run which may yield important feedback on how to improve any of the content or implementation methods of the study components.

Place-centered mapping involves making a base drawing of the space showing physical objects, observing the space, and indicating flow patterns, behaviors, and other data about people using the space.

Plagiarism unacknowledged use of another's words, ideas, or information.

Population all the members of a particular group of individuals that you have decided to study or to describe.

Positive psychology as identified by Martin Seligman, the scientific study of how an environment supports the five pillars of human well-being: positive emotions, engagement/flow (creativity), relationships, meaning/purpose, and achievement.

Positivism/Post-positivist a philosophical perspective based on objective truth in which authentic knowledge or empirical evidence is that which is produced or verified through controlled experiments, systematic observation, and logical proof.

Post-Occupancy Evaluation (POE) a variety of research methods used to collect data on the use of a project after it is completed and is occupied; may include end-user satisfaction surveys, observation, or sensors to measure air quality, energy efficiency, and other physical aspects of the built environment.

Potential end-user a person who possesses the characteristics of someone who may use the space, who volunteers to participate in your study.

Praxis a Greek term for the interrelationship between thinking and acting and reflecting on the results of our actions.

Precedent research a comprehensive review of projects, artwork, artifacts, or similar boundary objects used to inform and inspire associated visual media and other forms of creative work.

Precedent study a project that exemplifies innovation in architecture or design in its structural, technological, or formal (shape, texture, or material) exploration.

Predictive analytics a term used in marking and business-related research which means to uncover patterns in processed data, to propose a theory or to tentatively confirm or refute a causal occurrence.

Primary source immediate, temporally concurrent, or first-hand account of an event or a topic such as original written document, photograph, audio or visual recording of an event, diary, news report, dataset, or statistic.

Probe an interviewer's strategy using a verbal ("I see") or nonverbal (slight nod) prompt to elicit further elaboration of response by an interviewee.

Professional capital refers to the value of an individual, a combination of their talent, experience, social relationships, and decision-making ability when evaluating their potential contribution to a business, organization, or endeavor.

Programming/pre-design phase the first step in the professional interior design process with five main tasks: to establish goals, collect information, uncover concepts, determine needs, and define the problems to solve. Data collection methods include asking questions, observation, and researching site possibilities and constraints. Outcome of this phase results in a written project program establishing performance requirements, aesthetics, and needs of the client and end-users of a proposed project.

Project program a document that assimilates and organizes information gathered by the programmer into a form that is usable by the designer as the basis for their schematic design. Also called programming document or design brief, it varies in terms of format, length, and type of detail.

Project type defines the primary function of the space. Broad categories include residential, commercial, institutional, with more specific types such as hospitality, retail, school, post office, and so forth.

Proposition established rules or relationships between theoretical components (constructs).

Proprioception part of the sensory system related to body movement and perception of effort, strength, and force.

Prospect and refuge theory expounded by Jay Appleton (1975) in which he identifies survival as the biological basis for feelings of comfort, appreciation, and beauty in an environment incorporating a clear view of available resources and along with elements promoting privacy, security, and/or safety.

Prospectus a document submitted to a publisher by an aspiring author which describes the rationale, outstanding features, intended audience, and comparison to existing books on the same subject matter for marketing considerations.

Prototype a representation of an item at full scale as close to the look and feel of the final product as possible for client or designer feedback.

Proxemics coined by Edward T. Hall (1966) to describe the study of non-verbal, body language as social norms, or learned cultural traits, yet also having a biological basis which manifests in the distance people keep around themselves as an invisible, dynamic, personal space bubble which changes due to circumstances and relationship with the people around them.

Psychographic variables attributes relating to personality, values, attitudes, interests, social class, or lifestyles. Also called IAO variables (for "Interests, Attitudes, and Opinions") and are typically compared with demographics and behavior.

Qualifier question preliminary or initial questions on a questionnaire that assess whether the respondent fits a list of certain predetermined qualifications, typically demographic information such as gender, age, education level, or regarding a person's lifestyle, habits, or experiences.

Qualitative a type of data which captures the character or attributes of a situation, place, or experience; a method for data collection which is suitable for gaining an in-depth understanding for a complex social or cultural issue due to its association with subjective experience, feelings, or beliefs.

Quantitative a type of data and a method of data collection or analysis which seeks to gain knowledge by connecting a phenomenon to a measurable and often numerical result and comparing these results.

Quasi-experimental similar to an experiment but one in which not all variables may be accounted for.

Questionnaire a series of topic-related questions written to help you discover participant opinions; *standardized* would mean that an identical series of questions is distributed to the participants.

Random sample selecting study participants by chance.

Ranking question asks respondents to assign an order of priority to their response to a list of choices.

Ratings scale a question type that uses an ordinal scale in addition to indicating frequency, intensity, or degree of agreement with ranges of "least to most," "low to high," or "agree to disagree."

Ratio scale compares quantitative data across different units of measure such as the conversion of pounds to kilograms or square footage to meters. It is very similar to interval scale with an added feature of having an absolute zero value.

Rationalization a self-serving, dishonest form of reasoning which justifies one's actions or confirms an individual's beliefs.

Raw data a mixture of different types of source or primary data which includes completed questionnaires, interview transcripts, photos, and so forth.

Reconstruction translating notes from an interview to full sentence quotes, summarizing and/or paraphrasing what the interviewee said immediately after conducting an interview.

Reflexivity a dynamic process of awareness, transparency, and explanation by the researcher necessary when conducting certain forms of human-centered research.

Research the systematic investigation into and study of materials and sources to collect information about a particular subject, establish facts, and reach new conclusions.

Research-informed design (RID) the most recent iteration of evidence-based design (EBD) which bases design decision-making on the results of scientific inquiry.

Research method tool or technique for gathering and processing data.

Research methodology the framework used to justify the data collection, processing, and analysis methods.

Research proposal a fully documented plan to conduct original research typically submitted for approval before beginning a study.

Research question an open-ended yet focused core of a study which seeks to expound on describing an existing phenomenon, relationships between phenomena or establish causation between two or more variables.

Research strategy a general plan that establishes what information you need, where it might be found, and how you will get it.

Research-Through-Design (RTD) refers to conducting scientific inquiry through the results of investigation by employing the methods, practices, and process of design, with the intention of generating new knowledge.

Results all processed data that serves to answer the research question posed in the study.

Rhetorical devices used in literature or prose writing such as *metaphor*, and *narrative*, to effectively inform, persuade, and motivate readers.

Sample a subgroup of a population that is thought or meant to be representative of the population. The way a sample is collected determines the type of sample such as random, purposive, stratified, convenient, etc.

Sanborn map historical map created for cities during the late 1800s and early 1900s by the Sanborn Fire Insurance company.

Satisfaction survey a list of questions to be answered at the completion of an end-user's experience to gauge the positive or negative reaction.

Scale relative size of a project or study.

Scale model a simulation built at a small scale to represent the interior design solution ranging in materials, craft, detail, and focus from study model (equivalent to a three-dimensional sketch) to finish model.

Schema in psychology, referring to pre-existing knowledge structures involving memory and behavior. An example of a schema might be how someone gets ready for work in the morning or how children behave in a classroom.

Scientific method a standardized method of procedure that has characterized natural science since the seventeenth century, consisting of systematic observation, measurement, experiment, and the formulation, testing, and modification of *hypotheses*.

Scope breadth, depth, and amount of detail included in a project or study.

Scratch notes quick jottings to capture things while observing, to be expanded immediately thereafter.

Script in psychology, a pre-existing knowledge structure involving event sequences, typically in social or transactional situations.

Secondary source refers to information that interprets primary sources such as books that are historical accounts done retrospectively, documentary films, reviews, or critiques of original works or accounts.

Self-reports a type of cognitive response generated by a participant of a study including verbal, written (journal), or visual (photographs, drawings, artwork).

Semantic differential question a question type with many descriptive words to measure attitudes and other subjective and affective reactions to concepts, objects, and events.

Sentence completion question begins with a prompt and gives the respondent an opportunity to answer in a creative way.

Shadowing person-centered behavioral observation method, typically in an office or institutional setting, following a staff member or visitor with prior consent of the organization and participants involved.

Simulation the examination of a problem by means of an intermediary device made to look, feel, or behave like what is to be studied. Simulated scenarios are often used to train people.

Social ecology the theory that people working together can solve global environmental issues.

Somatosensory receptors or perception related to sense organs, primarily those activating neurons in the skin and hair commonly referred to as the sense of touch.

Spreadsheets combine both purposes of a table by storing and displaying data in a grid, or matrix of cells, with the added value of formulas, an interactive expression that calculates values within or across cells, and functions, which are predefined formulas.

Standard deviation a measure of the range from the average.

Standardized questionnaire a prepared list of questions used to interview more than one person consecutively that can also be used in a survey design.

Statistical significance the claim that a result from data generated by testing or experimentation is not likely to occur randomly or by chance, typically mathematically established through a P-value or another relevant and accepted test.

Statistics numerical characteristics that measure relationships for the purpose of comparison, such as percentages, averages, and tendencies; *descriptive* refers to a variety of methods that are used to simplify, summarize, organize, identify, and visually display such data and *inferential* are used to make judgments of the probability of relationship.

Structural system elements working together to hold the building up against gravity and lateral forces; including the foundation and framing giving a building its underlying form.

Subjective ideas arising from the mind, based on, or influenced by, personal feelings, tastes, or opinions.

Summative aggregates all the accumulated data into one visual table or block of text.

Survey to query (people) to collect data for the analysis of some aspect of a group or an area; to do a statistical study of a sample population by asking questions about knowledge, opinions, preferences, and other aspects of people's lives using a standardized questionnaire.

Survey design the act of formulating and conducting a statistical study of a sample population by asking questions about knowledge, opinions, preferences, and other aspects of people's lives.

Survey study a comprehensive overview summarizing many cases of a phenomenon.

Syllogism a tool in reasoning and argument which uses a series of "if, then" statements (two premises and a conclusion) to seek truth through deductive inference.

Systematic observation a method designed to focus the researcher's attention on certain aspects of the people or the environment which involves determining the unit of analysis and visual notations or codes to record the instances observed.

Table a data structure that organizes information into rows and columns to store and display data in an easily read format.

Task scenario part of a usability test that lays out the representative criteria, actions, and behaviors to be observed and recorded to determine or define what is meant by usability.

Telos Greek term for an appeal to purpose.

Testimony an expert opinion or eye-witness account that serves as evidence.

Theoretical memo a thinking tool for the researcher, an attempt to connect an observation to a theoretical explanation.

Theory a system of ideas intended to explain something; a way of thinking, or a set of principles used to justify an action or practice.

Thesis a proposal, claim, or written paper on a particular subject put forward or presented for consideration, to be discussed, proven, or maintained against objections for the purpose of gaining knowledge.

Thesis project the identification of a problem and a proposed solution in a synthesized design scenario, or the studio component to further expand your creative research.

Thick description coined by Geertz (1973) to communicate details of the observations while simultaneously extracting or constructing the meaning of the information gathered.

Tone in writing, a literary attitude towards the research and the participants communicating either a sense of authority, level of formality, or casualness in language.

Topographic geographic features that determine the shape of the visible landscape including mountains, forests, and bodies of water.

Trace evidence the physical evidence left by the interaction of people and the environment which could consist of manipulation, addition, or removal of items and wear patterns.

Transcription a post-interview record that is a true representation of questions and answers of an interview typed after it has been audio-recorded; the act of documenting the typed version of an audio-recorded conversation.

Triangulation a strategy for increasing the level of validity by employing several different kinds of instruments to collect complementary data.

Typology a classification system based on categories.

Unit of inquiry/analysis the main entity you are going to compare in a study which may be an individual data point such as an exam score, a person, a group of people, an institution, a behavior, an interaction, or an artifact.

Universal Design (UD) the design of products and environments to be usable by all people, to the greatest extent possible, and without the need for adaptation or specialized design; a design process that enables and empowers a diverse population by improving human performance, health and wellness, and social participation.

Usability test participant end-users are observed using mock-ups or prototypes to evaluate whether a design or space is easy to use or "user friendly"; also called *pilot tests*.

Validity internal logic that cannot be proven false.

Value system conditions underlying one's point of view.

Variable an object, event, idea, feeling, time period, or any other type of category you are trying to measure.

Vertical thinking using reason, logic, and attention to detail to carefully proceed in one direction to solve a problem.

Vestibular part of the sensory system related to balance and position in space which helps form the body's perception of its relationship with gravity, motion, and relative speed.

Vignette a short dramatic description or story to illustrate a qualitative point or finding.

Virtual reality (VR) interaction in 3-dimensional digital spaces.

Visual interpretation question allows respondents to respond to an image (a photograph, drawing, or diagram) or to compare a series of photographs.

Visual metaphor a poetic figure of speech that expresses an understanding of one concept in terms of another to reveal some similarity or correlation between the two; used in interior design research to create an understanding or communicate through symbolic images.

Visual models diagrams used in research to illustrate a principle or theory.

Visual notation shorthand technique that you will use to codify the attributes and activities of the subjects under observation.

Vulnerable populations people with physical, psychological, or social impairments which may limit their ability to provide informed consent, or put them at a high risk when participating in a study.

Wayfinding/Place-legibility coined by Kevin Lynch (1960) the system by which conceptual navigational tools such as paths, edges, districts, nodes, and landmarks in an environment work together to form a unified whole for ease of navigation by occupants.

White paper published concise, authoritative report, or problem-solving guide typically proposing solutions to an issue from research funded or sponsored by companies which may be used to promote the benefits of their products or services.

Word cloud also known as a *tag cloud*, *wordle*, or *weighted list* which illustrates hierarchically how often a word appears in a transcript by assigning font size, color, or other graphic manipulation of text.

Worldview a general philosophical orientation which shapes an individual's understanding of the world and nature of research; also known as a *paradigm*.

Zaltman Metaphor Elicitation Technique (ZMET) a patented process for uncovering hidden concepts and distilling information into an emerging metaphor using interview techniques and images manipulation.

Zoning municipal code designations and other overlapping restrictions which regulate land use.

credits

Uncredited images are courtesy Fairchild Books.

Chapter 1

1.1	Courtesy Amanda Dowell and Lily B. Robinson
A1.1	Courtesy of Amanda Dowell
B 1.1a and b	Courtesy of Amanda Dowell
B 1.2	Courtesy of Amanda Dowell
B1.3a–e	Courtesy Mary Kristofich

Chapter 2

2.1	Courtesy Amanda Dowell
2.2	Courtesy Amanda Dowell and Lily B. Robinson
2.3	Courtesy of Lily B. Robinson
2.4a and b	Courtesy of Amanda Dowell and Lily B. Robinson
2.5	Courtesy of Amanda Dowell
2.6	Courtesy of Amanda Dowell
2.7	Courtesy of Lily B. Robinson
2.8	Courtesy of Lily B. Robinson
2.9	Courtesy Chris Halter
2.10	Courtesy Chris Halter
2.11	Courtesy Chris Halter
2.12	Courtesy Chris Halter
2.13	Courtesy Chris Halter
2.14	Courtesy of Amber Style
2.15	Courtesy Chris Halter
2.16a	ValeryEgorov/iStock.com
2.16b	Courtesy of Lily B. Robinson
A2.3	Courtesy of Lily B. Robinson
B2.1	Courtesy of Walter Pierce Bryce III
B2.2a and b	Hekman Digital Archive
B2.2c and d	Courtesy of Maria da Piedade Ferreira/Photo by Michael Hoschek for HFT Stuttgart

Chapter 3

3.1	Courtesy of Lily B. Robinson
3.2	Courtesy of Lily B. Robinson
3.3	Courtesy of Lily B. Robinson
3.4a	Courtesy of Alexandra T. Parman and Lily B. Robinson
3.4b	Courtesy of Lily B. Robinson
3.5	Courtesy of Lily B. Robinson
3.6	Courtesy of Lily B. Robinson
3.7	Courtesy of Amanda Dowell
A3.3	Courtesy of Lily B. Robinson

Chapter 4

4.1	Courtesy of Lily B. Robinson
4.2	Courtesy of Lily B. Robinson
4.3	Courtesy of Lily B. Robinson
4.4	Courtesy of Amanda Dowell
4.5	Courtesy of Lily B. Robinson
4.10	Courtesy of Lily B. Robinson
A4.2	Courtesy of Lily B. Robinson
A4.3	Courtesy of GoogleEarth
A4.5a and b	Courtesy of Lily B. Robinson
B4.2	Whitney R. Smith, Arts + Architecture, April 1946. © Travers Family Trust. Used with Permission

Chapter 5

5.1	Courtesy of Amanda Dowell
5.2	The Professor Is In: The Essential Guide to Turning Your PhD Into A Job
5.3	Courtesy of Lily B. Robinson
5.4	Courtesy of Lily B. Robinson
5.5	Courtesy of Lily B. Robinson
5.6	Courtesy of Lily B. Robinson
5.7	Courtesy of Lily B. Robinson
5.8	Courtesy of Lily B. Robinson
5.9	Courtesy of Lily B. Robinson
5.10	Courtesy of Lily B. Robinson
5.11	Courtesy Leanna Wolff
5.12	Courtesy of Allard Jansen Architecture+ Development
5.13	Courtesy of Lily B. Robinson
5.14	Courtesy of Lily B. Robinson
5.15	Courtesy of Lily B. Robinson
5.16	Courtesy of Lily B. Robinson
B5.1	Courtesy of Lily B. Robinson
B5.2	Courtesy Sara Plaisted

Chapter 6

6.1	Courtesy of Amanda Dowell
6.2	Courtesy of Lily B. Robinson
6.3	Courtesy of The Salk Institute
6.4	Courtesy of Fairchild Books
6.5	Courtesy of Lily B. Robinson
B6.1	Courtesy of Amanda Dowell
B6.2	Courtesy of fathom

Chapter 7

7.1	Courtesy of Lily B. Robinson
7.2	Courtesy of Lily B. Robinson
7.3	Courtesy of Lily B. Robinson
7.4	Courtesy of Lily B. Robinson
7.5	Courtesy of Lily B. Robinson
7.6	Courtesy of Lily B. Robinson
7.7	Courtesy of Lily B. Robinson
B7.1	Courtesy of Lily B. Robinson

Chapter 8

8.1	Courtesy of Lily B. Robinson
8.2	Courtesy of Annahi Barce
8.3	Courtesy of Annahi Barce
8.4a and b	Courtesy of San Diego Public Library Foundation
8.5	Courtesy of Lily B. Robinson
8.6	Courtesy of Lily B. Robinson
8.7	Courtesy of Meli Apone
8.8	Courtesy of Lily B. Robinson
8.9	Courtesy of Leanna Wolff
8.10	Courtesy of Erica Yaw
8.11a and b	Courtesy of Zakaria Djebbara; AD:MT, Aalborg University & BeMoBIL, Technical University Berlin
8.12	Courtesy of Zakaria Djebbara; AD:MT, Aalborg University & BeMoBIL, Technical University Berlin
B8.1	Courtesy of Lily B. Robinson
B8.2	Courtesy of Cherry/SEE/Reames Architects, Client Data Gathering Techniques: Edith Cherry, FAIA

Chapter 9

9.1	Courtesy of Lily B. Robinson
9.2a	Courtesy of Lily B. Robinson
9.2b	Courtesy of Lily B. Robinson
9.3	Courtesy of Lily B. Robinson
9.5a–b	Courtesy of Wilder Penfield
9.6	U.S. Department of Health & Human Services/ Center for Disease Control
9.7	Courtesy of Lily B. Robinson
9.8a and b	Courtesy of Hal Taylor
9.9	Courtesy of Lily B. Robinson
9.10	Courtesy of Lily B. Robinson
9.11	Courtesy of Lily B. Robinson
9.12	Courtesy of Lily B. Robinson
9.13	Courtesy of Jaime Serra Palou
A9.1	Courtesy of Lily B. Robinson
B9.1a–c	Courtesy of Jesse Mitchell

Chapter 10

10.1	Courtesy of Lily B. Robinson
10.2	Courtesy of Amanda Dowell
10.3	Courtesy of Lily B. Robinson
B10.1a and b	Courtesy of Meli Apone
B10.2	Ingrid Fetell Lee—The Aesthetics of Joy 2022
B10.3a–c	Humble Design, Inc. Treger Strasberg, Founder

index

Weisberg, Robert 11, 25, 28–9
white papers 94
Wolcott, Harry F. 218–19
word cloud 212
wordle 212
working bibliography 100
worldviews 63–6

writing
　books 240, 241–2, 244
　papers, theses and dissertations 232–7
　styles 99–100

X

X–Y plot 178

Y

Young, James Webb 11

Z

Zaltman Metaphor Elicitation Technique (ZMET) 158–9
zoning 123, 124